The Theatre of
BERNARD SHAW

VOL. II

VOLUME I

MRS. WARREN'S PROFESSION

ARMS AND THE MAN

CAESAR AND CLEOPATRA

MAN AND SUPERMAN

ANDROCLES AND THE LION

VOLUME II

O'FLAHERTY, V.C.

HEARTBREAK HOUSE

SAINT JOAN (WITH PREFACE)

THE SIMPLETON OF THE UNEXPECTED ISLES

"IN GOOD KING CHARLES'S GOLDEN DAYS"

Nondramatic writing

The Theatre of BERNARD SHAW

TEN PLAYS, CHOSEN AND DISCUSSED BY

Alan S. Downer

Princeton University

VOLUME II

DODD, MEAD & COMPANY

New York - Toronto

1961

Library of Congress catalog card number: 61-12006
Printed in the United States of America

NOTE

When Shaw's works first began appearing in London, and for many years thereafter, they were considered to be interesting mainly for the ideas they set forth, and a number of responsible critics roundly declared that they were tracts and not plays at all. The passing years have inevitably brought a widespread appreciation of Shaw as artist, indeed as a unique kind of playwright-philosopher. The present selection from his forty-four plays is intended to indicate, as far as any selection can do, the development of his dramatic technique from the early years, when he was adapting to his own use the methods of the conventional theatre, to the last years when he was writing in a style and for a theatre that he had made peculiarly his own.

Because the emphasis of this collection is upon Shaw's dramaturgy, his prefaces to most of the individual plays have been omitted; they frequently develop tangential arguments associated with the dramatic action but infrequently comment on the problems of the playwright. The preface to *Saint Joan* has been retained as clarifying Shaw's special approach to familiar subject matter.

The appendix presents a sampling of Shaw's dramatic theorizing from his nondramatic writings and practical criticism of the theatre of the nineties. The selections and the commentary are the work of Dr. Martin Meisel, for whose close knowledge of the material and enthusiastic collaboration I am doubly grateful. I wish also to express my gratitude to Professor Norman Philbrick for permission to use certain unpublished materials from his personal collection of Shaviana.

A.S.D.

CONTENTS

VOLUME II

O'FLAHERTY, V.C.

O'Flaherty, V.C. is one of a group of short plays written during the First World War as recruiting posters or entertainment for the troops. Shaw intended it to be performed by the Abbey Theatre in Dublin, but apparently events in the great world combined with chauvinism to prevent its acceptance. Like so many of Shaw's plays it was first seen in New York, at the 39th Street Theatre, June 21, 1920, with P. J. Kelly as O'Flaherty. On December 20 of the same year it was presented by the Incorporated Stage Society at the Lyric Theatre, Hammersmith, London.

O'FLAHERTY V.C.

AT the door of an Irish country house in a park. Fine summer weather: the summer of 1915. *The porch, painted white, projects into the drive; but the door is at the side and the front has a window. The porch faces east; and the door is in the north side of it. On the south side is a tree in which a thrush is singing. Under the window is a garden seat with an iron chair at each end of it.*

The last four bars of God Save the King are heard in the distance, followed by three cheers. Then the band strikes up It's a Long Way to Tipperary and recedes until it is out of hearing.

Private O'Flaherty V.C. comes wearily southward along the drive, and falls exhausted into the garden seat. The thrush utters a note of alarm and flies away. The tramp of a horse is heard.

A GENTLEMAN'S VOICE. Tim! Hi! Tim! [*He is heard dismounting*].

A LABORER'S VOICE. Yes, your honor.

THE GENTLEMAN'S VOICE. Take this horse to the stables, will you?

A LABORER'S VOICE. Right, your honor. Yup there. Gwan now. Gwan. [*The horse is led away*].

General Sir Pearce Madigan, an elderly baronet in khaki, beaming with enthusiasm, arrives. O'Flaherty rises and stands at attention.

SIR PEARCE. No, no, O'Flaherty: none of that now. Youre off duty. Remember that though I am a general of forty years service, that little Cross of yours gives you a higher rank in the roll of glory than I can pretend to.

O'FLAHERTY [*relaxing*] I'm thankful to you, Sir Pearce; but I wouldnt have anyone think that the baronet of my native place would let a common soldier like me sit down in his presence without leave.

SIR PEARCE. Well, youre not a common soldier, O'Flaherty: youre a very uncommon one; and I'm proud to have you for my guest here today.

O'FLAHERTY. Sure I know, sir. You have to put up with a

lot from the like of me for the sake of the recruiting. All the quality shakes hands with me and says theyre proud to know me, just the way the king said when he pinned the Cross on me. And it's as true as I'm standing here, sir, the queen said to me "I hear you were born on the estate of General Madigan," she says; "and the General himself tells me you were always a fine young fellow." "Bedad, Mam," I says to her, "if the General knew all the rabbits I snared on him, and all the salmon I snatched on him, and all the cows I milked on him, he'd think me the finest ornament for the county jail he ever sent there for poaching."

SIR PEARCE [*laughing*] Youre welcome to them all, my lad. Come [*he makes him sit down again on the garden seat*]! sit down and enjoy your holiday [*he sits down on one of the iron chairs: the one at the doorless side of the porch*].

O'FLAHERTY. Holiday, is it? I'd give five shillings to be back in the trenches for the sake of a little rest and quiet. I never knew what hard work was til I took to recruiting. What with the standing on my legs all day, and the shaking hands, and the making speeches, and—whats worse—the listening to them, and the calling for cheers for king and country, and the saluting the flag til I'm stiff with it, and the listening to them playing God Save the King and Tipperary, and the trying to make my eyes look moist like a man in a picture book, I'm that bet that I hardly get a wink of sleep. I give you my word, Sir Pearce, that I never heard the tune of Tipperary in my life til I came back from Flanders; and already it's drove me to that pitch of tiredness of it that when a poor little innocent slip of a boy in the street the other night drew himself up and saluted and began whistling it at me, I clouted his head for him, God forgive me.

SIR PEARCE [*soothingly*] Yes, yes: I know. *I* know. One does get fed up with it: Ive been dog tired myself on parade many a time. But still, you know, theres a gratifying side to it, too. After all, he is our king; and it's our own country, isnt it?

O'FLAHERTY. Well, sir, to you that have an estate in it, it

would feel like your country. But the divil a perch of it ever I owned. And as to the king, God help him, my mother would have taken the skin off my back if I'd ever let on to have any other king than Parnell.

SIR PEARCE [*rising, painfully shocked*] Your mother! What are you dreaming about, O'Flaherty? A most loyal woman. Always most loyal. Whenever there is an illness in the Royal Family, she asks me every time we meet about the health of the patient as anxiously as if it were yourself, her only son.

O'FLAHERTY. Well, she's my mother; and I wont utter a word agen her. But I'm not saying a word of lie when I tell you that old woman is the biggest kanatt from here to the cross of Monasterboice. Sure she's the wildest Fenian and rebel, and always has been, that ever taught a poor innocent lad like myself to pray night and morning to St Patrick to clear the English out of Ireland the same as he cleared the snakes. Youll be surprised at my telling you that now, maybe, Sir Pearce?

SIR PEARCE [*unable to keep still, walking away from O'Flaherty*] Surprised! I'm more than surprised, O'Flaherty. I'm overwhelmed. [*Turning and facing him*] Are you—are you joking?

O'FLAHERTY. If youd been brought up by my mother, sir, youd know better than to joke about her. What I'm telling you is the truth; and I wouldnt tell it to you if I could see my way to get out of the fix I'll be in when my mother comes here this day to see her boy in his glory, and she after thinking all the time it was against the English I was fighting.

SIR PEARCE. Do you mean to say you told her such a monstrous falsehood as that you were fighting in the German army?

O'FLAHERTY. I never told her one word that wasnt the truth and nothing but the truth. I told her I was going to fight for the French and for the Russians; and sure who ever heard of the French or the Russians doing anything to the English but fighting them? That was how it was, sir. And sure the poor woman kissed me and went about the house singing in her old cracky voice that the French was on the sea, and theyd be here without delay, and the Orange will decay, says the Shan Van Vocht.

SIR PEARCE [*sitting down again, exhausted by his feelings*] Well, I never could have believed this. Never. What do you suppose will happen when she finds out?

O'FLAHERTY. She mustnt find out. It's not that she'd half kill me, as big as I am and as brave as I am. It's that I'm fond of her, and cant bring myself to break the heart in her. You may think it queer that a man should be fond of his mother, sir, and she having bet him from the time he could feel to the time she was too slow to ketch him; but I'm fond of her; and I'm not ashamed of it. Besides, didnt she win the Cross for me?

SIR PEARCE. Your mother! How?

O'FLAHERTY. By bringing me up to be more afraid of running away than of fighting. I was timid by nature; and when the other boys hurted me, I'd want to run away and cry. But she whaled me for disgracing the blood of the O'Flahertys until I'd have fought the divil himself sooner than face her after funking a fight. That was how I got to know that fighting was easier than it looked, and that the others was as much afeard of me as I was of them, and that if I only held out long enough theyd lose heart and give up. Thats the way I came to be so courageous. I tell you, Sir Pearce, if the German army had been brought up by my mother, the Kaiser would be dining in the banqueting hall at Buckingham Palace this day, and King George polishing his jack boots for him in the scullery.

SIR PEARCE. But I dont like this, O'Flaherty. You cant go on deceiving your mother, you know. It's not right.

O'FLAHERTY. Cant go on deceiving her, cant I? It's little you know what a son's love can do, sir. Did you ever notice what a ready liar I am?

SIR PEARCE. Well, in recruiting a man gets carried away. I stretch it a bit occasionally myself. After all, it's for king and country. But if you wont mind my saying it, O'Flaherty,

I think that story about your fighting the Kaiser and the twelve giants of the Prussian guard singlehanded would be the better for a little toning down. I dont ask you to drop it, you know; for it's popular, undoubtedly; but still, the truth is the truth. Dont you think it would fetch in almost as many recruits if you reduced the number of guardsmen to six?

O'FLAHERTY. Youre not used to telling lies like I am, sir. I got great practice at home with my mother. What with saving my skin when I was young and thoughtless, and sparing her feelings when I was old enough to understand them, Ive hardly told my mother the truth twice a year since I was born; and would you have me turn round on her and tell it now, when she's looking to have some peace and quiet in her old age?

SIR PEARCE [*troubled in his conscience*] Well, it's not my affair, of course, O'Flaherty. But hadnt you better talk to Father Quinlan about it?

O'FLAHERTY. Talk to Father Quinlan, is it! Do you know what Father Quinlan says to me this very morning?

SIR PEARCE. Oh, youve seen him already, have you? What did he say?

O'FLAHERTY. He says "You know, dont you" he says "that it's your duty, as a Christian and a good son of the Holy Church, to love your enemies?" he says. "I know it's my juty as a soldier to kill them" I says. "Thats right, Dinny," he says: "quite right. But" says he "you can kill them and do them a good turn afterwards to shew your love for them" he says; "and it's your duty to have a mass said for the souls of the hundreds of Germans you say you killed" says he; "for many and many of them were Bavarians and good Catholics" he says. "Is it me that must pay for masses for the souls of the Boshes?" I says. "Let the King of England pay for them" I says; "for it was his quarrel and not mine."

SIR PEARCE [*warmly*] It is the quarrel of every honest man and true patriot, O'Flaherty. Your mother must see that as clearly as I do. After all, she is a reasonable, well disposed woman, quite capable of understanding the right and the wrong of the war. Why cant you explain to her what the war is about?

O'FLAHERTY. Arra, sir, how the divil do I know what the war is about?

SIR PEARCE [*rising again and standing over him*] What! O'Flaherty: do you know what you are saying? You sit there wearing the Victoria Cross for having killed God knows how many Germans; and you tell me you dont know why you did it!

O'FLAHERTY. Asking your pardon, Sir Pearce. I tell you no such thing. I know quite well why I kilt them. I kilt them because I was afeard that, if I didnt, theyd kill me.

SIR PEARCE [*giving it up and sitting down again*] Yes, yes, of course; but have you no knowledge of the causes of the war? of the interests at stake? of the importance—I may almost say—in fact I will say—the sacred rights for which we are fighting? Dont you read the papers?

O'FLAHERTY. I do when I can get them. Theres not many newsboys crying the evening paper in the trenches. They do say, Sir Pearce, that we shall never beat the Boshes until we make Horatio Bottomley Lord Leftnant of England. Do you think thats true, sir?

SIR PEARCE. Rubbish, man! theres no Lord Lieutenant in England: the king is Lord Lieutenant. It's a simple question of patriotism. Does patriotism mean nothing to you?

O'FLAHERTY. It means different to me than what it would to you, sir. It means England and England's king to you. To me and the like of me, it means talking about the English just the way the English papers talk about the Boshes. And what good has it ever done here in Ireland? It's kept me ignorant because it filled up my mother's mind, and she thought it ought to fill up mine too. It's kept Ireland poor, because instead of trying to better ourselves we thought we was the fine fellows of patriots when we were speaking evil of Englishmen that was as poor as ourselves and maybe as good as ourselves. The Boshes I kilt was more knowledgable men than me: and what better am I now that Ive kilt them? What better is anybody?

SIR PEARCE [*huffed, turning a cold shoulder to him*] I am sorry the terrible experience of this war—the greatest war ever fought—has taught you no better, O'Flaherty.

O'FLAHERTY [*preserving his dignity*] I dont know about it's being a great war, sir. It's a big war; but thats not the same thing. Father Quinlan's new church is a big church: you might take the little old chapel out of the middle of it and not miss it. But my mother says there was more true religion in the old chapel. And the war has taught me that may be she was right.

SIR PEARCE [*grunts sulkily*]!!

O'FLAHERTY [*respectfully but doggedly*] And theres another thing it's taught me too, sir, that concerns you and me, if I may make bold to tell it to you.

SIR PEARCE [*still sulkily*] I hope it's nothing you oughtnt to say to me, O'Flaherty.

O'FLAHERTY. It's this, sir: that I'm able to sit here now and talk to you without humbugging you; and thats what not one of your tenants or your tenants' childer ever did to you before in all your long life. It's a true respect I'm shewing you at last, sir. Maybe youd rather have me humbug you and tell you lies as I used, just as the boys here, God help them, would rather have me tell them how I fought the Kaiser, that all the world knows I never saw in my life, than tell them the truth. But I cant take advantage of you the way I used, not even if I seem to be wanting in respect to you and cocked up by winning the Cross.

SIR PEARCE [*touched*] Not at all, O'Flaherty. Not at all.

O'FLAHERTY. Sure whats the Cross to me, barring the little pension it carries? Do you think I dont know that theres hundreds of men as brave as me that never had the luck to get anything for their bravery but a curse from the sergeant, and the blame for the faults of them that ought to have been their betters? Ive learnt more than youd think, sir; for how would a gentleman like you know what a poor ignorant conceited creature I was when I went from here into the wide world as a soldier? What use is all the lying, and pretending, and humbugging, and letting on, when the day comes to you that your comrade is killed in the trench beside you, and you dont as much as look round at him until you trip over his poor body, and then all you say is to ask why the hell the stretcher-bearers dont take it out of the way. Why should I read the papers to be humbugged and lied to by them that had the cunning to stay at home and send me to fight for them? Dont talk to me or to any soldier of the war being right. No war is right; and all the holy water that Father Quinlan ever blessed couldnt make one right. There, sir! Now you know what O'Flaherty V.C. thinks; and youre wiser so than the others that only knows what he done.

SIR PEARCE [*making the best of it, and turning good-humoredly to him again*] Well, what you did was brave and manly, anyhow.

O'FLAHERTY. God knows whether it was or not, better than you nor me, General. I hope He wont be too hard on me for it, anyhow.

SIR PEARCE [*sympathetically*] Oh yes: we all have to think seriously sometimes, especially when we're a little run down. I'm afraid weve been overworking you a bit over these recruiting meetings. However, we can knock off for the rest of the day; and tomorrow's Sunday. Ive had about as much as I can stand myself. [*He looks at his watch*]. It's teatime. I wonder whats keeping your mother.

O'FLAHERTY. It's nicely cocked up the old woman will be having tea at the same table as you, sir, instead of in the kitchen. She'll be after dressing in the heighth of grandeur; and stop she will at every house on the way to shew herself off and tell them where she's going, and fill the whole parish with spite and envy. But sure, she shouldnt keep you waiting, sir.

SIR PEARCE. Oh, thats all right: she must be indulged on an occasion like this. I'm sorry my wife is in London: she'd have been glad to welcome your mother.

O'FLAHERTY. Sure, I know she would, sir. She was always a kind friend to the poor. Little her ladyship knew, God help her, the depth of divilment that was in us: we were like a play to her. You see, sir, she was English: that was how it was. We was to her what the Pathans and Senegalese was to me when I first seen them: I couldnt think, somehow, that they were liars, and thieves, and backbiters, and drunkards, just like ourselves or any other Christians. Oh, her ladyship never knew all that was going on behind her back: how would she? When I was a weeshy child, she gave me the first penny I ever had in my hand; and I wanted to pray for her conversion that night the same as my mother made me pray for yours; and—

SIR PEARCE [*scandalized*] Do you mean to say that your mother made you pray for my conversion?

O'FLAHERTY. Sure and she wouldnt want to see a gentleman like you going to hell after she nursing your own son and bringing up my sister Annie on the bottle. That was how it was, sir. She'd rob you; and she'd lie to you; and she'd call down all the blessings of God on your head when she was selling you your own three geese that you thought had been ate by the fox the day after youd finished fattening them, sir; and all the time you were like a bit of her own flesh and blood to her. Often has she said she'd live to see you a good Catholic yet, leading victorious armies against the English and wearing the collar of gold that Malachi won from the proud invader. Oh, she's the romantic woman is my mother, and no mistake.

SIR PEARCE [*in great perturbation*] I really cant believe this, O'Flaherty. I could have sworn your mother was as honest a woman as ever breathed.

O'FLAHERTY. And so she is, sir. She's as honest as the day.

SIR PEARCE. Do you call it honest to steal my geese?

O'FLAHERTY. She didnt steal them, sir. It was me that stole them.

SIR PEARCE. Oh! And why the devil did you steal them?

O'FLAHERTY. Sure we needed them, sir. Often and often we had to sell our own geese to pay you the rent to satisfy your needs; and why shouldnt we sell your geese to satisfy ours?

SIR PEARCE. Well, damn me!

O'FLAHERTY [*sweetly*] Sure you had to get what you could out of us; and we had to get what we could out of you. God forgive us both!

SIR PEARCE. Really, O'Flaherty, the war seems to have upset you a little.

O'FLAHERTY. It's set me thinking, sir; and I'm not used to it. It's like the patriotism of the English. They never thought of being patriotic until the war broke out; and now the patriotism has took them so sudden and come so strange to them that they run about like frightened chickens, uttering all manner of nonsense. But please God theyll forget all about it when the war's over. Theyre getting tired of it already.

SIR PEARCE. No, no: it has uplifted us all in a wonderful way. The world will never be the same again, O'Flaherty. Not after a war like this.

O'FLAHERTY. So they all say, sir. I see no great differ myself. It's all the fright and the excitement; and when that quiets down theyll go back to their natural divilment and be the same as ever. It's like the vermin: itll wash off after a while.

SIR PEARCE [*rising and planting himself firmly behind the garden seat*] Well, the long and the short of it is, O'Flaherty, I must decline to be a party to any attempt to deceive your mother. I thoroughly disapprove of this feeling against the English, especially at a moment like the present. Even if your mother's political sympathies are really what you represent them to be, I should think that her gratitude to Gladstone ought to cure her of such disloyal prejudices.

O'FLAHERTY (*over his shoulder*) She says Gladstone was an Irishman, sir. What call would he have to meddle with Ireland as he did if he wasnt?

SIR PEARCE. What nonsense! Does she suppose Mr Asquith is an Irishman?

O'FLAHERTY. She wont give him any credit for Home Rule, sir. She says Redmond made him do it. She says you told her so.

SIR PEARCE [*convicted out of his own mouth*] Well, I never meant her to take it up in that ridiculous way. [*He moves to the end of the garden seat on O'Flaherty's left*] I'll give her a good talking to when she comes. I'm not going to stand any of her nonsense.

O'FLAHERTY. It's not a bit of use, sir. She says all the English generals is Irish. She says all the English poets and great men was Irish. She says the English never knew how to read their own books until we taught them. She says we're the lost tribes of the house of Israel and the chosen people of God. She says that the goddess Venus, that was born out of the foam of the sea, came up out of the water in Killiney Bay off Bray Head. She says that Moses built the seven churches, and that Lazarus was buried in Glasnevin.

SIR PEARCE. Bosh! How does she know he was? Did you ever ask her?

O'FLAHERTY. I did, sir, often.

SIR PEARCE. And what did she say?

O'FLAHERTY. She asked me how did I know he wasnt, and fetched me a clout on the side of my head.

SIR PEARCE. But have you never mentioned any famous Englishman to her, and asked her what she had to say about him?

O'FLAHERTY. The only one I could think of was Shakespear, sir; and she says he was born in Cork.

SIR PEARCE [*exhausted*] Well, I give it up [*he throws himself into the nearest chair*] The woman is—Oh, well! No matter.

O'FLAHERTY [*sympathetically*] Yes, sir: she's pigheaded and obstinate: theres no doubt about it. She's like the English: they think theres no one like themselves. It's the same with the Germans, though theyre educated and ought to know better. Youll never have a quiet world til you knock the patriotism out of the human race.

SIR PEARCE. Still, we—

O'FLAHERTY. Whisht, sir, for God's sake: here she is.

The General jumps up. Mrs O'Flaherty arrives, and comes between the two men. She is very clean, and carefully dressed in the oldfashioned peasant costume: black silk sunbonnet with a tiara of trimmings, and black cloak.

O'FLAHERTY [*rising shyly*] Good evening, mother.

MRS O'FLAHERTY [*severely*] You hold your whisht, and learn behavior while I pay my juty to his honor. [*To Sir Pearce, heartily*] And how is your honor's good self? And how is her ladyship and all the young ladies? Oh, it's right glad we are to see your honor back again and looking the picture of health.

SIR PEARCE [*forcing a note of extreme geniality*] Thank you, Mrs O'Flaherty. Well, you see weve brought you back your son safe and sound. I hope youre proud of him.

MRS O'FLAHERTY. And indeed and I am, your honor. It's the brave boy he is; and why wouldnt he be, brought up on your honor's estate and with you before his eyes for a pattern of the finest soldier in Ireland. Come and kiss your old mother, Dinny darlint. [*O'Flaherty does so sheepishly*]. Thats my own darling boy. And look at your fine new uniform stained already with the eggs youve been eating and the porter youve been drinking. [*She takes out her handkerchief; spits on it; and scrubs his lapel with it*]. Oh, it's the untidy slovenly one you always were. There! It wont be seen on the khaki: it's not like the old red coat that would shew up everything that dribbled down on it. [*To Sir Pearce*] And they tell me down at the lodge that her ladyship is staying in London, and that Miss Agnes is to be married to a fine young nobleman. Oh, it's your honor that is the lucky and happy father! It will be bad news for many of the young gentlemen of the quality round here, sir. Theres lots thought she was going to marry young Master Lawless—

SIR PEARCE. What! that—that—that bosthoon!

MRS O'FLAHERTY [*hilariously*] Let your honor alone for finding the right word! A big bosthoon he is indeed, your honor. Oh, to think of the times and times I have said that Miss Agnes would be my lady as her mother was before her! Didnt I, Dinny?

SIR PEARCE. And now, Mrs O'Flaherty, I daresay you have a great deal to say to Dennis that doesnt concern me. I'll just go in and order tea.

MRS O'FLAHERTY. Oh, why would your honor disturb yourself? Sure I can take the boy into the yard.

SIR PEARCE. Not at all. It wont disturb me in the least. And he's too big a boy to be taken into the yard now. He has made a front seat for himself. Eh? [*He goes into the house*].

MRS O'FLAHERTY. Sure he has that, your honor. God bless your honor! [*The General being now out of hearing, she turns threateningly to her son with one of those sudden Irish changes of manner which amaze and scandalize less flexible nations, and exclaims*] And what do you mean, you lying young scald, by telling me you were going to fight agen the English? Did you take me for a fool that couldnt find out, and the papers all full of you shaking hands with the English king at Buckingham Palace?

O'FLAHERTY. I didnt shake hands with him: he shook hands with me. Could I turn on the man in his own house, before his own wife, with his money in my pocket and in yours, and throw his civility back in his face?

MRS O'FLAHERTY. You would take the hand of a tyrant red with the blood of Ireland—

O'FLAHERTY. Arra hold your nonsense, mother: he's not half the tyrant you are, God help him. His hand was cleaner than mine that had the blood of his own relations on it, may be.

MRS O'FLAHERTY [*threateningly*] Is that a way to speak to your mother, you young spalpeen?

O'FLAHERTY [*stoutly*] It is so, if you wont talk sense to me. It's a nice thing for a poor boy to be made much of by kings and queens, and shook hands with by the heighth of his country's nobility in the capital cities of the world, and then to come home and be scolded and insulted by his own mother. I'll fight for who I like; and I'll shake hands with what kings I like; and if your own son is not good enough for you, you can go and look for another. Do you mind me now?

MRS O'FLAHERTY. And was it the Belgians learned you such brazen impudence?

O'FLAHERTY. The Belgians is good men; and the French ought to be more civil to them, let alone their being half murdered by the Boshes.

MRS O'FLAHERTY. Good men is it. Good men! to come over here when they were wounded because it was a Catholic country, and then to go to the Protestant Church because it didnt cost them anything, and some of them to never go near a church at all. Thats what you call good men!

O'FLAHERTY. Oh, youre the mighty fine politician, arnt you? Much you know about Belgians or foreign parts or the world youre living in, God help you!

MRS O'FLAHERTY. Why wouldnt I know better than you? Amment I your mother?

O'FLAHERTY. And if you are itself, how can you know what you never seen as well as me that was dug into the continent of Europe for six months, and was buried in the earth of it three times with the shells bursting on the top of me? I tell you I know what I'm about. I have my own reasons for taking part in this great conflict. I'd be ashamed to stay at home and not fight when everybody else is fighting.

MRS O'FLAHERTY. If you wanted to fight, why couldnt you fight in the German army?

O'FLAHERTY. Because they only get a penny a day.

MRS O'FLAHERTY. Well, and if they do itself, isnt there the French army?

O'FLAHERTY. They only get a hapenny a day.

MRS O'FLAHERTY [*much dashed*] Oh murder! They must be a mean lot, Dinny.

O'FLAHERTY [*sarcastic*] Maybe youd have me join the Turkish army, and worship the heathen Mahomet that put a corn in his ear and pretended it was a message from the heavens when the pigeon come to pick it out and eat it. I went where I could get the biggest allowance for you; and little thanks I get for it!

MRS O'FLAHERTY. Allowance, is it! Do you know what the thieving blackguards did on me? They came to me and they says, "Was your son a big eater?" they says. "Oh, he was that" says I: "ten shillings a week wouldnt keep him." Sure I thought the more I said the more theyd give me. "Then" says they, "thats ten shillings a week off your allowance" they says, "because you save that by the king feeding him." "Indeed!" says I: "I suppose if I'd six sons, youd stop three pound a week from me, and make out that I ought to pay you money instead of you paying me." "Theres a fallacy in your argument" they says.

O'FLAHERTY. A what?

MRS O'FLAHERTY. A fallacy: thats the word he said. I says to him, "It's a Pharisee I'm thinking you mean, sir; but you can keep your dirty money that your king grudges a poor old widow; and please God the English will be bet yet for the deadly sin of oppressing the poor"; and with that I shut the door in his face.

O'FLAHERTY [*furious*] Do you tell me they knocked ten shillings off you for my keep?

MRS O'FLAHERTY [*soothing him*] No, darlint: they only knocked off half a crown. I put up with it because Ive got the old age pension; and they know very well I'm only sixty-two; so Ive the better of them by half a crown a week anyhow.

O'FLAHERTY. It's a queer way of doing business. If theyd tell you straight out what they was going to give you, you wouldnt mind; but if there was twenty ways of telling the truth and only one way of telling a lie, the Government would find it out. It's in the nature of governments to tell lies.

Teresa Driscoll, a parlor maid, comes from the house.

TERESA. Youre to come up to the drawing room to have your tea, Mrs O'Flaherty.

MRS O'FLAHERTY. Mind you have a sup of good black tea

for me in the kitchen afterwards, acushla. That washy drawing room tea will give me the wind if I leave it on my stomach. [*She goes into the house, leaving the two young people alone together*].

O'FLAHERTY. Is that yourself, Tessie? And how are you?

TERESA. Nicely, thank you. And hows yourself?

O'FLAHERTY. Finely, thank God. [*He produces a gold chain*]. Look what Ive brought you, Tessie.

TERESA [*shrinking*] Sure I dont like to touch it, Denny. Did you take it off a dead man?

O'FLAHERTY. No: I took it off a live one; and thankful he was to me to be alive and kept a prisoner in ease and comfort, and me left fighting in peril of my life.

TERESA [*taking it*] Do you think it's real gold, Denny?

O'FLAHERTY. It's real German gold, anyhow.

TERESA. But German silver isnt real, Denny.

O'FLAHERTY [*his face darkening*] Well, it's the best the Bosh could do for me, anyhow.

TERESA. Do you think I might take it to the jeweller next market day and ask him?

O'FLAHERTY [*sulkily*] You may take it to the divil if you like.

TERESA. You neednt lose your temper about it. I only thought I'd like to know. The nice fool I'd look if I went about shewing off a chain that turned out to be only brass!

O'FLAHERTY. I think you might say Thank you.

TERESA. Do you? I think you might have said something more to me than "Is that yourself?" You couldnt say less to the postman.

O'FLAHERTY [*his brow clearing*] Oh, is that whats the matter? Here! come and take the taste of the brass out of my mouth. [*He seizes her and kisses her*].

Teresa, without losing her Irish dignity, takes the kiss as appreciatively as a connoisseur might take a glass of wine, and sits down with him on the garden seat.

TERESA [*as he squeezes her waist*] Thank God the priest cant see us here!

O'FLAHERTY. It's little they care for priests in France, alanna.

TERESA. And what had the queen on her, Denny, when she spoke to you in the palace?

O'FLAHERTY. She had a bonnet on without any strings to it. And she had a plakeen of embroidery down her bosom. And she had her waist where it used to be, and not where the other ladies had it. And she had little brooches in her ears, though she hadnt half the jewelry of Mrs Sullivan that keeps the popshop in Drumpogue. And she dresses her hair down over her forehead, in a fringe like. And she has an Irish look about her eyebrows. And she didnt know what to say to me, poor woman! and I didnt know what to say to her, God help me!

TERESA. Youll have a pension now with the Cross, wont you, Denny?

O'FLAHERTY. Sixpence three farthings a day.

TERESA. That isnt much.

O'FLAHERTY. I take out the rest in glory.

TERESA. And if youre wounded, youll have a wound pension, wont you?

O'FLAHERTY. I will, please God.

TERESA. Youre going out again, arnt you, Denny?

O'FLAHERTY. I cant help myself. I'd be shot for a deserter if I didnt go; and may be I'll be shot by the Boshes if I do go; so between the two of them I'm nicely fixed up.

MRS O'FLAHERTY [*calling from within the house*] Tessie! Tessie darlint!

TERESA [*disengaging herself from his arm and rising*] I'm wanted for the tea table. Youll have a pension anyhow, Denny, wont you, whether youre wounded or not?

MRS O'FLAHERTY. Come, child, come.

TERESA [*impatiently*] Oh, sure I'm coming. [*She tries to smile at Denny, not very convincingly, and hurries into the house*].

O'FLAHERTY [*alone*] And if I do get a pension itself, the divil a penny of it youll ever have the spending of.

MRS O'FLAHERTY [*as she comes from the porch*] Oh, it's a shame for you to keep the girl from her juties, Dinny. You might get her into trouble.

O'FLAHERTY. Much I care whether she gets into trouble or not! I pity the man that gets her into trouble. He'll get himself into worse.

MRS O'FLAHERTY. Whats that you tell me? Have you been falling out with her, and she a girl with a fortune of ten pounds?

O'FLAHERTY. Let her keep her fortune. I wouldnt touch her with the tongs if she had thousands and millions.

MRS O'FLAHERTY. Oh fie for shame, Dinny! why would you say the like of that of a decent honest girl, and one of the Driscolls too?

O'FLAHERTY. Why wouldnt I say it? She's thinking of nothing but to get me out there again to be wounded so that she may spend my pension, bad scran to her!

MRS O'FLAHERTY. Why, whats come over you, child, at all at all?

O'FLAHERTY. Knowledge and wisdom has come over me with pain and fear and trouble. Ive been made a fool of and imposed upon all my life. I thought that covetious sthreal in there was a walking angel; and now if ever I marry at all I'll marry a Frenchwoman.

MRS O'FLAHERTY [*fiercely*] Youll not, so; and dont you dar repeat such a thing to me.

O'FLAHERTY. Wont I, faith! Ive been as good as married to a couple of them already.

MRS O'FLAHERTY. The Lord be praised, what wickedness have you been up to, you young blackguard?

O'FLAHERTY. One of them Frenchwomen would cook you a meal twice in the day and all days and every day that Sir Pearce himself might go begging through Ireland for, and never see the like of. I'll have a French wife, I tell you; and when I settle down to be a farmer I'll have a French farm, with a field as big as the continent of Europe that ten of your dirty little fields here wouldnt so much as fill the ditch of.

MRS O'FLAHERTY [*furious*] Then it's a French mother you may go look for; for I'm done with you.

O'FLAHERTY. And it's no great loss youd be if it wasnt for my natural feelings for you; for it's only a silly ignorant old countrywoman you are with all your fine talk about Ireland: you that never stepped beyond the few acres of it you were born on!

MRS O'FLAHERTY [*tottering to the garden seat and shewing signs of breaking down*] Dinny darlint, why are you like this to me? Whats happened to you?

O'FLAHERTY [*gloomily*] Whats happened to everybody? thats what I want to know. Whats happened to you that I thought all the world of and was afeard of? Whats happened to Sir Pearce, that I thought was a great general, and that I now see to be no more fit to command an army than an old hen? Whats happened to Tessie, that I was mad to marry a year ago, and that I wouldnt take now with all Ireland for her fortune? I tell you the world's creation is crumbling in ruins about me; and then you come and ask whats happened to me?

MRS O'FLAHERTY [*giving way to wild grief*] Ochone! ochone! my son's turned agen me. Oh, whatll I do at all at all? Oh! oh! oh! oh!

SIR PEARCE [*running out of the house*] Whats this infernal noise? What on earth is the matter?

O'FLAHERTY. Arra hold your whisht, mother. Dont you see his honor?

MRS O'FLAHERTY. Oh, sir, I'm ruined and destroyed. Oh, wont you speak to Dinny, sir: I'm heart scalded with him. He wants to marry a Frenchwoman on me, and to go away and be a foreigner and desert his mother and betray his country. It's mad he is with the roaring of the cannons and he killing the Germans and the Germans killing him, bad cess to them! My boy is taken from me and turned agen me; and who is to take care of me in my old age after all Ive done for him, ochone! ochone!

O'FLAHERTY. Hold your noise, I tell you. Who's going to leave you? I'm going to take you with me. There now: does that satisfy you?

MRS O'FLAHERTY. Is it take me into a strange land among heathens and pagans and savages, and me not knowing a word of their language nor them of mine?

O'FLAHERTY. A good job they dont: may be theyll think youre talking sense.

MRS O'FLAHERTY. Ask me to die out of Ireland, is it? and the angels not to find me when they come for me!

O'FLAHERTY. And would you ask me to live in Ireland where Ive been imposed on and kept in ignorance, and to die where the divil himself wouldnt take me as a gift, let alone the blessed angels? You can come or stay. You can take your old way or take my young way. But stick in this place I will not among a lot of good-for-nothing divils thatll not do a hand's turn but watch the grass growing and build up the stone wall where the cow walked through it. And Sir Horace Plunkett breaking his heart all the time telling them how they might put the land into decent tillage like the French and Belgians.

SIR PEARCE. Yes: he's quite right, you know, Mrs O'Flaherty: quite right there.

MRS O'FLAHERTY. Well, sir, please God the war will last a long time yet; and may be I'll die before it's over and the separation allowance stops.

O'FLAHERTY. Thats all you care about. It's nothing but milch cows we men are for the women, with their separation allowances, ever since the war began, bad luck to them that made it!

TERESA [*coming from the porch between the General and Mrs O'Flaherty*] Hannah sent me out for to tell you, sir, that the tea will be black and the cake not fit to eat with the cold if yous all dont come at wanst.

MRS O'FLAHERTY [*breaking out again*] Oh, Tessie darlint, what have you been saying to Dinny at all at all? Oh! oh—

SIR PEARCE [*out of patience*] You cant discuss that here.

We shall have Tessie beginning now.

O'FLAHERTY. Thats right, sir: drive them in.

TERESA. I havnt said a word to him. He—

SIR PEARCE. Hold your tongue; and go in and attend to your business at the tea table.

TERESA. But amment I telling your honor that I never said a word to him? He gave me a beautiful gold chain. Here it is to shew your honour thats it's no lie I'm telling you.

SIR PEARCE. Whats this, O'Flaherty? Youve been looting some unfortunate officer.

O'FLAHERTY. No sir: I stole it from him of his own accord.

MRS O'FLAHERTY. Wouldnt your honor tell him that his mother has the first call on it? What would a slip of a girl like that be doing with a gold chain round her neck?

TERESA [*venomously*] Anyhow, I have a neck to put it round and not a hank of wrinkles.

At this unfortunate remark, Mrs O'Flaherty bounds from her seat; and an appalling tempest of wordy wrath breaks out. The remonstrances and commands of the General, and the protests and menaces of O'Flaherty, only increase the hubbub. They are soon all speaking at once at the top of their voices.

MRS O'FLAHERTY [*solo*] You impudent young heifer, how dar you say such a thing to me? [*Teresa retorts furiously; the men interfere; and the solo becomes a quartet, fortissimo*]. Ive a good mind to clout your ears for you to teach you manners. Be ashamed of yourself, do; and learn to know who youre speaking to. That I maytnt sin! but I dont know what the good God was thinking about when he made the like of you. Let me not see you casting sheep's eyes at my son again. There never was an O'Flaherty yet that would demean himself by keeping company with a dirty Driscoll; and if I see you next or nigh my house I'll put you in the ditch with a flea in your ear: mind that now.

THERESA. Is it me you offer such a name to, you foul-mouthed, dirty minded, lying, sloothering old sow, you? I wouldnt soil my tongue by calling you in your right name and telling Sir Pearce whats the common talk of the town about you. You and your O'Flahertys! setting yourself up agen the Driscolls that would never lower themselves to be seen in conversation with you at the fair. You can keep your ugly stingy lump of a son; for what he is but a common soldier? and God help the girl that gets him, say I! So the back of my hand to you, Mrs O'Flaherty; and that the cat may tear your ugly old face!

SIR PEARCE. Silence. Tessie: did you here me ordering you to go into the house? Mrs O'Flaherty! [*Louder*] Mrs O'Flaherty!! Will you just listen to me one moment? Please. [*Furiously*] Do you hear me speaking to you, woman? Are you human beings or are you wild beasts? Stop that noise immediately: do you hear? [*Yelling*] Are you going to do what I order you, or are you not? Scandalous! Disgraceful! This comes of being too familiar with you. O'Flaherty: shove them into the house. Out with the whole damned pack of you.

O'FLAHERTY [*to the women*] Here now: none of that, none of that. Go easy, I tell you. Hold your whisht, mother, will you, or youll be sorry for it after. [*To Teresa*] Is that the way for a decent young girl to speak? [*Despairingly*] Oh, for the Lord's sake, shut up, will yous? Have yous no respect for yourselves or your betters? [*Peremptorily*] Let me have no more of it, I tell you. Och! the divil's in the whole crew of you. In with you into the house this very minute and tear one another's eyes out in the kitchen if you like. In with you.

The two men seize the two women, and push them, still violently abusing one another, into the house. Sir Pearce slams the door upon them savagely. Immediately a heavenly silence falls on the summer afternoon. The two sit down out of breath; and for a long time nothing is said. Sir Pearce sits on an iron chair. O'Flaherty sits on the garden seat. The thrush begins to sing melodiously. O'Flaherty cocks his ears, and looks up at it. A smile spreads over his troubled features. Sir Pearce, with a long sigh, takes out his pipe, and begins to fill it.

O'FLAHERTY [*idyllically*] What a discontented sort of an

animal a man is, sir! Only a month ago, I was in the quiet of the country out at the front, with not a sound except the birds and the bellow of a cow in the distance as it might be, and the shrapnel making little clouds in the heavens, and the shells whistling, and may be a yell or two when one of us was hit; and would you believe it, sir, I complained of the noise and wanted to have a peaceful hour at home. Well: them two has taught me a lesson. This morning, sir, when I was telling the boys here how I was longing to be back taking my part for king and country with the others, I was lying, as you well knew, sir. Now I can go and say it with a clear conscience. Some likes war's alarums; and some likes home life. Ive tried both, sir; and I'm all for war's alarums now. I always was a quiet lad by natural disposition.

SIR PEARCE. Strictly between ourselves, O'Flaherty, and as one soldier to another [*O'Flaherty salutes, but without stiffening*], do you think we should have got an army without conscription if domestic life had been as happy as people say it is?

O'FLAHERTY. Well, between you and me and the wall, Sir Pearce, I think the less we say about that until the war's over, the better.

He winks at the General. The General strikes a match. The thrush sings. A jay laughs. The conversation drops.

HEARTBREAK HOUSE

Shaw began to write *Heartbreak House* in 1913 just after the London theatres had presented a number of plays by the great Russian dramatist, Anton Chekhov. As he had found the quintessence of Ibsenism to be the universal applicability of his basic themes, so Shaw found in Chekhov's decadent aristocrats dramatic types who knew no national boundaries. His new play was to be "A Fantasia in the Russian Manner on English Themes," and it grew out of an anecdote related by Lena Ashwell, an actress whose father had been first a sea captain and then a clergyman. It was to be a sort of freehand sketch rather than a well-made play. Shaw declared that it "began with an atmosphere and does not contain a word that was foreseen before it was written."

Although Shaw normally wrote with the efficiency of an experienced journalist, *Heartbreak House* was not completed until 1916. The outbreak of the First World War in 1914 appeared to him "a catastrophe of a magnitude so appalling, and a scope so unpredictable" that he began to wonder "whether the human animal, as he exists at present, is capable of solving the social problems raised by his own aggregation, or, as he calls it, civilization." Shaw's immediate reaction to the catastrophe was a series of lectures, interviews, pamphlets, and letters to the editor which caused him to be labeled traitor and monster. Perhaps it was the rejection of his "Common Sense" as much as the war itself that led to the despairing mood which changed *Heartbreak House* in mid-writing from affectionate satire to lamentation.

The play is at once symbolic and prophetic. The setting, like the play itself, begins as a kind of whim: a study or den built in the form of a ship to suit the taste of its owner, Captain Shotover. But, as the action develops, the setting evolves from the particular to the general, from Shotover's hideaway, to Europe, to civilization itself: a ship on the rocks. And just as *Androcles* can now be seen to have prophesied what would happen to man confronted with the First World War, *Heartbreak House* looks forward to the political muddling that was to follow it and to the horrors of blitzkrieg.

The play was first performed by the Theatre Guild in New York, November 10, 1920. Shotover was played by Albert Perry; his daughters, Lady Utterword by Lucille Watson and Hesione by Effie Shannon. Elisabeth Risdon was Ellie Dunn and Dudley Digges, Boss Mangan. The first London performance was at the Royal Court, October 18, 1921, with Brember Wills as Shotover, Edith Evans and Mary Grey as his daughters, Ellen O'Malley as Ellie, and Alfred Clark as Mangan.

HEARTBREAK HOUSE

ACT I

THE hilly country in the middle of the north edge of Sussex, looking very pleasant on a fine evening at the end of September, is seen through the windows of a room which has been built so as to resemble the after part of an old-fashioned high-pooped ship with a stern gallery; for the windows are ship built with heavy timbering, and run right across the room as continuously as the stability of the wall allows. A row of lockers under the windows provides an unupholstered window-seat interrupted by twin glass doors, respectively halfway between the stern post and the sides. Another door strains the illusion a little by being apparently in the ship's port side, and yet leading, not to the open sea, but to the entrance hall of the house. Between this door and the stern gallery are bookshelves. There are electric light switches beside the door leading to the hall and the glass doors in the stern gallery. Against the starboard wall is a carpenter's bench. The vice has a board in its jaws; and the floor is littered with shavings, overflowing from a waste-paper basket. A couple of planes and a centrebit are on the bench. In the same wall, between the bench and the windows, is a narrow doorway with a half door, above which a glimpse of the room beyond shews that it is a shelved pantry with bottles and kitchen crockery.

On the starboard side, but close to the middle, is a plain oak drawing-table with drawing-board, T-square, straightedges, set squares, mathematical instruments, saucers of water color, a tumbler of discolored water, Indian ink, pencils, and brushes on it. The drawing-board is set so that the draughtsman's chair has the window on its left hand. On the floor at the end of the table, on his right, is a ship's fire bucket. On the port side of the room, near the bookshelves, is a sofa with its back to the windows. It is a sturdy mahogany article, oddly upholstered in sailcloth, including the bolster, with a couple of blankets hanging over the back. Between the sofa and the drawing-table is a big wicker chair, with broad arms and a low sloping back, with its back to the light. A small but stout table of teak, with a round top and gate legs, stands against the port wall between the door and the bookcase. It is the only article in the room that suggests (not at all convincingly) a woman's hand in the furnishing. The uncarpeted floor of narrow boards is caulked and holystoned like a deck.

The garden to which the glass doors lead dips to the south before the landscape rises again to the hills. Emerging from the hollow is the cupola of an observatory. Between the observatory and the house is a flagstaff on a little esplanade, with a hammock on the east side and a long garden seat on the west.

A young lady, gloved and hatted, with a dust coat on, is sitting in the window-seat with her body twisted to enable her to look out at the view. One hand props her chin: the other hangs down with a volume of the Temple Shakespear in it, and her finger stuck in the page she has been reading.

A clock strikes six.

The young lady turns and looks at her watch. She rises with an air of one who waits and is almost at the end of her patience. She is a pretty girl, slender, fair, and intelligent looking, nicely but not expensively dressed, evidently not a smart idler.

With a sigh of weary resignation she comes to the draughtsman's chair; sits down; and begins to read Shakespear. Presently the book sinks to her lap; her eyes close; and she dozes into a slumber.

An elderly womanservant comes in from the hall with three unopened bottles of rum on a tray. She passes through and disappears in the pantry without noticing the young lady. She places the bottles on the shelf and fills her tray with empty bottles. As she returns with these, the young lady lets her book drop, awakening herself, and startling the womanservant so that she all but lets the tray fall.

THE WOMANSERVANT. God bless us! [*The young lady picks up the book and places it on the table*]. Sorry to wake you, miss, I'm sure; but you are a stranger to me. What might you be waiting here for now?

THE YOUNG LADY. Waiting for somebody to shew some signs of knowing that I have been invited here.

THE WOMANSERVANT. Oh, youre invited, are you? And has nobody come? Dear! dear!

THE YOUNG LADY. A wild-looking old gentleman came and looked in at the window; and I heard him calling out "Nurse: there is a young and attractive female waiting in the poop. Go and see what she wants." Are you the nurse?

THE WOMANSERVANT. Yes, miss: I'm Nurse Guinness. That was old Captain Shotover, Mrs Hushabye's father. I heard him roaring; but I thought it was for something else. I suppose it was Mrs Hushabye that invited you, ducky?

THE YOUNG LADY. I understood her to do so. But really I think I'd better go.

NURSE GUINNESS. Oh, dont think of such a thing, miss. If Mrs Hushabye has forgotten all about it, it will be a pleasant surprise for her to see you, wont it?

THE YOUNG LADY. It has been a very unpleasant surprise to me to find that nobody expects me.

NURSE GUINNESS. Youll get used to it, miss: this house is full of surprises for them that dont know our ways.

CAPTAIN SHOTOVER [*looking in from the hall suddenly: an ancient but still hardy man with an immense white beard, in a reefer jacket with a whistle hanging from his neck*] Nurse: there is a hold-all and a handbag on the front steps for everybody to fall over. Also a tennis racquet. Who the devil left them there?

THE YOUNG LADY. They are mine, I'm afraid.

THE CAPTAIN [*advancing to the drawing-table*] Nurse: who is this misguided and unfortunate young lady?

NURSE GUINNESS. She says Miss Hessy invited her, sir.

THE CAPTAIN. And had she no friend, no parents, to warn her against my daughter's invitations? This is a pretty sort of house, by heavens! A young and attractive lady is invited here. Her luggage is left on the steps for hours; and she herself is deposited in the poop and abandoned, tired and starving. This is our hospitality. These are our manners. No room ready. No hot water. No welcoming hostess. Our visitor is to sleep in the toolshed, and to wash in the duckpond.

NURSE GUINNESS. Now it's all right, Captain: I'll get the lady some tea; and her room shall be ready before she has finished it. [*To the young lady*] Take off your hat, ducky; and make yourself at home. [*She goes to the door leading to the hall*].

THE CAPTAIN [*as she passes him*] Ducky! Do you suppose, woman, that because this young lady has been insulted and neglected, you have the right to address her as you address my wretched children, whom you have brought up in ignorance of the commonest decencies of social intercourse?

NURSE GUINNESS. Never mind him, doty. [*Quite unconcerned, she goes out into the hall on her way to the kitchen*].

THE CAPTAIN. Madam: will you favor me with your name? [*He sits down in the big wicker chair*].

THE YOUNG LADY. My name is Ellie Dunn.

THE CAPTAIN. Dunn! I had a boatswain whose name was Dunn. He was originally a pirate in China. He set up as a ship's chandler with stores which I have every reason to believe he stole from me. No doubt he became rich. Are you his daughter?

ELLIE [*indignant*] No: certainly not. I am proud to be able to say that though my father has not been a successful man, nobody has ever had one word to say against him. I think my father is the best man I have ever known.

THE CAPTAIN. He must be greatly changed. Has he attained the seventh degree of concentration?

ELLIE. I dont understand.

THE CAPTAIN. But how could he, with a daughter? I, madam, have two daughters. One of them is Hesione Hushabye, who invited you here. I keep this house: she upsets it. I desire to attain the seventh degree of concentration: she invites visitors and leaves me to entertain them. [*Nurse Guinness returns with the tea-tray, which she places on the teak table*]. I have a second daughter who is, thank God, in a remote part of the Empire with her numskull of a husband. As a child she thought the figure-head of my ship, the Dauntless, the most beautiful thing on earth. He resembled it. He had the same expression: wooden yet enterprising. She married him, and will never set foot in this house again.

NURSE GUINNESS [*carrying the table, with the tea-things on it, to Ellie's side*] Indeed you never were more mistaken. She is in England this very moment. You have been told three times this week that she is coming home for a year for her health. And very glad you should be to see your own daughter again after all these years.

THE CAPTAIN. I am not glad. The natural term of the affection of the human animal for its offspring is six years. My daughter Ariadne was born when I was forty-six. I am now eighty-eight. If she comes, I am not at home. If she wants anything, let her take it. If she asks for me, let her be informed that I am extremely old, and have totally forgotten her.

NURSE GUINNESS. Thats no talk to offer to a young lady. Here, ducky, have some tea; and dont listen to him. [*She pours out a cup of tea*].

THE CAPTAIN [*rising wrathfully*] Now before high heaven they have given this innocent child Indian tea: the stuff they tan their own leather insides with. [*He seizes the cup and the tea-pot and empties both into the leathern bucket*].

ELLIE [*almost in tears*] Oh, please! I am so tired. I should have been glad of anything.

NURSE GUINNESS. Oh, what a thing to do! The poor lamb is ready to drop.

THE CAPTAIN. You shall have some of my tea. Do not touch that fly-blown cake: nobody eats it here except the dogs. [*He disappears into the pantry*].

NURSE GUINNESS. Theres a man for you! They say he sold himself to the devil in Zanzibar before he was a captain; and the older he grows the more I believe them.

A WOMAN'S VOICE [*in the hall*] Is anyone at home? Hesione! Nurse! Papa! Do come, somebody; and take in my luggage.

Thumping heard, as of an umbrella, on the wainscot.

NURSE GUINNESS. My gracious! It's Miss Addy, Lady Utterword, Mrs Hushabye's sister: the one I told the Captain about. [*Calling*] Coming, Miss, coming.

She carries the table back to its place by the door, and is hurrying out when she is intercepted by Lady Utterword, who bursts in much flustered. Lady Utterword, a blonde, is very handsome, very well dressed, and so precipitate in speech and action that the first impression (erroneous) is one of comic silliness.

LADY UTTERWORD. Oh, is that you, Nurse? How are you? You dont look a day older. Is nobody at home? Where is Hesione? Doesnt she expect me? Where are the servants? Whose luggage is that on the steps? Where's papa? Is everybody asleep? [*Seeing Ellie*] Oh! I beg your pardon. I suppose you are one of my nieces. [*Approaching her with outstretched arms*] Come and kiss your aunt, darling.

ELLIE. I'm only a visitor. It is my luggage on the steps.

NURSE GUINNESS. I'll go get you some fresh tea, ducky. [*She takes up the tray*].

ELLIE. But the old gentleman said he would make some himself.

NURSE GUINNESS. Bless you! he's forgotten what he went for already. His mind wanders from one thing to another.

LADY UTTERWORD. Papa, I suppose?

NURSE GUINNESS. Yes, Miss.

LADY UTTERWORD [*vehemently*] Dont be silly, Nurse. Dont call me Miss.

NURSE GUINNESS [*placidly*] No, lovey. [*She goes out*

with the tea-tray].

LADY UTTERWORD [*sitting down with a flounce on the sofa*] I know what you must feel. Oh, this house, this house! I come back to it after twenty-three years; and it is just the same: the luggage lying on the steps, the servants spoilt and impossible, nobody at home to receive anybody, no regular meals, nobody ever hungry because they are always gnawing bread and butter or munching apples, and, what is worse, the same disorder in ideas, in talk, in feeling. When I was a child I was used to it: I had never known anything better, though I was unhappy, and longed all the time—oh, how I longed!—to be respectable, to be a lady, to live as others did, not to have to think of everything for myself. I married at nineteen to escape from it. My husband is Sir Hastings Utterword, who has been governor of all the crown colonies in succession. I have always been the mistress of Government House. I have been so happy: I had forgotten that people could live like this. I wanted to see my father, my sister, my nephews and nieces (one ought to, you know), and I was looking forward to it. And now the state of the house! the way I'm received! the casual impudence of that woman Guinness, our old nurse! really Hesione might at least have been here: s o m e preparation might have been made for me. You must excuse my going on in this way; but I am really very much hurt and annoyed and disillusioned: and if I had realized it was to be like this, I wouldnt have come. I have a great mind to go away without another word. [*She is on the point of weeping*].

ELLIE [*also very miserable*] Nobody has been here to receive me either. I thought I ought to go away too. But how can I, Lady Utterword? My luggage is on the steps; and the station fly has gone.

The Captain emerges from the pantry with a tray of Chinese lacquer and a very fine tea-set on it. He rests it provisionally on the end of the table; snatches away the drawing-board, which he stands on the floor against the table legs; and puts the tray in the space thus cleared. Ellie pours out a cup greedily.

THE CAPTAIN. Your tea, young lady. What! another lady! I must fetch another cup. [*He makes for the pantry*].

LADY UTTERWORD [*rising from the sofa, suffused with emotion*] Papa! Dont you know me? I'm your daughter.

THE CAPTAIN. Nonsense! my daughter's upstairs asleep. [*He vanishes through the half door*].

Lady Utterword retires to the window to conceal her tears.

ELLIE [*going to her with the cup*] Dont be so distressed. Have this cup of tea. He is very old and very strange: he has been just like that to me. I know how dreadful it must be: my own father is all the world to me. Oh, I'm sure he didnt mean it.

The Captain returns with another cup.

THE CAPTAIN. Now we are complete. [*He places it on the tray*].

LADY UTTERWORD [*hysterically*] Papa: you cant have forgotten me. I am Ariadne. I'm little Paddy Patkins. Wont you kiss me? [*She goes to him and throws her arms round his neck*].

THE CAPTAIN [*woodenly enduring her embrace*] How can you be Ariadne? You are a middle-aged woman: well-preserved, madam, but no longer young.

LADY UTTERWORD. But think of all the years and years I have been away, papa. I have had to grow old, like other people.

THE CAPTAIN [*disengaging himself*] You should grow out of kissing strange men: they may be striving to attain the seventh degree of concentration.

LADY UTTERWORD. But I'm your daughter. You havnt seen me for years.

THE CAPTAIN. So much the worse! When our relatives are at home, we have to think of all their good points or it would be impossible to endure them. But when they are away, we console ourselves for their absence by dwelling on their vices. That is how I have come to think my absent daughter Ariadne a perfect fiend; so do not try to ingratiate yourself here by impersonating her. [*He walks firmly away to the other side of the room*].

LADY UTTERWORD. Ingratiating myself indeed! [*With dignity*] Very well, papa. [*She sits down at the drawing-table and pours out tea for herself*].

THE CAPTAIN. I am neglecting my social duties. You remember Dunn? Billy Dunn?

LADY UTTERWORD. Do you mean that villainous sailor who robbed you?

THE CAPTAIN [*introducing Ellie*] His daughter. [*He sits down on the sofa*].

ELLIE [*protesting*] No—

Nurse Guinness returns with fresh tea.

THE CAPTAIN. Take that hogwash away. Do you hear?

NURSE. Youve actually remembered about the tea! [*To Ellie*] O, miss, he didnt forget you after all! You h a v e made an impression.

THE CAPTAIN [*gloomily*] Youth! beauty! novelty! They are badly wanted in this house. I am excessively old. Hesione is only moderately young. Her children are not youthful.

LADY UTTERWORD. How can children be expected to be youthful in this house? Almost before we could speak we were filled with notions that might have been all very well for pagan philosophers of fifty, but were certainly quite unfit for respectable people of any age.

NURSE. You were always for respectability, Miss Addy.

LADY UTTERWORD. Nurse: will you please remember that I am Lady Utterword, and not Miss Addy, nor lovey, nor darling, nor doty? Do you hear?

NURSE. Yes, ducky: all right. I'll tell them all they must call you my lady. [*She takes her tray out with undisturbed placidity*].

LADY UTTERWORD. What comfort? what sense is there in having servants with no manners?

ELLIE [*rising and coming to the table to put down her*

empty cup] Lady Utterword: do you think Mrs Hushabye really expects me?

LADY UTTERWORD. Oh, dont ask me. You can see for yourself that Ive just arrived; her only sister, after twenty-three years absence! and it seems that *I* am not expected.

THE CAPTAIN. What does it matter whether the young lady is expected or not? She is welcome. There are beds: there is food. I'll find a room for her myself. [*He makes for the door*].

ELLIE [*following him to stop him*] Oh please— [*He goes out*]. Lady Utterword: I dont know what to do. Your father persists in believing that my father is some sailor who robbed him.

LADY UTTERWORD. You had better pretend not to notice it. My father is a very clever man; but he always forgot things; and now that he is old, of course he is worse. And I must warn you that it is sometimes very hard to feel quite sure that he really forgets.

Mrs Hushabye bursts into the room tempestuously, and embraces Ellie. She is a couple of years older than Lady Utterword, and even better looking. She has magnificent black hair, eyes like the fishpools of Heshbon, and a nobly modelled neck, short at the back and low between her shoulders in front. Unlike her sister she is uncorseted and dressed anyhow in a rich robe of black pile that shews off her white skin and statuesque contour.

MRS HUSHABYE. Ellie, my darling, my pettikins [*kissing her*]: how long have you been here? Ive been at home all the time: I was putting flowers and things in your room; and when I just sat down for a moment to try how comfortable the armchair was I went off to sleep. Papa woke me and told me you were here. Fancy your finding no one, and being neglected and abandoned. [*Kissing her again*] My poor love! [*She deposits Ellie on the sofa. Meanwhile Ariadne has left the table and come over to claim her share of attention*]. Oh! youve brought someone with you. Introduce me.

LADY UTTERWORD. Hesione: is it possible that y o u dont know me?

MRS HUSHABYE [*conventionally*] Of course I remember your face quite well. Where have we met?

LADY UTTERWORD. Didnt papa tell you I was here? Oh! this is really too much. [*She throws herself sulkily into the big chair*].

MRS HUSHABYE. Papa!

LADY UTTERWORD. Yes: Papa. O u r papa, you unfeeling wretch. [*Rising angrily*] I'll go straight to a hotel.

MRS HUSHABYE [*seizing her by the shoulders*] My goodness gracious goodness, you dont mean to say that youre Addy!

LADY UTTERWORD. I certainly am Addy; and I dont think I can be so changed that you would not have recognized me if you had any real affection for me. And papa didnt think me even worth mentioning!

MRS HUSHABYE. What a lark! Sit down. [*She pushes her back into the chair instead of kissing her, and posts herself behind it*]. You d o look a swell. Youre much handsomer than you used to be. Youve made the acquaintance of Ellie, of course. She is going to marry a perfect hog of a millionaire for the sake of her father, who is as poor as a church mouse; and you must help me to stop her.

ELLIE. Oh p l e a s e, Hesione.

MRS HUSHABYE. My pettikins, the man's coming here today with your father to begin persecuting you; and everybody will see the state of the case in ten minutes; so whats the use of making a secret of it?

ELLIE. He is not a hog, Hesione. You dont know how wonderfully good he was to my father, and how deeply grateful I am to him.

MRS HUSHABYE [*to Lady Utterword*] Her father is a very remarkable man, Addy. His name is Mazzini Dunn. Mazzini was a celebrity of some kind who knew Ellie's grandparents. They were both poets, like the Brownings; and when her father came into the world Mazzini said

"Another soldier born for freedom!" So they christened him Mazzini; and he has been fighting for freedom in his quiet way ever since. Thats why he is so poor.

ELLIE. I am proud of his poverty.

MRS HUSHABYE. Of course you are, pettikins. Why not leave him in it, and marry someone you love?

LADY UTTERWORD [*rising suddenly and explosively*] Hesione: are you going to kiss me or are you not?

MRS HUSHABYE. What do you want to be kissed for?

LADY UTTERWORD. I d o n t want to be kissed; but I do want you to behave properly and decently. We are sisters. We have been separated for twenty-three years. You o u g h t to kiss me.

MRS HUSHABYE. Tomorrow morning, dear, before you make up. I hate the smell of powder.

LADY UTTERWORD. Oh! you unfeeling— [*She is interrupted by the return of the captain*].

THE CAPTAIN [*to Ellie*] Your room is ready. [*Ellie rises*]. The sheets were damp; but I have changed them. [*He makes for the garden door on the port side*].

LADY UTTERWORD. Oh! What about m y sheets?

THE CAPTAIN [*halting at the door*] Take my advice: air them; or take them off and sleep in blankets. You shall sleep in Ariadne's old room.

LADY UTTERWORD. Indeed I shall do nothing of the sort. That little hole! I am entitled to the best spare room.

THE CAPTAIN [*continuing unmoved*] She married a numskull. She told me she would marry anyone to get away from home.

LADY UTTERWORD. You are pretending not to know me on purpose. I will leave the house.

Mazzini Dunn enters from the hall. He is a little elderly man with bulging credulous eyes and earnest manners. He is dressed in a blue serge jacket suit with an unbuttoned mackintosh over it, and carries a soft black hat of clerical cut.

ELLIE. At last! Captain Shotover: here is my father.

THE CAPTAIN. This! Nonsense! not a bit like him. [*He goes away through the garden, shutting the door sharply behind him*].

LADY UTTERWORD. I will not be ignored and pretended to be somebody else. I will have it out with papa now, this instant. [*To Mazzini*] Excuse me. [*She follows the Captain out, making a hasty bow to Mazzini, who returns it*].

MRS HUSHABYE [*hospitably, shaking hands*] How good of you to come, Mr Dunn! You dont mind papa, do you? He is as mad as a hatter, you know, but quite harmless, and extremely clever. You will have some delightful talks with him.

MAZZINI. I hope so. [*To Ellie*] So here you are, Ellie, dear. [*He draws her arm affectionately through his*]. I must thank you, Mrs Hushabye, for your kindness to my daughter. I'm afraid she would have had no holiday if you had not invited her.

MRS HUSHABYE. Not at all. Very nice of her to come and attract young people to the house for us.

MAZZINI [*smiling*] I'm afraid Ellie is not interested in young men, Mrs Hushabye. Her taste is on the graver, solider side.

MRS HUSHABYE [*with a sudden rather hard brightness in her manner*] Wont you take off your overcoat, Mr Dunn? You will find a cupboard for coats and hats and things in the corner of the hall.

MAZZINI [*hastily releasing Ellie*] Yes—thank you—I had better— [*He goes out*].

MRS HUSHABYE [*emphatically*] The old brute!

ELLIE. Who?

MRS. HUSHABYE. Who! Him. He. It. [*Pointing after Mazzini*]. "Graver, solider tastes," indeed!

ELLIE [*aghast*] You dont mean that you were speaking like that of my father!

MRS HUSHABYE. I was. You know I was.

ELLIE [*with dignity*] I will leave your house at once.

[*She turns to the door*].

MRS HUSHABYE. If you attempt it, I'll tell your father why.

ELLIE [*turning again*] Oh! How can you treat a visitor like this, Mrs Hushabye?

MRS HUSHABYE. I thought you were going to call me Hesione.

ELLIE. Certainly not now?

MRS HUSHABYE. Very well: I'll tell your father.

ELLIE [*distressed*] Oh!

MRS HUSHABYE. If you turn a hair—if you take his part against me and against your own heart for a moment, I'll give that born soldier of freedom a piece of my mind that will stand him on his selfish old head for a week.

ELLIE. Hesione! My father selfish! How little you know—

She is interrupted by Mazzini, who returns, excited and perspiring.

MAZZINI. Ellie: Mangan has come: I thought youd like to know. Excuse me, Mrs Hushabye: the strange old gentleman—

MRS HUSHABYE. Papa. Quite so.

MAZZINI. Oh, I beg your pardon: of course: I was a little confused by his manner. He is making Mangan help him with something in the garden; and he wants me to—

A powerful whistle is heard.

THE CAPTAIN'S VOICE. Bosun ahoy! [*The whistle is repeated*].

MAZZINI [*flustered*] Oh dear! I believe he is whistling for me. [*He hurries out*].

MRS HUSHABYE. Now m y father is a wonderful man if you like.

ELLIE. Hesione: listen to me. You dont understand. My father and Mr Mangan were boys together. Mr Ma—

MRS HUSHABYE. I dont care what they were: we must sit down if you are going to begin as far back as that. [*She snatches at Ellie's waist, and makes her sit down on the sofa beside her*]. Now, pettikins: tell me all about Mr Mangan. They call him Boss Mangan, dont they? He is a Napoleon of industry and disgustingly rich, isnt he? Why isnt your father rich?

ELLIE. My poor father should never have been in business. His parents were poets; and they gave him the noblest ideas; but they could not afford to give him a profession.

MRS HUSHABYE. Fancy your grandparents, with their eyes in fine frenzy rolling! And so your poor father had to go into business. Hasnt he succeeded in it?

ELLIE. He always used to say he could succeed if he only had some capital. He fought his way along, to keep a roof over our heads and bring us up well; but it was always a struggle: always the same difficulty of not having capital enough. I dont know how to describe it to you.

MRS HUSHABYE. Poor Ellie! I know. Pulling the devil by the tail.

ELLIE [*hurt*] Oh no. Not like that. It was at least dignified.

MRS HUSHABYE. That made it all the harder, didnt it? *I* shouldn't have pulled the devil by the tail with dignity. I should have pulled hard—[*between her teeth*] h a r d. Well? Go on.

ELLIE. At last it seemed that all our troubles were at an end. Mr Mangan did an extraordinarily noble thing out of pure friendship for my father and respect for his character. He asked him how much capital he wanted, and gave it to him. I dont mean that he lent it to him, or that he invested it in his business. He just simply made him a present of it. Wasnt that splendid of him?

MRS HUSHABYE. On condition that you married him?

ELLIE. Oh no, no, no. This was when I was a child. He had never even seen me: he never came to our house. It was absolutely disinterested. Pure generosity.

MRS HUSHABYE. Oh! I beg the gentleman's pardon. Well, what became of the money?

ELLIE. We all got new clothes and moved into another

house. And I went to another school for two years.

MRS HUSHABYE. Only two years?

ELLIE. That was all; for at the end of two years my father was utterly ruined.

MRS HUSHABYE. How?

ELLIE. I dont know. I never could understand. But it was dreadful. When we were poor my father had never been in debt. But when he launched out into business on a large scale, he had to incur liabilities. When the business went into liquidation he owed more money than Mr Mangan had given him.

MRS HUSHABYE. Bit off more than he could chew, I suppose.

ELLIE. I think you are a little unfeeling about it.

MRS HUSHABYE. My pettikins: you mustnt mind my way of talking. I was quite as sensitive and particular as you once; but I have picked up so much slang from the children that I am really hardly presentable. I suppose your father had no head for business, and made a mess of it.

ELLIE. Oh, that just shews how entirely you are mistaken about him. The business turned out a great success. It now pays forty-four per cent after deducting the excess profits tax.

MRS HUSHABYE. Then why arnt you rolling in money?

ELLIE. I dont know. It seems very unfair to me. You see, my father was made bankrupt. It nearly broke his heart, because he had persuaded several of his friends to put money into the business. He was sure it would succeed; and events proved that he was quite right. But they all lost their money. It was dreadful. I dont know what we should have done but for Mr Mangan.

MRS HUSHABYE. What! Did the Boss come to the rescue again, after all his money being thrown away?

ELLIE. He did indeed, and never uttered a reproach to my father. He bought what was left of the business—the buildings and the machinery and things—from the official trustee for enough money to enable my father to pay six and eightpence in the pound and get his discharge. Everyone pitied papa so much, and saw so plainly that he was an honorable man, that they let him off at six-and-eight pence instead of ten shillings. Then Mr Mangan started a company to take up the business, and made my father a manager in it to save us from starvation; for I wasnt earning anything then.

MRS HUSHABYE. Quite a romance. And when did the Boss develop the tender passion?

ELLIE. Oh, that was years after, quite lately. He took the chair one night at a sort of people's concert. I was singing there. As an amateur, you know: half a guinea for expenses and three songs with three encores. He was so pleased with my singing that he asked might he walk home with me. I never saw anyone so taken aback as he was when I took him home and introduced him to my father: his own manager. It was then that my father told me how nobly he had behaved. Of course it was considered a great chance for me, as he is so rich. And—and—we drifted into a sort of understanding—I suppose I should call it an engagement— [*She is distressed and cannot go on*].

MRS HUSHABYE [*rising and marching about*] You may have drifted into it; but you will bounce out of it, my pettikins, if I am to have anything to do with it.

ELLIE [*hopelessly*] No: it's no use. I am bound in honor and gratitude. I will go through with it.

MRS HUSHABYE [*behind the sofa, scolding down at her*] You know, of course, that it's not honorable or grateful to marry a man you dont love. Do you love this Mangan man?

ELLIE. Yes. At least—

MRS HUSHABYE. I dont want to know about "the least": I want to know the worst. Girls of your age fall in love with all sorts of impossible people, especially old people.

ELLIE. I like Mr Mangan very much; and I shall always be—

MRS HUSHABYE [*impatiently completing the sentence and prancing away intolerantly to starboard*] —grateful to him for his kindness to dear father. I know. Anybody else?

ELLIE. What do you mean?

MRS HUSHABYE. Anybody else? Are you in love with anybody else?

ELLIE. Of course not.

MRS HUSHABYE. Humph! [*The book on the drawing-table catches her eye. She picks it up, and evidently finds the title very unexpected. She looks at Ellie, and asks, quaintly*]. Quite sure youre not in love with an actor?

ELLIE. No, no. Why? What put such a thing into your head?

MRS HUSHABYE. This is yours, isnt it? Why else should you be reading Othello?

ELLIE. My father taught me to love Shakespear.

MRS HUSHABYE [*flinging the book down on the table*] Really! your father does seem to be about the limit.

ELLIE [*naïvely*] Do you never read Shakespear, Hesione? That seems to me so extraordinary. I like Othello.

MRS HUSHABYE. Do you indeed? He was jealous, wasnt he?

ELLIE. Oh, not that. I think all the part about jealousy is horrible. But dont you think it must have been a wonderful experience for Desdemona, brought up so quietly at home, to meet a man who had been out in the world doing all sorts of brave things and having terrible adventures, and yet finding something in her that made him love to sit and talk with her and tell her about them?

MRS HUSHABYE. Thats your idea of romance, is it?

ELLIE. Not romance, exactly. It might really happen.

Ellie's eyes shew that she is not arguing, but in a day-dream. Mrs Hushabye, watching her inquisitively, goes deliberately back to the sofa and resumes her seat beside her.

MRS HUSHABYE. Ellie darling: have you noticed that some of those stories that Othello told Desdemona couldnt have happened?

ELLIE. Oh no. Shakespear thought they could have happened.

MRS HUSHABYE. Hm! Desdemona thought they could have happened. But they didnt.

ELLIE. Why do you look so enigmatic about it? You are such a sphinx: I never know what you mean.

MRS HUSHABYE. Desdemona would have found him out if she had lived, you know. I wonder was that why he strangled her!

ELLIE. Othello was not telling lies.

MRS HUSHABYE. How do you know?

ELLIE. Shakespear would have said if he was. Hesione: there are men who have done wonderful things: men like Othello, only, of course, white, and very handsome, and—

MRS HUSHABYE. Ah! Now we're coming to it. Tell me all about him. I knew there must be somebody, or youd never have been so miserable about Mangan: youd have thought it quite a lark to marry him.

ELLIE [*blushing vividly*] Hesione: you are dreadful. But I dont want to make a secret of it, though of course I dont tell everybody. Besides, I dont know him.

MRS HUSHABYE. Dont know him! What does that mean?

ELLIE. Well, of course I know him to speak to.

MRS HUSHABYE. But you want to know him ever so much more intimately, eh?

ELLIE. No no: I know him quite—almost intimately.

MRS HUSHABYE. You dont know him; and you know him almost intimately. How lucid!

ELLIE. I mean that he does not call on us. I—I got into conversation with him by chance at a concert.

MRS HUSHABYE. You seem to have rather a gay time at your concerts, Ellie.

ELLIE. Not at all: we talk to everyone in the green-room waiting for our turns. I thought he was one of the artists: he looked so splendid. But he was only one of the committee. I happened to tell him that I was copying a picture at the National Gallery. I make a little money that way. I cant paint much; but as it's always the same picture

I can do it pretty quickly and get two or three pounds for it. It happened that he came to the National Gallery one day.

MRS HUSHABYE. One student's day. Paid sixpence to stumble about through a crowd of easels, when he might have come in next day for nothing and found the floor clear! Quite by accident?

ELLIE [*triumphantly*] No. On purpose. He liked talking to me. He knows lots of the most splendid people. Fashionable women who are all in love with him. But he ran away from them to see me at the National Gallery and persuade me to come with him for a drive round Richmond Park in a taxi.

MRS HUSHABYE. My pettikins, you have been going it. It's wonderful what you good girls can do without anyone saying a word.

ELLIE. I am not in society, Hesione. If I didnt make acquaintances in that way I shouldnt have any at all.

MRS HUSHABYE. Well, no harm if you know how to take care of yourself. May I ask his name?

ELLIE [*slowly and musically*] Marcus Darnley.

MRS HUSHABYE [*echoing the music*] Marcus Darnley! What a splendid name!

ELLIE. Oh, I'm so glad you think so. I think so too; but I was afraid it was only a silly fancy of my own.

MRS HUSHABYE. Hm! Is he one of the Aberdeen Darnleys?

ELLIE. Nobody knows. Just fancy! He was found in an antique chest—

MRS HUSHABYE. A what?

ELLIE. An antique chest, one summer morning in a rose garden, after a night of the most terrible thunderstorm.

MRS HUSHABYE. What on earth was he doing in the chest? Did he get into it because he was afraid of the lightning?

ELLIE. Oh no, no: he was a baby. The name Marcus Darnley was embroidered on his babyclothes. And five hundred pounds in gold.

MRS HUSHABYE [*looking hard at her*] Ellie!

ELLIE. The garden of the Viscount—

MRS HUSHABYE. —de Rougemont?

ELLIE [*innocently*] No: de Larochejaquelin. A French family. A vicomte. His life has been one long romance. A tiger—

MRS HUSHABYE. Slain by his own hand?

ELLIE. Oh no: nothing vulgar like that. He saved the life of the tiger from a hunting party: one of King Edward's hunting parties in India. The King was furious: that was why he never had his military services properly recognized. But he doesnt care. He is a Socialist and despises rank, and has been in three revolutions fighting on the barricades.

MRS HUSHABYE. How can you sit there telling me such lies? You, Ellie, of all people! And I thought you were a perfectly simple, straightforward, good girl.

ELLIE [*rising, dignified but very angry*] Do you mean to say you dont believe me?

MRS HUSHABYE. Of course I dont believe you. Youre inventing every word of it. Do you take me for a fool?

Ellie stares at her. Her candor is so obvious that Mrs Hushabye is puzzled.

ELLIE. Goodbye, Hesione. I'm very sorry. I see now that it sounds very improbable as I tell it. But I cant stay if you think that way about me.

MRS HUSHABYE [*catching her dress*] You shant go. I couldnt be so mistaken: I know too well what liars are like. Somebody has really told you all this.

ELLIE [*flushing*] Hesione: dont say that you dont believe h i m. I couldnt bear that.

MRS HUSHABYE [*soothing her*] Of course I believe him, dearest. But you should have broken it to me by degrees. [*Drawing her back to her seat*] Now tell me all about him. Are you in love with him?

ELLIE. Oh no. I'm not so foolish. I dont fall in love with people. I'm not so silly as you think.

MRS HUSHABYE. I see. Only something to think about—

to give some interest and pleasure to life.

ELLIE. Just so. Thats all, really.

MRS HUSHABYE. It makes the hours go fast, doesnt it? No tedious waiting to go to sleep at nights and wondering whether you will have a bad night. How delightful it makes waking up in the morning! How much better than the happiest dream! All life transfigured! No more wishing one had an interesting book to read, because life is so much happier than any book! No desire but to be alone and not to have to talk to anyone: to be alone and just think about it.

ELLIE [*embracing her*] Hesione: you are a witch. How do you know? Oh, you are the most sympathetic woman in the world.

MRS HUSHABYE [*caressing her*] Pettikins, my pettikins: how I envy you! and how I pity you!

ELLIE. Pity me! Oh, why?

A very handsome man of fifty, with mousquetaire moustaches, wearing a rather dandified curly brimmed hat, and carrying an elaborate walking-stick, comes into the room from the hall, and stops short at sight of the women on the sofa.

ELLIE [*seeing him and rising in glad surprise*] Oh! Hesione: this is Mr Marcus Darnley.

MRS HUSHABYE [*rising*] What a lark! He is my husband.

ELLIE. But how— [*She stops suddenly; then turns pale and sways*].

MRS HUSHABYE [*catching her and sitting down with her on the sofa*] Steady, my pettikins.

THE MAN [*with a mixture of confusion and effrontery, depositing his hat and stick on the teak table*] My real name, Miss Dunn, is Hector Hushabye. I leave you to judge whether that is a name any sensitive man would care to confess to. I never use it when I can possibly help it. I have been away for nearly a month; and I had no idea you knew my wife, or that you were coming here. I am none the less delighted to find you in our little house.

ELLIE [*in great distress*] I dont know what to do. Please, may I speak to papa? Do leave me. I cant bear it.

MRS HUSHABYE. Be off, Hector.

HECTOR. I—

MRS HUSHABYE. Quick, quick. Get out.

HECTOR. If you think it better— [*He goes out, taking his hat with him but leaving the stick on the table*].

MRS HUSHABYE [*laying Ellie down at the end of the sofa*] Now, pettikins, he is gone. Theres nobody but me. You can let yourself go. Dont try to control yourself. Have a good cry.

ELLIE [*raising her head*] Damn!

MRS HUSHABYE. Splendid! Oh, what a relief! I thought you were going to be broken-hearted. Never mind me. Damn him again.

ELLIE. I am not damning him: I am damning myself for being such a fool. [*Rising*] How could I let myself be taken in so? [*She begins prowling to and fro, her bloom gone, looking curiously older and harder*].

MRS HUSHABYE [*cheerfully*] Why not, pettikins? Very few young women can resist Hector. I couldnt when I was your age. He is really rather splendid, you know.

ELLIE [*turning on her*] Splendid! Yes: splendid l o o k i n g , of course. But how can you love a liar?

MRS HUSHABYE. I dont know. But you can, fortunately. Otherwise there wouldnt be much love in the world.

ELLIE. But to lie like that! To be a boaster! a coward!

MRS HUSHABYE [*rising in alarm*] Pettikins: none of that, if you please. If you hint the slightest doubt of Hector's courage, he will go straight off and do the most horribly dangerous things to convince himself that he isnt a coward. He has a dreadful trick of getting out of one third-floor window and coming in at another, just to test his nerve. He has a whole drawerful of Albert Medals for saving people's lives.

ELLIE. He never told me that.

MRS HUSHABYE. He never boasts of anything he really

did: he cant bear it; and it makes him shy if anyone else does. All his stories are made-up stories.

ELLIE [*coming to her*] Do you mean that he is really brave, and really has adventures, and yet tells lies about things that he never did and that never happened?

MRS HUSHABYE. Yes, pettikins, I do. People dont have their virtues and vices in sets: they have them anyhow: all mixed.

ELLIE [*staring at her thoughtfully*] Theres something odd about this house, Hesione, and even about you. I dont know why I'm talking to you so calmly. I have a horrible fear that my heart is broken, but that heartbreak is not like what I thought it must be.

MRS HUSHABYE [*fondling her*] It's only life educating you, pettikins. How do you feel about Boss Mangan now?

ELLIE [*disengaging herself with an expression of distaste*] Oh, how can you remind me of him, Hesione?

MRS HUSHABYE. Sorry, dear. I think I hear Hector coming back. You dont mind now, do you, dear?

ELLIE. Not in the least. I'm quite cured.

Mazzini Dunn and Hector come in from the hall.

HECTOR [*as he opens the door and allows Mazzini to pass in*] One second more, and she would have been a dead woman!

MAZZINI. Dear! dear! what an escape! Ellie, my love: Mr Hushabye has just been telling me the most extraordinary—

ELLIE. Yes: Ive heard it. [*She crosses to the other side of the room*].

HECTOR [*following her*] Not this one: I'll tell it to you after dinner. I think youll like it. The truth is, I made it up for you, and was looking forward to the pleasure of telling it to you. But in a moment of impatience at being turned out of the room, I threw it away on your father.

ELLIE [*turning at bay with her back to the carpenter's bench, scornfully self-possessed*] It was not thrown away. He believes it. I should not have believed it.

MAZZINI [*benevolently*] Ellie is very naughty, Mr Hushabye. Of course she does not really think that. [*He goes to the bookshelves, and inspects the titles of the volumes*].

Boss Mangan comes in from the hall, followed by the Captain. Mangan, carefully frock-coated as for church or for a directors' meeting, is about fiftyfive, with a careworn, mistrustful expression, standing a little on an entirely imaginary dignity, with a dull complexion, straight, lustreless hair, and features so entirely commonplace that it is impossible to describe them.

CAPTAIN SHOTOVER [*to Mrs Hushabye, introducing the newcomer*] Says his name is Mangan. Not ablebodied.

MRS HUSHABYE [*graciously*] How do you do, Mr Mangan?

MANGAN [*shaking hands*] Very pleased.

CAPTAIN SHOTOVER. Dunn's lost his muscle, but recovered his nerve. Men seldom do after three attacks of delirium tremens. [*He goes into the pantry*].

MRS HUSHABYE. I congratulate you, Mr Dunn.

MAZZINI [*dazed*] I am a lifelong teetotaler.

MRS HUSHABYE. You will find it far less trouble to let papa have his own way than try to explain.

MAZZINI. But three attacks of delirium tremens, really!

MRS HUSHABYE [*to Mangan*] Do you know my husband, Mr. Mangan? [*She indicates Hector*].

MANGAN [*going to Hector, who meets him with outstretched hand*] Very pleased. [*Turning to Ellie*] I hope, Miss Ellie, you have not found the journey down too fatiguing. [*They shake hands*].

MRS HUSHABYE. Hector: shew Mr Dunn his room.

HECTOR. Certainly. Come along, Mr Dunn. [*He takes Mazzini out*].

ELLIE. You havnt shewn me my room yet, Hesione.

MRS HUSHABYE. How stupid of me! Come along. Make yourself quite at home, Mr Mangan. Papa will entertain you. [*She calls to the Captain in the pantry*] Papa: come and explain the house to Mr Mangan.

She goes out with Ellie. The Captain comes from the pantry.

CAPTAIN SHOTOVER. Youre going to marry Dunn's daughter. Dont. Youre too old.

MANGAN [*staggered*] Well! Thats fairly blunt, Captain.

CAPTAIN SHOTOVER. It's true.

MANGAN. She doesnt think so.

CAPTAIN SHOTOVER. She does.

MANGAN. Older men than I have—

CAPTAIN SHOTOVER [*finishing the sentence for him*]—made fools of themselves. That, also, is true.

MANGAN [*asserting himself*] I dont see that this is any business of yours.

CAPTAIN SHOTOVER. It is everybody's business. The stars in their courses are shaken when such things happen.

MANGAN. I'm going to marry her all the same.

CAPTAIN SHOTOVER. How do you know?

MANGAN [*playing the strong man*] I intend to. I mean to. See? I never made up my mind to do a thing yet that I didnt bring it off. Thats the sort of man I am; and there will be a better understanding between us when you make up your mind to that, Captain.

CAPTAIN SHOTOVER. You frequent picture palaces.

MANGAN. Perhaps I do. Who told you?

CAPTAIN SHOTOVER. Talk like a man, not like a movy. You mean that you make a hundred thousand a year.

MANGAN. I dont boast. But when I meet a man that makes a hundred thousand a year, I take off my hat to that man, and stretch out my hand to him and call him brother.

CAPTAIN SHOTOVER. Then you also make a hundred thousand a year, hey?

MANGAN. No. I cant say that. Fifty thousand, perhaps.

CAPTAIN SHOTOVER. His half brother only. [*He turns away from Mangan with his usual abruptness, and collects the empty tea-cups on the Chinese tray*].

MANGAN [*irritated*] See here, Captain Shotover. I dont quite understand my position here. I came here on your daughter's invitation. Am I in her house or in yours?

CAPTAIN SHOTOVER. You are beneath the dome of heaven, in the house of God. What is true within these walls is true outside them. Go out on the seas; climb the mountains; wander through the valleys. She is still too young.

MANGAN [*weakening*] But I'm very little over fifty.

CAPTAIN SHOTOVER. You are still less under sixty. Boss Mangan: you will not marry the pirate's child. [*He carries the tray away into the pantry*].

MANGAN [*following him to the half door*] What pirate's child? What are you talking about?

CAPTAIN SHOTOVER [*in the pantry*] Ellie Dunn. You will not marry her.

MANGAN. Who will stop me?

CAPTAIN SHOTOVER [*emerging*] My daughter. [*He makes for the door leading to the hall*].

MANGAN [*following him*] Mrs Hushabye! Do you mean to say she brought me down here to break it off?

CAPTAIN SHOTOVER [*stopping and turning on him*] I know nothing more than I have seen in her eye. She w i l l break it off. Take my advice: marry a West Indian negress: they make excellent wives. I was married to one myself for two years.

MANGAN. Well, I a m damned!

CAPTAIN SHOTOVER. I thought so. I was, too, for many years. The negress redeemed me.

MANGAN [*feebly*] This is queer. I ought to walk out of this house.

CAPTAIN SHOTOVER. Why?

MANGAN. Well, many men would be offended by your style of talking.

CAPTAIN SHOTOVER. Nonsense! It's the other sort of talking that makes quarrels. Nobody ever quarrels with me.

A gentleman, whose firstrate tailoring and frictionless

manners proclaim the wellbred West Ender, comes in from the hall. He has an engaging air of being young and unmarried, but on close inspection is found to be at least over forty.

THE GENTLEMAN. Excuse my intruding in this fashion; but there is no knocker on the door; and the bell does not seem to ring.

CAPTAIN SHOTOVER. Why should there be a knocker? Why should the bell ring? The door is open.

THE GENTLEMAN. Precisely. So I ventured to come in.

CAPTAIN SHOTOVER. Quite right. I will see about a room for you. [*He makes for the door*].

THE GENTLEMAN [*stopping him*] But I'm afraid you dont know who I am.

CAPTAIN SHOTOVER. Do you suppose that at my age I make distinctions between one fellowcreature and another? [*He goes out. Mangan and the newcomer stare at one another*].

MANGAN. Strange character, Captain Shotover, sir.

THE GENTLEMAN. Very.

CAPTAIN SHOTOVER [*shouting outside*] Hesione: another person has arrived and wants a room. Man about town, well dressed, fifty.

THE GENTLEMAN. Fancy Hesione's feelings! May I ask are you a member of the family?

MANGAN. No.

THE GENTLEMAN. I am. At least a connexion.

Mrs Hushabye comes back.

MRS HUSHABYE. How do you do? How good of you to come!

THE GENTLEMAN. I am very glad indeed to make your acquaintance, Hesione. [*Instead of taking her hand he kisses her. At the same moment the Captain appears in the doorway*]. You will excuse my kissing your daughter, Captain, when I tell you that—

CAPTAIN SHOTOVER. Stuff! Everyone kisses my daughter. Kiss her as much as you like. [*He makes for the pantry*].

THE GENTLEMAN. Thank you. One moment, Captain. [*The Captain halts and turns. The gentleman goes to him affably*]. Do you happen to remember—but probably you dont, as it occurred many years ago—that your younger daughter married a numskull?

CAPTAIN SHOTOVER. Yes. She said she'd marry anybody to get away from this house. I should not have recognized you: your head is no longer like a walnut. Your aspect is softened. You have been boiled in bread and milk for years and years, like other married men. Poor devil! [*He disappears into the pantry*].

MRS HUSHABYE [*going past Mangan to the gentleman and scrutinizing him*]. I dont believe you are Hastings Utterword.

THE GENTLEMAN. I am not.

MRS HUSHABYE. Then what business had you to kiss me?

THE GENTLEMAN. I thought I would like to. The fact is, I am Randall Utterword, the unworthy younger brother of Hastings. I was abroad diplomatizing when he was married.

LADY UTTERWORD [*dashing in*] Hesione: where is the key of the wardrobe in my room? My diamonds are in my dressing-bag: I must lock it up— [*Recognizing the stranger with a shock*] Randall: how dare you? [*She marches at him past Mrs Hushabye, who retreats and joins Mangan near the sofa*].

RANDALL. How dare I what? I am not doing anything.

LADY UTTERWORD. Who told you I was here?

RANDALL. Hastings. You had just left when I called on you at Claridge's; so I followed you down here. You are looking extremely well.

LADY UTTERWORD. Dont presume to tell me so.

MRS HUSHABYE. What is wrong with Mr Randall, Addy?

LADY UTTERWORD [*recollecting herself*] Oh, nothing. But he has no right to come bothering you and papa without being invited. [*She goes to the window-seat and sits down, turning away from them ill-humoredly and looking into the garden, where Hector and Ellie are now seen strolling together*].

MRS HUSHABYE. I think you have not met Mr Mangan, Addy.

LADY UTTERWORD [*turning her head and nodding coldly to Mangan*] I beg your pardon. Randall: you have flustered me so: I made a perfect fool of myself.

MRS HUSHABYE. Lady Utterword. My sister. My y o u n g e r sister.

MANGAN [*bowing*] Pleased to meet you, Lady Utterword.

LADY UTTERWORD [*with marked interest*] Who is that gentleman walking in the garden with Miss Dunn?

MRS HUSHABYE. I dont know. She quarrelled mortally with my husband only ten minutes ago; and I didnt know anyone else had come. It must be a visitor. [*She goes to the window to look*]. Oh, it i s Hector. Theyve made it up.

LADY UTTERWORD. Your husband! That handsome man?

MRS HUSHABYE. Well, why shouldnt my husband be a handsome man?

RANDALL [*joining them at the window*] One's husband never is, Ariadne. [*He sits by Lady Utterword, on her right*].

MRS HUSHABYE. One's sister's husband always is, Mr Randall.

LADY UTTERWORD. Dont be vulgar, Randall. And you, Hesione, are just as bad.

Ellie and Hector come in from the garden by the starboard door. Randall rises. Ellie retires into the corner near the pantry. Hector comes forward; and Lady Utterword rises looking her very best.

MRS HUSHABYE. Hector: this is Addy.

HECTOR [*apparently surprised*] Not this lady.

LADY UTTERWORD [*smiling*] Why not?

HECTOR [*looking at her with a piercing glance of deep but respectful admiration, his moustache bristling*] I thought— [*Pulling himself together*] I beg your pardon, Lady Utterword. I am extremely glad to welcome you at last under our roof. [*He offers his hand with grave courtesy*].

MRS HUSHABYE. She wants to be kissed, Hector.

LADY UTTERWORD. Hesione! [*But she still smiles*].

MRS HUSHABYE. Call her Addy; and kiss her like a good brother-in-law; and have done with it. [*She leaves them to themselves*].

HECTOR. Behave yourself, Hesione. Lady Utterword is entitled not only to hospitality but to civilization.

LADY UTTERWORD [*gratefully*] Thank you, Hector. [*They shake hands cordially*].

Mazzini Dunn is seen crossing the garden from starboard to port.

CAPTAIN SHOTOVER [*coming from the pantry and addressing Ellie*] Your father has washed himself.

ELLIE [*quite self-possessed*] He often does, Captain Shotover.

CAPTAIN SHOTOVER. A strange conversion! I saw him through the pantry window.

Mazzini Dunn enters through the port window door, newly washed and brushed, and stops, smiling benevolently, between Mangan and Mrs Hushabye.

MRS HUSHABYE [*introducing*] Mr Mazzini Dunn, Lady Ut—oh, I forgot: youve met. [*Indicating Ellie*] Miss Dunn.

MAZZINI [*walking across the room to take Ellie's hand, and beaming at his own naughty irony*] I have met Miss Dunn also. She is my daughter. [*He draws her arm through his caressingly*].

MRS HUSHABYE. Of course: how stupid! Mr Utterword, my sister's-er—

RANDALL [*shaking hands agreeably*] Her brother-in-law, Mr Dunn. How do you do?

MRS HUSHABYE. This is my husband.

HECTOR. We have met, dear. Dont introduce us any more. [*He moves away to the big chair, and adds*] Wont you sit down, Lady Utterword? [*She does so very graciously*].

MRS HUSHABYE. Sorry. I hate it: it's like making people shew their tickets.

MAZZINI [*sententiously*] How little it tells us, after all! The great question is, not who we are, but what we are.

CAPTAIN SHOTOVER. Ha! What are you?

MAZZINI [*taken aback*] What am I?

CAPTAIN SHOTOVER. A thief, a pirate, and a murderer.

MAZZINI. I assure you you are mistaken.

CAPTAIN SHOTOVER. An adventurous life; but what does it end in? Respectability. A ladylike daughter. The language and appearance of a city missionary. Let it be a warning to all of you. [*He goes out through the garden*].

DUNN. I hope nobody here believes that I am a thief, a pirate, or a murderer. Mrs Hushabye: will you excuse me a moment? I must really go and explain. [*He follows the Captain*].

MRS HUSHABYE [*as he goes*] It's no use. Youd really better— [*But Dunn has vanished*]. We had better all go out and look for some tea. We never have regular tea; but you can always get some when you want: the servants keep it stewing all day. The kitchen veranda is the best place to ask. May I shew you? [*She goes to the starboard door*].

RANDALL [*going with her*] Thank you, I dont think I'll take any tea this afternoon. But if you will shew me the garden—?

MRS HUSHABYE. Theres nothing to see in the garden except papa's observatory, and a gravel pit with a cave where he keeps dynamite and things of that sort. However, it's pleasanter out of doors; so come along.

RANDALL. Dynamite! Isnt that rather risky?

MRS HUSHABYE. Well, we dont sit in the gravel pit when theres a thunderstorm.

LADY UTTERWORD. Thats something new. What is the dynamite for?

HECTOR. To blow up the human race if it goes too far. He is trying to discover a psychic ray that will explode all the explosives at the will of a Mahatma.

ELLIE. The Captain's tea is delicious, Mr Utterword.

MRS HUSHABYE [*stopping in the doorway*] Do you mean to say that youve had some of my father's tea? that you got round him before you were ten minutes in the house?

ELLIE. I did.

MRS HUSHABYE. You little devil! [*She goes out with Randall*].

MANGAN. Wont you come, Miss Ellie?

ELLIE. I'm too tired. I'll take a book up to my room and rest a little. [*She goes to the bookshelf*].

MANGAN. Right. You cant do better. But I'm disappointed. [*He follows Randall and Mrs Hushabye*].

Ellie, Hector, and Lady Utterword are left. Hector is close to Lady Utterword. They look at Ellie, waiting for her to go.

ELLIE [*looking at the title of a book*] Do you like stories of adventure, Lady Utterword?

LADY UTTERWORD [*patronizingly*] Of course, dear.

ELLIE. Then I'll leave you to Mr Hushabye. [*She goes out through the hall*].

HECTOR. That girl is mad about tales of adventure. The lies I have to tell her!

LADY UTTERWORD [*not interested in Ellie*] When you saw me what did you mean by saying that you thought, and then stopping short? What did you think?

HECTOR [*folding his arms and looking down at her magnetically*] May I tell you?

LADY UTTERWORD. Of course.

HECTOR. It will not sound very civil. I was on the point of saying "I thought you were a plain woman."

LADY UTTERWORD. Oh for shame, Hector! What right

had you to notice whether I am plain or not?

HECTOR. Listen to me, Ariadne. Until today I have seen only photographs of you; and no photograph can give the strange fascination of the daughters of that supernatural old man. There is some damnable quality in them that destroys men's moral sense, and carries them beyond honor and dishonor. You know that, dont you?

LADY UTTERWORD. Perhaps I do, Hector. But let me warn you once for all that I am a rigidly conventional woman. You may think because I'm a Shotover that I'm a Bohemian, because we are all so horribly Bohemian. But I'm not. I hate and loathe Bohemianism. No child brought up in a strict Puritan household ever suffered from Puritanism as I suffered from our Bohemianism.

HECTOR. Our children are like that. They spend their holidays in the houses of their respectable schoolfellows.

LADY UTTERWORD. I shall invite them for Christmas.

HECTOR. Their absence leaves us both without our natural chaperons.

LADY UTTERWORD. Children are certainly very inconvenient sometimes. But intelligent people can always manage, unless they are Bohemians.

HECTOR. You are no Bohemian; but you are no Puritan either: your attraction is alive and powerful. What sort of woman do you count yourself?

LADY UTTERWORD. I am a woman of the world, Hector; and I can assure you that if you will only take the trouble always to do the perfectly correct thing, and to say the perfectly correct thing, you can do just what you like. An ill-conducted, careless woman gets simply no chance. An ill-conducted, careless man is never allowed within arms length of any woman worth knowing.

HECTOR. I see. You are neither a Bohemian woman nor a Puritan woman. You are a dangerous woman.

LADY UTTERWORD. On the contrary, I am a safe woman.

HECTOR. You are a most accursedly attractive woman. Mind: I am not making love to you. I do not like being attracted. But you had better know how I feel if you are going to stay here.

LADY UTTERWORD. You are an exceedingly clever lady-killer, Hector. And terribly handsome. I am quite a good player, myself, at that game. Is it quite understood that we are only playing?

HECTOR. Quite. I am deliberately playing the fool, out of sheer worthlessness.

LADY UTTERWORD [*rising brightly*] Well, you are my brother-in-law. Hesione asked you to kiss me. [*He seizes her in his arms, and kisses her strenuously*]. Oh! that was a little more than play, brother-in-law. [*She pushes him suddenly away*]. You shall not do that again.

HECTOR. In effect, you got your claws deeper into me than I intended.

MRS HUSHABYE [*coming in from the garden*] Dont let me disturb you: I only want a cap to put on daddiest. The sun is setting; and he'll catch cold. [*She makes for the door leading to the hall*].

LADY UTTERWORD. Your husband is quite charming, darling. He has actually condescended to kiss me at last. I shall go into the garden: it's cooler now. [*She goes out by the port door*].

MRS HUSHABYE. Take care, dear child. I dont believe any man can kiss Addy without falling in love with her. [*She goes into the hall*].

HECTOR [*striking himself on the chest*] Fool! Goat!

Mrs Hushabye comes back with the Captain's cap.

HECTOR. Your sister is an extremely enterprising old girl. Wheres Miss Dunn!

MRS HUSHABYE. Mangan says she has gone up to her room for a nap. Addy wont let you talk to Ellie: she has marked you for her own.

HECTOR. She has the diabolical family fascination. I began making love to her automatically. What am I to do? I cant fall in love; and I cant hurt a woman's feelings by telling her so when she falls in love with me. And as women are always falling in love with my moustache I get landed in all sorts of tedious and terrifying flirtations in which I'm not a bit in earnest.

MRS HUSHABYE. Oh, neither is Addy. She has never been in love in her life, though she has always been trying to fall in head over ears. She is worse than you, because you had one real go at least, with me.

HECTOR. That was a confounded madness. I cant believe that such an amazing experience is common. It has left its mark on me. I believe that is why I have never been able to repeat it.

MRS HUSHABYE [*laughing and caressing his arm*] We were frightfully in love with one another, Hector. It was such an enchanting dream that I have never been able to grudge it to you or anyone else since. I have invited all sorts of pretty women to the house on the chance of giving you another turn. But it has never come off.

HECTOR. I dont know that I want it to come off. It was damned dangerous. You fascinated me; but I loved you; so it was heaven. This sister of yours fascinates me; but I hate her; so it is hell. I shall kill her if she persists.

MRS HUSHABYE. Nothing will kill Addy: she is as strong as a horse. [*Releasing him*] Now *I* am going off to fascinate somebody.

HECTOR. The Foreign Office toff? Randall?

MRS HUSHABYE. Goodness gracious, no! Why should I fascinate him?

HECTOR. I presume you dont mean the bloated capitalist, Mangan?

MRS HUSHABYE. Hm! I think he had better be fascinated by me than by Ellie. [*She is going into the garden when the Captain comes in from it with some sticks in his hand*]. What have you got there, daddiest?

CAPTAIN SHOTOVER. Dynamite.

MRS HUSHABYE. Youve been to the gravel pit. Dont drop it about the house: theres a dear. [*She goes into the garden, where the evening light is now very red*].

HECTOR. Listen, O sage. How long dare you concentrate on a feeling without risking having it fixed in your consciousness all the rest of your life?

CAPTAIN SHOTOVER. Ninety minutes. An hour and a half. [*He goes into the pantry*].

Hector, left alone, contracts his brows, and falls into a daydream. He does not move for some time. Then he folds his arms. Then, throwing his hands behind him, and gripping one with the other, he strides tragically once to and fro. Suddenly he snatches his walking-stick from the teak table, and draws it; for it is a sword-stick. He fights a desperate duel with an imaginary antagonist, and after many vicissitudes runs him through the body up to the hilt. He sheathes his sword and throws it on the sofa, falling into another reverie as he does so. He looks straight into the eyes of an imaginary woman; seizes her by the arms; and says in a deep and thrilling tone "Do you love me!" *The Captain comes out of the pantry at this moment; and Hector, caught with his arms stretched out and his fists clenched, has to account for his attitude by going through a series of gymnastic exercises.*

CAPTAIN SHOTOVER. That sort of strength is no good. You will never be as strong as a gorilla.

HECTOR. What is the dynamite for?

CAPTAIN SHOTOVER. To kill fellows like Mangan.

HECTOR. No use. They will always be able to buy more dynamite than you.

CAPTAIN SHOTOVER. I will make a dynamite that he cannot explode.

HECTOR. And that you can, eh?

CAPTAIN SHOTOVER. Yes: when I have attained the seventh degree of concentration.

HECTOR. Whats the use of that? You never do attain it.

CAPTAIN SHOTOVER. What then is to be done? Are we to be kept for ever in the mud by these hogs to whom the universe is nothing but a machine for greasing their bristles and filling their snouts?

HECTOR. Are Mangan's bristles worse than Randall's lovelocks?

CAPTAIN SHOTOVER. We must win powers of life and death over them both. I refuse to die until I have invented the means.

HECTOR. Who are we that we should judge them?

CAPTAIN SHOTOVER. What are they that they should judge us? Yet they do, unhesitatingly. There is enmity between our seed and their seed. They know it and act on it, strangling our souls. They believe in themselves. When we believe in ourselves, we shall kill them.

HECTOR. It is the same seed. You forget that your pirate has a very nice daughter. Mangan's son may be a Plato: Randall's a Shelley. What was my father?

CAPTAIN SHOTOVER. The damndest scoundrel I ever met. [*He replaces the drawing-board; sits down at the table; and begins to mix a wash of color*].

HECTOR. Precisely. Well, dare you kill his innocent grandchildren?

CAPTAIN SHOTOVER. They are mine also.

HECTOR. Just so. We are members one of another. [*He throws himself carelessly on the sofa*]. I tell you I have often thought of this killing of human vermin. Many men have thought of it. Decent men are like Daniel in the lion's den: their survival is a miracle; and they do not always survive. We live among the Mangans and Randalls and Billie Dunns as they, poor devils, live among the disease germs and the doctors and the lawyers and the parsons and the restaurant chefs and the tradesmen and the servants and all the rest of the parasites and blackmailers. What are our terrors to theirs? Give me the power to kill them; and I'll spare them in sheer—

CAPTAIN SHOTOVER [*cutting in sharply*] Fellow feeling?

HECTOR. No. I should kill myself if I believed that. I must believe that my spark, small as it is, is divine, and that the red light over their door is hell fire. I should spare them in simple magnanimous pity.

CAPTAIN SHOTOVER. You cant spare them until you have the power to kill them. At present they have the power to kill you. There are millions of blacks over the water for them to train and let loose on us. Theyre going to do it. Theyre doing it already.

HECTOR. They are too stupid to use their power.

CAPTAIN SHOTOVER [*throwing down his brush and coming to the end of the sofa*] Do not deceive yourself: they do use it. We kill the better half of ourselves every day to propitiate them. The knowledge that these people are there to render all our aspirations barren prevents us having the aspirations. And when we are tempted to seek their destruction they bring forth demons to delude us, disguised as pretty daughters, and singers and poets and the like, for whose sake we spare them.

HECTOR [*sitting up and leaning towards him*] May not Hesione be such a demon, brought forth by you lest I should slay you?

CAPTAIN SHOTOVER. That is possible. She has used you up, and left you nothing but dreams, as some women do.

HECTOR. Vampire women, demon women.

CAPTAIN SHOTOVER. Men think the world well lost for them, and lose it accordingly. Who are the men that do things? The husbands of the shrew and of the drunkard, the men with the thorn in the flesh. [*Walking distractedly away towards the pantry*] I must think these things out. [*Turning suddenly*] But I go on with the dynamite none the less. I will discover a ray mightier than any X-ray: a mind ray that will explode the ammunition in the belt of my adversary before he can point his gun at me. And I must hurry. I am old: I have no time to waste in talk. [*He is about to go into the pantry, and Hector is making for the hall, when Hesione comes back*].

MRS HUSHABYE. Daddiest: you and Hector must come and help me to entertain all these people. What on earth were you shouting about?

HECTOR [*stopping in the act of turning the door handle*] He is madder than usual.

MRS HUSHABYE. We all are.

HECTOR. I must change. [*He resumes his door opening*].

MRS HUSHABYE. Stop, stop. Come back, both of you. Come back. [*They return, reluctantly*]. Money is running short.

HECTOR. Money! Where are my April dividends?

MRS HUSHABYE. Where is the snow that fell last year?

CAPTAIN SHOTOVER. Where is all the money you had for that patent lifeboat I invented?

MRS HUSHABYE. Five hundred pounds; and I have made it last since Easter!

CAPTAIN SHOTOVER. Since Easter! Barely four months! Monstrous extravagance! I could live for seven years on £500.

MRS HUSHABYE. Not keeping open house as we do here, daddiest.

CAPTAIN SHOTOVER. Only £500 for that lifeboat! I got twelve thousand for the invention before that.

MRS HUSHABYE. Yes, dear; but that was for the ship with the magnetic keel that sucked up submarines. Living at the rate we do, you cannot afford life-saving inventions. Cant you think of something that will murder half Europe at one bang?

CAPTAIN SHOTOVER. No. I am ageing fast. My mind does not dwell on slaughter as it did when I was a boy. Why doesnt your husband invent something? He does nothing but tell lies to women.

HECTOR. Well, that is a form of invention, is it not? However, you are right: I ought to support my wife.

MRS HUSHABYE. Indeed you shall do nothing of the sort: I should never see you from breakfast to dinner. I want my husband.

HECTOR [*bitterly*] I might as well be your lapdog.

MRS HUSHABYE. Do you want to be my breadwinner,

like the other poor husbands?

HECTOR. No, by thunder! What a damned creature a husband is anyhow!

MRS HUSHABYE [*to the Captain*] What about that harpoon cannon?

CAPTAIN SHOTOVER. No use. It kills whales, not men.

MRS HUSHABYE. Why not? You fire the harpoon out of a cannon. It sticks in the enemy's general; you wind him in; and there you are.

HECTOR. You are your father's daughter, Hesione.

CAPTAIN SHOTOVER. There is something in it. Not to wind in generals: they are not dangerous. But one could fire a grapnel and wind in a machine gun or even a tank. I will think it out.

MRS HUSHABYE [*squeezing the Captain's arm affectionately*] Saved! You a r e a darling, daddiest. Now we must go back to these dreadful people and entertain them.

CAPTAIN SHOTOVER. They have had no dinner. Dont forget that.

HECTOR. Neither have I. And it is dark: it must be all hours.

MRS HUSHABYE. Oh, Guinness will produce some sort of dinner for them. The servants always take jolly good care that there is food in the house.

CAPTAIN SHOTOVER [*raising a strange wail in the darkness*] What a house! What a daughter!

MRS HUSHABYE [*raving*] What a father!

HECTOR [*following suit*] What a husband!

CAPTAIN SHOTOVER. Is there no thunder in heaven?

HECTOR. Is there no beauty, no bravery, on earth?

MRS HUSHABYE. What do men want? They have their food, their firesides, their clothes mended, and our love at the end of the day. Why are they not satisfied? Why do they envy us the pain with which we bring them into the world, and make strange dangers and torments for themselves to be even with us?

CAPTAIN SHOTOVER [*weirdly chanting*]

I builded a house for my daughters, and opened the doors thereof,
That men might come for their choosing, and their betters spring from their love;
But one of them married a numskull;

HECTOR [*taking up the rhythm*]
The other a liar wed;

MRS HUSHABYE [*completing the stanza*]
And now must she lie beside him, even as she made her bed.

LADY UTTERWORD [*calling from the garden*] Hesione! Hesione! Where are you?

HECTOR. The cat is on the tiles.

MRS HUSHABYE. Coming, darling, coming. [*She goes quickly into the garden*].

The Captain goes back to his place at the table.

HECTOR [*going into the hall*] Shall I turn up the lights for you?

CAPTAIN SHOTOVER. No. Give me deeper darkness. Money is not made in the light.

END OF ACT I

ACT II

THE same room, with the lights turned up and the curtains drawn. Ellie comes in, followed by Mangan. Both are dressed for dinner. She strolls to the drawing-table. He comes between the table and the wicker chair.

MANGAN. What a dinner! I dont call it a dinner: I call it a meal.

ELLIE. I am accustomed to meals, Mr Mangan, and very lucky to get them. Besides, the captain cooked some macaroni for me.

MANGAN [*shuddering liverishly*] Too rich: I cant eat such things. I suppose it's because I have to work so much with my brain. Thats the worst of being a man of business: you are always thinking, thinking, thinking. By the way, now that we are alone, may I take the opportunity to come to a little understanding with you?

ELLIE [*settling into the draughtsman's seat*] Certainly. I should like to.

MANGAN [*taken aback*] Should you? That surprises me; for I thought I noticed this afternoon that you avoided me all you could. Not for the first time either.

ELLIE. I was very tired and upset. I wasn't used to the ways of this extraordinary house. Please forgive me.

MANGAN. Oh, thats all right: I dont mind. But Captain Shotover has been talking to me about you. You and me, you know.

ELLIE [*interested*] The Captain! What did he say?

MANGAN. Well, he noticed the difference between our ages.

ELLIE. He notices everything.

MANGAN. You dont mind, then?

ELLIE. Of course I know quite well that our engagement—

MANGAN. Oh! you call it an engagement.

ELLIE. Well, isnt it?

MANGAN. Oh, yes, yes: no doubt it is if you hold to it.

This is the first time youve used the word; and I didnt quite know where we stood: thats all. [*He sits down in the wicker chair; and resigns himself to allow her to lead the conversation*]. You were saying—?

ELLIE. Was I? I forget. Tell me. Do you like this part of the country? I heard you ask Mr Hushabye at dinner whether there are any nice houses to let down here.

MANGAN. I like the place. The air suits me. I shouldnt be surprised if I settled down here.

ELLIE. Nothing would please me better. The air suits me too. And I want to be near Hesione.

MANGAN [*with growing uneasiness*] The air may suit us; but the question is, should we suit one another? Have you thought about that?

ELLIE. Mr. Mangan: we must be sensible, mustnt we? It's no use pretending that we are Romeo and Juliet. But we can get on very well together if we choose to make the best of it. Your kindness of heart will make it easy for me.

MANGAN [*leaning forward, with the beginning of something like deliberate unpleasantness in his voice*] Kindness of heart, eh? I ruined your father, didnt I?

ELLIE. Oh, not intentionally.

MANGAN. Yes I did. Ruined him on purpose.

ELLIE. On purpose!

MANGAN. Not out of ill-nature, you know. And youll admit that I kept a job for him when I had finished with him. But business is business; and I ruined him as a matter of business.

ELLIE. I dont understand how that can be. Are you trying to make me feel that I need not be grateful to you, so that I may choose freely?

MANGAN [*rising aggressively*] No. I mean what I say.

ELLIE. But how could it possibly do you any good to ruin my father? The money he lost was yours.

MANGAN [*with a sour laugh*] W a s mine! It i s mine, Miss Ellie, and all the money the other fellows lost too. [*He shoves his hands into his pockets and shews his teeth*].

I just smoked them out like a hive of bees. What do you say to that? A bit of a shock, eh?

ELLIE. It would have been, this morning. N o w! you cant think how little it matters. But it's quite interesting. Only, you must explain it to me. I dont understand it. [*Propping her elbows on the drawing-board and her chin on her hands, she composes herself to listen with a combination of conscious curiosity with unconscious contempt which provokes him to more and more unpleasantness, and an attempt at patronage of her ignorance*].

MANGAN. Of course you dont understand: what do you know about business? You just listen and learn. Your father's business was a new business; and I dont start new businesses: I let other fellows start them. They put all their money and their friends' money into starting them. They wear out their souls and bodies trying to make a success of them. Theyre what you call enthusiasts. But the first dead lift of the thing is too much for them; and they havnt enough financial experience. In a year or so they have either to let the whole show go bust, or sell out to a new lot of fellows for a few deferred ordinary shares: that is, if theyre lucky enough to get anything at all. As likely as not the very same thing happens to the new lot. They put in more money and a couple of years more work; and then perhaps t h e y have to sell out to a third lot. If it's really a big thing the third lot will have to sell out too, and leave t h e i r work and t h e i r money behind them. And thats where the real business man comes in: where I come in. But I'm cleverer than some: I dont mind dropping a little money to start the process. I took your father's measure. I saw that he had a sound idea, and that he would work himself silly for it if he got the chance. I saw that he was a child in business, and was dead certain to outrun his expenses and be in too great a hurry to wait for his market. I knew that the surest way to ruin a man who doesnt know how to handle money is to give him some. I explained my idea to some friends in the city, and they found the money;

for I take no risks in ideas, even when theyre my own. Your father and the friends that ventured their money with him were no more to me than a heap of squeezed lemons. Youve been wasting your gratitude: my kind heart is all rot. I'm sick of it. When I see your father beaming at me with his moist, grateful eyes, regularly wallowing in gratitude, I sometimes feel I must tell him the truth or burst. What stops me is that I know he wouldnt believe me. He'd think it was my modesty, as you did just now. He'd think anything rather than the truth, which is that he's a blamed fool, and I am a man that knows how to take care of himself. [*He throws himself back into the big chair with large self-approval*]. Now what do you think of me, Miss Ellie?

ELLIE [*dropping her hands*] How strange! that my mother, who knew nothing at all about business, should have been quite right about you! She always said—not before papa, of course, but to us children—that you were just that sort of man.

MANGAN [*sitting up, much hurt*] Oh! did she? And yet she'd have let you marry me.

ELLIE. Well, you see, Mr Mangan, my mother married a very good man—for whatever you may think of my father as a man of business, he is the soul of goodness—and she is not at all keen on my doing the same.

MANGAN. Anyhow, you dont want to marry me now, do you?

ELLIE [*very calmly*] Oh, I think so. Why not?

MANGAN [*rising aghast*] Why not!

ELLIE. I dont see why we shouldnt get on very well together.

MANGAN. Well, but look here, you know— [*He stops, quite at a loss*].

ELLIE [*patiently*] Well?

MANGAN. Well, I thought you were rather particular about people's characters.

ELLIE. If we women were particular about men's characters, we should never get married at all, Mr Mangan.

MANGAN. A child like you talking of "we women"! What next! Youre not in earnest?

ELLIE. Yes I am. Arnt you?

MANGAN. You mean to hold me to it?

ELLIE. Do you wish to back out of it?

MANGAN. Oh no. Not exactly back out of it.

ELLIE. Well?

He has nothing to say. With a long whispered whistle, he drops into the wicker chair and stares before him like a beggared gambler. But a cunning look soon comes into his face. He leans over towards her on his right elbow, and speaks in a low steady voice.

MANGAN. Suppose I told you I was in love with another woman!

ELLIE [*echoing him*] Suppose I told you I was in love with another man!

MANGAN [*bouncing angrily out of his chair*] I'm not joking.

ELLIE. Who told you *I* was?

MANGAN. I tell you I'm serious. Youre too young to be serious; but youll have to believe me. I want to be near your friend Mrs Hushabye. I'm in love with her. Now the murder's out.

ELLIE. I want to be near your friend Mr Hushabye. I'm in love with him. [*She rises and adds with a frank air*] Now we are in one another's confidence, we shall be real friends. Thank you for telling me.

MANGAN [*almost beside himself*] Do you think I'll be made a convenience of like this?

ELLIE. Come, Mr Mangan! you made a business convenience of my father. Well, a woman's business is marriage. Why shouldnt I make a domestic convenience of you?

MANGAN. Because I dont choose, see? Because I'm not a silly gull like your father. Thats why.

ELLIE [*with serene contempt*] You are not good enough to clean my father's boots, Mr Mangan; and I am paying you a great compliment in condescending to make a convenience of you, as you call it. Of course you are free to throw over our engagement if you like; but, if you do, youll never enter Hesione's house again: I will take care of that.

MANGAN [*gasping*] You little devil, youve done me. [*On the point of collapsing into the big chair again he recovers himself*] Wait a bit, though: youre not so cute as you think. You cant beat Boss Mangan as easy as that. Suppose I go straight to Mrs Hushabye and tell her that youre in love with her husband.

ELLIE. She knows it.

MANGAN. You told her!!!

ELLIE. She told me.

MANGAN [*clutching at his bursting temples*] Oh, this is a crazy house. Or else I'm going clean off my chump. Is she making a swop with you—she to have your husband and you to have hers?

ELLIE. Well, you dont want us both, do you?

MANGAN [*throwing himself into the chair distractedly*] My brain wont stand it. My head's going to split. Help! Help me to hold it. Quick: hold it: squeeze it. Save me. [*Ellie comes behind his chair; clasps his head hard for a moment; then begins to draw her hands from his forehead back to his ears*]. Thank you. [*Drowsily*] Thats very refreshing. [*Waking a little*] Don't you hypnotize me, though. Ive seen men made fools of by hypnotism.

ELLIE [*steadily*] Be quiet. Ive seen men made fools of without hypnotism.

MANGAN [*humbly*] You dont dislike touching me, I hope. You never touched me before, I noticed.

ELLIE. Not since you fell in love naturally with a grown-up nice woman, who will never expect you to make love to her. And I will never expect him to make love to me.

MANGAN. He may, though.

ELLIE [*making her passes rhythmically*] Hush. Go to

sleep. Do you hear? You are to go to sleep, go to sleep, go to sleep; be quiet, deeply deeply quiet; sleep, sleep, sleep, sleep, sleep.

He falls asleep. Ellie steals away; turns the light out; and goes into the garden.

Nurse Guinness opens the door and is seen in the light which comes in from the hall.

GUINNESS [*speaking to someone outside*] Mr Mangan's not here, ducky: theres no one here. It's all dark.

MRS HUSHABYE [*without*] Try the garden. Mr Dunn and I will be in my boudoir. Shew him the way.

GUINNESS. Yes, ducky. [*She makes for the garden door in the dark; stumbles over the sleeping Mangan; and screams*]. Ahoo! Oh Lord, sir! I beg your pardon, I'm sure: I didnt see you in the dark. Who is it? [*She goes back to the door and turns on the light*]. Oh, Mr Mangan, sir, I hope I havnt hurt you plumping into your lap like that. [*Coming to him*] I was looking for you, sir. Mrs Hushabye says will you please— [*Noticing that he remains quite insensible*] Oh, my good Lord, I hope I havnt killed him. Sir! Mr Mangan! Sir! [*She shakes him; and he is rolling inertly off the chair on the floor when she holds him up and props him against the cushion*]. Miss Hessy! Miss Hessy! Quick, doty darling. Miss Hessy! [*Mrs Hushabye comes in from the hall, followed by Mazzini Dunn*]. Oh, Miss Hessy, Ive been and killed him.

Mazzini runs round the back of the chair to Mangan's right hand, and sees that the nurse's words are apparently only too true.

MAZZINI. What tempted you to commit such a crime, woman?

MRS HUSHABYE [*trying not to laugh*] Do you mean you did it on purpose?

GUINNESS. Now is it likely I'd kill any man on purpose? I fell over him in the dark; and I'm a pretty tidy weight. He never spoke nor moved until I shook him; and then he would have dropped dead on the floor. Isnt it tiresome?

MRS HUSHABYE [*going past the nurse to Mangan's side, and inspecting him less credulously than Mazzini*] Nonsense! he is not dead: he is only asleep. I can see him breathing.

GUINNESS. But why wont he wake?

MAZZINI [*speaking very politely into Mangan's ear*] Mangan! My dear Mangan! [*He blows into Mangan's ear*].

MRS HUSHABYE. Thats no good. [*She shakes him vigorously*]. Mr Mangan: wake up. Do you hear? [*He begins to roll over*]. Oh! Nurse, nurse: he's falling: help me.

Nurse Guinness rushes to the rescue. With Mazzini's assistance, Mangan is propped safely up again.

GUINNESS [*behind the chair; bending over to test the case with her nose*] Would he be drunk, do you think, pet?

MRS HUSHABYE. Had he any of papa's rum?

MAZZINI. It cant be that: he is most abstemious. I am afraid he drank too much formerly, and has to drink too little now. You know, Mrs Hushabye, I really think he has been hypnotized.

GUINNESS. Hip no what, sir?

MAZZINI. One evening at home, after we had seen a hypnotizing performance, the children began playing at it; and Ellie stroked my head. I assure you I went off dead asleep; and they had to send for a professional to wake me up after I had slept eighteen hours. They had to carry me upstairs; and as the poor children were not very strong, they let me slip; and I rolled right down the whole flight and never woke up. [*Mrs Hushabye splutters*]. Oh, you may laugh, Mrs Hushabye; but I might have been killed.

MRS HUSHABYE. I couldnt have helped laughing even if you had been, Mr Dunn. So Ellie has hypnotized him. What fun!

MAZZINI. Oh no, no, no. It was such a terrible lesson to her: nothing would induce her to try such a thing again.

MRS HUSHABYE. Then who did it? *I* didnt.

MAZZINI. I thought perhaps the Captain might have

done it unintentionally. He is so fearfully magnetic: I feel vibrations whenever he comes close to me.

GUINNESS. The Captain will get him out of it anyhow, sir: I'll back him for that. I'll go fetch him. [*She makes for the pantry*].

MRS HUSHABYE. Wait a bit. [*To Mazzini*] You say he is all right for eighteen hours?

MAZZINI. Well, *I* was asleep for eighteen hours.

MRS HUSHABYE. Were you any the worse for it?

MAZZINI. I dont quite remember. They had poured brandy down my throat, you see; and—

MRS HUSHABYE. Quite. Anyhow, you survived. Nurse, darling: go and ask Miss Dunn to come to us here. Say I want to speak to her particularly. You will find her with Mr Hushabye probably.

GUINNESS. I think not, ducky: Miss Addy is with him. But I'll find her and send her to you. [*She goes out into the garden*].

MRS HUSHABYE [*calling Mazzini's attention to the figure on the chair*] Now, Mr Dunn, look. Just look. Look hard. Do you still intend to sacrifice your daughter to that thing?

MAZZINI [*troubled*] You have completely upset me, Mrs Hushabye, by all you have said to me. That anyone could imagine that I—*I*, a consecrated soldier of freedom, if I may say so—could sacrifice Ellie to anybody or anyone, or that I should ever have dreamed of forcing her inclinations in any way, is a most painful blow to my—well, I suppose you would say to my good opinion of myself.

MRS HUSHABYE [*rather stolidly*] Sorry.

MAZZINI [*looking forlornly at the body*] What is your objection to poor Mangan, Mrs Hushabye? He looks all right to me. But then I am so accustomed to him.

MRS HUSHABYE. Have you no heart? Have you no sense? Look at the brute! Think of poor weak innocent Ellie in the clutches of this slavedriver, who spends his life making thousands of rough violent workmen bend to his will and sweat for him: a man accustomed to have great masses of iron beaten into shape for him by steam-hammers! to fight with women and girls over a halfpenny an hour ruthlessly! a captain of industry, I think you call him, dont you? Are you going to fling your delicate, sweet, helpless child into such a beast's claws just because he will keep her in an expensive house and make her wear diamonds to shew how rich he is?

MAZZINI [*staring at her in wide-eyed amazement*] Bless you, dear Mrs Hushabye, what romantic ideas of business you have! Poor dear Mangan isnt a bit like that.

MRS HUSHABYE [*scornfully*] Poor dear Mangan indeed!

MAZZINI. But he doesnt know anything about machinery. He never goes near the men: he couldnt manage them: he is afraid of them. I never can get him to take the least interest in the works: he hardly knows more about them than you do. People are cruelly unjust to Mangan: they think he is all rugged strength just because his manners are bad.

MRS HUSHABYE. Do you mean to tell me he isnt strong enough to crush poor little Ellie?

MAZZINI. Of course it's very hard to say how any marriage will turn out; but speaking for myself, I should say that he wont have a dog's chance against Ellie. You know, Ellie has remarkable strength of character. I think it is because I taught her to like Shakespear when she was very young.

MRS HUSHABYE [*contemptuously*] Shakespear! The next thing you will tell me is that you could have made a great deal more money than Mangan. [*She retires to the sofa, and sits down at the port end of it in the worst of humors*].

MAZZINI [*following her and taking the other end*] No: I'm no good at making money. I dont care enough for it, somehow. I'm not ambitious! that must be it. Mangan is wonderful about money: he thinks of nothing else. He is so dreadfully afraid of being poor. I am always thinking of other things: even at the works I think of the things we are doing and not of what they cost. And the worst of it is, poor Mangan doesnt know what to do with his money when he gets it. He is such a baby that he doesnt know even what to eat and drink: he has ruined his liver eating and drinking the wrong things; and now he can hardly eat at all. Ellie will diet him splendidly. You will be surprised when you come to know him better: he is really the most helpless of mortals. You get quite a protective feeling towards him.

MRS HUSHABYE. Then who manages his business, pray?

MAZZINI. I do. And of course other people like me.

MRS HUSHABYE. Footling people, you mean.

MAZZINI. I suppose youd think us so.

MRS HUSHABYE. And pray why dont you do without him if youre all so much cleverer?

MAZZINI. Oh, we couldnt: we should ruin the business in a year. I've tried; and I know. We should spend too much on everything. We should improve the quality of the goods and make them too dear. We should be sentimental about the hard cases among the workpeople. But Mangan keeps us in order. He is down on us about every extra halfpenny. We could never do without him. You see, he will sit up all night thinking of how to save sixpence. Wont Ellie make him jump, though, when she takes his house in hand!

MRS HUSHABYE. Then the creature is a fraud even as a captain of industry!

MAZZINI. I am afraid all the captains of industry are what *you* call frauds, Mrs Hushabye. Of course there are some manufacturers who really do understand their own works; but they dont make as high a rate of profit as Mangan does. I assure you Mangan is quite a good fellow in his way. He means well.

MRS HUSHABYE. He doesnt look well. He is not in his first youth, is he?

MAZZINI. After all, no husband is in his first youth for

very long, Mrs Hushabye. And men cant afford to marry in their first youth nowadays.

MRS HUSHABYE. Now if *I* said that, it would sound witty. Why cant y o u say it wittily? What on earth is the matter with you? Why dont you inspire everybody with confidence? with respect?

MAZZINI [*humbly*] I think that what is the matter with me is that I am poor. You dont know what that means at home. Mind: I dont say they have ever complained. Theyve all been wonderful: theyve been proud of my poverty. Theyve even joked about it quite often. But my wife has had a very poor time of it. She has been quite resigned—

MRS HUSHABYE [*shuddering involuntarily*]!!

MAZZINI. There! You see, Mrs Hushabye. I dont want Ellie to live on resignation.

MRS HUSHABYE. Do you want her to have to resign herself to living with a man she doesnt love?

MAZZINI [*wistfully*] Are you sure that would be worse than living with a man she did love, if he was a footling person?

MRS HUSHABYE [*relaxing her contemptuous attitude, quite interested in Mazzini now*] You know, I really think you must love Ellie very much; for you become quite clever when you talk about her.

MAZZINI. I didnt know I was so very stupid on other subjects.

MRS HUSHABYE. You are, sometimes.

MAZZINI [*turning his head away; for his eyes are wet*] I have learnt a good deal about myself from you, Mrs Hushabye; and I'm afraid I shall not be the happier for your plain speaking. But if you thought I needed it to make me think of Ellie's happiness you were very much mistaken.

MRS HUSHABYE [*leaning towards him kindly*] Have I been a beast?

MAZZINI [*pulling himself together*] It doesnt matter about me, Mrs Hushabye. I think you like Ellie; and that is enough for me.

MRS HUSHABYE. I'm beginning to like you a little. I perfectly loathed you at first. I thought you the most odious, self-satisfied, boresome elderly prig I ever met.

MAZZINI [*resigned, and now quite cheerful*] I daresay I am all that. I never have been a favorite with gorgeous women like you. They always frighten me.

MRS HUSHABYE [*pleased*] Am I a gorgeous woman, Mazzini? I shall fall in love with you presently.

MAZZINI [*with placid gallantry*] No you wont, Hesione. But you would be quite safe. Would you believe it that quite a lot of women have flirted with me because I am quite safe? But they get tired of me for the same reason.

MRS HUSHABYE [*mischievously*]. Take care. You may not be so safe as you think.

MAZZINI. Oh yes, quite safe. You see, I have been in love really: the sort of love that only happens once. [*Softly*] Thats why Ellie is such a lovely girl.

MRS HUSHABYE. Well, really, you a r e coming out. Are you quite sure you wont let me tempt you into a second grand passion?

MAZZINI. Quite. It wouldnt be natural. The fact is, you dont strike on my box, Mrs Hushabye; and I certainly dont strike on yours.

MRS HUSHABYE. I see. Your marriage was a safety match.

MAZZINI. What a very witty application of the expression I used! I should never have thought of it.

Ellie comes in from the garden, looking anything but happy.

MRS HUSHABYE [*rising*] Oh! here is Ellie at last. [*She goes behind the sofa*].

ELLIE [*on the threshold of the starboard door*] Guinness said you wanted me: you and papa.

MRS HUSHABYE. You have kept us waiting so long that it almost came to—well, never mind. Your father is a very wonderful man [*she ruffles his hair affectionately*]: the only one I ever met who could resist me when I made myself really agreeable. [*She comes to the big chair, on Mangan's left*]. Come here. I have something to shew you. [*Ellie strolls listlessly to the other side of the chair*]. Look.

ELLIE [*contemplating Mangan without interest*] I know. He is only asleep. We had a talk after dinner; and he fell asleep in the middle of it.

MRS HUSHABYE. You did it, Ellie. You put him asleep.

MAZZINI [*rising quickly and coming to the back of the chair*] Oh, I hope not. Did you, Ellie?

ELLIE [*wearily*] He asked me to.

MAZZINI. But it's dangerous. You know what happened to me.

ELLIE [*utterly indifferent*] Oh, I daresay I can wake him. If not, somebody else can.

MRS HUSHABYE. It doesnt matter, anyhow, because I have at last persuaded your father that you dont want to marry him.

ELLIE [*suddenly coming out of her listlessness, much vexed*] But why did you do that, Hesione? I do want to marry him. I fully intend to marry him.

MAZZINI. Are you quite sure, Ellie? Mrs Hushabye has made me feel that I may have been thoughtless and selfish about it.

ELLIE [*very clearly and steadily*] Papa. When Mrs Hushabye takes it on herself to explain to you what I think or dont think, shut your ears tight; and shut your eyes too. Hesione knows nothing about me: she hasnt the least notion of the sort of person I am, and never will. I promise you I wont do anything I dont want to do and mean to do for my own sake.

MAZZINI. You are quite, quite sure?

ELLIE. Quite, quite sure. Now you must go away and leave me to talk to Mrs Hushabye.

MAZZINI. But I should like to hear. Shall I be in the way?

ELLIE [*inexorable*] I had rather talk to her alone.

MAZZINI [*affectionately*] Oh, well, I know what a nuisance parents are, dear. I will be good and go. [*He goes to the garden door*]. By the way, do you remember the address of that professional who woke me up? Dont you think I had better telegraph to him?

MRS HUSHABYE [*moving towards the sofa*] It's too late to telegraph tonight.

MAZZINI. I suppose so. I do hope he'll wake up in the course of the night. [*He goes out into the garden*].

ELLIE [*turning vigorously on Hesione the moment her father is out of the room*] Hesione: what the devil do you mean by making mischief with my father about Mangan?

MRS HUSHABYE [*promptly losing her temper*] Dont you dare speak to me like that, you little minx. Remember that you are in my house.

ELLIE. Stuff! Why dont you mind your own business? What is it to you whether I choose to marry Mangan or not?

MRS HUSHABYE. Do you suppose you can bully me, you miserable little matrimonial adventurer?

ELLIE. Every woman who hasnt any money is a matrimonial adventurer. It's easy for you to talk: you have never known what it is to want money; and you can pick up men as if they were daisies. I am poor and respectable—

MRS HUSHABYE [*interrupting*] Ho! respectable! How did you pick up Mangan? How did you pick up my husband? You have the audacity to tell me that I am a—a—a—

ELLIE. A siren. So you are. You were born to lead men by the nose: if you werent, Marcus would have waited for me, perhaps.

MRS HUSHABYE [*suddenly melting and half laughing*] Oh, my poor Ellie, my pettikins, my unhappy darling! I am so sorry about Hector. But what can I do? It's not my fault: I'd give him to you if I could.

ELLIE. I dont blame you for that.

MRS HUSHABYE. What a brute I was to quarrel with you and call you names! Do kiss me and say youre not angry with me.

ELLIE [*fiercely*] Oh, dont slop and gush and be sentimental. Dont you see that unless I can be hard—as hard as nails—I shall go mad? I dont care a damn about your calling me names: do you think a woman in my situation can feel a few hard words?

MRS HUSHABYE. Poor little woman! Poor little situation!

ELLIE. I suppose you think youre being sympathetic. You are just foolish and stupid and selfish. You see me getting a smasher right in the face that kills a whole part of my life: the best part that can never come again; and you think you can help me over it by a little coaxing and kissing. When I want all the strength I can get to lean on: something iron, something stony, I dont care how cruel it is, you go all mushy and want to slobber over me. I'm not angry; I'm not unfriendly; but for God's sake do pull yourself together; and dont think that because youre on velvet and always have been, women who are in hell can take it as easily as you.

MRS HUSHABYE [*shrugging her shoulders*] Very well. [*She sits down on the sofa in her old place*]. But I warn you that when I am neither coaxing and kissing nor laughing, I am just wondering how much longer I can stand living in this cruel, damnable world. You object to the siren: well, I drop the siren. You want to rest your wounded bosom against a grindstone. Well [*folding her arms*], here is the grindstone.

ELLIE [*sitting down beside her, appeased*] Thats better: you really have the trick of falling in with everyone's mood; but you dont understand, because you are not the sort of woman for whom there is only one man and only one chance.

MRS HUSHABYE. I certainly dont understand how your marrying that object [*indicating Mangan*] will console you for not being able to marry Hector.

ELLIE. Perhaps you dont understand why I was quite

a nice girl this morning, and am now neither a girl nor particularly nice.

MRS HUSHABYE. Oh yes, I do. It's because you have made up your mind to do something despicable and wicked.

ELLIE. I dont think so, Hesione. I must make the best of my ruined house.

MRS HUSHABYE. Pooh! Youll get over it. Your house isnt ruined.

ELLIE. Of course I shall get over it. You dont suppose I'm going to sit down and die of a broken heart, I hope, or be an old maid living on a pittance from the Sick and Indigent Room-keepers' Association. But my heart i s broken, all the same. What I mean by that is that I know that what has happened to me with Marcus will not happen to me ever again. In the world for me there is Marcus and a lot of other men of whom one is just the same as another. Well, if I cant have love, thats no reason why I should have poverty. If Mangan has nothing else, he has money.

MRS HUSHABYE. And are there no y o u n g men with money?

ELLIE. Not within my reach. Besides, a young man would have the right to expect love from me, and would perhaps leave me when he found I could not give it to him. Rich young men can get rid of their wives, you know, pretty cheaply. But this object, as you call him, can expect nothing more from me than I am prepared to give him.

MRS HUSHABYE. He will be your owner, remember. If he buys you, he will make the bargain pay him and not you. Ask your father.

ELLIE [*rising and strolling to the chair to contemplate their subject*] You need not trouble on that score, Hesione. I have more to give Boss Mangan than he has to give me: it is I who am buying him, and at a pretty good price too, I think. Women are better at that sort of bargain than men. I have taken the Boss's measure; and ten Boss Mangans shall not prevent me doing far more as I please as his wife than I have ever been able to do as a poor girl. [*Stooping to the recumbent figure*] Shall they, Boss? I think not. [*She passes on to the drawing-table, and leans against the end of it, facing the windows*]. I shall not have to spend most of my time wondering how long my gloves will last, anyhow.

MRS HUSHABYE [*rising superbly*] Ellie: you are a wicked sordid little beast. And to think that I actually condescended to fascinate that creature there to save you from him! Well, let me tell you this: if you make this disgusting match, you will never see Hector again if I can help it.

ELLIE [*unmoved*] I nailed Mangan by telling him that if he did not marry me he should never see you again. [*She lifts herself on her wrists and seats herself on the end of the table*].

MRS HUSHABYE [*recoiling*] Oh!

ELLIE. So you see I am not unprepared for your playing that trump against me. Well, you just try it: thats all. I should have made a man of Marcus, not a household pet.

MRS HUSHABYE [*flaming*] You dare!

ELLIE [*looking almost dangerous*] Set him thinking about me if y o u dare.

MRS HUSHABYE. Well, of all the impudent little fiends I ever met! Hector says there is a certain point at which the only answer you can give to a man who breaks all the rules is to knock him down. What would you say if I were to box your ears?

ELLIE [*calmly*] I should pull your hair.

MRS HUSHABYE [*mischievously*] That wouldnt hurt me. Perhaps it comes off at night.

ELLIE [*so taken aback that she drops off the table and runs to her*] Oh, you dont mean to say, Hesione, that your beautiful black hair is false?

MRS HUSHABYE [*patting it*] Dont tell Hector. He believes in it.

ELLIE [*groaning*] Oh! Even the hair that ensnared him false! Everything false!

MRS HUSHABYE. Pull it and try. Other women can

snare men in their hair; but I can swing a baby on mine. Aha! you cant do that, Goldylocks.

ELLIE [*heartbroken*] No. You have stolen my babies.

MRS HUSHABYE. Pettikins: dont make me cry. You know, what you said about my making a household pet of him is a little true. Perhaps he ought to have waited for you. Would any other woman on earth forgive you?

ELLIE. Oh, what right had you to take him all for yourself! [*Pulling herself together*] There! You couldnt help it: neither of us could help it. He couldnt help it. No: dont say anything more: I cant bear it. Let us wake the object. [*She begins stroking Mangan's head, reversing the movement with which she put him to sleep*]. Wake up, do you hear? You are to wake up at once. Wake up, wake up, wake—

MANGAN [*bouncing out of the chair in a fury and turning on them*] Wake up! So you think Ive been asleep, do you? [*He kicks the chair violently back out of his way, and gets between them*]. You throw me into a trance so that I cant move hand or foot—I might have been buried alive! it's a mercy I wasnt—and then you think I was only asleep. If youd let me drop the two times you rolled me about, my nose would have been flattened for life against the floor. But Ive found you all out, anyhow. I know the sort of people I'm among now. Ive heard every word youve said, you and your precious father, and [*to Mrs Hushabye*] you too. So I'm an object, am I? I'm a thing, am I? I'm a fool that hasnt sense enough to feed myself properly, am I? I'm afraid of the men that would starve if it werent for the wages I give them, am I? I'm nothing but a disgusting old skinflint to be made a convenience of by designing women and fool managers of my works, am I? I'm—

MRS HUSHABYE [*with the most elegant aplomb*] Sh-sh-sh-sh-sh! Mr Mangan: you are bound in honor to obliterate from your mind all you heard while you were pretending to be asleep. It was not meant for you to hear.

MANGAN. Pretending to be asleep! Do you think if I

was only pretending that I'd have sprawled there helpless, and listened to such unfairness, such lies, such injustice and plotting and backbiting and slandering of me, if I could have up and told you what I thought of you! I wonder I didnt burst.

MRS HUSHABYE [*sweetly*] You dreamt it all, Mr Mangan. We were only saying how beautifully peaceful you looked in your sleep. That was all, wasnt it, Ellie? Believe me, Mr Mangan, all those unpleasant things came into your mind in the last half second before you woke. Ellie rubbed your hair the wrong way; and the disagreeable sensation suggested a disagreeable dream.

MANGAN [*doggedly*] I believe in dreams.

MRS HUSHABYE. So do I. But they go by contraries, dont they?

MANGAN [*depths of emotion suddenly welling up in him*] I shant forget, to my dying day, that when you gave me the glad eye that time in the garden, you were making a fool of me. That was a dirty low mean thing to do. You had no right to let me come near you if I disgusted you. It isnt my fault if I'm old and havnt a moustache like a bronze candlestick as your husband has. There are things no decent woman would do to a man—like a man hitting a woman in the breast.

Hesione, utterly shamed, sits down on the sofa and covers her face with her hands. Mangan sits down also on his chair and begins to cry like a child. Ellie stares at them. Mrs Hushabye, at the distressing sound he makes, takes down her hands and looks at him. She rises and runs to him.

MRS HUSHABYE. Dont cry: I cant bear it. Have I broken your heart? I didnt know you had one. How could I?

MANGAN. I'm a man aint I?

MRS HUSHABYE [*half coaxing, half rallying, altogether tenderly*] Oh no: not what I call a man. Only a Boss: just that and nothing else. What business has a Boss with a heart?

MANGAN. Then youre not a bit sorry for what you did,

nor ashamed?

MRS HUSHABYE. I was ashamed for the first time in my life when you said that about hitting a woman in the breast, and I found out what I'd done. My very bones blushed red. Youve had your revenge, Boss. Arnt you satisfied?

MANGAN. Serve you right! Do you hear? Serve you right! Youre just cruel. Cruel.

MRS HUSHABYE. Yes: cruelty would be delicious if one could only find some sort of cruelty that didnt really hurt. By the way [*sitting down beside him on the arm of the chair*], whats your name? It's not really Boss, is it?

MANGAN [*shortly*] If you want to know, my name's Alfred.

MRS HUSHABYE [*springing up*] Alfred! Ellie: he was christened after Tennyson!!!

MANGAN [*rising*] I was christened after my uncle, and never had a penny from him, damn him! What of it?

MRS HUSHABYE. It comes to me suddenly that you are a real person: that you had a mother, like anyone else. [*Putting her hands on his shoulders and surveying him*] Little Alf!

MANGAN. Well, you have a nerve.

MRS HUSHABYE. And you have a heart, Alfy, a whimpering little heart, but a real one. [*Releasing him suddenly*] Now run and make it up with Ellie. She has had time to think what to say to you, which is more than I had. [*She goes out quickly into the garden by the port door*].

MANGAN. That woman has a pair of hands that go right through you.

ELLIE. Still in love with her, in spite of all we said about you?

MANGAN. Are all women like you two? Do they never think of anything about a man except what they can get out of him? You werent even thinking that about me. You were only thinking whether your gloves would last.

ELLIE. I shall not have to think about that when we are married.

MANGAN. And you think I am going to marry you after what I heard there!

ELLIE. You heard nothing from me that I did not tell you before.

MANGAN. Perhaps you think I cant do without you.

ELLIE. I think you would feel lonely without us all now, after coming to know us so well.

MANGAN [*with something like a yell of despair*] Am I never to have the last word?

CAPTAIN SHOTOVER [*appearing at the starboard garden door*] There is a soul in torment here. What is the matter?

MANGAN. This girl doesnt want to spend her life wondering how long her gloves will last.

CAPTAIN SHOTOVER [*passing through*] Dont wear any. I never do. [*He goes into the pantry*].

LADY UTTERWORD [*appearing at the port garden door, in a handsome dinner dress*] Is anything the matter?

ELLIE. This gentleman wants to know is he never to have the last word?

LADY UTTERWORD [*coming forward to the sofa*] I should let him have it, my dear. The important thing is not to have the last word, but to have your own way.

MANGAN. She wants both.

LADY UTTERWORD. She wont get them, Mr Mangan. Providence always has the last word.

MANGAN [*desperately*] Now y o u are going to come religion over me. In this house a man's mind might as well be a football. I'm going. [*He makes for the hall, but is stopped by a hail from the Captain, who has just emerged from his pantry*].

CAPTAIN SHOTOVER. Whither away, Boss Mangan?

MANGAN. To hell out of this house: let that be enough for you and all here.

CAPTAIN SHOTOVER. You were welcome to come: you are free to go. The wide earth, the high seas, the spacious skies are waiting for you outside.

LADY UTTERWORD. But your things, Mr Mangan. Your

bags, your comb and brushes, your pyjamas—

HECTOR [*who has just appeared in the port doorway in a handsome Arab costume*] Why should the escaping slave take his chains with him?

MANGAN. Thats right, Hushabye. Keep the pyjamas, my lady; and much good may they do you.

HECTOR [*advancing to Lady Utterword's left hand*] Let us all go out into the night and leave everything behind us.

MANGAN. You stay where you are, the lot of you. I want no company, especially female company.

ELLIE. Let him go. He is unhappy here. He is angry with us.

CAPTAIN SHOTOVER. Go, Boss Mangan; and when you have found the land where there is happiness and where there are no women, send me its latitude and longitude; and I will join you there.

LADY UTTERWORD. You will certainly not be comfortable without your luggage, Mr Mangan.

ELLIE [*impatient*] Go, go: why dont you go? It is a heavenly night: you can sleep on the heath. Take my waterproof to lie on: it is hanging up in the hall.

HECTOR. Breakfast at nine, unless you prefer to breakfast with the Captain at six.

ELLIE. Good night, Alfred.

HECTOR. Alfred! [*He runs back to the door and calls into the garden*] Randall: Mangan's Christian name is Alfred.

RANDALL [*appearing in the starboard doorway in evening dress*] Then Hesione wins her bet.

Mrs Hushabye appears in the port doorway. She throws her left arm round Hector's neck; draws him with her to the back of the sofa; and throws her right arm round Lady Utterword's neck.

MRS HUSHABYE. They wouldnt believe me, Alf.

They contemplate him.

MANGAN. Is there any more of you coming in to look at

me, as if I was the latest thing in a menagerie?

MRS HUSHABYE. You a r e the latest thing in this menagerie.

Before Mangan can retort, a fall of furniture is heard from upstairs; then a pistol shot, and a yell of pain. The staring group breaks up in consternation.

MAZZINI'S VOICE [*from above*] Help! A burglar! Help!

HECTOR [*his eyes blazing*] A burglar!!!

MRS HUSHABYE. No, Hector: youll be shot. [*But it is too late: he has dashed out past Mangan, who hastily moves towards the bookshelves out of his way*].

CAPTAIN SHOTOVER [*blowing his whistle*] All hands aloft! [*He strides out after Hector*].

LADY UTTERWORD. My diamonds! [*She follows the Captain*].

RANDALL [*rushing after her*] No, Ariadne. Let me.

ELLIE. Oh, is papa shot? [*She runs out*].

MRS HUSHABYE. Are you frightened, Alf?

MANGAN. No. It aint my house, thank God.

MRS HUSHABYE. If they catch a burglar, shall we have to go into court as witnesses, and be asked all sorts of questions about our private lives?

MANGAN. You wont be believed if you tell the truth.

Mazzini, terribly upset, with a duelling pistol in his hand, comes from the hall, and makes his way to the drawing-table.

MAZZINI. Oh, my dear Mrs Hushabye, I might have killed him. [*He throws the pistol on the table and staggers round to the chair*]. I hope you wont believe I really intended to.

Hector comes in, marching an old and villainous looking man before him by the collar. He plants him in the middle of the room and releases him.

Ellie follows, and immediately runs across to the back of her father's chair and pats his shoulders.

RANDALL [*entering with a poker*] Keep your eye on this

door, Mangan. I'll look after the other. [*He goes to the starboard door and stands on guard there*].

Lady Utterword comes in after Randall, and goes between Mrs Hushabye and Mangan.

Nurse Guinness brings up the rear, and waits near the door, on Mangan's left.

MRS HUSHABYE. What has happened?

MAZZINI. Your housekeeper told me there was somebody upstairs, and gave me a pistol that Mr Hushabye had been practising with. I thought it would frighten him; but it went off at a touch.

THE BURGLAR. Yes, and took the skin off my ear. Precious near took the top off my head. Why dont you have a proper revolver instead of a thing like that, that goes off if you as much as blow on it?

HECTOR. One of my duelling pistols. Sorry.

MAZZINI. He put his hands up and said it was a fair cop.

THE BURGLAR. So it was. Send for the police.

HECTOR. No, by thunder! It was not a fair cop. We were four to one.

MRS HUSHABYE. What will they do to him?

THE BURGLAR. Ten years. Beginning with solitary. Ten years off my life. I shant serve it all: I'm too old. It will see me out.

LADY UTTERWORD. You should have thought of that before you stole my diamonds.

THE BURGLAR. Well, youve got them back, lady: havnt you? Can you give me back the years of my life you are going to take from me?

MRS HUSHABYE. Oh, we cant bury a man alive for ten years for a few diamonds.

THE BURGLAR. Ten little shining diamonds! Ten long black years!

LADY UTTERWORD. Think of what it is for us to be dragged through the horrors of a criminal court, and have all our family affairs in the papers! If you were a native, and Hastings could order you a good beating and send you away, I shouldnt mind; but here in England there is no real protection for any respectable person.

THE BURGLAR. I'm too old to be giv a hiding, lady. Send for the police and have done with it. It's only just and right you should.

RANDALL [*who has relaxed his vigilance on seeing the burglar so pacifically disposed, and comes forward swinging the poker between his fingers like a well-folded umbrella*] It is neither just nor right that we should be put to a lot of inconvenience to gratify your moral enthusiasm, my friend. You had better get out, while you have the chance.

THE BURGLAR [*inexorably*] No. I must work my sin off my conscience. This has come as a sort of call to me. Let me spend the rest of my life repenting in a cell. I shall have my reward above.

MANGAN [*exasperated*] The very burglars cant behave naturally in this house.

HECTOR. My good sir: you must work out your salvation at somebody else's expense. Nobody here is going to charge you.

THE BURGLAR. Oh, you wont charge me, wont you?

HECTOR. No. I'm sorry to be inhospitable; but will you kindly leave the house?

THE BURGLAR. Right. I'll go to the police station and give myself up. [*He turns resolutely to the door; but Hector stops him*].

<table>
<tr><td>HECTOR.</td><td>Oh no. You mustnt do that.</td></tr>
<tr><td>RANDALL.</td><td>No, no. Clear out, man, cant you; and dont be a fool.</td></tr>
<tr><td>MRS HUSHABYE.</td><td>Dont be so silly. Cant you repent at home?</td></tr>
</table>

LADY UTTERWORD. You will have to do as you are told.

THE BURGLAR. It's compounding a felony, you know.

MRS HUSHABYE. This is utterly ridiculous. Are we to be forced to prosecute this man when we dont want to?

THE BURGLAR. Am I to be robbed of my salvation to save you the trouble of spending a day at the sessions? Is that justice? Is it right? Is it fair to me?

MAZZINI [*rising and leaning across the table persuasively as if it were a pulpit desk or a shop counter*] Come, come! let me shew you how you can turn your very crimes to account. Why not set up as a locksmith? You must know more about locks than most honest men?

THE BURGLAR. Thats true, sir. But I couldnt set up as a locksmith under twenty pounds.

RANDALL. Well, you can easily steal twenty pounds. You will find it in the nearest bank.

THE BURGLAR [*horrified*] Oh what a thing for a gentleman to put into the head of a poor criminal scrambling out of the bottomless pit as it were! Oh, shame on you, sir! Oh, God forgive you! [*He throws himself into the big chair and covers his face as if in prayer*].

LADY UTTERWORD. Really, Randall!

HECTOR. It seems to me that we shall have to take up a collection for this inopportunely contrite sinner.

LADY UTTERWORD. But twenty pounds is ridiculous.

THE BURGLAR [*looking up quickly*] I shall have to buy a lot of tools, lady.

LADY UTTERWORD. Nonsense: you have your burgling kit.

THE BURGLAR. Whats a jimmy and a centrebit and an acetylene welding plant and a bunch of skeleton keys? I shall want a forge, and a smithy, and a shop, and fittings. I cant hardly do it for twenty.

HECTOR. My worthy friend, we havnt got twenty pounds.

THE BURGLAR [*now master of the situation*] You can raise it among you, cant you?

MRS HUSHABYE. Give him a sovereign, Hector, and get rid of him.

HECTOR [*giving him a pound*] There! Off with you.

THE BURGLAR [*rising and taking the money very ungratefully*] I wont promise nothing. You have more on you than a quid: all the lot of you, I mean.

LADY UTTERWORD [*vigorously*] Oh, let us prosecute him and have done with it. I have a conscience too, I hope; and I do not feel at all sure that we have any right to let him go, especially if he is going to be greedy and impertinent.

THE BURGLAR [*quickly*] All right, lady, all right. Ive no wish to be anything but agreeable. Good evening, ladies and gentlemen; and thank you kindly.

He is hurrying out when he is confronted in the doorway by Captain Shotover.

CAPTAIN SHOTOVER [*fixing the burglar with a piercing regard*] Whats this? Are there two of you?

THE BURGLAR [*falling on his knees before the Captain in abject terror*] Oh my good Lord, what have I done? Dont tell me its your house Ive broken into, Captain Shotover.

The Captain seizes him by the collar; drags him to his feet; and leads him to the middle of the group, Hector falling back beside his wife to make way for them.

CAPTAIN SHOTOVER [*turning him towards Ellie*] Is that your daughter? [*He releases him*].

THE BURGLAR. Well, how do I know, Captain? You know the sort of life you and me has led. Any young lady of that age might be my daughter anywhere in the wide world, as you might say.

CAPTAIN SHOTOVER [*to Mazzini*] You are not Billy Dunn. This is Billy Dunn. Why have you imposed on me?

THE BURGLAR [*indignantly to Mazzini*] Have you been giving yourself out to be me? You, that nigh blew my head off! Shooting yourself, in a manner of speaking!

MAZZINI. My dear Captain Shotover, ever since I came into this house I have done hardly anything else but assure you that I am not Mr William Dunn, but Mazzini Dunn, a very different person.

THE BURGLAR. He dont belong to my branch, Captain. Theres two sets in the family: the thinking Dunns and the drinking Dunns, each going their own ways. I'm a drinking

Dunn: he's a thinking Dunn. But that didnt give him any right to shoot me.

CAPTAIN SHOTOVER. So youve turned burglar, have you?

THE BURGLAR. No, Captain: I wouldnt disgrace our old sea calling by such a thing. I am no burglar.

LADY UTTERWORD. What were you doing with my diamonds?

GUINNESS. What did you break into the house for if youre no burglar?

RANDALL. Mistook the house for your own and came in by the wrong window, eh?

THE BURGLAR. Well, it's no use my telling you a lie: I can take in most captains, but not Captain Shotover, because he sold himself to the devil in Zanzibar, and can divine water, spot gold, explode a cartridge in your pocket with a glance of his eye, and see the truth hidden in the heart of man. But I'm no burglar.

CAPTAIN SHOTOVER. Are you an honest man?

THE BURGLAR. I dont set up to be better than my fellow-creatures, and never did, as you well know, Captain. But what I do is innocent and pious. I enquire about for houses where the right sort of people live. I work it on them same as I worked it here. I break into the house; put a few spoons or diamonds in my pocket; make a noise; get caught; and take up a collection. And you wouldnt believe how hard it is to get caught when youre actually trying to. I have knocked over all the chairs in a room without a soul paying any attention to me. In the end I have had to walk out and leave the job.

RANDALL. When that happens, do you put back the spoons and diamonds?

THE BURGLAR. Well, I dont fly in the face of Providence, if thats what you want to know.

CAPTAIN SHOTOVER. Guinness: you remember this man?

GUINNESS. I should think I do, seeing I was married to him, the blackguard!

HESIONE } [*exclaiming* { Married to him!
LADY UTTERWORD } *together*] { Guinness!!

THE BURGLAR. It wasnt legal. Ive been married to no end of women. No use coming that over me.

CAPTAIN SHOTOVER. Take him to the forecastle. [*He flings him to the door with a strength beyond his years*].

GUINNESS. I suppose you mean the kitchen. They wont have him there. Do you expect servants to keep company with thieves and all sorts?

CAPTAIN SHOTOVER. Land-thieves and water-thieves are the same flesh and blood. I'll have no boatswain on my quarter-deck. Off with you both.

THE BURGLAR. Yes, Captain. [*He goes out humbly*].

MAZZINI. Will it be safe to have him in the house like that?

GUINNESS. Why didnt you shoot him, sir? If I'd known who he was, I'd have shot him myself. [*She goes out*].

MRS HUSHABYE. Do sit down, everybody. [*She sits down on the sofa*].

They all move except Ellie. Mazzini resumes his seat. Randall sits down in the window seat near the starboard door, again making a pendulum of his poker, and studying it as Galileo might have done. Hector sits on his left, in the middle. Mangan, forgotten, sits in the port corner. Lady Utterword takes the big chair. Captain Shotover goes into the pantry in deep abstraction. They all look after him; and Lady Utterword coughs consciously.

MRS HUSHABYE. So Billy Dunn was poor nurse's little romance. I knew there had been somebody.

RANDALL. They will fight their battles over again and enjoy themselves immensely.

LADY UTTERWORD [*irritably*] You are not married; and you know nothing about it, Randall. Hold your tongue.

RANDALL. Tyrant!

MRS HUSHABYE. Well, we have had a very exciting evening. Everything will be an anticlimax after it. We'd better all go to bed.

RANDALL. Another burglar may turn up.

MAZZINI. Oh, impossible! I hope not.

RANDALL. Why not? There is more than one burglar in England.

MRS HUSHABYE. What do you say, Alf?

MANGAN [*huffily*] Oh, I dont matter. I'm forgotten. The burglar has put my nose out of joint. Shove me into a corner and have done with me.

MRS HUSHABYE [*jumping up mischievously, and going to him*] Would you like a walk on the heath, Alfred? With me?

ELLIE. Go, Mr Mangan. It will do you good. Hesione will soothe you.

MRS HUSHABYE [*slipping her arm under his and pulling him upright*] Come, Alfred. There is a moon: it's like the night in Tristan and Isolde. [*She caresses his arm and draws him to the port garden door*].

MANGAN [*writhing but yielding*] How you can have the face—the heart— [*He breaks down and is heard sobbing as she takes him out*].

LADY UTTERWORD. What an extraordinary way to behave! What is the matter with the man?

ELLIE [*in a strangely calm voice, staring into an imaginary distance*] His heart is breaking: that is all. [*The Captain appears at the pantry door, listening*]. It is a curious sensation: the sort of pain that goes mercifully beyond our powers of feeling. When your heart is broken, your boats are burned: nothing matters any more. It is the end of happiness and the beginning of peace.

LADY UTTERWORD [*suddenly rising in a rage, to the astonishment of the rest*] How dare you?

HECTOR. Good heavens! Whats the matter?

RANDALL [*in a warning whisper*] Tch—tch—tch! Steady.

ELLIE [*surprised and haughty*] I was not addressing you particularly, Lady Utterword. And I am not accustomed to be asked how dare I.

LADY UTTERWORD. Of course not. Anyone can see how badly you have been brought up.

MAZZINI. Oh, I hope not, Lady Utterword. Really!

LADY UTTERWORD. I know very well what you meant. The impudence!

ELLIE. What on earth do you mean?

CAPTAIN SHOTOVER [*advancing to the table*] She means that her heart will not break. She has been longing all her life for someone to break it. At last she has become afraid she has none to break.

LADY UTTERWORD [*flinging herself on her knees and throwing her arms round him*] Papa: dont say you think Ive no heart.

CAPTAIN SHOTOVER [*raising her with grim tenderness*] If you had no heart how could you want to have it broken, child?

HECTOR [*rising with a bound*] Lady Utterword: you are not to be trusted. You have made a scene. [*He runs out into the garden through the starboard door*].

LADY UTTERWORD. Oh! Hector, Hector! [*She runs out after him*].

RANDALL. Only nerves, I assure you. [*He rises and follows her, waving the poker in his agitation*]. Ariadne! Ariadne! For God's sake be careful. You will— [*He is gone*].

MAZZINI [*rising*] How distressing! Can I do anything, I wonder?

CAPTAIN SHOTOVER [*promptly taking his chair and setting to work at the drawing-board*] No. Go to bed. Goodnight.

MAZZINI [*bewildered*] Oh! Perhaps you are right.

ELLIE. Goodnight, dearest. [*She kisses him*].

MAZZINI. Goodnight, love. [*He makes for the door, but turns aside to the bookshelves*]. I'll just take a book. [*He takes one*]. Goodnight. [*He goes out, leaving Ellie alone with the Captain*].

The Captain is intent on his drawing. Ellie, standing

sentry over his chair, contemplates him for a moment.

ELLIE. Does nothing ever disturb you, Captain Shotover?

CAPTAIN SHOTOVER. Ive stood on the bridge for eighteen hours in a typhoon. Life here is stormier; but I can stand it.

ELLIE. Do you think I ought to marry Mr Mangan?

CAPTAIN SHOTOVER [*never looking up*] One rock is as good as another to be wrecked on.

ELLIE. I am not in love with him.

CAPTAIN SHOTOVER. Who said you were?

ELLIE. You are not surprised?

CAPTAIN SHOTOVER. Surprised! At m y age!

ELLIE. It seems to me quite fair. He wants me for one thing: I want him for another.

CAPTAIN SHOTOVER. Money?

ELLIE. Yes.

CAPTAIN SHOTOVER. Well, one turns the cheek: the other kisses it. One provides the cash: the other spends it.

ELLIE. Who will have the best of the bargain, I wonder?

CAPTAIN SHOTOVER. You. These fellows live in an office all day. You will have to put up with him from dinner to breakfast; but you will both be asleep most of that time. All day you will be quit of him; and you will be shopping with his money. If that is too much for you, marry a seafaring man: you will be bothered with him only three weeks in the year, perhaps.

ELLIE. That would be best of all, I suppose.

CAPTAIN SHOTOVER. It's a dangerous thing to be married right up to the hilt, like my daughter's husband. The man is at home all day, like a damned soul in hell.

ELLIE. I never thought of that before.

CAPTAIN SHOTOVER. If youre marrying for business, you cant be too businesslike.

ELLIE. Why do women always want other women's husbands?

CAPTAIN SHOTOVER. Why do horse-thieves prefer a

horse that is broken-in to one that is wild?

ELLIE [*with a short laugh*] I suppose so. What a vile world it is!

CAPTAIN SHOTOVER. It doesnt concern me. I'm nearly out of it.

ELLIE. And I'm only just beginning.

CAPTAIN SHOTOVER. Yes; so look ahead.

ELLIE. Well, I think I am being very prudent.

CAPTAIN SHOTOVER. I didnt say prudent. I said look ahead.

ELLIE. Whats the difference?

CAPTAIN SHOTOVER. It's prudent to gain the whole world and lose your own soul. But dont forget that your soul sticks to you if you stick to it; but the world has a way of slipping through your fingers.

ELLIE [*wearily, leaving him and beginning to wander restlessly about the room*] I'm sorry, Captain Shotover; but it's no use talking like that to me. Old-fashioned people are no use to me. Old-fashioned people think you can have a soul without money. They think the less money you have, the more soul you have. Young people nowadays know better. A soul is a very expensive thing to keep: much more so than a motor car.

CAPTAIN SHOTOVER. Is it? How much does your soul eat?

ELLIE. Oh, a lot. It eats music and pictures and books and mountains and lakes and beautiful things to wear and nice people to be with. In this country you cant have them without lots of money: that is why our souls are so horribly starved.

CAPTAIN SHOTOVER. Mangan's soul lives on pigs' food.

ELLIE. Yes: money is thrown away on him. I suppose his soul was starved when he was young. But it will not be thrown away on me. It is just because I want to save my soul that I am marrying for money. All the women who are not fools do.

CAPTAIN SHOTOVER. There are other ways of getting

money. Why dont you steal it?

ELLIE. Because I dont want to go to prison.

CAPTAIN SHOTOVER. Is that the only reason? Are you quite sure honesty has nothing to do with it?

ELLIE. Oh, you are very old-fashioned, Captain. Does any modern girl believe that the legal and illegal ways of getting money are the honest and dishonest ways? Mangan robbed my father and my father's friends. I should rob all the money back from Mangan if the police would let me. As they wont, I must get it back by marrying him.

CAPTAIN SHOTOVER. I cant argue: I'm too old: my mind is made up and finished. All I can tell you is that, old-fashioned or new-fashioned, if you sell yourself, you deal your soul a blow that all the books and pictures and concerts and scenery in the world wont heal. [*He gets up suddenly and makes for the pantry*].

ELLIE [*running after him and seizing him by the sleeve*] Then why did you sell yourself to the devil in Zanzibar?

CAPTAIN SHOTOVER [*stopping, startled*] What?

ELLIE. You shall not run away before you answer. I have found out that trick of yours. If you sold yourself, why shouldnt I?

CAPTAIN SHOTOVER. I had to deal with men so degraded that they wouldnt obey me unless I swore at them and kicked them and beat them with my fists. Foolish people took young thieves off the streets; flung them into a training ship where they were taught to fear the cane instead of fearing God; and thought theyd made men and sailors of them by private subscription. I tricked these thieves into believing I'd sold myself to the devil. It saved my soul from the kicking and swearing that was damning me by inches.

ELLIE [*releasing him*] I shall pretend to sell myself to Boss Mangan to save my soul from the poverty that is damning m e by inches.

CAPTAIN SHOTOVER. Riches will damn you ten times deeper. Riches wont save even your body.

ELLIE. Old-fashioned again. We know now that the

soul is the body, and the body the soul. They tell us they are different because they want to persuade us that we can keep our souls if we let them make slaves of our bodies. I am afraid you are no use to me, Captain.

CAPTAIN SHOTOVER. What did you expect? A Savior, eh? Are you old-fashioned enough to believe in that?

ELLIE. No. But I thought you were very wise, and might help me. Now I have found you out. You pretend to be busy, and think of fine things to say, and run in and out to surprise people by saying them, and get away before they can answer you.

CAPTAIN SHOTOVER. It confuses me to be answered. It discourages me. I cannot bear men and women. I h a v e to run away. I must run away now. [*He tries to*].

ELLIE [*again seizing his arm*] You shall not run away from me. I can hypnotize you. You are the only person in the house I can say what I like to. I know you are fond of me. Sit down. [*She draws him to the sofa*].

CAPTAIN SHOTOVER [*yielding*] Take care: I am in my dotage. Old men are dangerous: it doesnt matter to them what is going to happen to the world.

They sit side by side on the sofa. She leans affectionately against him with her head on his shoulder and her eyes half closed.

ELLIE [*dreamily*] I should have thought nothing else mattered to old men. They cant be very interested in what is going to happen to themselves.

CAPTAIN SHOTOVER. A man's interest in the world is only the overflow from his interest in himself. When you are a child your vessel is not yet full; so you care for nothing but your own affairs. When you grow up, your vessel overflows; and you are a politician, a philosopher, or an explorer and adventurer. In old age the vessel dries up: there is no overflow: you are a child again. I can give you the memories of my ancient wisdom: mere scraps and leavings; but I no longer really care for anything but my own little wants and hobbies. I sit here working out my old ideas as a means of destroying my fellow-creatures. I see my daughters and their men living foolish lives of romance and sentiment and snobbery. I see you, the younger generation, turning from their romance and sentiment and snobbery to money and comfort and hard common sense. I was ten times happier on the bridge in the typhoon, or frozen into Arctic ice for months in darkness, than you or they have ever been. You are looking for a rich husband. At your age I looked for hardship, danger, horror, and death, that I might feel the life in me more intensely. I did not let the fear of death govern my life; and my reward was, I had my life. You are going to let the fear of poverty govern your life; and your reward will be that you will eat, but you will not live.

ELLIE [*sitting up impatiently*] But what can I do? I am not a sea captain: I cant stand on bridges in typhoons, or go slaughtering seals and whales in Greenland's icy mountains. They wont let women be captains. Do you want me to be a stewardess?

CAPTAIN SHOTOVER. There are worse lives. The stewardesses could come ashore if they liked; but they sail and sail and sail.

ELLIE. What could they do ashore but marry for money? I dont want to be a stewardess: I am too bad a sailor. Think of something else for me.

CAPTAIN SHOTOVER. I cant think so long and continuously. I am too old. I must go in and out. [*He tries to rise*].

ELLIE [*pulling him back*] You shall not. You are happy here, arnt you?

CAPTAIN SHOTOVER. I tell you it's dangerous to keep me. I cant keep awake and alert.

ELLIE. What do you run away for? To sleep?

CAPTAIN SHOTOVER. No. To get a glass of rum.

ELLIE [*frightfully disillusioned*] Is t h a t it? How disgusting! Do you like being drunk?

CAPTAIN SHOTOVER. No: I dread being drunk more than anything in the world. To be drunk means to have dreams; to go soft; to be easily pleased and deceived; to fall into the clutches of women. Drink does that for you when you are young. But when you are old: very very old, like me, the dreams come by themselves. You dont know how terrible that is: you are young: you sleep at night only, and sleep soundly. But later on you will sleep in the afternoon. Later still you will sleep even in the morning; and you will awake tired, tired of life. You will never be free from dozing and dreams: the dreams will steal upon your work every ten minutes unless you can awaken yourself with rum. I drink now to keep sober; but the dreams are conquering: rum is not what it was: I have had ten glasses since you came; and it might be so much water. Go get me another: Guinness knows where it is. You had better see for yourself the horror of an old man drinking.

ELLIE. You shall not drink. Dream. I like you to dream. You must never be in the real world when we talk together.

CAPTAIN SHOTOVER. I am too weary to resist or too weak. I am in my second childhood. I do not see you as you really are. I cant remember what I really am. I feel nothing but the accursed happiness I have dreaded all my life long: the happiness that comes as life goes, the happiness of yielding and dreaming instead of resisting and doing, the sweetness of the fruit that is going rotten.

ELLIE. You dread it almost as much as I used to dread losing my dreams and having to fight and do things. But that is all over for me: m y dreams are dashed to pieces. I should like to marry a very old, very rich man. I should like to marry you. I had much rather marry you than marry Mangan. Are you very rich?

CAPTAIN SHOTOVER. No. Living from hand to mouth. And I have a wife somewhere in Jamaica: a black one. My first wife. Unless she's dead.

ELLIE. What a pity! I feel so happy with you. [*She takes his hand, almost unconsciously, and pats it*]. I thought I should never feel happy again.

CAPTAIN SHOTOVER. Why?

ELLIE. Dont you know?

CAPTAIN SHOTOVER. No.

ELLIE. Heartbreak. I fell in love with Hector, and didnt know he was married.

CAPTAIN SHOTOVER. Heartbreak? Are you one of those who are so sufficient to themselves that they are only happy when they are stripped of everything, even of hope?

ELLIE [*gripping the hand*] It seems so; for I feel now as if there was nothing I could not do, because I want nothing.

CAPTAIN SHOTOVER. Thats the only real strength. Thats genius. Thats better than rum.

ELLIE [*throwing away his hand*] Rum! Why did you spoil it?

Hector and Randall come in from the garden through the starboard door.

HECTOR. I beg your pardon. We did not know there was anyone here.

ELLIE [*rising*] That means that you want to tell Mr Randall the story about the tiger. Come, Captain: I want to talk to my father; and you had better come with me.

CAPTAIN SHOTOVER [*rising*] Nonsense! the man is in bed.

ELLIE. Aha! Ive caught you. My real father has gone to bed; but the father you gave me is in the kitchen. You knew quite well all along. Come. [*She draws him out into the garden with her through the port door*].

HECTOR. Thats an extraordinary girl. She has the Ancient Mariner on a string like a Pekinese dog.

RANDALL. Now that they have gone, shall we have a friendly chat?

HECTOR. You are in what is supposed to be my house. I am at your disposal.

Hector sits down in the draughtsman's chair, turning it to face Randall, who remains standing, leaning at his ease against the carpenter's bench.

RANDALL. I take it that we may be quite frank. I mean about Lady Utterword.

HECTOR. *You* may. I have nothing to be frank about. I never met her until this afternoon.

RANDALL [*straightening up*] What! But you are her sister's husband.

HECTOR. Well, if you come to that, you are her husband's brother.

RANDALL. But you seem to be on intimate terms with her.

HECTOR. So do you.

RANDALL. Yes; but I *am* on intimate terms with her. I have known her for years.

HECTOR. It took her years to get to the same point with you that she got to with me in five minutes, it seems.

RANDALL [*vexed*] Really, Ariadne is the limit. [*He moves away huffishly towards the windows*].

HECTOR [*coolly*] She is, as I remarked to Hesione, a very enterprising woman.

RANDALL [*returning, much troubled*] You see, Hushabye, you are what women consider a good-looking man.

HECTOR. I cultivated that appearance in the days of my vanity; and Hesione insists on my keeping it up. She makes me wear these ridiculous things [*indicating his Arab costume*] because she thinks me absurd in evening dress.

RANDALL. Still, you *do* keep it up, old chap. Now, I assure you I have not an atom of jealousy in my disposition—

HECTOR. The question would seem to be rather whether your brother has any touch of that sort.

RANDALL. What! Hastings! Oh, dont trouble about Hastings. He has the gift of being able to work sixteen hours a day at the dullest detail, and actually likes it. That gets him to the top wherever he goes. As long as Ariadne takes care that he is fed regularly, he is only too thankful to anyone who will keep her in good humor for him.

HECTOR. And as she has all the Shotover fascination, there is plenty of competition for the job, eh?

RANDALL [*angrily*] She encourages them. Her conduct is perfectly scandalous. I assure you, my dear fellow, I havnt an atom of jealousy in my composition; but she makes herself the talk of every place she goes to by her thoughtlessness. It's nothing more: she doesnt really care for the men she keeps hanging about her; but how is the world to know that? It's not fair to Hastings. It's not fair to me.

HECTOR. Her theory is that her conduct is so correct—

RANDALL. Correct! She does nothing but make scenes from morning till night. You be careful, old chap. She will get you into trouble: that is, she would if she really cared for you.

HECTOR. Doesnt she?

RANDALL. Not a scrap. She may want your scalp to add to her collection; but her true affection has been engaged years ago. You had really better be careful.

HECTOR. Do you suffer much from this jealousy?

RANDALL. Jealousy! I jealous! My dear fellow, havnt I told you that there is not an atom of—

HECTOR. Yes. And Lady Utterword told me she never made scenes. Well, dont waste your jealousy on my moustache. Never waste jealousy on a real man: it is the imaginary hero that supplants us all in the long run. Besides, jealousy does not belong to your easy man-of-the-world pose, which you carry so well in other respects.

RANDALL. Really, Hushabye, I think a man may be allowed to be a gentleman without being accused of posing.

HECTOR. It is a pose like any other. In this house we know all the poses: our game is to find out the man under the pose. The man under your pose is apparently Ellie's favorite, Othello.

RANDALL. Some of your games in this house are damned annoying, let me tell you.

HECTOR. Yes: I have been their victim for many years. I used to writhe under them at first; but I became accustomed to them. At last I learned to play them.

RANDALL. If it's all the same to you, I had rather you didnt play them on me. You evidently dont quite understand my character, or my notions of good form.

HECTOR. Is it your notion of good form to give away Lady Utterword?

RANDALL [*a childishly plaintive note breaking into his huff*] I have not said a word against Lady Utterword. This is just the conspiracy over again.

HECTOR. What conspiracy?

RANDALL. You know very well, sir. A conspiracy to make me out to be pettish and jealous and childish and everything I am not. Everyone knows I am just the opposite.

HECTOR [*rising*] Something in the air of the house has upset you. It often does have that effect. [*He goes to the garden door and calls Lady Utterword with commanding emphasis*] Ariadne!

LADY UTTERWORD [*at some distance*] Yes.

RANDALL. What are you calling her for? I want to speak—

LADY UTTERWORD [*arriving breathless*] Yes. You really are a terribly commanding person. Whats the matter?

HECTOR. I do not know how to manage your friend Randall. No doubt you do.

LADY UTTERWORD. Randall: have you been making yourself ridiculous, as usual? I can see it in your face. Really, you are the most pettish creature.

RANDALL. You know quite well, Ariadne, that I have not an ounce of pettishness in my disposition. I have made myself perfectly pleasant here. I have remained absolutely cool and imperturbable in the face of a burglar. Imperturbability is almost too strong a point of mine. But [*putting his foot down with a stamp, and walking angrily up and down the room*] I insist on being treated with a certain consideration. I will not allow Hushabye to take liberties with me. I will not stand your encouraging people as you do.

HECTOR. The man has a rooted delusion that he is your husband.

LADY UTTERWORD. I know. He is jealous. As if he had any right to be! He compromises me everywhere. He makes scenes all over the place. Randall: I will not allow it.

I simply will not allow it. You had no right to discuss me with Hector. I will not be discussed by men.

HECTOR. Be reasonable, Ariadne. Your fatal gift of beauty forces men to discuss you.

LADY UTTERWORD. Oh indeed! what about your fatal gift of beauty?

HECTOR. How can I help it?

LADY UTTERWORD. You could cut off your moustache: I cant cut off my nose. I get my whole life messed up with people falling in love with me. And then Randall says I run after men.

RANDALL. I—

LADY UTTERWORD. Yes you do: you said it just now. Why cant you think of something else than women? Napoleon was quite right when he said that women are the occupation of the idle man. Well, if ever there was an idle man on earth, his name is Randall Utterword.

RANDALL. Ariad—

LADY UTTERWORD [*overwhelming him with a torrent of words*] Oh yes you are: it's no use denying it. What have you ever done? What good are you? You are as much trouble in the house as a child of three. You couldnt live without your valet.

RANDALL. This is—

LADY UTTERWORD. Laziness! You are laziness incarnate. You are selfishness itself. You are the most uninteresting man on earth. You cant even gossip about anything but yourself and your grievances and your ailments and the people who have offended you. [*Turning to Hector*] Do you know what they call him, Hector?

HECTOR } [*speaking together*] { Please dont tell me.
RANDALL } { I'll not stand it—

LADY UTTERWORD. Randall the Rotter: that is his name in good society.

RANDALL [*shouting*] I'll not bear it, I tell you. Will you listen to me, you infernal— [*He chokes*].

LADY UTTERWORD. Well: go on. What were you going

to call me? An infernal what? Which unpleasant animal is it to be this time?

RANDALL [*foaming*] There is no animal in the world so hateful as a woman can be. You are a maddening devil. Hushabye: you will not believe me when I tell you that I have loved this demon all my life; but God knows I have paid for it. [*He sits down in the draughtsman's chair, weeping*].

LADY UTTERWORD [*standing over him with triumphant contempt*] Cry-baby!

HECTOR [*gravely, coming to him*] My friend: the Shotover sisters have two strange powers over men. They can make them love; and they can make them cry. Thank your stars that you are not married to one of them.

LADY UTTERWORD [*haughtily*] And pray, Hector—

HECTOR [*suddenly catching her round the shoulders; swinging her right round him and away from Randall; and gripping her throat with the other hand*] Ariadne: if you attempt to start on me, I'll choke you: do you hear? The cat-and-mouse game with the other sex is a good game; but I can play your head off at it. [*He throws her, not at all gently, into the big chair, and proceeds, less fiercely but firmly*]. It is true that Napoleon said that woman is the occupation of the idle man. But he added that she is the relaxation of the warrior. Well, *I* am the warrior. So take care.

LADY UTTERWORD [*not in the least put out, and rather pleased by his violence*] My dear Hector: I have only done what you asked me to do.

HECTOR. How do you make that out, pray?

LADY UTTERWORD. You called me in to manage Randall, didnt you? You said you couldnt manage him yourself.

HECTOR. Well, what if I did? I did not ask you to drive the man mad.

LADY UTTERWORD. He isnt mad. Thats the way to manage him. If you were a mother, youd understand.

HECTOR. Mother! What are you up to now?

LADY UTTERWORD. It's quite simple. When the children got nerves and were naughty, I smacked them just enough to give them a good cry and a healthy nervous shock. They went to sleep and were quite good afterwards. Well, I cant smack Randall: he is too big; so when he gets nerves and is naughty, I just rag him till he cries. He will be all right now. Look: he is half asleep already. [*Which is quite true*].

RANDALL [*waking up indignantly*] I'm not. You are most cruel, Ariadne. [*Sentimentally*] But I suppose I must forgive you, as usual. [*He checks himself in the act of yawning*].

LADY UTTERWORD [*to Hector*] Is the explanation satisfactory, dread warrior?

HECTOR. Some day I shall kill you, if you go too far. I thought you were a fool.

LADY UTTERWORD [*laughing*] Everybody does, at first. But I am not such a fool as I look. [*She rises complacently*]. Now, Randall: go to bed. You will be a good boy in the morning.

RANDALL [*only very faintly rebellious*] I'll go to bed when I like. It isnt ten yet.

LADY UTTERWORD. It is long past ten. See that he goes to bed at once, Hector. [*She goes into the garden*].

HECTOR. Is there any slavery on earth viler than this slavery of men to women?

RANDALL [*rising resolutely*] I'll not speak to her tomorrow. I'll not speak to her for another week. I'll give her s u c h a lesson. I'll go straight to bed without bidding her goodnight. [*He makes for the door leading to the hall*].

HECTOR. You are under a spell, man. Old Shotover sold himself to the devil in Zanzibar. The devil gave him a black witch for a wife; and these two demon daughters are their mystical progeny. I am tied to Hesione's apron-string; but I'm her husband; and if I did go stark staring mad about her, at least we became man and wife. But why should you let yourself be dragged about and beaten by Ariadne as a toy donkey is dragged about and beaten by a child? What do you get by it? Are you her lover?

RANDALL. You must not misunderstand me. In a higher sense—in a Platonic sense—

HECTOR. Psha! Platonic sense! She makes you her servant; and when pay-day comes round, she bilks you: that is what you mean.

RANDALL [*feebly*] Well, if I dont mind, I dont see what business it is of yours. Besides, I tell you I am going to punish her. You shall see: *I* know how to deal with women. I'm really very sleepy. Say goodnight to Mrs Hushabye for me, will you, like a good chap. Goodnight. [*He hurries out*].

HECTOR. Poor wretch! Oh women! women! women! [*He lifts his fists in invocation to heaven*]. Fall. Fall and crush. [*He goes out into the garden*].

END OF ACT II

ACT III

I*N the garden, Hector, as he comes out through the glass door of the poop, finds Lady Utterword lying voluptuously in the hammock on the east side of the flagstaff, in the circle of light cast by the electric arc, which is like a moon in its opal globe. Beneath the head of the hammock, a campstool. On the other side of the flagstaff, on the long garden seat, Captain Shotover is asleep, with Ellie beside him, leaning affectionately against him on his right hand. On his left is a deck chair. Behind them in the gloom, Hesione is strolling about with Mangan. It is a fine still night, moonless.*

LADY UTTERWORD. What a lovely night! It seems made for us.

HECTOR. The night takes no interest in us. What are we to the night? [*He sits down moodily in the deck chair*].

ELLIE [*dreamily, nestling against the Captain*] Its beauty soaks into my nerves. In the night there is peace for the old and hope for the young.

HECTOR. Is that remark your own?

ELLIE. No. Only the last thing the Captain said before he went to sleep.

CAPTAIN SHOTOVER. I'm not asleep.

HECTOR. Randall is. Also Mr Mazzini Dunn. Mangan too, probably.

MANGAN. No.

HECTOR. Oh, you are there. I thought Hesione would have sent you to bed by this time.

MRS HUSHABYE [*coming to the back of the garden seat, into the light, with Mangan*] I think I shall. He keeps telling me he has a presentiment that he is going to die. I never met a man so greedy for sympathy.

MANGAN [*plaintively*] But I have a presentiment. I really have. And you wouldnt listen.

MRS HUSHABYE. I was listening for something else. There was a sort of splendid drumming in the sky. Did none of you hear it? It came from a distance and then died away.

MANGAN. I tell you it was a train.

MRS HUSHABYE. And *I* tell you, Alf, there is no train at this hour. The last is nine fortyfive.

MANGAN. But a goods train.

MRS HUSHABYE. Not on our little line. They tack a truck on to the passenger train. What can it have been, Hector?

HECTOR. Heaven's threatening growl of disgust at us useless futile creatures. [*Fiercely*] I tell you, one of two things must happen. Either out of that darkness some new creation will come to supplant us as we have supplanted the animals, or the heavens will fall in thunder and destroy us.

LADY UTTERWORD [*in a cool instructive manner, wallowing comfortably in her hammock*] We have not supplanted the animals, Hector. Why do you ask heaven to destroy this house, which could be made quite comfortable if Hesione had any notion of how to live? Dont you know what is wrong with it?

HECTOR. We are wrong with it. There is no sense in us. We are useless, dangerous, and ought to be abolished.

LADY UTTERWORD. Nonsense! Hastings told me the very first day he came here, nearly twentyfour years ago, what is wrong with the house.

CAPTAIN SHOTOVER. What! The numskull said there was something wrong with my house!

LADY UTTERWORD. I said Hastings said it; and he is not in the least a numskull.

CAPTAIN SHOTOVER. Whats wrong with my house?

LADY UTTERWORD. Just what is wrong with a ship, papa. Wasnt it clever of Hastings to see that?

CAPTAIN SHOTOVER. The man's a fool. Theres nothing wrong with a ship.

LADY UTTERWORD. Yes there is.

MRS HUSHABYE. But what is it? Dont be aggravating, Addy.

LADY UTTERWORD. Guess.

HECTOR. Demons. Daughters of the witch of Zanzibar. Demons.

LADY UTTERWORD. Not a bit. I assure you, all this house needs to make it a sensible, healthy, pleasant house, with good appetites and sound sleep in it, is horses.

MRS HUSHABYE. Horses! What rubbish!

LADY UTTERWORD. Yes: horses. Why have we never been able to let this house? Because there are no proper stables. Go anywhere in England where there are natural, wholesome, contented, and really nice English people; and what do you always find? That the stables are the real centre of the household; and that if any visitor wants to play the piano the whole room has to be upset before it can be opened, there are so many things piled on it. I never lived until I learned to ride; and I shall never ride really well because I didnt begin as a child. There are only two classes in good society in England: the equestrian classes and the neurotic classes. It isnt mere convention: everybody can see that the people who hunt are the right people and the people who dont are the wrong ones.

CAPTAIN SHOTOVER. There is some truth in this. My ship made a man of me; and a ship is the horse of the sea.

LADY UTTERWORD. Exactly how Hastings explained your being a gentleman.

CAPTAIN SHOTOVER. Not bad for a numskull. Bring the man here with you next time: I must talk to him.

LADY UTTERWORD. Why is Randall such an obvious rotter? He is well bred; he has been at a public school and a university; he has been in the Foreign Office; he knows the best people and has lived all his life among them. Why is he so unsatisfactory, so contemptible? Why cant he get a valet to stay with him longer than a few months? Just because he is too lazy and pleasure-loving to hunt and shoot. He strums the piano, and sketches, and runs after married women, and reads literary books and poems. He actually plays the flute: but I never let him bring it into my house.

If he would only— [*She is interrupted by the melancholy strains of a flute coming from an open window above. She raises herself indignantly in the hammock*]. Randall: you have not gone to bed. Have you been listening? [*The flute replies pertly*]:

How vulgar! Go to bed instantly, Randall: how dare you? [*The window is slammed down. She subsides*]. How can anyone care for such a creature!

MRS HUSHABYE. Addy: do you think Ellie ought to marry poor Alfred merely for his money?

MANGAN [*much alarmed*] Whats that? Mrs. Hushabye: are my affairs to be discussed like this before everybody?

LADY UTTERWORD. I dont think Randall is listening now.

MANGAN. Everybody is listening. It isnt right.

MRS HUSHABYE. But in the dark, what does it matter? Ellie doesnt mind. Do you, Ellie?

ELLIE. Not in the least. What is your opinion, Lady Utterword? You have so much good sense.

MANGAN. But it isnt right. It— [*Mrs Hushabye puts her hand on his mouth*]. Oh, very well.

LADY UTTERWORD. How much money have you, Mr Mangan?

MANGAN. Really— No: I cant stand this.

LADY UTTERWORD. Nonsense, Mr Mangan! It all turns on your income, doesnt it?

MANGAN. Well, if you come to that, how much money has she?

ELLIE. None.

LADY UTTERWORD. You are answered, Mr Mangan. And now, as you have made Miss Dunn throw her cards on the table, you cannot refuse to shew your own.

MRS HUSHABYE. Come, Alf! out with it! How much?

MANGAN [*baited out of all prudence*] Well, if you want

to know, I have no money and never had any.

MRS HUSHABYE. Alfred: you mustnt tell naughty stories.

MANGAN. I'm not telling you stories. I'm telling you the raw truth.

LADY UTTERWORD. Then what do you live on, Mr Mangan?

MANGAN. Travelling expenses. And a trifle of commission.

CAPTAIN SHOTOVER. What more have any of us but travelling expenses for our life's journey?

MRS HUSHABYE. But you have factories and capital and things?

MANGAN. People think I have. People think I'm an industrial Napoleon. Thats why Miss Ellie wants to marry me. But I tell you I have nothing.

ELLIE. Do you mean that the factories are like Marcus's tigers? That they dont exist?

MANGAN. They exist all right enough. But theyre not mine. They belong to syndicates and shareholders and all sorts of lazy good-for-nothing capitalists. I get money from such people to start the factories. I find people like Miss Dunn's father to work them, and keep a tight hand so as to make them pay. Of course I make them keep me going pretty well; but it's a dog's life; and I dont own anything.

MRS HUSHABYE. Alfred, Alfred: you are making a poor mouth of it to get out of marrying Ellie.

MANGAN. I'm telling the truth about my money for the first time in my life; and it's the first time my word has ever been doubted.

LADY UTTERWORD. How sad! Why dont you go in for politics, Mr Mangan?

MANGAN. Go in for politics! Where have you been living? I a m in politics.

LADY UTTERWORD. I'm sure I beg your pardon. I never heard of you.

MANGAN. Let me tell you, Lady Utterword, that the

Prime Minister of this country asked me to join the Government without even going through the nonsense of an election, as the dictator of a great public department.

LADY UTTERWORD. As a Conservative or a Liberal?

MANGAN. No such nonsense. As a practical business man. [*They all burst out laughing*]. What are you all laughing at?

MRS HUSHABYE. Oh, Alfred, Alfred!

ELLIE. You! who have to get my father to do everything for you!

MRS HUSHABYE. You! who are afraid of your own workmen!

HECTOR. You! with whom three women have been playing cat and mouse all the evening!

LADY UTTERWORD. You must have given an immense sum to the party funds, Mr Mangan.

MANGAN. Not a penny out of my own pocket. The syndicate found the money: they knew how useful I should be to them in the Government.

LADY UTTERWORD. This is most interesting and unexpected, Mr Mangan. And what have your administrative achievements been, so far?

MANGAN. Achievements? Well, I dont know what you call achievements; but Ive jolly well put a stop to the games of the other fellows in the other departments. Every man of them thought he was going to save the country all by himself, and do me out of the credit and out of my chance of a title. I took good care that if they wouldnt let me do it they shouldnt do it themselves either. I may not know anything about my own machinery; but I know how to stick a ramrod into the other fellow's. And now they all look the biggest fools going.

HECTOR. And in heaven's name, what do you look like?

MANGAN. I look like the fellow that was too clever for all the others, dont I? If that isnt a triumph of practical business, what is?

HECTOR. Is this England, or is it a madhouse?

LADY UTTERWORD. Do you expect to save the country, Mr Mangan?

MANGAN. Well, who else will? Will your Mr Randall save it?

LADY UTTERWORD. Randall the rotter! Certainly not.

MANGAN. Will your brother-in-law save it with his moustache and his fine talk?

HECTOR. Yes, if they will let me.

MANGAN [*sneering*] Ah! W i l l they let you?

HECTOR. No. They prefer you.

MANGAN. Very well then, as youre in a world where I'm appreciated and youre not, youd best be civil to me, hadnt you? Who else is there but me?

LADY UTTERWORD. There is Hastings. Get rid of your ridiculous sham democracy; and give Hastings the necessary powers, and a good supply of bamboo to bring the British native to his senses: he will save the country with the greatest ease.

CAPTAIN SHOTOVER. It had better be lost. Any fool can govern with a stick in his hand. *I* could govern that way. It is not God's way. The man is a numskull.

LADY UTTERWORD. The man is worth all of you rolled into one. What do y o u say, Miss Dunn?

ELLIE. I think my father would do very well if people did not put upon him and cheat him and despise him because he is so good.

MANGAN [*contemptuously*] I think I see Mazzini Dunn getting into parliament or pushing his way into the Government. Weve not come to that yet, thank God! What do you say, Mrs Hushabye?

MRS HUSHABYE. Oh, *I* say it matters very little which of you governs the country so long as we govern you.

HECTOR. We? Who is we, pray?

MRS HUSHABYE. The devil's granddaughters, dear. The lovely women.

HECTOR [*raising his hands as before*] Fall, I say; and deliver us from the lures of Satan!

ELLIE. There seems to be nothing real in the world except my father and Shakespear. Marcus's tigers are false; Mr Mangan's millions are false; there is nothing really strong and true about Hesione but her beautiful black hair; and Lady Utterword's is too pretty to be real. The one thing that was left to me was the Captain's seventh degree of concentration; and that turns out to be—

CAPTAIN SHOTOVER. Rum.

LADY UTTERWORD [*placidly*] A good deal of my hair is quite genuine. The Duchess of Dithering offered me fifty guineas for this [*touching her forehead*] under the impression that it was a transformation; but it is all natural except the color.

MANGAN [*wildly*] Look here: I'm going to take off all my clothes. [*He begins tearing off his coat*].

LADY UTTERWORD.	[*in consternation*]	Mr Mangan!
CAPTAIN SHOTOVER.		Whats that?
HECTOR.		Ha! ha! Do. Do.
ELLIE.		Please dont.

MRS HUSHABYE [*catching his arm and stopping him*] Alfred: for shame! Are you mad?

MANGAN. Shame! What shame is there in this house? Let's all strip stark naked. We may as well do the thing thoroughly when we're about it. Weve stripped ourselves morally naked: well, let us strip ourselves physically naked as well, and see how we like it. I tell you I cant bear this. I was brought up to be respectable. I dont mind the women dyeing their hair and the men drinking: it's human nature. But it's not human nature to tell everybody about it. Every time one of you opens your mouth I go like this [*he cowers as if to avoid a missile*] afraid of what will come next. How are we to have any self-respect if we dont keep it up that we're better than we really are?

LADY UTTERWORD. I quite sympathize with you, Mr

Mangan. I have been through it all; and I know by experience that men and women are delicate plants and must be cultivated under glass. Our family habit of throwing stones in all directions and letting the air in is not only unbearably rude, but positively dangerous. Still, there is no use catching physical colds as well as moral ones; so please keep your clothes on.

MANGAN. I'll do as I like: not what you tell me. Am I a child or a grown man? I wont stand this mothering tyranny. I'll go back to the city, where I'm respected and made much of.

MRS HUSHABYE. Goodbye, Alf. Think of us sometimes in the city. Think of Ellie's youth!

ELLIE. Think of Hesione's eyes and hair!

CAPTAIN SHOTOVER. Think of this garden in which you are not a dog barking to keep the truth out!

HECTOR. Think of Lady Utterword's beauty! her good sense! her style!

LADY UTTERWORD. Flatterer. Think, Mr Mangan, whether you can really do any better for yourself elsewhere: that is the essential point, isnt it?

MANGAN [*surrendering*] All right: all right. I'm done. Have it your own way. Only let me alone. I dont know whether I'm on my head or my heels when you all start on me like this. I'll stay. I'll marry her. I'll do anything for a quiet life. Are you satisfied now?

ELLIE. No. I never really intended to make you marry me, Mr Mangan. Never in the depths of my soul. I only wanted to feel my strength: to know that you could not escape if I chose to take you.

MANGAN [*indignantly*] What! Do you mean to say you are going to throw me over after my acting so handsome?

LADY UTTERWORD. I should not be too hasty, Miss Dunn. You can throw Mr Mangan over at any time up to the last moment. Very few men in his position go bankrupt.

You can live very comfortably on his reputation for immense wealth.

ELLIE. I cannot commit bigamy, Lady Utterword.

MRS HUSHABYE.		Bigamy! Whatever on earth are you talking about, Ellie?
LADY UTTERWORD.	[*exclaiming all together*]	Bigamy! What do you mean, Miss Dunn?
MANGAN.		Bigamy! Do you mean to say youre married already?
HECTOR.		Bigamy! This is some enigma.

ELLIE. Only half an hour ago I became Captain Shotover's white wife.

MRS HUSHABYE. Ellie! What nonsense! Where?

ELLIE. In heaven, where all true marriages are made.

LADY UTTERWORD. Really, Miss Dunn! Really, papa!

MANGAN. He told me *I* was too old! And him a mummy!

HECTOR [*quoting Shelley*]

"Their altar the grassy earth outspread,
And their priest the muttering wind."

ELLIE. Yes: I, Ellie Dunn, give my broken heart and my strong sound soul to its natural captain, my spiritual husband and second father.

She draws the Captain's arm through hers, and pats his hand. The Captain remains fast asleep.

MRS HUSHABYE. Oh, thats very clever of you, pettikins. V e r y clever. Alfred: you could never have lived up to Ellie. You must be content with a little share of me.

MANGAN [*sniffing and wiping his eyes*] It isnt kind— [*His emotion chokes him*].

LADY UTTERWORD. You are well out of it, Mr Mangan. Miss Dunn is the most conceited young woman I have met since I came back to England.

MRS HUSHABYE. Oh, Ellie isnt conceited. Are you, pettikins?

ELLIE. I know my strength now, Hesione.

MANGAN. Brazen, I call you. Brazen.

MRS HUSHABYE. Tut tut, Alfred: dont be rude. Dont you feel how lovely this marriage night is, made in heaven? Arnt you happy, you and Hector? Open your eyes: Addy and Ellie look beautiful enough to please the most fastidious man: we live and love and have not a care in the world. We women have managed all that for you. Why in the name of common sense do you go on as if you were two miserable wretches?

CAPTAIN SHOTOVER. I tell you happiness is no good. You can be happy when you are only half alive. I am happier now I am half dead than ever I was in my prime. But there is no blessing on my happiness.

ELLIE [*her face lighting up*] Life with a blessing! that is what I want. Now I know the real reason why I couldnt marry Mr Mangan: there would be no blessing on our marriage. There is a blessing on my broken heart. There is a blessing on your beauty, Hesione. There is a blessing on your father's spirit. Even on the lies of Marcus there is a blessing; but on Mr Mangan's money there is none.

MANGAN. I dont understand a word of that.

ELLIE. Neither do I. But I know it means something.

MANGAN. Dont say there was any difficulty about the blessing. I was ready to get a bishop to marry us.

MRS HUSHABYE. Isnt he a fool, pettikins?

HECTOR [*fiercely*] Do not scorn the man. We are all fools.

Mazzini, in pyjamas and a richly colored silk dressing-gown, comes from the house, on Lady Utterword's side.

MRS HUSHABYE. Oh! here comes the only man who ever resisted me. Whats the matter, Mr Dunn? Is the house on fire?

MAZZINI. Oh no: nothing's the matter: but really it's

impossible to go to sleep with such an interesting conversation going on under one's window, and on such a beautiful night too. I just had to come down and join you all. What has it all been about?

MRS HUSHABYE. Oh, wonderful things, soldier of freedom.

HECTOR. For example, Mangan, as a practical business man, has tried to undress himself and has failed ignominiously; whilst you, as an idealist, have succeeded brilliantly.

MAZZINI. I hope you dont mind my being like this, Mrs Hushabye. [*He sits down on the campstool*].

MRS HUSHABYE. On the contrary, I could wish you always like that.

LADY UTTERWORD. Your daughter's match is off, Mr Dunn. It seems that Mr Mangan, whom we all supposed to be a man of property, owns absolutely nothing.

MAZZINI. Well of course I knew that, Lady Utterword. But if people believe in him and are always giving him money, whereas they dont believe in me and never give me any, how can I ask poor Ellie to depend on what I can do for her?

MANGAN. Dont you run away with this idea that I have nothing. I—

HECTOR. Oh, dont explain. We understand. You have a couple of thousand pounds in exchequer bills, 50,000 shares worth tenpence a dozen, and half a dozen tabloids of cyanide of potassium to poison yourself with when you are found out. Thats the reality of your millions.

MAZZINI. Oh no, no, no. He is quite honest: the businesses are genuine and perfectly legal.

HECTOR [*disgusted*] Yah! Not even a great swindler!

MANGAN. So you think. But Ive been too many for some honest men, for all that.

LADY UTTERWORD. There is no pleasing you, Mr Mangan. You are determined to be neither rich nor poor, honest nor dishonest.

MANGAN. There you go again. Ever since I came into this silly house I have been made to look like a fool, though I'm as good a man in this house as in the city.

ELLIE [*musically*] Yes: this silly house, this strangely happy house, this agonizing house, this house without foundations. I shall call it Heartbreak House.

MRS HUSHABYE. Stop, Ellie; or I shall howl like an animal.

MANGAN [*breaks into a low snivelling*] !!!

MRS HUSHABYE. There! you have set Alfred off.

ELLIE. I like him best when he is howling.

CAPTAIN SHOTOVER. Silence! [*Mangan subsides into silence*]. I say, let the heart break in silence.

HECTOR. Do you accept that name for your house?

CAPTAIN SHOTOVER. It is not my house: it is only my kennel.

HECTOR. We have been too long here. We do not live in this house: we haunt it.

LADY UTTERWORD [*heart torn*] It is dreadful to think how you have been here all these years while I have gone round the world. I escaped young; but it has drawn me back. It wants to break my heart too. But it shant. I have left you and it behind. It was silly of me to come back. I felt sentimental about papa and Hesione and the old place. I felt them calling to me.

MAZZINI. But what a very natural and kindly and charming human feeling, Lady Utterword!

LADY UTTERWORD. So I thought, Mr Dunn. But I know now that it was only the last of my influenza. I found that I was not remembered and not wanted.

CAPTAIN SHOTOVER. You left because you did not want us. Was there no heartbreak in that for your father? You tore yourself up by the roots; and the ground healed up and brought forth fresh plants and forgot you. What right had you to come back and probe old wounds?

MRS HUSHABYE. You were a complete stranger to me at first, Addy; but now I feel as if you had never been away.

LADY UTTERWORD. Thank you, Hesione; but the influenza is quite cured. The place may be Heartbreak House to you, Miss Dunn, and to this gentleman from the city who seems to have so little self-control; but to me it is only a very ill-regulated and rather untidy villa without any stables.

HECTOR. Inhabited by—?

ELLIE. A crazy old sea captain and a young singer who adores him.

MRS HUSHABYE. A sluttish female, trying to stave off a double chin and an elderly spread, vainly wooing a born soldier of freedom.

MAZZINI. Oh, really, Mrs Hushabye—

MANGAN. A member of His Majesty's Government that everybody sets down as a nincompoop: dont forget him, Lady Utterword.

LADY UTTERWORD. And a very fascinating gentleman whose chief occupation is to be married to my sister.

HECTOR. All heartbroken imbeciles.

MAZZINI. Oh no. Surely, if I may say so, rather a favorable specimen of what is best in our English culture. You are very charming people, most advanced, unprejudiced, frank, humane, unconventional, democratic, free-thinking, and everything that is delightful to thoughtful people.

MRS HUSHABYE. You do us proud, Mazzini.

MAZZINI. I am not flattering, really. Where else could I feel perfectly at ease in my pyjamas? I sometimes dream that I am in very distinguished society, and suddenly I have nothing on but my pyjamas! Sometimes I havnt even pyjamas. And I always feel overwhelmed with confusion. But here, I dont mind in the least: it seems quite natural.

LADY UTTERWORD. An infallible sign that you are not now in really distinguished society, Mr Dunn. If you were in my house, you w o u l d feel embarrassed.

MAZZINI. I shall take particular care to keep out of your house, Lady Utterword.

LADY UTTERWORD. You will be quite wrong, Mr Dunn. I should make you very comfortable; and you would not have the trouble and anxiety of wondering whether you should wear your purple and gold or your green and crimson dressing-gown at dinner. You complicate life instead of simplifying it by doing these ridiculous things.

ELLIE. Y o u r house is not Heartbreak House: is it, Lady Utterword?

HECTOR. Yet she breaks hearts, easy as her house is. That poor devil upstairs with his flute howls when she twists his heart, just as Mangan howls when my wife twists his.

LADY UTTERWORD. That is because Randall has nothing to do but have his heart broken. It is a change from having his head shampooed. Catch anyone breaking Hastings' heart!

CAPTAIN SHOTOVER. The numskull wins, after all.

LADY UTTERWORD. I shall go back to my numskull with the greatest satisfaction when I am tired of you all, clever as you are.

MANGAN [*huffily*] I never set up to be clever.

LADY UTTERWORD. I forgot you, Mr Mangan.

MANGAN. Well, I dont see that quite, either.

LADY UTTERWORD. You may not be clever, Mr Mangan; but you are successful.

MANGAN. But I dont want to be regarded merely as a successful man. I have an imagination like anyone else. I have a presentiment—

MRS HUSHABYE. Oh, you are impossible, Alfred. Here I am devoting myself to you; and you think of nothing but your ridiculous presentiment. You bore me. Come and talk poetry to me under the stars. [*She drags him away into the darkness*].

MANGAN [*tearfully, as he disappears*] Yes: it's all very well to make fun of me; but if you only knew—

HECTOR [*impatiently*] How is all this going to end?

MAZZINI. It wont end, Mr Hushabye. Life doesnt end: it goes on.

ELLIE. Oh, it cant go on for ever. I'm always expecting something. I dont know what it is; but life must come to a point sometime.

LADY UTTERWORD. The point for a young woman of your age is a baby.

HECTOR. Yes, but, damn it, I have the same feeling; and *I* cant have a baby.

LADY UTTERWORD. By deputy, Hector.

HECTOR. But I h a v e children. All that is over and done with for me: and yet I too feel that this cant last. We sit here talking, and leave everything to Mangan and to chance and to the devil. Think of the powers of destruction that Mangan and his mutual admiration gang wield! It's madness: it's like giving a torpedo to a badly brought up child to play at earthquakes with.

MAZZINI. I know. I used often to think about that when I was young.

HECTOR. Think! Whats the good of thinking about it? Why didnt you do something?

MAZZINI. But I did. I joined societies and made speeches and wrote pamphlets. That was all I could do. But, you know, though the people in the societies thought they knew more than Mangan, most of them wouldnt have joined if they had known as much. You see they had never had any money to handle or any men to manage. Every year I expected a revolution, or some frightful smash-up: it seemed impossible that we could blunder and muddle on any longer. But nothing happened, except, of course, the usual poverty and crime and drink that we are used to. Nothing ever does happen. It's amazing how well we get along, all things considered.

LADY UTTERWORD. Perhaps somebody cleverer than you and Mr Mangan was at work all the time.

MAZZINI. Perhaps so. Though I was brought up not to

believe in anything, I often feel that there is a great deal to be said for the theory of an overruling Providence, after all.

LADY UTTERWORD. Providence! I meant Hastings.

MAZZINI. Oh, I beg your pardon, Lady Utterword.

CAPTAIN SHOTOVER. Every drunken skipper trusts to Providence. But one of the ways of Providence with drunken skippers is to run them on the rocks.

MAZZINI. Very true, no doubt, at sea. But in politics, I assure you, they only run into jellyfish. Nothing happens.

CAPTAIN SHOTOVER. At sea nothing happens to the sea. Nothing happens to the sky. The sun comes up from the east and goes down to the west. The moon grows from a sickle to an arc lamp, and comes later and later until she is lost in the light as other things are lost in the darkness. After the typhoon, the flying-fish glitter in the sunshine like birds. It's amazing how t h e y get along, all things considered. Nothing happens, except something not worth mentioning.

ELLIE. What is that, O Captain, my captain?

CAPTAIN SHOTOVER [*savagely*] Nothing but the smash of the drunken skipper's ship on the rocks, the splintering of her rotten timbers, the tearing of her rusty plates, the drowning of the crew like rats in a trap.

ELLIE. Moral: dont take rum.

CAPTAIN SHOTOVER [*vehemently*] That is a lie, child. Let a man drink ten barrels of rum a day, he is not a drunken skipper until he is a drifting skipper. Whilst he can lay his course and stand on his bridge and steer it, he is no drunkard. It is the man who lies drinking in his bunk and trusts to Providence that I call the drunken skipper, though he drank nothing but the waters of the River Jordan.

ELLIE. Splendid! And you havnt had a drop for an hour. You see you dont need it: your own spirit is not dead.

CAPTAIN SHOTOVER. Echoes: nothing but echoes. The last shot was fired years ago.

HECTOR. And this ship that we are all in? This soul's prison we call England?

CAPTAIN SHOTOVER. The captain is in his bunk, drinking bottled ditch-water; and the crew is gambling in the forecastle. She will strike and sink and split. Do you think the laws of God will be suspended in favor of England because you were born in it?

HECTOR. Well, I dont mean to be drowned like a rat in a trap. I still have the will to live. What am I to do?

CAPTAIN SHOTOVER. Do? Nothing simpler. Learn your business as an Englishman.

HECTOR. And what may my business as an Englishman be, pray?

CAPTAIN SHOTOVER. Navigation. Learn it and live; or leave it and be damned.

ELLIE. Quiet, quiet: youll tire yourself.

MAZZINI. I thought all that once, Captain; but I assure you nothing will happen.

A dull distant explosion is heard.

HECTOR [*starting up*] What was that?

CAPTAIN SHOTOVER. Something happening. [*He blows his whistle*]. Breakers ahead!

The light goes out.

HECTOR [*furiously*] Who put that light out? Who dared put that light out?

NURSE GUINNESS [*running in from the house to the middle of the esplanade*] I did, sir. The police have telephoned to say we'll be summoned if we dont put that light out: it can be seen for miles.

HECTOR. It shall be seen for a hundred miles. [*He dashes into the house*].

NURSE GUINNESS. The rectory is nothing but a heap of bricks, they say. Unless we can give the rector a bed he has nowhere to lay his head this night.

CAPTAIN SHOTOVER. The Church is on the rocks, breaking up. I told him it would unless it headed for God's open sea.

NURSE GUINNESS. And you are all to go down to the cellars.

CAPTAIN SHOTOVER. Go there yourself, you and all the crew. Batten down the hatches.

NURSE GUINNESS. And hide beside the coward I married! I'll go on the roof first. [*The lamp lights up again*]. There! Mr Hushabye's turned it on again.

THE BURGLAR [*hurrying in and appealing to Nurse Guinness*] Here: wheres the way to that gravel pit? The boot-boy says theres a cave in the gravel pit. Them cellars is no use. Wheres the gravel pit, Captain?

NURSE GUINNESS. Go straight on past the flagstaff until you fall into it and break your dirty neck. [*She pushes him contemptuously towards the flagstaff, and herself goes to the foot of the hammock and waits there, as it were by Ariadne's cradle*].

Another and louder explosion is heard. The burglar stops and stands trembling.

ELLIE [*rising*] That was nearer.

CAPTAIN SHOTOVER. The next one will get us. [*He rises*]. Stand by, all hands, for judgment.

THE BURGLAR. Oh my Lordy God! [*He rushes away frantically past the flagstaff into the gloom*].

MRS HUSHABYE [*emerging panting from the darkness*] Who was that running away? [*She comes to Ellie*]. Did you hear the explosions? And the sound in the sky: it's splendid: it's like an orchestra: it's like Beethoven.

ELLIE. By thunder, Hesione: it i s Beethoven.

She and Hesione throw themselves into one another's arms in wild excitement. The light increases.

MAZZINI [*anxiously*] The light is getting brighter.

NURSE GUINNESS [*looking up at the house*] It's Mr Hushabye turning on all the lights in the house and tearing down the curtains.

RANDALL [*rushing in in his pyjamas, distractedly waving a flute*] Ariadne: my soul, my precious, go down to the cellars: I beg and implore you, go down to the cellars!

LADY UTTERWORD [*quite composed in her hammock*] The governor's wife in the cellars with the servants! Really, Randall!

RANDALL. But what shall I do if you are killed?

LADY UTTERWORD. You will probably be killed, too, Randall. Now play your flute to shew that you are not afraid; and be good. Play us Keep the home fires burning.

NURSE GUINNESS [*grimly*] T h e y l l keep the home fires burning for us: them up there.

RANDALL [*having tried to play*] My lips are trembling. I cant get a sound.

MAZZINI. I hope poor Mangan is safe.

MRS HUSHABYE. He is hiding in the cave in the gravel pit.

CAPTAIN SHOTOVER. My dynamite drew him there. It is the hand of God.

HECTOR [*returning from the house and striding across to his former place*] There is not half light enough. We should be blazing to the skies.

ELLIE [*tense with excitement*] Set fire to the house, Marcus.

MRS HUSHABYE. My house! No.

HECTOR. I thought of that; but it would not be ready in time.

CAPTAIN SHOTOVER. The judgment has come. Courage will not save you; but it will shew that your souls are still alive.

MRS HUSHABYE. Sh-sh! Listen: do you hear it now? It's magnificent.

They all turn away from the house and look up, listening.

HECTOR [*gravely*] Miss Dunn: you can do no good here. We of this house are only moths flying into the candle. You had better go down to the cellar.

ELLIE [*scornfully*] I d o n t think.

MAZZINI. Ellie, dear, there is no disgrace in going to

the cellar. An officer would order his soldiers to take cover. Mr Hushabye is behaving like an amateur. Mangan and the burglar are acting very sensibly; and it is they who will survive.

ELLIE. Let them. I shall behave like an amateur. But why should you run any risk?

MAZZINI. Think of the risk those poor fellows up there are running!

NURSE GUINNESS. Think of t h e m, indeed, the murdering blackguards! What next?

A terrific explosion shakes the earth. They reel back into their seats, or clutch the nearest support. They hear the falling of the shattered glass from the windows.

MAZZINI. Is anyone hurt?

HECTOR. Where did it fall?

NURSE GUINNESS [*in hideous triumph*] Right in the gravel pit: I seen it. Serve un right! I seen it. [*She runs away towards the gravel pit, laughing harshly*].

HECTOR. One husband gone.

CAPTAIN SHOTOVER. Thirty pounds of good dynamite wasted.

MAZZINI. Oh, poor Mangan!

HECTOR. Are you immortal that you need pity him? Our turn next.

They wait in silence and intense expectation. Hesione and Ellie hold each other's hand tight.

A distant explosion is heard.

MRS HUSHABYE [*relaxing her grip*] Oh! they have passed us.

LADY UTTERWORD. The danger is over, Randall. Go to bed.

CAPTAIN SHOTOVER. Turn in, all hands. The ship is safe. [*He sits down and goes asleep*].

ELLIE [*disappointedly*] Safe!

HECTOR [*disgustedly*] Yes, safe. And how damnably dull the world has become again suddenly! [*He sits down*].

MAZZINI [*sitting down*] I was quite wrong, after all. It

is we who have survived; and Mangan and the burglar—

HECTOR. —the two burglars—

LADY UTTERWORD. —the two practical men of business—

MAZZINI. —both gone. And the poor clergyman will have to get a new house.

MRS HUSHABYE. But what a glorious experience! I hope theyll come again tomorrow night.

ELLIE [*radiant at the prospect*] Oh, I hope so.

Randall at last succeeds in keeping the home fires burning on his flute.

CURTAIN

SAINT JOAN

In 1913 Shaw wrote to an actress, "I shall do a Joan play some day. . . . I should have God about to damn the English for their share in her betrayal and Joan producing an end of burnt stick in arrest of Judgment. . . . That soldier is the only redeeming figure in the whole business. English literature must be saved (by an Irishman, as usual) from the disgrace of having nothing to show concerning Joan except the piffling libel in Henry VI, which reminds me that one of my scenes will be Voltaire and Shakespeare running down by-streets in heaven to avoid meeting Joan." Although *Saint Joan* was not actually written until ten years later, it is apparent that from the first Shaw had thought of it as something more than a simple chronicle play, after the traditional Shakespearean pattern, and that the post-mortem adventures of Joan were to be as significant as the events of her lifetime.

There has been much debate about this aspect of the play, and Shaw in his Preface answers, definitively, those managers and critics who would prefer that the Epilogue be omitted. To do so would probably weaken the statement of the theme, but it would also deprive the audience of the most typically Shavian part of the whole. The Epilogue is completely *sui generis;* it is not historical realism, or expressionism, or symbolism. If it begins, like the third act of *Man and Superman,* as a kind of dream vision, it moves, as in the earlier play, far beyond the capacity of a single dreamer. The Epilogue demonstrates the sureness of Shaw's technical imagination, his ability to do with his stage exactly what the dramatic material demands, to enlarge the capabilities of the theatre rather than to work contentedly within its limitations. He thus practices in his art what he preaches in his doctrine.

Despite Shaw's declared preference for *Back to Methuselah,* production statistics will probably show *Saint Joan* to be his "World Classic." It was first performed by the Theatre Guild in New York, December 28, 1923, with Winifred Lenihan as The Maid, Philip Leigh as The Dauphin, A. H. Van Buren as Warwick, Ian Maclaren as Cauchon, Joseph Macaulay as The Inquisitor, and Henry Travers as de Stogumber. For its first London performance at the New Theatre, March 26, 1924, Sybil Thorndike took the role of Joan, with Ernest Thesiger as The Dauphin, Lewis Casson as de Stogumber, and Raymond Massey as Captain La Hire.

PREFACE TO SAINT JOAN

JOAN THE ORIGINAL AND PRESUMPTUOUS

JOAN OF ARC, a village girl from the Vosges, was born about 1412; burnt for heresy, witchcraft, and sorcery in 1431; rehabilitated after a fashion in 1456; designated venerable in 1904; declared Blessed in 1908; and finally canonized in 1920. She is the most notable Warrior Saint in the Christian calendar, and the queerest fish among the eccentric worthies of the Middle Ages. Though a professed and most pious Catholic, and the projector of a Crusade against the Husites, she was in fact one of the first Protestant martyrs. She was also one of the first apostles of Nationalism, and the first French practitioner of Napoleonic realism in warfare as distinguished from the sporting ransom gambling chivalry of her time. She was the pioneer of rational dressing for women, and, like Queen Christina of Sweden two centuries later, to say nothing of Catalina de Erauso and innumerable obscure heroines who have disguised themselves as men to serve as soldiers and sailors, she refused to accept the specific woman's lot, and dressed and fought and lived as men did.

As she contrived to assert herself in all these ways with such force that she was famous throughout western Europe before she was out of her teens (indeed she never got out of them), it is hardly surprising that she was judicially burnt, ostensibly for a number of capital crimes which we no longer punish as such, but essentially for what we call unwomanly and insufferable presumption. At eighteen Joan's pretensions were beyond those of the proudest Pope or the haughtiest emperor. She claimed to be the ambassador and plenipotentiary of God, and to be, in effect, a member of the Church Triumphant whilst still in the flesh on earth. She patronized her own king, and summoned the English king to repentance and obedience to her commands. She lectured, talked down, and overruled statesmen and prelates. She poohpoohed the plans of generals, leading their troops to victory on plans of her own. She had an unbounded and quite unconcealed contempt for official opinion, judgment, and authority, and for War Office tactics and strategy. Had she been a sage and monarch in whom the most venerable hierarchy and the most illustrious dynasty converged, her pretensions and proceedings would have been as trying to the official mind as the pretensions of Caesar were to Cassius. As her actual condition was pure upstart, there were only two opinions about her. One was that she was miraculous: the other that she was unbearable.

JOAN AND SOCRATES

If Joan had been malicious, selfish, cowardly or stupid, she would have been one of the most odious persons known to history instead of one of the most attractive. If she had been old enough to know the effect she was producing on the men whom she humiliated by being right when they were wrong, and had learned to flatter and manage them, she might have lived as long as Queen Elizabeth. But she was too young and rustical and inexperienced to have any such arts. When she was thwarted by men whom she thought fools, she made no secret of her opinion of them or her impatience with their folly; and she was naïve enough to expect them to be obliged to her for setting them right and keeping them out of mischief. Now it is always hard for superior wits to understand the fury roused by their exposures of the stupidities of comparative dullards. Even Socrates, for all his age and experience, did not defend himself at his trial like a man who understood the long accumulated fury that had burst on him, and was clamoring for his death. His accuser, if born 2300 years later, might have been picked out of any first class carriage on a suburban railway during the evening or morning rush from or to the City; for he had really nothing to say except that he and his like could not endure being shewn up as idiots every time Socrates opened his mouth. Socrates, unconscious of this, was paralyzed by his sense that somehow he was missing the point of the attack. He petered out after he had established the fact that he was an old soldier and a man of honorable life, and that his accuser was a silly snob. He had no suspicion of the extent to which his mental superiority had roused fear and hatred against him in the hearts of men towards whom he was conscious of nothing but good will and good service.

CONTRAST WITH NAPOLEON

If Socrates was as innocent as this at the age of seventy, it may be imagined how innocent Joan was at the age of seventeen. Now Socrates was a man of argument, operating slowly and peacefully on men's minds, whereas Joan was a woman of action, operating with impetuous violence on their bodies. That, no doubt, is why the contemporaries of Socrates endured him so long, and why Joan was destroyed before she was fully grown. But both of them combined terrifying ability with a frankness, personal modesty, and benevolence which made the furious dislike to which they fell victims absolutely unreasonable, and therefore inapprehensible by themselves. Napoleon, also possessed of terrifying ability, but neither frank nor disinterested, had no illusions as to the nature of his popularity. When he was asked how the world would take his death, he said it would give a gasp of relief. But it is not so easy for mental giants who neither hate nor intend to injure their fellows to realize that nevertheless their fellows hate mental giants and would like to destroy them, not only enviously because the juxtaposition of a superior wounds their vanity, but quite humbly and honestly because it frightens them. Fear will drive men to any extreme; and the fear inspired by a superior being is a mystery which cannot be reasoned away. Being immeasurable it is unbearable when there is no presumption or guarantee of its benevolence and moral responsibility: in other words, when it has no official status. The legal and conventional superiority of Herod and Pilate, and of Annas and Caiaphas, inspires fear; but the fear, being a reasonable fear of measurable and avoidable consequences which seem salutary and protective, is bearable; whilst the strange superiority of Christ and the fear it inspires elicit a shriek of

Crucify Him from all who cannot divine its benevolence. Socrates has to drink the hemlock, Christ to hang on the cross, and Joan to burn at the stake, whilst Napoleon, though he ends in St Helena, at least dies in his bed there; and many terrifying but quite comprehensible official scoundrels die natural deaths in all the glory of the kingdoms of this world, proving that it is far more dangerous to be a saint than to be a conqueror. Those who have been both, like Mahomet and Joan, have found that it is the conqueror who must save the saint, and that defeat and capture mean martyrdom. Joan was burnt without a hand lifted on her own side to save her. The comrades she had led to victory and the enemies she had disgraced and defeated, the French king she had crowned and the English king whose crown she had kicked into the Loire, were equally glad to be rid of her.

WAS JOAN INNOCENT OR GUILTY?

As this result could have been produced by a crapulous inferiority as well as by a sublime superiority, the question which of the two was operative in Joan's case has to be faced. It was decided against her by her contemporaries after a very careful and conscientious trial; and the reversal of the verdict twentyfive years later, in form a rehabilitation of Joan, was really only a confirmation of the validity of the coronation of Charles VII. It is the more impressive reversal by a unanimous Posterity, culminating in her canonization, that has quashed the original proceedings, and put her judges on their trial, which, so far, has been much more unfair than their trial of her. Nevertheless the rehabilitation of 1456, corrupt job as it was, really did produce evidence enough to satisfy all reasonable critics that Joan was not a common termagant, not a harlot, not a witch, not a blasphemer, no more an idolater than the Pope himself, and not ill conducted in any sense apart from her soldiering, her wearing of men's clothes, and her audacity, but on the contrary goodhumored, an intact virgin, very pious, very temperate (we should call her meal of bread soaked in the common wine which is the drinking water of France ascetic), very kindly, and, though a brave and hardy soldier, unable to endure loose language or licentious conduct. She went to the stake without a stain on her character except the overweening presumption, the superbity as they called it, that led her thither. It would therefore be waste of time now to prove that the Joan of the first part of the Elizabethan chronicle play of Henry VI (supposed to have been tinkered by Shakespear)grossly libels her in its concluding scenes in deference to Jingo patriotism. The mud that was thrown at her has dropped off by this time so completely that there is no need for any modern writer to wash up after it. What is far more difficult to get rid of is the mud that is being thrown at her judges, and the whitewash which disfigures her beyond recognition. When Jingo scurrility had done its worst to her, sectarian scurrility (in this case Protestant scurrility) used her stake to beat the Roman Catholic Church and the Inquisition. The easiest way to make these institutions the villains of a melodrama was to make The Maid its heroine. That melodrama may be dismissed as rubbish. Joan got a far fairer trial from the Church and the Inquisition than any prisoner of her type and in her situation gets nowadays in any official secular court; and the decision was strictly according to law. And she was not a melodramatic heroine: that is, a physically beautiful lovelorn parasite on an equally beautiful hero, but a genius and a saint, about as completely the opposite of a melodramatic heroine as it is possible for a human being to be.

Let us be clear about the meaning of the terms. A genius is a person who, seeing farther and probing deeper than other people, has a different set of ethical valuations from theirs, and has energy enough to give effect to this extra vision and its valuations in whatever manner best suits his or her specific talents. A saint is one who' having practised heroic virtues, and enjoyed revelations or powers of the order which The Church classes technically as supernatural, is eligible for canonization. If a historian is an Anti-Feminist, and does not believe women to be capable of genius in the traditional masculine departments, he will never make anything of Joan, whose genius was turned to practical account mainly in soldiering and politics. If he is Rationalist enough to deny that saints exist, and to hold that new ideas cannot come otherwise than by conscious ratiocination, he will never catch Joan's likeness. Her ideal biographer must be free from nineteenth century prejudices and biases; must understand the Middle Ages, the Roman Catholic Church, and the Holy Roman Empire much more intimately than our Whig historians have ever understood them; and must be capable of throwing off sex partialities and their romance, and regarding woman as the female of the human species, and not as a different kind of animal with specific charms and specific imbecilities.

JOAN'S GOOD LOOKS

To put the last point roughly, any book about Joan which begins by describing her as a beauty may be at once classed as a romance. Not one of Joan's comrades, in village, court, or camp, even when they were straining themselves to please the king by praising her, ever claimed that she was pretty. All the men who alluded to the matter declared most emphatically that she was unattractive sexually to a degree that seemed to them miraculous, considering that she was in the bloom of youth, and neither ugly, awkward, deformed, nor unpleasant in her person. The evident truth is that like most women of her hardy managing type she seemed neutral in the conflict of sex because men were too much afraid of her to fall in love with her. She herself was not sexless: in spite of the virginity she had vowed up to a point, and preserved to her death, she never excluded the possibility of marriage for herself. But marriage, with its preliminary of the attraction, pursuit, and capture of a husband, was not her business: she had something else to do. Byron's formula, "Man's love is of man's life a thing apart: 'tis woman's whole existence" did not apply to her any more than to George Washington or any other masculine worker on the heroic scale. Had she lived in our time, picture postcards might have been sold of her as a general: they would not have been sold of her as a sultana. Nevertheless there is one reason for crediting her with a very remarkable face. A sculptor of her time in Orleans made a statue of a helmeted young woman with a face that is unique in art in point of being evidently not an ideal face but a portrait, and yet so uncommon as to be unlike any real woman one has ever seen. It is surmised that Joan served unconsciously as the sculptor's model. There is no proof of this; but those extraordinarily spaced eyes raise so powerfully the question "If this woman be not Joan, who is she?" that I dispense with further evidence, and challenge those who disagree with me to prove a negative. It is a wonderful face, but quite neutral from the point of view of the operatic beauty fancier.

Such a fancier may perhaps be finally chilled by the prosaic fact that Joan was the defendant in a suit for breach of promise of marriage, and that she conducted her own case and won it.

JOAN'S SOCIAL POSITION

By class Joan was the daughter of a working farmer who was one of the headmen of his village, and transacted its feudal business for it with the neighboring squires and their lawyers. When the castle in which the villagers were entitled to take refuge from raids became derelict, he organized a combination of half a dozen farmers to obtain possession of it so as to occupy it when there was any danger of invasion. As a child, Joan could please herself at times with being the young lady of this castle. Her mother and brothers were able to follow and share her fortune at court without making themselves notably ridiculous. These facts leave us no excuse for the popular romance that turns every heroine into either a princess or a beggarmaid. In the somewhat similar case of Shakespear a whole inverted pyramid of wasted research has been based on the assumption that he was an illiterate laborer, in the face of the plainest evidence that his father was a man of business, and at one time a very prosperous one, married to a woman of some social pretensions. There is the same tendency to drive Joan into the position of a hired shepherd girl, though a hired shepherd girl in Domrémy would have deferred to her as the young lady of the farm.

The difference between Joan's case and Shakespear's is that Shakespear was not illiterate. He had been to school, and knew as much Latin and Greek as most university passmen retain: that is, for practical purposes, none at all. Joan was absolutely illiterate. "I do not know A from B" she said. But many princesses at that time and for long after might have said the same. Marie Antoinette, for instance, at Joan's age could not spell her own name correctly. But this does not mean that Joan was an ignorant person, or that she suffered from the diffidence and sense of social disadvantage now felt by people who cannot read or write. If she could not write letters, she could and did dictate them and attach full and indeed excessive importance to them. When she was called a shepherd lass to her face she very warmly resented it, and challenged any woman to compete with her in the household arts of the mistresses of well furnished houses. She understood the political and military situation in France much better than most of our newspaper fed university women-graduates understand the corresponding situation of their own country today. Her first convert was the neighboring commandant at Vaucouleurs; and she converted him by telling him about the defeat of the Dauphin's troops at the Battle of Herrings so long before he had official news of it that he concluded she must have had a divine revelation. This knowledge of and interest in public affairs was nothing extraordinary among farmers in a warswept countryside. Politicians came to the door too often sword in hand to be disregarded: Joan's people could not afford to be ignorant of what was going on in the feudal world. They were not rich; and Joan worked on the farm as her father did, driving the sheep to pasture and so forth; but there is no evidence or suggestion of sordid poverty, and no reason to believe that Joan had to work as a hired servant works, or indeed to work at all when she preferred to go to confession, or dawdle about waiting for visions and listening to the church bells to hear voices in them. In short, much more of a young lady, and even of an intellectual, than most of the daughters of our petty bourgeoisie.

JOAN'S VOICES AND VISIONS

Joan's voices and visions have played many tricks with her reputation. They have been held to prove that she was mad, that she was a liar and impostor, that she was a sorceress (she was burned for this), and finally that she was a saint. They do not prove any of these things; but the variety of the conclusions reached shew how little our matter-of-fact historians know about other people's minds, or even about their own. There are people in the world whose imagination is so vivid that when they have an idea it comes to them as an audible voice, sometimes uttered by a visible figure. Criminal lunatic asylums are occupied largely by murderers who have obeyed voices. Thus a woman may hear voices telling her that she must cut her husband's throat and strangle her child as they lie asleep; and she may feel obliged to do what she is told. By a medico-legal superstition it is held in our courts that criminals whose temptations present themselves under these illusions are not responsible for their actions, and must be treated as insane. But the seers of visions and the hearers of revelations are not always criminals. The inspirations and intuitions and unconsciously reasoned conclusions of genius sometimes assume similar illusions. Socrates, Luther, Swedenborg, Blake saw visions and heard voices just as Saint Francis and Saint Joan did. If Newton's imagination had been of the same vividly dramatic kind he might have seen the ghost of Pythagoras walk into the orchard and explain why the apples were falling. Such an illusion would have invalidated neither the theory of gravitation nor Newton's general sanity. What is more, the visionary method of making the discovery would not be a whit more miraculous than the normal method. The test of sanity is not the normality of the method but the reasonableness of the discovery. If Newton had been informed by Pythagoras that the moon was made of green cheese, then Newton would have been locked up. Gravitation, being a reasoned hypothesis which fitted remarkably well into the Copernican version of the observed physical facts of the universe, established Newton's reputation for extraordinary intelligence, and would have done so no matter how fantastically he had arrived at it. Yet his theory of gravitation is not so impressive a mental feat as his astounding chronology, which established him as the king of mental conjurors, but a Bedlamite king whose authority no one now accepts. On the subject of the eleventh horn of the beast seen by the prophet Daniel he was more fantastic than Joan, because his imagination was not dramatic but mathematical and therefore extraordinarily susceptible to numbers: indeed if all his works were lost except his chronology we should say that he was as mad as a hatter. As it is, who dares diagnose Newton as a madman?

In the same way Joan must be judged a sane woman in spite of her voices because they never gave her any advice that might not have come to her from her mother wit exactly as gravitation came to Newton. We can all see now, especially since the late war threw so many of our women into military life, that Joan's campaigning could not have been carried on in petticoats. This was not only because she did a man's work, but because it was morally necessary that sex should be left out of the question as between her and her comrades-in-arms. She gave this reason herself when she was pressed on the subject; and the fact that this entirely reasonable necessity came to her imagination first as an order from God delivered through the mouth of Saint Catherine does not prove that she was mad. The soundness of the order proves that she was unusually sane; but its form proves that her dramatic imagination played tricks with her senses. Her policy was also quite sound: nobody disputes that the relief of Orleans, followed up by the coronation at Rheims of the Dauphin as a counterblow to the suspicions then current of his legitimacy and consequently of his title, were military and political masterstrokes that saved France. They might have been planned by Napoleon or any other illusionproof genius. They came to Joan as an instruction from her Counsel, as she called her visionary saints; but she was none the less an able leader of men for imagining her ideas in this way.

THE EVOLUTIONARY APPETITE

What then is the modern view of Joan's voices and visions and messages from God? The nineteenth century said that they were delusions, but that as she was a pretty girl, and had been abominably ill-treated and finally done to death by a superstitious rabble of medieval priests hounded on by a corrupt political bishop, it must be assumed that she was the innocent dupe of these delusions. The twentieth century finds this explanation too vapidly commonplace, and demands something more mystic. I think the twentieth century is right, because an explanation which amounts to Joan being mentally defective instead of, as she obviously was, mentally excessive, will not wash. I cannot believe, nor, if I could, could I expect all my readers to believe, as Joan did, that three ocularly visible well dressed persons, named respectively Saint Catherine, Saint Margaret, and Saint Michael, came down from heaven and gave her certain instructions with which they were charged by God for her. Not that such a belief would be more improbable or fantastic than some modern beliefs which we all swallow; but there are fashions and family habits in belief, and it happens that, my fashion being Victorian and my family habit Protestant, I find myself unable to attach any such objective validity to the form of Joan's visions.

But that there are forces at work which use individuals for purposes far transcending the purpose of keeping these individuals alive and prosperous and respectable and safe and happy in the middle station in life, which is all any good bourgeois can reasonably require, is established by the fact that men will, in the pursuit of knowledge and of social readjustments for which they will not be a penny the better, and are indeed often many pence the worse, face poverty, infamy, exile, imprisonment, dreadful hardship, and death. Even the selfish pursuit of personal power does not nerve men to the efforts and sacrifices which are eagerly made in pursuit of extensions of our power over nature, though these extensions may not touch the personal life of the seeker at any point. There is no more mystery about this appetite for knowledge and power than about the appetite for food: both are known as facts and as facts only, the difference between them being that the appetite for food is necessary to the life of the hungry man and is therefore a personal appetite, whereas the other is an appetite for evolution, and therefore a superpersonal need.

The diverse manners in which our imaginations dramatize the approach of the superpersonal forces is a problem for the psychologist, not for the historian. Only, the historian must understand that visionaries are neither impostors nor lunatics. It is one thing to say that the figure Joan recognized as St Catherine was not really St Catherine, but the dramatization by Joan's imagination of that pressure upon her of the driving force that is behind evolution which I have just called the evolutionary appetite. It is quite another to class her visions with the vision of two moons seen by a drunken person, or with Brocken spectres, echoes and the like. Saint Catherine's instructions were far too cogent for that; and the simplest French peasant who believes in apparitions of celestial personages to favored mortals is nearer to the scientific truth about Joan than the Rationalist and Materialist historians and essayists who feel obliged to set down a girl who saw saints and heard them talking to her as either crazy or mendacious. If Joan was mad, all Christendom was mad too; for people who believe devoutly in the existence of celestial personages are every whit as mad in that sense as the people who think they see them. Luther, when he threw his inkhorn at the devil, was no more mad than any other Augustinian monk: he had a more vivid imagination, and had perhaps eaten and slept less: that was all.

THE MERE ICONOGRAPHY DOES NOT MATTER

All the popular religions in the world are made apprehensible by an array of legendary personages, with an Almighty Father, and sometimes a mother and divine child, as the central figures. These are presented to the mind's eye in childhood; and the result is a hallucination which persists strongly throughout life when it has been well impressed. Thus all the thinking of the hallucinated adult about the fountain of inspiration which is continually flowing in the universe, or about the promptings of virtue and the revulsions of shame: in short, about aspiration and conscience, both of which forces are matters of fact more obvious than electro-magnetism, is thinking in terms of the celestial vision. And when in the case of exceptionally imaginative persons, especially those practising certain appropriate austerities, the hallucination extends from the mind's eye to the body's, the visionary sees Krishna or the Buddha or the Blessed Virgin or St Catherine as the case may be.

THE MODERN EDUCATION WHICH JOAN ESCAPED

It is important to everyone nowadays to understand this, because modern science is making short work of the hallucinations without regard to the vital importance of the things they symbolize. If Joan were reborn today she would be sent, first to a convent school in which she would be mildly taught to connect inspiration and conscience with St Catherine and St Michael exactly as she was in the fifteenth century, and then finished up with a very energetic training in the gospel of Saints Louis Pasteur and Paul Bert, who would tell her (possibly in visions but more probably in pamphlets) not to be a superstitious little fool, and to empty out St Catherine and the rest of the Catholic hagiology as an obsolete iconography of exploded myths. It would be rubbed into her that Galileo was a martyr, and his persecutors incorrigible ignoramuses, and that St Teresa's hormones had gone astray and left her incurably hyperpituitary or hyperadrenal or hysteroid or epileptoid or anything but asteroid. She would have been convinced by precept and experiment that baptism and receiving the body of her Lord were contemptible superstitions, and that vaccination and vivisection were enlightened practices. Behind her new Saints Louis and Paul there would be not only Science purifying Religion and being purified by it, but hypochondria, melancholia, cowardice, stupidity, cruelty, muckraking curiosity, knowledge without wisdom, and everything that the eternal soul in Nature loathes, instead of the virtues of which St Catherine was the figure head. As to the new rites, which would be the saner Joan? the one who carried little children to be baptized of water and the spirit, or the one who sent the police to force their parents to have the most villainous racial poison we know thrust into their veins? the one who told them the story of the angel and Mary, or the one who questioned them as to their experiences of the Edipus complex? the one to whom the consecrated wafer was the very body of the virtue that was her salvation, or the one who looked forward to a precise and convenient regulation of her health and her desires by a nicely calculated diet of thyroid extract, adrenalin, thymin, pituitrin, and insulin, with pick-me-ups of hormone stimulants, the blood being first carefully fortified with antibodies against all possible infections by inoculations of infected bacteria and serum from infected animals, and against old age by surgical extirpation of the reproductive ducts or weekly doses of monkey gland?

It is true that behind all these quackeries there is a certain body of genuine scientific physiology. But was there any the less a certain body of genuine psychology behind St Catherine and the Holy Ghost? And which is the healthier mind? the saintly mind or the monkey gland mind? Does not the present cry of Back to the Middle Ages, which has been incubating ever since the pre-Raphaelite movement began, mean that it is no longer our Academy pictures that are intolerable, but our credulities that have not the excuse of being superstitions, our cruelties that have not the excuse of barbarism, our persecutions that have not the excuse of religious faith, our shameless substitution of successful swindlers and scoundrels and quacks for saints as objects of worship, and our deafness and blindness to the calls and visions of the inexorable power that made us, and will destroy us if we disregard it? To Joan and her contemporaries we should appear as a drove of Gadarene swine, possessed by all the unclean spirits cast out by the faith and civilization of the Middle Ages, running violently down a steep place into a hell of high explosives. For us to set up our condition as a standard of sanity, and declare Joan mad because she never condescended to it, is to prove that we are not only lost but irredeemable. Let us then once for all drop all nonsense about Joan being cracked, and accept her as at least as sane as Florence Nightingale, who also combined a very simple iconography of religious belief with a mind so exceptionally powerful that it kept her in continual trouble with the medical and military panjandrums of her time.

FAILURES OF THE VOICES

That the voices and visions were illusory, and their wisdom all Joan's own, is shewn by the occasions on which they failed her, notably during her trial, when they assured her that she would be rescued. Here her hopes flattered her; but they were not unreasonable: her military colleague La Hire was in command of a considerable force not so very far off; and if the Armagnacs, as her party was called, had really wanted to rescue her, and had put anything like her own vigor into the enterprise, they could have attempted it with very fair chances of success. She did not understand that they were glad to be rid of her, nor that the rescue of a prisoner from the hands of the Church was a much more serious business for a medieval captain, or even a medieval king, than its mere physical difficulty as a military exploit suggested. According to her lights her expectation of a rescue was reasonable; therefore she heard Madame Saint Catherine assuring her it would happen, that being her way of finding out and making up her own mind. When it became evident that she had miscalculated: when she was led to the stake, and La Hire was not thundering at the gates of Rouen nor charging Warwick's men at arms, she threw over Saint Catherine at once, and recanted. Nothing could be more sane or practical. It was not until she discovered that she had gained nothing by her recantation but close imprisonment for life that she withdrew it, and deliberately and explicitly chose burning instead: a decision which shewed not only the extraordinary decision of her character, but also a Rationalism carried to its ultimate human test of suicide. Yet even in this the illusion persisted; and she announced her relapse as dictated to her by her voices.

JOAN A GALTONIC VISUALIZER

The most sceptical scientific reader may therefore accept as a flat fact, carrying no implication of unsoundness of mind, that Joan was what Francis Galton and other modern investigators of human faculty call a visualizer. She saw imaginary saints just as some other people see imaginary diagrams and landscapes with numbers dotted about them, and are thereby able to perform feats of memory and arithmetic impossible to non-visualizers. Visualizers will understand this at once. Non-visualizers who have never read Galton will be puzzled and incredulous. But a very little inquiry among their acquaintances will reveal to them that the mind's eye is more or less a magic lantern, and that the street is full of normally sane people who have hallucinations of all sorts which they believe to be part of the normal permanent equipment of all human beings.

JOAN'S MANLINESS AND MILITARISM

Joan's other abnormality, too common among uncommon things to be properly called a peculiarity, was her craze for soldiering and the masculine life. Her father tried to frighten her out of it by threatening to drown her if she ran away with the soldiers, and ordering her brothers to drown her if he were not on the spot. This extravagance was clearly not serious: it must have been addressed to a child young enough to imagine that he was in earnest. Joan must therefore as a child have wanted to run away and be a soldier. The awful prospect of being thrown into the Meuse and drowned by a terrible father and her big brothers kept her quiet until the father had lost his terrors and the brothers yielded to her natural leadership; and by that time she had sense enough to know that the masculine and military life was not a mere matter of running away from home. But the taste for it never left her, and was fundamental in determining her career.

If anyone doubts this, let him ask himself why a maid charged with a special mission from heaven to the Dauphin (this was how Joan saw her very able plan for retrieving the desperate situation of the uncrowned king) should not have simply gone to the court as a maid, in woman's dress, and urged her counsel upon him in a woman's way, as other women with similar missions had come to his mad father and his wise grandfather. Why did she insist on having a soldier's dress and arms and sword and horse and equipment, and on treating her escort of soldiers as comrades, sleeping side by side with them on the floor at night as if there were no difference of sex between them? It may be answered that this was the safest way of travelling through a country infested with hostile troops and bands of marauding deserters from both sides. Such an answer has no weight because it applies to all the women who travelled in France at that time, and who never dreamt of travelling otherwise than as women. But even if we accept it, how does it account for the fact that when the danger was over, and she could present herself at court in feminine attire with perfect safety and obviously with greater propriety, she presented herself in her man's dress, and instead of urging Charles, like Queen Victoria urging the War Office to send Roberts to the Transvaal, to send D'Alençon, De Rais, La Hire and the rest to the relief of Dunois at Orleans, insisted that she must go herself and lead the assault in person? Why did she give exhibitions of her dexterity in handling a lance, and of her seat as a rider? Why did she accept presents of armor and chargers and masculine surcoats, and in every action repudiate the conventional character of a woman? The simple answer to all these questions is that she was the sort of woman that wants to lead a man's life. They are to be found wherever there are armies on foot or navies on the seas, serving in male disguise, eluding detection for astonishingly long periods, and sometimes, no doubt, escaping it entirely. When they are in a position to defy public opinion they throw off all concealment. You have your Rosa Bonheur painting in male blouse and trousers, and George Sand living a man's life and almost compelling her Chopins and De Mussets to live women's lives to amuse her. Had Joan not been one of those "unwomanly women," she might have been canonized much sooner.

But it is not necessary to wear trousers and smoke big cigars to live a man's life any more than it is necessary to wear petticoats to live a woman's. There are plenty of gowned and bodiced women in ordinary civil life who manage their own affairs and other people's, including those of their menfolk, and are entirely masculine in their tastes and pursuits. There always were such women, even in the Victorian days when women had fewer legal rights than men, and our modern women magistrates, mayors, and members of Parliament were unknown. In reactionary Russia in our own century a woman soldier organized an effective regiment of amazons, which disappeared only because it was Aldershottian enough to be against the Revolution. The exemption of women from military service is founded, not on any natural inaptitude that men do not share, but on the fact that communities cannot reproduce themselves without plenty of women. Men are more largely dispensable, and are sacrificed accordingly.

WAS JOAN SUICIDAL?

These two abnormalities were the only ones that were irresistibly prepotent in Joan; and they brought her to the stake. Neither of them was peculiar to her. There was nothing peculiar about her except the vigor and scope of her mind and character, and the intensity of her vital energy. She was accused of a suicidal tendency; and it is a fact that when she attempted to escape from Beaurevoir Castle by jumping from a tower said to be sixty feet high, she took a risk beyond reason, though she recovered from the crash after a few days fasting. Her death was deliberately chosen as an alternative to life without liberty. In battle she challenged death as Wellington did at Waterloo, and as Nelson habitually did when he walked his quarter deck during his battles with all his decorations in full blaze. As neither Nelson nor Wellington nor any of those who have performed desperate feats, and preferred death to captivity, has been accused of suicidal mania, Joan need not be suspected of it. In the Beaurevoir affair there was more at stake than her freedom. She was distracted by the news that Compiègne was about to fall; and she was convinced that she could save it if only she could get free. Still, the leap was so perilous that her conscience was not quite easy about it; and she expressed this, as usual, by saying that Saint Catherine had forbidden her to do it, but forgave her afterwards for her disobedience.

JOAN SUMMED UP

We may accept and admire Joan, then, as a sane and shrewd country girl of extraordinary strength of mind and hardihood of body. Everything she did was thoroughly calculated; and though the process was so rapid that she was hardly conscious of it, and ascribed it all to her voices, she was a woman of policy and not of blind impulse. In war she was as much a realist as Napoleon: she had his eye for artillery and his knowledge of what it could do. She did not expect besieged cities to fall Jerichowise at the sound of her trumpet, but, like Wellington, adapted her methods of attack to the peculiarities of the defence; and she anticipated the Napoleonic calculation that if you only hold on long enough the other fellow will give in: for example, her final triumph at Orleans was achieved after her commander Dunois had sounded the retreat at the end of a day's fighting without a decision. She was never for a moment what so many romancers and playwrights have pretended: a romantic young lady. She was a thorough daughter of the soil in her peasantlike matter-of-factness and doggedness, and her acceptance of great lords and kings and prelates as such without idolatry or snobbery, seeing at a glance how much they were individually good for. She had the respectable countrywoman's sense of the value of public decency, and would not tolerate foul language and neglect of religious observances, nor allow disreputable women to hang about her soldiers. She had one pious ejaculation "En nom Dé!" and one meaningless oath "Par mon martin"; and this much swearing she allowed to the incorrigibly blasphemous La Hire equally with herself. The value of this prudery was so great in restoring the self-respect of the badly demoralized army that, like most of her policy, it justified itself as soundly calculated. She talked to and dealt with people of all classes, from laborers to kings, without embarrassment or affectation, and got them to do what she wanted when they were not afraid or corrupt. She could coax and she could hustle, her tongue having a soft side and a sharp edge. She was very capable: a born boss.

JOAN'S IMMATURITY AND IGNORANCE

All this, however, must be taken with one heavy qualification. She was only a girl in her teens. If we could think of her as a managing woman of fifty we should seize her type at once; for we have plenty of managing women among us of that age who illustrate perfectly the sort of person she would have become had she lived. But she, being only a lass when all is said, lacked their knowledge of men's vanities and of the weight and proportion of social forces. She knew nothing of iron hands in velvet gloves: she just used her fists. She thought political changes much easier than they are, and, like Mahomet in his innocence of any world but the tribal world, wrote letters to kings calling on them to make millennial rearrangements. Consequently it was only in the enterprises that were really simple and compassable by swift physical force, like the coronation and the Orleans campaign, that she was successful.

Her want of academic education disabled her when she had to deal with such elaborately artificial structures as the great ecclesiastical and social institutions of the Middle Ages. She had a horror of heretics without suspecting that she was herself a heresiarch, one of the precursors of a schism that rent Europe in two, and cost centuries of bloodshed that is not yet staunched. She objected to foreigners on the sensible ground that they were not in their proper place in France; but she had no notion of how this brought her into conflict with Catholicism and Feudalism, both essentially international. She worked by commonsense; and where scholarship was the only clue to institutions she was in the dark, and broke her shins against them, all the more rudely because of her enormous self-confidence, which made her the least cautious of human beings in civil affairs.

This combination of inept youth and academic ignorance with great natural capacity, push, courage, devotion, originality and oddity, fully accounts for all the facts in Joan's career, and makes her a credible historical and human phenomenon; but it clashes most discordantly both with the idolatrous romance that has grown up round her, and the belittling scepticism that reacts against that romance.

THE MAID IN LITERATURE

English readers would probably like to know how these idolizations and reactions have affected the books they are most familiar with about Joan. There is the first part of the Shakesperean, or pseudo-Shakesperean trilogy of Henry VI, in which Joan is one of the leading characters. This portrait of Joan is not more authentic than the descriptions in the London papers of George Washington in 1780, of

Napoleon in 1803, of the German Crown Prince in 1915, or of Lenin in 1917. It ends in mere scurrility. The impression left by it is that the playwright, having begun by an attempt to make Joan a beautiful and romantic figure, was told by his scandalized company that English patriotism would never stand a sympathetic representation of a French conqueror of English troops, and that unless he at once introduced all the old charges against Joan of being a sorceress and a harlot, and assumed her to be guilty of all of them, his play could not be produced. As likely as not, this is what actually happened: indeed there is only one other apparent way of accounting for the sympathetic representation of Joan as a heroine culminating in her eloquent appeal to the Duke of Burgundy, followed by the blackguardly scurrility of the concluding scenes. That other way is to assume that the original play was wholly scurrilous, and that Shakespear touched up the earlier scenes. As the work belongs to a period at which he was only beginning his practice as a tinker of old works, before his own style was fully formed and hardened, it is impossible to verify this guess. His finger is not unmistakably evident in the play, which is poor and base in its moral tone; but he may have tried to redeem it from downright infamy by shedding a momentary glamor on the figure of The Maid.

When we jump over two centuries to Schiller, we find Die Jungfrau von Orleans drowned in a witch's caldron of raging romance. Schiller's Joan has not a single point of contact with the real Joan, nor indeed with any mortal woman that ever walked this earth. There is really nothing to be said of his play but that it is not about Joan at all, and can hardly be said to pretend to be; for he makes her die on the battlefield, finding her burning unbearable. Before Schiller came Voltaire, who burlesqued Homer in a mock epic called La Pucelle. It is the fashion to dismiss this with virtuous indignation as an obscene libel; and I certainly cannot defend it against the charge of extravagant indecorum. But its purpose was not to depict Joan, but to kill with ridicule everything that Voltaire righteously hated in the institutions and fashions of his own day. He made Joan ridiculous, but not contemptible nor (comparatively) unchaste; and as he also made Homer and St Peter and St Denis and the brave Dunois ridiculous, and the other heroines of the poem very unchaste indeed, he may be said to have let Joan off very easily. But indeed the personal adventures of the characters are so outrageous, and so Homerically free from any pretence at or even possibility of historical veracity, that those who affect to take them seriously only make themselves Pecksniffian. Samuel Butler believed The Iliad to be a burlesque of Greek Jingoism and Greek religion, written by a hostage or a slave; and La Pucelle makes Butler's theory almost convincing. Voltaire represents Agnes Sorel, the Dauphin's mistress, whom Joan never met, as a woman with a consuming passion for the chastest concubinal fidelity, whose fate it was to be continually falling into the hands of licentious foes and suffering the worst extremities of rapine. The combats in which Joan rides a flying donkey, or in which, taken unaware with no clothes on, she defends Agnes with her sword, and inflicts appropriate mutilations on her assailants, can be laughed at as they are intended to be without scruple; for no sane person could mistake them for sober history; and it may be that their ribald irreverence is more wholesome than the beglamored sentimentality of Schiller. Certainly Voltaire should not have asserted that Joan's father was a priest; but when he was out to *écraser l'infâme* (the French Church) he stuck at nothing.

So far, the literary representations of The Maid were legendary. But the publication by Quicherat in 1841 of the reports of her trial and rehabilitation placed the subject on a new footing. These entirely realistic documents created a living interest in Joan which Voltaire's mock Homerics and Schiller's romantic nonsense missed. Typical products of that interest in America and England are the histories of Joan by Mark Twain and Andrew Lang. Mark Twain was converted to downright worship of Joan directly by Quicherat. Later on, another man of genius, Anatole France, reacted against the Quicheratic wave of enthusiasm, and wrote a Life of Joan in which he attributed Joan's ideas to clerical prompting and her military success to an adroit use of her by Dunois as a *mascotte*: in short, he denied that she had any serious military or political ability. At this Andrew saw red, and went for Anatole's scalp in a rival Life of her which should be read as a corrective to the other. Lang had no difficulty in shewing that Joan's ability was not an unnatural fiction to be explained away as an illusion manufactured by priests and soldiers, but a straightforward fact.

It has been lightly pleaded in explanation that Anatole France is a Parisian of the art world, into whose scheme of things the able, hardheaded, hardhanded female, though she dominates provincial France and business Paris, does not enter; whereas Lang was a Scot, and every Scot knows that the grey mare is as likely as not to be the better horse. But this explanation does not convince me. I cannot believe that Anatole France does not know what everybody knows. I wish everybody knew all that he knows. One feels antipathies at work in his book. He is not anti-Joan; but he is anti-clerical, anti-mystic, and fundamentally unable to believe that there ever was any such person as the real Joan.

Mark Twain's Joan, skirted to the ground, and with as many petticoats as Noah's wife in a toy ark, is an attempt to combine Bayard with Esther Summerson from Bleak House into an unimpeachable American school teacher in armor. Like Esther Summerson she makes her creator ridiculous, and yet, being the work of a man of genius, remains a credible human goodygoody in spite of her creator's infatuation. It is the description rather than the valuation that is wrong. Andrew Lang and Mark Twain are equally determined to make Joan a beautiful and most ladylike Victorian; but both of them recognize and insist on her capacity for leadership, though the Scots scholar is less romantic about it than the Mississippi pilot. But then Lang was, by lifelong professional habit, a critic of biographies rather than a biographer, whereas Mark Twain writes his biography frankly in the form of a romance.

PROTESTANT MISUNDERSTANDINGS OF THE MIDDLE AGES

They had, however, one disability in common. To understand Joan's history it is not enough to understand her character: you must understand her environment as well. Joan in a nineteenth-twentieth century environment is as incongruous a figure as she would appear were she to walk down Piccadilly today in her fifteenth century armor. To see her in her proper perspective you must understand Christendom and the Catholic Church, the Holy Roman Empire and the Feudal System, as they existed and were understood in the Middle Ages. If you confuse the Middle Ages with the Dark Ages, and are in the habit of ridiculing your aunt for wearing "medieval clothes," meaning those in vogue in the eighteen-nineties, and are quite convinced that the world has progressed enormously, both morally and mechanically, since Joan's time, then you will never understand why Joan was burnt, much less feel that you might have voted for burning her yourself if you had been a member of the court that tried her; and until you feel that you know nothing essential about her.

That the Mississippi pilot should have broken down on this misunderstanding is natural enough. Mark Twain, the Innocent Abroad, who saw the lovely churches of the Middle Ages without a throb of emotion, author of A Yankee at the Court of King Arthur, in which the heroes and heroines of medieval chivalry are guys seen through the eyes of a street arab, was clearly out of court from the beginning. Andrew Lang was better read; but, like Walter Scott, he enjoyed medieval history as a string of Border romances rather than as the record of a high European civilization based on a catholic faith. Both of them were baptized as Protestants, and impressed by all their schooling and most of their reading with the belief that Catholic bishops who burnt heretics were persecutors capable of any villainy; that all heretics were Albigensians or Husites or Jews or Protestants of the highest character; and that the Inquisition was a Chamber of Horrors invented expressly and exclusively for such burnings. Accordingly we find them representing Peter Cauchon, Bishop of Beauvais, the judge who sent Joan to the stake, as an unconscionable scoundrel, and all the questions put to her as "traps" to ensnare and destroy her. And they assume unhesitatingly that the two or three score of canons and doctors of law and divinity who sat with Cauchon as assessors, were exact reproductions of him on slightly less elevated chairs and with a different headdress.

COMPARATIVE FAIRNESS OF JOAN'S TRIAL

The truth is that Cauchon was threatened and insulted by the English for being too considerate to Joan. A recent French writer denies that Joan was burnt, and holds that Cauchon spirited her away and burnt somebody or something else in her place, and that the pretender who subsequently personated her at Orleans and elsewhere was not a pretender but the real authentic Joan. He is able to cite Cauchon's pro-Joan partiality in support of his view. As to the assessors, the objection to them is not that they were a row of uniform rascals, but that they were political partisans of Joan's enemies. This is a valid objection to all such trials; but in the absence of neutral tribunals they are unavoidable. A trial by Joan's French partisans would have been as unfair as the trial by her French opponents; and an equally mixed tribunal would have produced a deadlock. Such recent trials as those of Edith Cavell by a German tribunal and Roger Casement by an English one were open to the same objection; but they went forward to the death nevertheless, because neutral tribunals were not available. Edith, like Joan, was an arch heretic: in the middle of the war she declared before the world that "Patriotism is not enough." She nursed enemies back to health, and assisted their prisoners to escape, making it abundantly clear that she would help any fugitive or distressed person without asking whose side he was on, and acknowledging no distinction before Christ between Tommy and Jerry and Pitou the *poilu*. Well might Edith have wished that she could bring the Middle Ages back, and have fifty civilians, learned in the law or vowed to the service of God, to support two skilled judges in trying her case according to the Catholic law of Christendom, and to argue it out with her at sitting after sitting for many weeks. The modern military Inquisition was not so squeamish. It shot her out of hand; and her countrymen, seeing in this a good opportunity for lecturing the enemy on his intolerance, put up a statue to her, but took particular care not to inscribe on the pedestal "Patriotism is not enough," for which omission, and the lie it implies, they will need Edith's intercession when they are themselves brought to judgment, if any heavenly power thinks such moral cowards capable of pleading to an intelligible indictment.

The point need be no further labored. Joan was persecuted essentially as she would be persecuted today. The change from burning to hanging or shooting may strike us as a change for the better. The change from careful trial under ordinary law to recklessly summary military terrorism may strike us a change for the worse. But as far as toleration is concerned the trial and execution in Rouen in 1431 might have been an event of today; and we may charge our consciences accordingly. If Joan had to be dealt with by us in London she would be treated with no more toleration than Miss Sylvia Pankhurst, or the Peculiar People, or the parents who keep their children from the elementary school, or any of the others who cross the line we have to draw, rightly or wrongly, between the tolerable and the intolerable.

JOAN NOT TRIED AS A POLITICAL OFFENDER

Besides, Joan's trial was not, like Casement's, a national political trial. Ecclesiastical courts and the courts of the Inquisition (Joan was tried by a combination of the two) were Courts Christian: that is, international courts; and she was tried, not as a traitress, but as a heretic, blasphemer, sorceress and idolater. Her alleged offences were not political offences against England, nor against the Burgundian faction in France, but against God and against the common morality of Christendom. And although the idea we call Nationalism was so foreign to the medieval conception of Christian society that it might almost have been directly charged against Joan as an additional heresy, yet it was not so charged; and it is unreasonable to suppose that the political bias of a body of Frenchmen like the assessors would on this point have run strongly in favor of the English foreigners (even if they had been making themselves particularly agreeable in France instead of just the contrary) against a Frenchwoman who had vanquished them.

The tragic part of the trial was that Joan, like most prisoners tried for anything but the simplest breaches of the ten commandments, did not understand what they were accusing her of. She was much more like Mark Twain than like Peter Cauchon. Her attachment to the Church was very different from the Bishop's, and does not, in fact, bear close examination from his point of view. She delighted in the solaces the Church offers to sensitive souls: to her, confession and communion were luxuries beside which the vulgar pleasures of the senses were trash. Her prayers were wonderful conversations with her three saints. Her piety seemed superhuman to the formally dutiful people whose religion was only a task to them. But when the Church was not offering her her favorite luxuries, but calling on her to accept its interpretation of God's will, and to sacrifice her own, she flatly refused, and made it clear that her notion of a Catholic Church was one in which the Pope was Pope Joan. How could the Church tolerate that, when it had just destroyed Hus, and had watched the career of Wycliffe with a growing anger that would have brought him, too, to the stake, had he not died a natural death before the wrath fell on him in his grave? Neither Hus nor Wycliffe was as bluntly defiant as Joan: both were reformers of the Church like Luther; whilst Joan, like Mrs Eddy, was quite prepared to supersede St Peter as the rock on which the Church was built, and, like Mahomet, was always ready with a private revelation from God to settle every question and fit every occasion.

The enormity of Joan's pretension was proved by her own unconsciousness of it, which we call her innocence, and her friends called her simplicity. Her solutions of the problems presented to her seemed, and indeed mostly were, the plainest commonsense, and their revelation to her by her Voices was to her a simple matter of fact. How could plain commonsense and simple fact seem to her to be that hideous thing, heresy? When rival prophetesses came into the field, she was down on them at once for liars and humbugs; but she never thought of them as heretics. She was in a state of invincible ignorance as to the Church's view; and the Church could not tolerate her pretensions without either waiving its authority or giving her a place beside the Trinity during her lifetime and in her teens, which was unthinkable. Thus an irresistible force met an immovable obstacle, and developed the heat that consumed poor Joan.

Mark and Andrew would have shared her innocence and her fate had they been dealt with by the Inquisition: that is why their accounts of the trial are as absurd as hers might have been could she have written one. All that can be said for their assumption that Cauchon was a vulgar villain, and that the questions put to Joan were traps, is that it has the support of the inquiry which rehabilitated her twentyfive years later. But this rehabilitation was as corrupt as the contrary proceeding applied to Cromwell by our Restoration reactionaries. Cauchon had been dug up, and his body thrown into the common sewer. Nothing was easier than to accuse him of cozenage, and declare the whole trial void on that account. That was what everybody wanted, from Charles the Victorious, whose credit was bound up with The Maid's, to the patriotic Nationalist populace, who idolized Joan's memory. The English were gone; and a verdict in their favor would have been an outrage on the throne and on the patriotism which Joan had set on foot.

We have none of these overwhelming motives of political convenience and popularity to bias us. For us the first trial stands valid and the rehabilitation would be negligible but for the mass of sincere testimony it produced as to Joan's engaging personal character. The question then arises: how did The Church get over the verdict at the first trial when it canonized Joan five hundred years later?

THE CHURCH UNCOMPROMISED BY ITS AMENDS

Easily enough. In the Catholic Church, far more than in law, there is no wrong without a remedy. It does not defer to Joanesque private judgment as such, the supremacy of private judgment for the individual being the quintessence of Protestantism; nevertheless it finds a place for private judgment *in excelsis* by admitting that the highest wisdom may come as a divine revelation to an individual. On sufficient evidence it will declare that individual a saint. Thus, as revelation may come by way of an enlightenment of the private judgment no less than by the words of a celestial personage appearing in a vision, a saint may be defined as a person of heroic virtue whose private judgment is privileged. Many innovating saints, notably Francis and Clare, have been in conflict with the Church during their lives, and have thus raised the question whether they were heretics or saints. Francis might have gone to the stake had he lived longer. It is therefore by no means impossible for a person to be excommunicated as a heretic, and on further consideration canonized as a saint. Excommunication by a provincial ecclesiastical court is not one of the acts for which the Church claims infallibility. Perhaps I had better inform my Protestant readers that the famous Dogma of Papal Infallibility is by far the most modest pretension of the kind in existence. Compared with our infallible democracies, our infallible medical councils, our infallible astronomers, our infallible judges, and our infallible parliaments, the Pope is on his knees in the dust confessing his ignorance before the throne of God, asking only that as to certain historical matters on which he has clearly more sources of information open to him than anyone else his decision shall be taken as final. The Church may, and perhaps some day will, canonize Galileo without compromising such infallibility as it claims for the Pope, if not without compromising the infallibility claimed for the Book of Joshua by simple souls whose rational faith in more important things has become bound up with a quite irrational faith in the chronicle of Joshua's campaigns as a treatise on physics. Therefore the Church will probably not canonize Galileo yet awhile, though it might do worse. But it has been able to canonize Joan without any compromise at all. She never doubted that the sun went round the earth: she had seen it do so too often.

Still, there was a great wrong done to Joan and to the conscience of the world by her burning. *Tout comprendre, c'est tout pardonner*, which is the Devil's sentimentality, cannot excuse it. When we have admitted that the tribunal was not only honest and legal, but exceptionally merciful in respect of sparing Joan the torture which was customary when she was obdurate as to taking the oath, and that Cauchon was far more self-disciplined and conscientious both as priest and lawyer than any English judge ever dreams of being in a political case in which his party and class prejudices are involved, the human fact remains that the burning of Joan of Arc was a horror, and that a historian who would defend it would defend anything. The final criticism of its physical side is implied in the refusal of the Marquesas islanders to be persuaded that the English did not eat Joan. Why, they ask, should anyone take the trouble to roast a human being except with that object? They cannot conceive its being a pleasure. As we have no answer for them that is not shameful to us, let us blush for our more complicated and pretentious savagery before we proceed to unravel the business further, and see what other lessons it contains for us.

CRUELTY, MODERN AND MEDIEVAL

First, let us get rid of the notion that the mere physical cruelty of the burning has any special significance. Joan was burnt just as dozens of less interesting heretics were burnt in her time. Christ, in being crucified, only shared the fate of thousands of forgotten malefactors. They have no pre-eminence in mere physical pain: much more horrible executions than theirs are on record, to say nothing of the agonies of so-called natural death as its worst.

Joan was burnt more than five hundred years ago. More than three hundred years later: that is, only about a hundred years before I was born, a woman was burnt on Stephen's Green in my native city of Dublin for coining, which was held to be treason. In my preface to the recent volume on English Prisons under Local Government, by Sidney and Beatrice Webb, I have mentioned that when I was already a grown man I saw Richard Wagner conduct two concerts, and that when Richard Wagner was a young man he saw and avoided a crowd of people hastening to see a soldier broken on the wheel by the more cruel of the two ways of carrying out that hideous method of execution. Also that the penalty of hanging, drawing, and quartering, unmentionable in its details, was abolished so recently that there are men living who have been sentenced to it. We are still flogging criminals, and clamoring for more flogging. Not even the most sensationally frightful of these atrocities inflicted on its victim the misery, degradation, and conscious waste and loss of life suffered in our modern prisons, especially the model ones, without, as far as I can see, rousing any more compunction than the burning of heretics did in the Middle Ages. We have not even the excuse of getting some fun out of our prisons as the Middle Ages did out of their stakes and wheels and gibbets. Joan herself judged this matter when she had to choose between imprisonment and the stake, and chose the stake. And thereby she deprived The Church of the plea that it was guiltless of her death, which was the work of the secular arm. The Church should have confined itself to excommunicating her. There it was within its rights: she had refused to accept its authority or comply with its conditions; and it could say with truth "You are not one of us: go forth and find the religion that suits you, or found one for yourself." It had no right to say "You may return to us now that you have recanted; but you shall stay in a dungeon all the rest of your life." Unfortunately, The Church did not believe that there was any genuine soul saving religion outside itself; and it was deeply corrupted, as all the Churches were and still are, by primitive Calibanism (in Browning's sense), or the propitiation of a dreaded deity by suffering and sacrifice. Its method was not cruelty for cruelty's sake, but cruelty for the salvation of Joan's soul. Joan, however, believed that the saving of her soul was her own business, and not that of *les gens d'église*. By using that term as she did, mistrustfully and contemptuously, she announced herself as, in germ, an anti-Clerical as thoroughgoing as Voltaire or Anatole France. Had she said in so many words "To the dustbin with the Church Militant and its blackcoated officials: I recognize only the Church Triumphant in heaven," she would hardly have put her view more plainly.

CATHOLIC ANTI-CLERICALISM

I must not leave it to be inferred here that one cannot be an anti-Clerical and a good Catholic too. All the reforming Popes have been vehement anti-Clericals, veritable scourges of the clergy. All the great Orders arose from dissatisfaction with the priests: that of the Franciscans with priestly snobbery, that of the Dominicans with priestly laziness and Laodiceanism, that of the Jesuits with priestly apathy and ignorance and indiscipline. The most bigoted Ulster Orangeman or Leicester Low Church bourgeois (as described by Mr Henry Nevinson) is a mere Gallio compared to Machiavelli, who, though no Protestant, was a fierce anti-Clerical. Any Catholic may, and many Catholics do, denounce any priest or body of priests, as lazy, drunken, idle, dissolute, and unworthy of their great Church and their function as the pastors of their flocks of human souls. But to say that the souls of the people are no business of the Churchmen is to go a step further, a step across the Rubicon. Joan virtually took that step.

CATHOLICISM NOT YET CATHOLIC ENOUGH

And so, if we admit, as we must, that the burning of Joan was a mistake, we must broaden Catholicism sufficiently to include her in its charter. Our Churches must admit that no official organization of mortal men whose vocation does not carry with it extraordinary mental powers (and this is all that any Church Militant can in the face of fact and history pretend to be), can keep pace with the private judgment of persons of genius except when, by a very rare accident, the genius happens to be Pope, and not even then unless he is an exceedingly overbearing Pope. The Churches must learn humility as well as teach it. The Apostolic Succession cannot be secured or confined by the laying on of hands: the tongues of fire have descended on heathens and outcasts too often for that, leaving anointed Churchmen to scandalize History as worldly rascals. When the Church Militant behaves as if it were already the Church Triumphant, it makes these appalling blunders about Joan and Bruno and Galileo and the rest which make it so difficult for a Freethinker to join it; and a Church which has no place for Freethinkers: nay, which does not inculcate and encourage freethinking with a complete belief that thought, when really free, must by its own law take the path that leads to The Church's bosom, not only has no future in modern culture, but obviously has no faith in the valid science of its own tenets, and is guilty of the heresy that theology and science are two different and opposite impulses, rivals for human allegiance.

I have before me the letter of a Catholic priest. "In your play," he writes, "I see the dramatic presentation of the conflict of the Regal, sacerdotal, and Prophetical powers, in which Joan was crushed. To me it is not the victory of any one of them over the others that will bring peace and the

Reign of the Saints in the Kingdom of God, but their fruitful interaction in a costly but noble state of tension." The Pope himself could not put it better; nor can I. We must accept the tension, and maintain it nobly without letting ourselves be tempted to relieve it by burning the thread. This is Joan's lesson to The Church; and its formulation by the hand of a priest emboldens me to claim that her canonization was a magnificently Catholic gesture as the canonization of a Protestant saint by the Church of Rome. But its special value and virtue cannot be apparent until it is known and understood as such. If any simple priest for whom this is too hard a saying tells me that it was not so intended, I shall remind him that the Church is in the hands of God, and not, as simple priests imagine, God in the hands of the Church; so if he answers too confidently for God's intentions he may be asked "Hast thou entered into the springs of the sea? or hast thou walked in the recesses of the deep?" And Joan's own answer is also the answer of old: "Though He slay me, yet will I trust in Him; *but I will maintain my own ways before Him.*"

THE LAW OF CHANGE IS THE LAW OF GOD

When Joan maintained her own ways she claimed, like Job, that there was not only God and the Church to be considered, but the Word made Flesh: that is, the unaveraged individual, representing life possibly at its highest actual human evolution and possibly at its lowest, but never at its merely mathematical average. Now there is no deification of the democratic average in the theory of the Church: it is an avowed hierarchy in which the members are sifted until at the end of the process an individual stands supreme as the Vicar of Christ. But when the process is examined it appears that its successive steps of selection and election are of the superior by the inferior (the cardinal vice of democracy), with the result that great popes are as rare and accidental as great kings, and that it has sometimes been safer for an aspirant to the Chair and the Keys to pass as a moribund dotard than as an energetic saint. At best very few popes have been canonized, or could be without letting down the standard of sanctity set by the self-elected saints.

No other result could have been reasonably expected; for it is not possible that an official organization of the spiritual needs of millions of men and women, mostly poor and ignorant, should compete successfully in the selection of its principals with the direct choice of the Holy Ghost as it flashes with unerring aim upon the individual. Nor can any College of Cardinals pray effectively that its choice may be inspired. The conscious prayer of the inferior may be that his choice may light on a greater than himself; but the sub-conscious intention of his self-preserving individuality must be to find a trustworthy servant for his own purposes. The saints and prophets, though they may be accidentally in this or that official position or rank, are always really self-selected, like Joan. And since neither Church nor State, by the secular necessities of its constitution, can guarantee even the recognition of such self-chosen missions, there is nothing for us but to make it a point of honour to privilege heresy to the last bearable degree on the simple ground that all evolution in thought and conduct must at first appear as heresy and misconduct. In short, though all society is founded on intolerance, all improvement is founded on tolerance, or the recognition of the fact that the law of evolution is Ibsen's law of change. And as the law of God in any sense of the word which can now command a faith proof against science is a law of evolution, it follows that the law of God is a law of change, and that when the Churches set themselves against change as such, they are setting themselves against the law of God.

CREDULITY, MODERN AND MEDIEVAL

When Abernethy, the famous doctor, was asked why he indulged himself with all the habits he warned his patients against as unhealthy, he replied that his business was that of a direction post, which points out the way to a place, but does not go thither itself. He might have added that neither does it compel the traveller to go thither, nor prevent him from seeking some other way. Unfortunately our clerical direction posts always do coerce the traveller when they have the political power to do so. When the Church was a temporal as well as a spiritual power, and for long after to the full extent to which it could control or influence the temporal power, it enforced conformity by persecutions that were all the more ruthless because their intention was so excellent. Today, when the doctor has succeeded to the priest, and can do practically what he likes with parliament and the press through the blind faith in him which has succeeded to the far more critical faith in the parson, legal compulsion to take the doctor's prescription, however poisonous, is carried to an extent that would have horrified the Inquisition and staggered Archbishop Laud. Our credulity is grosser than that of the Middle Ages, because the priest had no such direct pecuniary interest in our sins as the doctor has in our diseases: he did not starve when all was well with his flock, nor prosper when they were perishing, as our private commercial doctors must. Also the medieval cleric believed that something extremely unpleasant would happen to him after death if he was unscrupulous, a belief now practically extinct among persons receiving a dogmatically materialist education. Our professional corporations are Trade Unions without souls to be damned; and they will soon drive us to remind them that they have bodies to be kicked. The Vatican was never soulless: at worst it was a political conspiracy to make the Church supreme temporally as well as spiritually. Therefore the question raised by Joan's burning is a burning question still, though the penalties involved are not so sensational. That is why I am probing it. If it were only an historical curiosity I would not waste my readers' time and my own on it for five minutes.

TOLERATION, MODERN AND MEDIEVAL

The more closely we grapple with it the more difficult it becomes. At first sight we are disposed to repeat that Joan should have been excommunicated and then left to go her own way, though she would have protested vehemently against so cruel a deprivation of her spiritual food; for confession, absolution, and the body of her Lord were first necessaries of life to her. Such a spirit as Joan's might have got over that difficulty as the Church of England got over the Bulls of Pope Leo, by making a Church of her own, and affirming it to be the temple of the true and original faith from which her persecutors had strayed. But as such a proceeding was, in the eyes of both Church and State at that time, a spreading of damnation and anarchy, its toleration involved a greater strain on faith in freedom than political and ecclesiastical human nature could bear. It is easy to say that the Church should have waited for the alleged evil results instead of assuming that they would occur, and what they would be. That sounds simple enough; but if a modern Public Health Authority were to leave people entirely to their own devices in the matter of sanitation, saying, "We have nothing to do with drainage or your views about drainage; but if you catch smallpox or typhus we will prosecute you and have you punished very severely like the authorities in Butler's Erewhon," it would either be removed to the County Asylum or reminded that A's neglect of sanitation may kill the child of B two miles off, or start an epidemic in which the most conscientious sanitarians may perish.

We must face the fact that society is founded on intolerance. There are glaring cases of the abuse of intolerance; but they are quite as characteristic of our own age as of the Middle Ages. The typical modern example and contrast is compulsory inoculation replacing what was virtually compulsory baptism. But compulsion to inoculate is objected to as a crudely unscientific and mischievous anti-sanitary quackery, not in the least because we think it wrong to compel people to protect their children from disease. Its opponents would make it a crime, and will probably succeed in doing so; and that will be just as intolerant as making it compulsory. Neither the Pasteurians nor their opponents the Sanitarians would leave parents free to bring up their children naked, though that course also has some plausible advocates. We may prate of toleration as we will; but society must always draw a line somewhere between allowable conduct and insanity or crime, in spite of the risk of mistaking sages for lunatics and saviors for blasphemers. We must persecute, even to the death; and all we can do to mitigate the danger of persecution is, first, to be very careful what we persecute, and second, to bear in mind that unless there is a large liberty to shock conventional people, and a well informed sense of the value of originality, individuality, and eccentricity, the result will be apparent stagnation covering a repression of evolutionary forces which will eventually explode with extravagant and probably destructive violence.

VARIABILITY OF TOLERATION

The degree of tolerance attainable at any moment depends on the strain under which society is maintaining its cohesion. In war, for instance, we suppress the gospels and put Quakers in prison, muzzle the newspapers, and make it a serious offence to shew a light at night. Under the strain of invasion the French Government in 1792 struck off 4000 heads, mostly on grounds that would not in time of settled peace have provoked any Government to chloroform a dog; and in 1920 the British Government slaughtered and burnt in Ireland to persecute the advocates of a constitutional change which it had presently to effect itself. Later on the Fascisti in Italy did everything that the Black and Tans did in Ireland, with some grotesquely ferocious variations, under the strain of an unskilled attempt at industrial revolution by Socialists who understood Socialism even less than Capitalists understand Capitalism. In the United States an incredibly savage persecution of Russians took place during the scare spread by the Russian Bolshevik revolution after 1917. These instances could easily be multiplied; but they are enough to shew that between a maximum of indulgent toleration and a ruthlessly intolerant Terrorism there is a scale through which toleration is continually rising or falling, and that there was not the smallest ground for the self-complacent conviction of the nineteenth century that it was more tolerant than the fifteenth, or that such an event as the execution of Joan could not possibly occur in what we call our own more enlightened times. Thousands of women, each of them a thousand times less dangerous and terrifying to our Governments than Joan was to the Government of her day, have within the last ten years been slaughtered, starved to death, burnt out of house and home, and what not that Persecution and Terror could do to them, in the course of Crusades far more tyrannically pretentious than the medieval Crusades which proposed nothing more hyperbolical than the rescue of the Holy Sepulchre from the Saracens. The Inquisition, with its English equivalent the Star Chamber, are gone in the sense that their names are now disused; but can any of the modern substitutes for the Inquisition, the Special Tribunals and Commissions, the punitive expeditions, the suspensions of the Habeas Corpus Act, the proclamations of martial law and of minor states of siege, and the rest of them, claim that their victims have as fair a trial, as well considered a body of law to govern their cases, or as conscientious a judge to insist on strict legality of procedure as Joan had from the Inquisition and from the spirit of the Middle Ages even when her country was under the heaviest strain of civil and foreign war? From us she would have had no trial and no law except a Defence of The Realm Act suspending all law; and for judge she would have had, at best, a bothered major, and at worst a promoted advocate in ermine and scarlet to whom the scruples of a trained ecclesiastic like Cauchon would seem ridiculous and ungentlemanly.

THE CONFLICT BETWEEN GENIUS AND DISCIPLINE

Having thus brought the matter home to ourselves, we may now consider the special feature of Joan's mental constitution which made her so unmanageable. What is to be done on the one hand with rulers who will not give any reason for their orders, and on the other with people who cannot understand the reasons when they are given? The government of the world, political, industrial, and domestic, has to be carried on mostly by the giving and obeying of orders under just these conditions. "Dont argue: do as you are told" has to be said not only to children and soldiers, but practically to everybody. Fortunately most people do not want to argue: they are only too glad to be saved the trouble of thinking for themselves. And the ablest and most independent thinkers are content to understand their own special department. In other departments they will unhesitatingly ask for and accept the instructions of a policeman or the advice of a tailor without demanding or desiring explanations.

Nevertheless, there must be some ground for attaching authority to an order. A child will obey its parents, a soldier his officer, a philosopher a railway porter, and a workman a foreman, all without question, because it is generally accepted that those who give the orders understand what they are about, and are duly authorized and even obliged to give them, and because, in the practical emergencies of daily life, there is no time for lessons and explanations, or for arguments as to their validity. Such obediences are as necessary to the continuous operation of our social system as the revolutions of the earth are to the succession of night and day. But they are not so spontaneous as they seem: they have to be very carefully arranged and maintained. A bishop will defer to and obey a king; but let a curate venture to give him an order, however necessary and sensible, and the bishop will forget his cloth and damn the curate's impudence. The more obedient a man is to accredited authority the more jealous he is of allowing any unauthorized person to order him about.

With all this in mind, consider the career of Joan. She was a village girl, in authority over sheep and pigs, dogs and chickens, and to some extent over her father's hired laborers when he hired any, but over no one else on earth. Outside the farm she had no authority, no prestige, no claim to the smallest deference. Yet she ordered everybody about, from her uncle to the king, the archbishop, and the military General Staff. Her uncle obeyed her like a sheep, and took her to the castle of the local commander, who, on being ordered about, tried to assert himself, but soon collapsed and obeyed. And so on up to the king, as we have seen. This would have been unbearably irritating even if her orders had been offered as rational solutions of the desperate difficulties in which her social superiors found themselves just then. But they were not so offered. Nor were they offered as the expression of Joan's arbitrary will. It was never "I say so," but always "God says so."

JOAN AS THEOCRAT

Leaders who take that line have no trouble with some people, and no end of trouble with others. They need never fear a lukewarm reception. Either they are messengers of God, or they are blasphemous impostors. In the Middle Ages the general belief in witchcraft greatly intensified this contrast, because when an apparent miracle happened (as in the case of the wind changing at Orleans) it proved the divine mission to the credulous, and proved a contract with the devil to the sceptical. All through, Joan had to depend on those who accepted her as an incarnate angel against those who added to an intense resentment of her presumption a bigoted abhorrence of her as a witch. To this abhorrence we must add the extreme irritation of those who did not believe in the voices, and regarded her as a liar and impostor. It is hard to conceive anything more infuriating to a statesman or a military commander, or to a court favorite, than to be overruled at every turn, or to be robbed of the ear of the reigning sovereign, by an impudent young upstart practising on the credulity of the populace and the vanity and silliness of an immature prince by exploiting a few of those lucky coincidences which pass as miracles with uncritical people. Not only were the envy, snobbery, and competitive ambition of the baser natures exacerbated by Joan's success, but among the friendly ones that were clever enough to be critical a quite reasonable scepticism and mistrust of her ability, founded on a fair observation of her obvious ignorance and temerity, were at work against her. And as she met all remonstrances and all criticisms, not with arguments or persuasion, but with a flat appeal to the authority of God and a claim to be in God's special confidence, she must have seemed, to all who were not infatuated by her, so insufferable that nothing but an unbroken chain of overwhelming successes in the military and political field could have saved her from the wrath that finally destroyed her.

UNBROKEN SUCCESS ESSENTIAL IN THEOCRACY

To forge such a chain she needed to be the King, the Archbishop of Rheims, the Bastard of Orleans, and herself into the bargain; and that was impossible. From the moment when she failed to stimulate Charles to follow up his coronation with a swoop on Paris she was lost. The fact that she insisted on this whilst the king and the rest timidly and foolishly thought they could square the Duke of Burgundy, and effect a combination with him against the English, made her a terrifying nuisance to them; and from that time onward she could do nothing but prowl about the battlefields waiting for some lucky chance to sweep the captains into a big move. But it was to the enemy that the chance came: she was taken prisoner by the Burgundians fighting before Compiègne, and at once discovered that she had not a friend in the political world. Had she escaped she would probably have fought on until the English were gone, and then had to shake the dust of the court off her feet, and retire to Domrémy as Garibaldi had to retire to Caprera.

MODERN DISTORTIONS OF JOAN'S HISTORY

This, I think, is all that we can now pretend to say about the prose of Joan's career. The romance of her rise, the tragedy of her execution, and the comedy of the attempts of posterity to make amends for that execution, belong to my play and not to my preface, which must be confined to a sober essay on the facts. That such an essay is badly needed can be ascertained by examining any of our standard works of reference. They give accurately enough the facts about the visit to Vaucouleurs, the annunciation to Charles at Chinon, the raising of the siege of Orleans and the subsequent battles, the coronation at Rheims, the capture at Compiegne, and the trial and execution at Rouen, with their dates and the names of the people concerned; but they all break down on the melodramatic legend of the wicked bishop and the entrapped maiden and the rest of it. It would be far less misleading if they were wrong as to the facts, and right in their view of the facts. As it is, they illustrate the too little considered truth that the fashion in which we think changes like the fashion of our clothes, and that it is difficult, if not impossible, for most people to think otherwise than in the fashion of their own period.

HISTORY ALWAYS OUT OF DATE

This, by the way, is why children are never taught contemporary history. Their history books deal with periods of which the thinking has passed out of fashion, and the circumstances no longer apply to active life. For example, they are taught history about Washington, and told lies about Lenin. In Washington's time they were told lies (the same lies) about Washington, and taught history about Cromwell. In the fifteenth and sixteenth centuries they were told lies about Joan, and by this time might very well be told the truth about her. Unfortunately the lies did not cease when the political circumstances became obsolete. The Reformation, which Joan had unconsciously anticipated, kept the questions which arose in her case burning up to our own day (you can see plenty of the burnt houses still in Ireland), with the result that Joan has remained the subject of anti-Clerical lies, of specifically Protestant lies, and of Roman Catholic evasions of her unconscious Protestantism. The truth sticks in our throats with all the sauces it is served with: it will never go down until we take it without any sauce at all.

THE REAL JOAN NOT MARVELLOUS ENOUGH FOR US

But even in its simplicity, the faith demanded by Joan is one which the anti-metaphysical temper of nineteenth century civilization, which remains powerful in England and America, and is tyrannical in France, contemptuously refuses her. We do not, like her contemporaries, rush to the opposite extreme in a recoil from her as from a witch self-sold to the devil, because we do not believe in the devil nor in the possibility of commercial contracts with him. Our credulity, though enormous, is not boundless; and our stock of it is quite used up by our mediums, clairvoyants, hand readers, slate writers, Christian Scientists, psycho-analysts, electronic vibration diviners, therapeutists of all schools registered and unregistered, astrologers, astronomers who tell us that the sun is nearly a hundred million miles away and that Betelgeuse is ten times as big as the whole universe, physicists who balance Betelgeuse by describing the incredible smallness of the atom, and a host of other marvel mongers whose credulity would have dissolved the Middle Ages in a roar of sceptical merriment. In the Middle Ages people believed that the earth was flat, for which they had at least the evidence of their senses: we believe it to be round, not because as many as one per cent of us could give the physical reasons for so quaint a belief, but because modern science has convinced us that nothing that is obvious is true, and that everything that is magical, improbable, extraordinary, gigantic, microscopic, heartless, or outrageous is scientific.

I must not, by the way, be taken as implying that the earth is flat, or that all or any of our amazing credulities are delusions or impostures. I am only defending my own age against the charge of being less imaginative than the Middle Ages. I affirm that the nineteenth century, and still more the twentieth, can knock the fifteenth into a cocked hat in point of susceptibility to marvels and miracles and saints and prophets and magicians and monsters and fairy tales of all kinds. The proportion of marvel to immediately credible statement in the latest edition of the Encyclopædia Britannica is enormously greater than in the Bible. The medieval doctors of divinity who did not pretend to settle how many angels could dance on the point of a needle cut a very poor figure as far as romantic credulity is concerned beside the modern physicists who have settled to the billionth of a millimetre every movement and position in the dance of the electrons. Not for worlds would I question the precise accuracy of these calculations or the existence of electrons (whatever they may be). The fate of Joan is a warning to me against such heresy. But why the men who believe in electrons should regard themselves as less credulous than the men who believed in angels is not apparent to me. If they refuse to believe, with the Rouen assessors of 1431, that Joan was a witch, it is not because that explanation is too marvellous, but because it is not marvellous enough.

THE STAGE LIMITS OF HISTORICAL REPRESENTATION

For the story of Joan I refer the reader to the play which follows. It contains all that need be known about her; but as it is for stage use I have had to condense into three and a half hours a series of events which in their historical happening were spread over four times as many months; for the theatre imposes unities of time and place from which Nature in her boundless wastefulness is free. Therefore the reader must not suppose that Joan really put Robert de Baudricourt in her pocket in fifteen minutes, nor that her excommunication, recantation, relapse, and death at the stake were a matter of half an hour or so. Neither do I claim more for my dramatizations of Joan's contemporaries than that some of them are probably slightly more like the originals than those imaginary portraits of all the Popes from Saint Peter onward through the Dark Ages which are still gravely exhibited in the Uffizi in Florence (or were when I was there last). My Dunois would do equally well for the Duc d'Alençon. Both left descriptions of Joan so similar that, as a man always describes himself unconsciously whenever he describes anyone else, I have inferred that these good-natured young men were very like one another in mind; so I have lumped the twain into a single figure, thereby saving the theatre manager a salary and a suit of armor. Dunois' face, still on record at Châteaudun, is a suggestive help. But I really know no more about these men and their circle than Shakespear knew about Falconbridge and the Duke of Austria, or about Macbeth and Macduff. In view of the things they did in history, and have to do again in the play, I can only invent appropriate characters for them in Shakespear's manner.

A VOID IN THE ELIZABETHAN DRAMA

I have, however, one advantage over the Elizabethans. I write in full view of the Middle Ages, which may be said to have been rediscovered in the middle of the nineteenth century after an eclipse of about four hundred and fifty years. The Renascence of antique literature and art in the sixteenth century, and the lusty growth of Capitalism, between them buried the Middle Ages; and their resurrection is a second Renascence. Now there is not a breath of medieval atmosphere in Shakespear's histories. His John of Gaunt is like a study of the old age of Drake. Although he was a Catholic by family tradition, his figures are all intensely Protestant, individualist, sceptical, self-centered in everything but their love affairs, and completely personal and selfish even in them. His kings are not statesmen: his cardinals have no religion: a novice can read his plays from one end to the other without learning that the world is finally governed by forces expressing themselves in religions and laws which make epochs rather than by vulgarly ambitious individuals who make rows. The divinity which shapes our ends, rough hew them how we will, is mentioned fatalistically only to be forgotten immediately like a passing vague apprehension. To Shakespear as to Mark Twain, Cauchon would have been a tyrant and a bully instead of a Catholic, and the inquisitor Lemaître would have been a Sadist instead of a lawyer. Warwick would have had no more feudal quality than his successor the King Maker has in the play of Henry VI. We should have seen them all completely satisfied that if they would only to their own selves be true they could not then be false to any man (a precept which represents the reaction against medievalism at its intensest) as if they were beings in the air, without public responsibilities of any kind. All Shakespear's characters are so: that is why they seem natural to our middle classes, who are comfortable and irresponsible at other people's expense, and are neither ashamed of that condition nor even conscious of it. Nature abhors this vacuum in Shakespear; and I have taken care to let the medieval atmosphere blow through my play freely. Those who see it performed will not mistake the startling event it records for a mere personal accident. They will have before them not only the visible and human puppets, but the Church, the Inquisition, the Feudal System, with divine inspiration always beating against their too inelastic limits: all more terrible in their dramatic force than any of the little mortal figures clanking about in plate armor or moving silently in the frocks and hoods of the order of St Dominic.

TRAGEDY, NOT MELODRAMA

There are no villains in the piece. Crime, like disease, is not interesting: it is something to be done away with by general consent, and that is all about it. It is what men do at their best, with good intentions, and what normal men and women find that they must and will do in spite of their intentions, that really concern us. The rascally bishop and the cruel inquisitor of Mark Twain and Andrew Lang are as dull as pickpockets; and they reduce Joan to the level of the even less interesting person whose pocket is picked. I have represented both of them as capable and eloquent exponents of The Church Militant and The Church Litigant, because only by doing so can I maintain my drama on the level of high tragedy and save it from becoming a mere police court sensation. A villain in a play can never be anything more than a *diabolus ex machina*, possibly a more exciting expedient than a *deus ex machina*, but both equally mechanical, and therefore interesting only as mechanism. It is, I repeat, what normally innocent people do that concerns us; and if Joan had not been burnt by normally innocent people in the energy of their righteousness her death at their hands would have no more significance than the Tokyo earthquake, which burnt a great many maidens. The tragedy of such murders is that they are not committed by murderers. They are judicial murders, pious murders; and this contradiction at once brings an element of comedy into the tragedy: the angels may weep at the murder, but the gods laugh at the murderers.

THE INEVITABLE FLATTERIES OF TRAGEDY

Here then we have a reason why my drama of Saint Joan's career, though it may give the essential truth of it, gives an inexact picture of some accidental facts. It goes almost without saying that the old Jeanne d'Arc melodramas, reducing everything to a conflict of villain and hero, or in Joan's case villain and heroine, not only miss the point entirely, but falsify the characters, making Cauchon a scoundrel, Joan a prima donna, and Dunois a lover. But the writer of high tragedy and comedy, aiming at the innermost attainable truth, must needs flatter Cauchon nearly as much as the melodramatist vilifies him. Although there is, as far as I have been able to discover, nothing against Cauchon that convicts him of bad faith or exceptional severity in his judicial relations with Joan, or of as much anti-prisoner, pro-police, class and sectarian bias as we now take for granted in our own courts, yet there is hardly more warrant for classing him as a great Catholic churchman, completely proof against the passions roused by the temporal situation. Neither does the inquisitor Lemaître, in such scanty accounts of him as are now recoverable, appear quite so able a master of his duties and of the case before him as I have given him credit for being. But it is the business of the stage to make its figures more intelligible to themselves than they would be in real life; for by no other means can they be made intelligible to the audience. And in this case Cauchon and Lemaître have to make intelligible not only themselves but the Church and the Inquisition, just as Warwick has to make the feudal system intelligible, the three between them having thus to make a twentieth-century audience conscious of an epoch fundamentally different from its own. Obviously the real Cauchon, Lemaître, and Warwick could not have done this: they were part of the Middle Ages themselves, and therefore as unconscious of its peculiarities as of the atomic formula of the air they breathed. But the play would be unintelligible if I had not endowed them with enough of this consciousness to enable them to explain their attitude to the twentieth century. All I claim is that by this inevitable sacrifice of verisimilitude I have secured in the only possible way sufficient veracity to justify me in claiming that as far as I can gather from the available documentation, and from such powers of divination as I possess, the things I represent these three exponents of the drama as saying are the things they actually would have said if they had known what they were really doing. And beyond this neither drama nor history can go in my hands.

SOME WELL-MEANT PROPOSALS FOR THE IMPROVEMENT OF THE PLAY

I have to thank several critics on both sides of the Atlantic, including some whose admiration for my play is most generously enthusiastic, for their heartfelt instructions as to how it can be improved. They point out that by the excision of the epilogue and all the references to such undramatic and tedious matters as the Church, the feudal system, the Inquisition, the theory of heresy and so forth, all of which, they point out, would be ruthlessly blue pencilled by any experienced manager, the play could be considerably shortened. I think they are mistaken. The experienced knights of the blue pencil, having saved an hour and a half by disembowelling the play, would at once proceed to waste two hours in building elaborate scenery, having real water in the river Loire and a real bridge across it, and staging an obviously sham fight for possession of it, with the victorious French led by Joan on a real horse. The coronation would eclipse all previous theatrical displays, shewing, first, the procession through the streets of Rheims, and then the service in the cathedral, with special music written for both. Joan would be burnt on the stage, as Mr Matheson Lang always is in The Wandering Jew, on the principle that it does not matter in the least why a woman is burnt provided she is burnt, and people can pay to see it done. The intervals between the acts whilst these splendors were being built up and then demolished by the stage carpenters would seem eternal, to the great profit of the refreshment bars. And the weary and demoralized audience would lose their last trains and curse me for writing such inordinately long and intolerably dreary and meaningless plays. But the applause of the press would be unanimous. Nobody who knows the stage history of Shakespear will doubt that this is what would happen if I knew my business so little as to listen to these well intentioned but disastrous counsellors: indeed it probably will happen when I am no longer in control of the performing rights. So perhaps it will be as well for the public to see the play while I am still alive.

THE EPILOGUE

As to the epilogue, I could hardly be expected to stultify myself by implying that Joan's history in the world ended unhappily with her execution, instead of beginning there. It was necessary by hook or crook to shew the canonized Joan as well as the incinerated one; for many a woman has got herself burnt by carelessly whisking a muslin skirt into the drawing room fireplace, but getting canonized is a different matter, and a more important one. So I am afraid the epilogue must stand.

TO THE CRITICS, LEST THEY SHOULD FEEL IGNORED

To a professional critic (I have been one myself) theatregoing is the curse of Adam. The play is the evil he is paid to endure in the sweat of his brow; and the sooner it is over, the better. This would seem to place him in irreconcilable opposition to the paying playgoer, from whose point of view the longer the play, the more entertainment he gets for his money. It does in fact so place him, especially in the provinces, where the playgoer goes to the theatre for the sake of the play solely, and insists so effectively on a certain number of hours' entertainment that touring managers are sometimes seriously embarrassed by the brevity of the London plays they have to deal in.

For in London the critics are reinforced by a considerable body of persons who go to the theatre as many others go to church, to display their best clothes and compare them with other people's; to be in the fashion, and have something to talk about at dinner parties; to adore a pet performer; to pass the evening anywhere rather than at home: in short, for any or every reason except interest in dramatic art as such. In fashionable centres the number of irreligious people who go to church, of unmusical people who go to concerts and operas, and of undramatic people who go to the theatre, is so prodigious that sermons have been cut down to ten minutes and plays to two hours; and, even at that, congregations sit longing for the benediction and audiences for the final curtain, so that they may get away to the lunch or supper they really crave for, after arriving as late as (or later than) the hour of beginning can possibly be made for them.

Thus from the stalls and in the Press an atmosphere of hypocrisy spreads. Nobody says straight out that genuine drama is a tedious nuisance, and that to ask people to endure more than two hours of it (with two long intervals of relief) is an intolerable imposition. Nobody says "I hate classical tragedy and comedy as I hate sermons and symphonies; but I like police news and divorce news and any kind of dancing or decoration that has an aphrodisiac effect on me or on my wife or husband. And whatever superior people may pretend, I cannot associate pleasure with any sort of intellectual activity; and I dont believe anyone else can either." Such things are not said; yet nine-tenths of what is offered as criticism of the drama in the metropolitan Press of Europe and America is nothing but a muddled paraphrase of it. If it does not mean that, it means nothing.

I do not complain of this, though it complains very unreasonably of me. But I can take no more notice of it than Einstein of the people who are incapable of mathematics. I write in the classical manner for those who pay for admission to a theatre because they like classical comedy or tragedy for its own sake, and like it so much when it is good of its kind and well done that they tear themselves away from it with reluctance to catch the very latest train or omnibus that will take them home. Far from arriving late from an eight or half-past eight o'clock dinner so as to escape at least the first half-hour of the performance, they stand in queues outside the theatre doors for hours beforehand in bitingly cold weather to secure a seat. In countries where a play lasts a week, they bring baskets of provisions and sit it out. These are the patrons on whom I depend for my bread. I do not give them performances twelve hours long, because circumstances do not at present make such entertainments feasible; though a performance beginning after breakfast and ending at sunset is as possible physically and artistically in Surrey or Middlesex as in Ober-Ammergau; and an all-night sitting in a theatre would be at least as enjoyable as an all-night sitting in the House of Commons, and much more useful. But in St Joan I have done my best by going to the well-established classical limit of three and a half hours practically continuous playing, barring the one interval imposed by considerations which have nothing to do with art. I know that this is hard on the pseudo-critics and on the fashionable people whose playgoing is a hypocrisy. I cannot help feeling some compassion for them when they assure me that my play, though a great play, must fail hopelessly, because it does not begin at a quarter to nine and end at eleven. The facts are overwhelmingly against them. They forget that all men are not as they are. Still, I am sorry for them; and though I cannot for their sakes undo my work and help the people who hate the theatre to drive out the people who love it, yet I may point out to them that they have several remedies in their own hands. They can escape the first part of the play by their usual practice of arriving late. They can escape the epilogue by not waiting for it. And if the irreducible minimum thus attained is still too painful, they can stay away altogether. But I deprecate this extreme course, because it is good neither for my pocket nor for their own souls. Already a few of them, noticing that what matters is not the absolute length of time occupied by a play, but the speed with which that times passes, are discovering that the theatre, though purgatorial in its Aristotelian moments, is not necessarily always the dull place they have so often found it. What do its discomforts matter when the play makes us forget them?

Ayot St Lawrence,
May 1924.

SAINT JOAN

SCENE I

A FINE spring morning on the river Meuse, between Lorraine and Champagne, in the year 1429 A.D., *in the castle of Vaucouleurs.*

Captain Robert de Baudricourt, a military squire, handsome and physically energetic, but with no will of his own, is disguising that defect in his usual fashion by storming terribly at his steward, a trodden worm, scanty of flesh, scanty of hair, who might be any age from 18 *to* 55, *being the sort of man whom age cannot wither because he has never bloomed.*

The two are in a sunny stone chamber on the first floor of the castle. At a plain strong oak table, seated in chair to match, the captain presents his left profile. The steward stands facing him at the other side of the table, if so deprecatory a stance as his can be called standing. The mullioned thirteenth-century window is open behind him. Near it in the corner is a turret with a narrow arched doorway leading to a winding stair which descends to the courtyard. There is a stout fourlegged stool under the table, and a wooden chest under the window.

ROBERT. No eggs! No eggs!! Thousand thunders, man, what do you mean by no eggs?

STEWARD. Sir: it is not my fault. It is the act of God.

ROBERT. Blasphemy. You tell me there are no eggs; and you blame your Maker for it.

STEWARD. Sir: what can I do? I cannot lay eggs.

ROBERT [*sarcastic*] Ha! You jest about it.

STEWARD. No, sir, God knows. We all have to go without eggs just as you have, sir. The hens will not lay.

ROBERT. Indeed! [*Rising*] Now listen to me, you.

STEWARD [*humbly*] Yes, sir.

ROBERT. What am I?

STEWARD. What are you, sir?

ROBERT [*coming at him*] Yes: what am I? Am I Robert, squire of Baudricourt and captain of this castle of Vaucouleurs; or am I a cowboy?

STEWARD. Oh, sir, you know you are a greater man here

than the king himself.

ROBERT. Precisely. And now, do you know what you are?

STEWARD. I am nobody, sir, except that I have the honor to be your steward.

ROBERT [*driving him to the wall, adjective by adjective*] You have not only the honor of being my steward, but the privilege of being the worst, most incompetent, drivelling snivelling jibbering jabbering idiot of a steward in France. [*He strides back to the table*].

STEWARD [*cowering on the chest*] Yes, sir: to a great man like you I must seem like that.

ROBERT [*turning*] My fault, I suppose. Eh?

STEWARD [*coming to him deprecatingly*] Oh, sir: you always give my most innocent words such a turn!

ROBERT. I will give your neck a turn if you dare tell me, when I ask you how many eggs there are, that you cannot lay any.

STEWARD [*protesting*] Oh sir, oh sir—

ROBERT. No: not oh sir, oh sir, but no sir, no sir. My three Barbary hens and the black are the best layers in Champagne. And you come and tell me that there are no eggs! Who stole them? Tell me that, before I kick you out through the castle gate for a liar and a seller of my goods to thieves. The milk was short yesterday, too: do not forget that.

STEWARD [*desperate*] I know, sir. I know only too well. There is no milk: there are no eggs: tomorrow there will be nothing.

ROBERT. Nothing! You will steal the lot: eh?

STEWARD. No, sir: nobody will steal anything. But there is a spell on us: we are bewitched.

ROBERT. That story is not good enough for me. Robert de Baudricourt burns witches and hangs thieves. Go. Bring me four dozen eggs and two gallons of milk here in this room before noon, or Heaven have mercy on your bones! I will teach you to make a fool of me. [*He resumes his seat with an air of finality*].

STEWARD. Sir: I tell you there are no eggs. There will be

none—not if you were to kill me for it—as long as The Maid is at the door.

ROBERT. The Maid! What maid? What are you talking about?

STEWARD. The girl from Lorraine, sir. From Domrémy.

ROBERT [*rising in fearful wrath*] Thirty thousand thunders! Fifty thousand devils! Do you mean to say that that girl, who had the impudence to ask to see me two days ago, and whom I told you to send back to her father with my orders that he was to give her a good hiding, is here still?

STEWARD. I have told her to go, sir. She wont.

ROBERT. I did not tell you to tell her to go: I told you to throw her out. You have fifty men-at-arms and a dozen lumps of ablebodied servants to carry out my orders. Are they afraid of her?

STEWARD. She is so positive, sir.

ROBERT [*seizing him by the scruff of the neck*] Positive! Now see here. I am going to throw you downstairs.

STEWARD. No, sir. Please.

ROBERT. Well, stop me by being positive. It's quite easy: any slut of a girl can do it.

STEWARD [*hanging limp in his hands*] Sir, sir: you cannot get rid of her by throwing me out. [*Robert has to let him drop. He squats on his knees on the floor, contemplating his master resignedly*]. You see, sir, you are much more positive than I am. But so is she.

ROBERT. I am stronger than you are, you fool.

STEWARD. No, sir: it isnt that: it's your strong character, sir. She is weaker than we are: she is only a slip of a girl; but we cannot make her go.

ROBERT. You parcel of curs: you are afraid of her.

STEWARD [*rising cautiously*] No, sir: we are afraid of you; but she puts courage into us. She really doesnt seem to be afraid of anything. Perhaps you could frighten her, sir.

ROBERT [*grimly*] Perhaps. Where is she now?

STEWARD. Down in the courtyard, sir, talking to the soldiers as usual. She is always talking to the soldiers except when she is praying.

ROBERT. Praying! Ha! You believe she prays, you idiot. I know the sort of girl that is always talking to soldiers. She shall talk to me a bit. [*He goes to the window and shouts fiercely through it*] Hallo, you there!

A GIRL'S VOICE [*bright, strong and rough*] Is it me, sir?

ROBERT. Yes, you.

THE VOICE. Be you captain?

ROBERT. Yes, damn your impudence, I be captain. Come up here. [*To the soldiers in the yard*] Shew her the way, you. And shove her along quick. [*He leaves the window, and returns to his place at the table, where he sits magisterially*].

STEWARD [*whispering*] She wants to go and be a soldier herself. She wants you to give her soldier's clothes. Armor, sir! And a sword! Actually! [*He steals behind Robert*].

Joan appears in the turret doorway. She is an ablebodied country girl of 17 *or* 18, *respectably dressed in red, with an uncommon face: eyes very wide apart and bulging as they often do in very imaginative people, a long well-shaped nose with wide nostrils, a short upper lip, resolute but full-lipped mouth, and handsome fighting chin. She comes eagerly to the table, delighted at having penetrated to Baudricourt's presence at last, and full of hope as to the result. His scowl does not check or frighten her in the least. Her voice is normally a hearty coaxing voice, very confident, very appealing, very hard to resist.*

JOAN [*bobbing a curtsey*] Good morning, captain squire. Captain: you are to give me a horse and armor and some soldiers, and send me to the Dauphin. Those are your orders from my Lord.

ROBERT [*outraged*] Orders from *your* lord! And who the devil may your lord be? Go back to him, and tell him that I am neither duke nor peer at his orders: I am squire of Baudricourt; and I take no orders except from the king.

JOAN [*reassuringly*] Yes, squire: that is all right. My Lord is the King of Heaven.

ROBERT. Why, the girl's mad. [*To the steward*] Why didnt you tell me so, you blockhead?

STEWARD. Sir: do not anger her: give her what she wants.

JOAN [*impatient, but friendly*] They all say I am mad until I talk to them, squire. But you see that it is the will of God that you are to do what He has put into my mind.

ROBERT. It is the will of God that I shall send you back to your father with orders to put you under lock and key and thrash the madness out of you. What have you to say to that?

JOAN. You think you will, squire; but you will find it all coming quite different. You said you would not see me; but here I am.

STEWARD [*appealing*] Yes, sir. You see, sir.

ROBERT. Hold your tongue, you.

STEWARD [*abjectly*] Yes, sir.

ROBERT [*to Joan, with a sour loss of confidence*] So you are presuming on my seeing you, are you?

JOAN [*sweetly*] Yes, squire.

ROBERT [*feeling that he has lost ground, brings down his two fists squarely on the table, and inflates his chest imposingly to cure the unwelcome and only too familiar sensation*] Now listen to me. I am going to assert myself.

JOAN [*busily*] Please do, squire. The horse will cost sixteen francs. It is a good deal of money; but I can save it on the armor. I can find a soldier's armor that will fit me well enough: I am very hardy; and I do not need beautiful armor made to my measure like you wear. I shall not want many soldiers: the Dauphin will give me all I need to raise the siege of Orleans.

ROBERT [*flabbergasted*] To raise the siege of Orleans!

JOAN [*simply*] Yes, squire: that is what God is sending me to do. Three men will be enough for you to send with me if they are good men and gentle to me. They have promised to come with me. Polly and Jack and—

ROBERT. Polly!! You impudent baggage, do you dare call squire Bertrand de Poulengey Polly to my face?

JOAN. His friends call him so, squire: I did not know he had any other name. Jack—

ROBERT. That is Monsieur John of Metz, I suppose?

JOAN. Yes, squire. Jack will come willingly: he is a very kind gentleman, and gives me money to give to the poor. I think John Godsave will come, and Dick the Archer, and their servants John of Honecourt and Julian. There will be no trouble for you, squire: I have arranged it all: you have only to give the order.

ROBERT [*contemplating her in a stupor of amazement*] Well, I am damned!

JOAN [*with unruffled sweetness*] No, squire: God is very merciful; and the blessed saints Catherine and Margaret, who speak to me every day [*he gapes*], will intercede for you. You will go to paradise; and your name will be remembered for ever as my first helper.

ROBERT [*to the steward, still much bothered, but changing his tone as he pursues a new clue*] Is this true about Monsieur de Poulengey?

STEWARD [*eagerly*] Yes, sir, and about Monsieur de Metz too. They both want to go with her.

ROBERT [*thoughtful*] Mf! [*He goes to the window, and shouts into the courtyard*] Hallo! You there: send Monsieur de Poulengey to me, will you? [*He turns to Joan*]. Get out; and wait in the yard.

JOAN [*smiling brightly at him*] Right, squire. [*She goes out*].

ROBERT [*to the steward*] Go with her, you, you dithering imbecile. Stay within call; and keep your eye on her. I shall have her up here again.

STEWARD. Do so in God's name, sir. Think of those hens, the best layers in Champagne; and—

ROBERT. Think of my boot; and take your backside out of reach of it.

The steward retreats hastily and finds himself confronted in the doorway by Bertrand de Poulengey, a lymphatic French gentleman-at-arms, aged 36 or thereabout, employed in the department of the provost-marshal, dreamily absent-minded, seldom speaking unless spoken to, and then slow and obstinate in reply: altogether in contrast to the self-assertive, loud-mouthed, super-

ficially energetic, fundamentally will-less Robert. The steward makes way for him, and vanishes.

Poulengey salutes, and stands awaiting orders.

ROBERT [*genially*] It isnt service, Polly. A friendly talk. Sit down. [*He hooks the stool from under the table with his instep*].

Poulengey relaxing, comes into the room; places the stool between the table and the window; and sits down ruminatively. Robert, half sitting on the end of the table, begins the friendly talk.

ROBERT. Now listen to me, Polly. I must talk to you like a father.

Poulengey looks up at him gravely for a moment, but says nothing.

ROBERT. It's about this girl you are interested in. Now, I have seen her. I have talked to her. First, she's mad. That doesnt matter. Second, she's not a farm wench. She's a bourgeoise. That matters a good deal. I know her class exactly. Her father came here last year to represent his village in a lawsuit: he is one of their notables. A farmer. Not a gentleman farmer: he makes money by it, and lives by it. Still, not a laborer. Not a mechanic. He might have a cousin a lawyer, or in the Church. People of this sort may be of no account socially; but they can give a lot of bother to the authorities. That is to say, to me. Now no doubt it seems to you a very simple thing to take this girl away, humbugging her into the belief that you are taking her to the Dauphin. But if you get her into trouble, you may get me into no end of a mess, as I am her father's lord, and responsible for her protection. So friends or no friends, Polly, hands off her.

POULENGEY [*with deliberate impressiveness*] I should as soon think of the Blessed Virgin herself in that way, as of this girl.

ROBERT [*coming off the table*] But she says you and Jack and Dick have offered to go with her. What for? You are not going to tell me that you take her crazy notion of going to the Dauphin seriously, are you?

POULENGEY [*slowly*] There is something about her. They

are pretty foulmouthed and foulminded down there in the guardroom, some of them. But there hasnt been a word that has anything to do with her being a woman. They have stopped swearing before her. There is something. Something. It may be worth trying.

ROBERT. Oh, come, Polly! pull yourself together. Commonsense was never your strong point; but this is a little too much. [*He retreats disgustedly*].

POULENGEY [*unmoved*] What is the good of commonsense? If we had any commonsense we should join the Duke of Burgundy and the English king. They hold half the country, right down to the Loire. They have Paris. They have this castle: you know very well that we had to surrender it to the Duke of Bedford, and that you are only holding it on parole. The Dauphin is in Chinon, like a rat in a corner, except that he wont fight. We dont even know that he is the Dauphin: his mother says he isnt; and she ought to know. Think of that! the queen denying the legitimacy of her own son!

ROBERT. Well, she married her daughter to the English king. Can you blame the woman?

POULENGEY. I blame nobody. But thanks to her, the Dauphin is down and out; and we may as well face it. The English will take Orleans: the Bastard will not be able to stop them.

ROBERT. He beat the English the year before last at Montargis. I was with him.

POULENGEY. No matter: his men are cowed now; and he cant work miracles. And I tell you that nothing can save our side now but a miracle.

ROBERT. Miracles are all right, Polly. The only difficulty about them is that they dont happen nowadays.

POULENGEY. I used to think so. I am not so sure now. [*Rising, and moving ruminatively towards the window*] At all events this is not a time to leave any stone unturned. There is something about the girl.

ROBERT. Oh! You think the girl can work miracles, do

you?

POULENGEY. I think the girl herself is a bit of a miracle. Anyhow, she is the last card left in our hand. Better play her than throw up the game. [*He wanders to the turret*].

ROBERT [*wavering*] You really think that?

POULENGEY [*turning*] Is there anything else left for us to think?

ROBERT [*going to him*] Look here, Polly. If you were in my place would you let a girl like that do you out of sixteen francs for a horse?

POULENGEY. I will pay for the horse.

ROBERT. You will!

POULENGEY. Yes: I will back my opinion.

ROBERT. You will really gamble on a forlorn hope to the tune of sixteen francs?

POULENGEY. It is not a gamble.

ROBERT. What else is it?

POULENGEY. It is a certainty. Her words and her ardent faith in God have put fire into me.

ROBERT [*giving him up*] Whew! You are as mad as she is.

POULENGEY [*obstinately*] We want a few mad people now. See where the sane ones have landed us!

ROBERT [*his irresoluteness now openly swamping his affected decisiveness*] I shall feel like a precious fool. Still, if you feel sure—?

POULENGEY. I feel sure enough to take her to Chinon—unless you stop me.

ROBERT. This is not fair. You are putting the responsibility on me.

POULENGEY. It is on you whichever way you decide.

ROBERT. Yes: thats just it. Which way am I to decide? You dont see how awkward this is for me. [*Snatching at a dilatory step with an unconscious hope that Joan will make up his mind for him*] Do you think I ought to have another talk to her?

POULENGEY [*rising*] Yes. [*He goes to the window and calls*] Joan!

JOAN'S VOICE. Will he let us go, Polly?

POULENGEY. Come up. Come in. [*Turning to Robert*] Shall I leave you with her?

ROBERT. No: stay here; and back me up.

Poulengey sits down on the chest. Robert goes back to his magisterial chair, but remains standing to inflate himself more imposingly. Joan comes in, full of good news.

JOAN. Jack will go halves for the horse.

ROBERT. Well!! [*He sits, deflated*]

POULENGEY [*Gravely*] Sit down, Joan.

JOAN [*checked a little, and looking to Robert*] May I?

ROBERT. Do what you are told.

Joan curtsies and sits down on the stool between them. Robert outfaces his perplexity with his most peremptory air.

ROBERT. What is your name?

JOAN [*chattily*] They always call me Jenny in Lorraine. Here in France I am Joan. The soldiers call me The Maid.

ROBERT. What is your surname?

JOAN. Surname? What is that? My father sometimes calls himself d'Arc; but I know nothing about it. You met my father. He—

ROBERT. Yes, yes: I remember. You come from Domrémy in Lorraine, I think.

JOAN. Yes; but what does it matter? we all speak French.

ROBERT. Dont ask questions: answer them. How old are you?

JOAN. Seventeen: so they tell me. It might be nineteen. I dont remember.

ROBERT. What did you mean when you said that St Catherine and St Margaret talked to you every day?

JOAN. They do.

ROBERT. What are they like?

JOAN [*suddenly obstinate*] I will tell you nothing about that: they have not given me leave.

ROBERT. But you actually see them; and they talk to you just as I am talking to you?

JOAN. No: it is quite different. I cannot tell you: you

must not talk to me about my voices.

ROBERT. How do you mean? voices?

JOAN. I hear voices telling me what to do. They come from God.

ROBERT. They come from your imagination.

JOAN. Of course. That is how the messages of God come to us.

POULENGEY. Checkmate.

ROBERT. No fear! [*To Joan*] So God says you are to raise the siege of Orleans?

JOAN. And to crown the Dauphin in Rheims Cathedral.

ROBERT [*gasping*] Crown the D——! Gosh!

JOAN. And to make the English leave France.

ROBERT [*sarcastic*] Anything else?

JOAN [*charming*] Not just at present, thank you, squire.

ROBERT. I suppose you think raising a siege is as easy as chasing a cow out of a meadow. You think soldiering is anybody's job?

JOAN. I do not think it can be very difficult if God is on your side, and you are willing to put your life in His hand. But many soldiers are very simple.

ROBERT [*grimly*] Simple! Did you ever see English soldiers fighting?

JOAN. They are only men. God made them just like us; but He gave them their own country and their own language; and it is not His will that they should come into our country and try to speak our language.

ROBERT. Who has been putting such nonsense into your head? Dont you know that soldiers are subject to their feudal lord, and that it is nothing to them or to you whether he is the duke of Burgundy or the king of England or the king of France? What has their language to do with it?

JOAN. I do not understand that a bit. We are all subject to the King of Heaven; and He gave us our countries and our languages, and meant us to keep to them. If it were not so it would be murder to kill an Englishman in battle; and you, squire, would be in great danger of hell fire. You must not think about your duty to your feudal lord, but about your duty to God.

POULENGEY. It's no use, Robert: she can choke you like that every time.

ROBERT. Can she, by Saint Dennis! We shall see. [*To Joan*] We are not talking about God: we are talking about practical affairs. I ask you again, girl, have you ever seen English soldiers fighting? Have you ever seen them plundering, burning, turning the countryside into a desert? Have you heard no tales of their Black Prince who was blacker than the devil himself, or of the English king's father?

JOAN. You must not be afraid, Robert—

ROBERT. Damn you, I am not afraid. And who gave you leave to call me Robert?

JOAN. You were called so in church in the name of our Lord. All the other names are your father's or your brother's or anybody's.

ROBERT. Tcha!

JOAN. Listen to me, squire. At Domrémy we had to fly to the next village to escape from the English soldiers. Three of them were left behind, wounded. I came to know these three poor goddams quite well. They had not half my strength.

ROBERT. Do you know why they are called goddams?

JOAN. No. Everyone calls them goddams.

ROBERT. It is because they are always calling on their God to condemn their souls to perdition. That is what goddam means in their language. How do you like it?

JOAN. God will be merciful to them; and they will act like His good children when they go back to the country He made for them, and made them for. I have heard the tales of the Black Prince. The moment he touched the soil of our country the devil entered into him and made him a black fiend. But at home, in the place made for him by God, he was good. It is always so. If I went into England against the will of God to conquer England, and tried to live there and speak its language, the devil would enter into me; and when I was old I should shudder to remember the wickednesses I did.

ROBERT. Perhaps. But the more devil you were the better you might fight. That is why the goddams will take Orleans. And you cannot stop them, nor ten thousand like you.

JOAN. One thousand like me can stop them. Ten like me can stop them with God on our side. [*She rises impetuously, and goes at him, unable to sit quiet any longer*]. You do not understand, squire. Our soldiers are always beaten because they are fighting only to save their skins; and the shortest way to save your skin is to run away. Our knights are thinking only of the money they will make in ransoms: it is not kill or be killed with them, but pay or be paid. But I will teach them all to fight that the will of God may be done in France; and then they will drive the poor goddams before them like sheep. You and Polly will live to see the day when there will not be an English soldier on the soil of France; and there will be but one king there: not the feudal English king, but God's French one.

ROBERT [*to Poulengey*] This may be all rot, Polly; but the troops might swallow it, though nothing that we can say seems able to put any fight into them. Even the Dauphin might swallow it. And if she can put fight into him, she can put it into anybody.

POULENGEY. I can see no harm in trying. Can you? And there is something about the girl—

ROBERT [*turning to Joan*] Now listen you to me; and [*desperately*] dont cut in before I have time to think.

JOAN [*plumping down on the stool again, like an obedient schoolgirl*] Yes, squire.

ROBERT. Your orders are, that you are to go to Chinon under the escort of this gentleman and three of his friends.

JOAN [*radiant, clasping her hands*] Oh, squire! Your head is all circled with light, like a saint's.

POULENGEY. How is she to get into the royal presence?

ROBERT [*who has looked up for his halo rather apprehensively*] I dont know: how did she get into my presence? If the Dauphin can keep her out he is a better man than I take him for. [*Rising*] I will send her to Chinon; and she can say I sent her. Then let come what may: I can do no more.

JOAN. And the dress? I may have a soldier's dress, maynt I, squire?

ROBERT. Have what you please. I wash my hands of it.

JOAN [*wildly excited by her success*] Come, Polly. [*She dashes out*].

ROBERT [*shaking Poulengey's hand*] Goodbye, old man, I am taking a big chance. Few other men would have done it. But as you say, there is something about her.

POULENGEY. Yes: there is something about her. Goodbye. [*He goes out*].

Robert, still very doubtful whether he has not been made a fool of by a crazy female, and a social inferior to boot, scratches his head and slowly comes back from the door.

The steward runs in with a basket.

STEWARD. Sir, sir—

ROBERT. What now?

STEWARD. The hens are laying like mad, sir. Five dozen eggs!

ROBERT [*stiffens convulsively; crosses himself; and forms with his pale lips the words*] Christ in heaven! [*Aloud but breathless*] She did come from God.

SCENE II

CHINON, in Touraine. An end of the throne-room in the castle, curtained off to make an antechamber. The Archbishop of Rheims, close on 50, a full-fed political prelate with nothing of the ecclesiastic about him except his imposing bearing, and the Lord Chamberlain, Monseigneur de la Trémouille, a monstrous arrogant wineskin of a man, are waiting for the Dauphin. There is a door in the wall to the right of the two men. It is late in the afternoon on the 8th of March, 1429. The Archbishop stands with dignity whilst the Chamberlain, on his left, fumes about in the worst of tempers.

LA TRÉMOUILLE. What the devil does the Dauphin mean by keeping us waiting like this? I dont know how you have the patience to stand there like a stone idol.

THE ARCHBISHOP. You see, I am an archbishop; and an archbishop is a sort of idol. At any rate he has to learn to keep still and suffer fools patiently. Besides, my dear Lord Chamberlain, it is the Dauphin's royal privilege to keep you waiting, is it not?

LA TRÉMOUILLE. Dauphin be damned! saving your reverence. Do you know how much money he owes me?

THE ARCHBISHOP. Much more than he owes me, I have no doubt, because you are a much richer man. But I take it he owes you all you could afford to lend him. That is what he owes me.

LA TRÉMOUILLE. Twentyseven thousand: that was his last haul. A cool twentyseven thousand!

THE ARCHBISHOP. What becomes of it all? He never has a suit of clothes that I would throw to a curate.

LA TRÉMOUILLE. He dines on a chicken or a scrap of mutton. He borrows my last penny; and there is nothing to shew for it. [*A page appears in the doorway*]. At last!

THE PAGE. No, my lord: it is not His Majesty. Monsieur de Rais is approaching.

LA TRÉMOUILLE. Young Bluebeard! Why announce him?

THE PAGE. Captain La Hire is with him. Something has

happened, I think.

Gilles de Rais, a young man of 25, very smart and self-possessed, and sporting the extravagance of a little curled beard dyed blue at a clean-shaven court, comes in. He is determined to make himself agreeable, but lacks natural joyousness, and is not really pleasant. In fact when he defies the Church some eleven years later he is accused of trying to extract pleasure from horrible cruelties, and hanged. So far, however, there is no shadow of the gallows on him. He advances gaily to the Archbishop. The page withdraws.

BLUEBEARD. Your faithful lamb, Archbishop. Good day, my lord. Do you know what has happened to La Hire?

LA TRÉMOUILLE. He has sworn himself into a fit, perhaps.

BLUEBEARD. No: just the opposite. Foul Mouthed Frank, the only man in Touraine who could beat him at swearing, was told by a soldier that he shouldnt use such language when he was at the point of death.

THE ARCHBISHOP. Nor at any other point. But was Foul Mouthed Frank on the point of death?

BLUEBEARD. Yes: he has just fallen into a well and been drowned. La Hire is frightened out of his wits.

Captain La Hire comes in: a war dog with no court manners and pronounced camp ones.

BLUEBEARD. I have just been telling the Chamberlain and the Archbishop. The Archbishop says you are a lost man.

LA HIRE [*striding past Bluebeard, and planting himself between the Archbishop and La Trémouille*] This is nothing to joke about. It is worse than we thought. It was not a soldier, but an angel dressed as a soldier.

THE ARCHBISHOP
THE CHAMBERLAIN
BLUEBEARD } [*exclaiming all together*] An angel!

LA HIRE. Yes, an angel. She has made her way from Champagne with half a dozen men through the thick of everything: Burgundians, Goddams, deserters, robbers, and Lord knows who; and they never met a soul except the country folk. I know one of them: de Poulengey. He says she's an angel. If ever I utter an oath again may my soul be blasted to eternal damnation!

THE ARCHBISHOP. A very pious beginning, Captain.

Bluebeard and La Trémouille laugh at him. The page returns.

THE PAGE. His Majesty.

They stand perfunctorily at court attention. The Dauphin, aged 26, *really King Charles the Seventh since the death of his father, but as yet uncrowned, comes in through the curtains with a paper in his hands. He is a poor creature physically; and the current fashion of shaving closely, and hiding every scrap of hair under the head-covering or headdress, both by women and men, makes the worst of his appearance. He has little narrow eyes, near together, a long pendulous nose that droops over his thick short upper lip, and the expression of a young dog accustomed to be kicked, yet incorrigible and irrepressible. But he is neither vulgar nor stupid; and he has a cheeky humor which enables him to hold his own in conversation. Just at present he is excited, like a child with a new toy. He comes to the Archbishop's left hand. Bluebeard and La Hire retire towards the curtains.*

CHARLES. Oh, Archbishop, do you know what Robert de Baudricourt is sending me from Vaucouleurs?

THE ARCHBISHOP [*contemptuously*] I am not interested in the newest toys.

CHARLES [*indignantly*] It isnt a toy. [*Sulkily*] However, I can get on very well without your interest.

THE ARCHBISHOP. Your Highness is taking offence very unnecessarily.

CHARLES. Thank you. You are always ready with a lecture, arnt you?

LA TRÉMOUILLE [*roughly*] Enough grumbling. What have you got there?

CHARLES. What is that to you?

LA TRÉMOUILLE. It is my business to know what is passing between you and the garrison at Vaucouleurs. [*He snatches the paper from the Dauphin's hand, and begins reading it with some difficulty, following the words with his finger and spelling them out syllable by syllable.*]

CHARLES [*mortified*] You all think you can treat me as you please because I owe you money, and because I am no good at fighting. But I have the blood royal in my veins.

THE ARCHBISHOP. Even that has been questioned, your Highness. One hardly recognizes in you the grandson of Charles the Wise.

CHARLES. I want to hear no more of my grandfather. He was so wise that he used up the whole family stock of wisdom for five generations, and left me the poor fool I am, bullied and insulted by all of you.

THE ARCHBISHOP. Control yourself, sir. These outbursts of petulance are not seemly.

CHARLES. Another lecture! Thank you. What a pity it is that though you are an archbishop saints and angels dont come to see y o u!

THE ARCHBISHOP. What do you mean?

CHARLES. Aha! Ask that bully there [*pointing to La Trémouille*].

LA TRÉMOUILLE [*furious*] Hold your tongue. Do you hear?

CHARLES. Oh, I hear. You neednt shout. The whole castle can hear. Why dont you go and shout at the English, and beat them for me?

LA TRÉMOUILLE [*raising his fist*] You young—

CHARLES [*running behind the Archbishop*] Dont you raise your hand to me. It's high treason.

LA HIRE. Steady, Duke! Steady!

THE ARCHBISHOP [*resolutely*] Come, come! this will not do. My lord Chamberlain: please! please! we must keep some sort of order. [*To the Dauphin*] And you, sir: if you cannot rule your kingdom, at least try to rule yourself.

CHARLES. Another lecture! Thank you.

LA TRÉMOUILLE [*handing the paper to the Archbishop*] Here: read the accursed thing for me. He has sent the blood boiling into my head: I cant distinguish the letters.

CHARLES [*coming back and peering round La Trémouille's left shoulder*] I will read it for you if you like. I c a n read, you know.

LA TRÉMOUILLE [*with intense contempt, not at all stung by the taunt*] Yes: reading is about all you are fit for. Can you make it out, Archbishop?

THE ARCHBISHOP. I should have expected more commonsense from De Baudricourt. He is sending some cracked country lass here—

CHARLES [*interrupting*] No: he is sending a saint: an angel. And she is coming to me: to me, the king, and not to you, Archbishop, holy as you are. She knows the blood royal if you dont. [*He struts up to the curtains between Bluebeard and La Hire*].

THE ARCHBISHOP. You cannot be allowed to see this crazy wench.

CHARLES [*turning*] But I am the king; and I will.

LA TRÉMOUILLE [*brutally*] Then she cannot be allowed to see you. Now!

CHARLES. I tell you I will. I am going to put my foot down—

BLUEBEARD [*laughing at him*] Naughty! What would your wise grandfather say?

CHARLES. That just shews your ignorance, Bluebeard. My grandfather had a saint who used to float in the air when she was praying, and told him everything he wanted to know. My poor father had two saints, Marie de Maillé and the Gasque of Avignon. It is in our family; and I dont care what you say: I will have my saint too.

THE ARCHBISHOP. This creature is not a saint. She is not even a respectable woman. She does not wear women's clothes. She is dressed like a soldier, and rides round the country with soldiers. Do you suppose such a person can be admitted to your Highness's court?

LA HIRE. Stop. [*Going to the Archbishop*] Did you say a girl in armor, like a soldier?

THE ARCHBISHOP. So De Baudricourt describes her.

LA HIRE. But by all the devils in hell—Oh, God forgive me, what am I saying?— by Our Lady and all the saints, this must be the angel that struck Foul Mouthed Frank dead for swearing.

CHARLES. [*triumphantly*] You see! A miracle!

LA HIRE. She may strike the lot of us dead if we cross her. For Heaven's sake, Archbishop, be careful what you are doing.

THE ARCHBISHOP [*severely*] Rubbish! Nobody has been struck dead. A drunken blackguard who has been rebuked a hundred times for swearing has fallen into a well, and been drowned. A mere coincidence.

LA HIRE. I do not know what a coincidence is. I do know that the man is dead, and that she told him he was going to die.

THE ARCHBISHOP. We are all going to die, Captain.

LA HIRE [*crossing himself*] I hope not. [*He backs out of the conversation*].

BLUEBEARD. We can easily find out whether she is an angel or not. Let us arrange when she comes that I shall be the Dauphin, and see whether she will find me out.

CHARLES. Yes: I agree to that. If she cannot find the blood royal I will have nothing to do with her.

THE ARCHBISHOP. It is for the Church to make saints: let De Baudricourt mind his own business, and not dare usurp the function of his priest. I say the girl shall not be admitted.

BLUEBEARD. But, Archbishop—

THE ARCHBISHOP [*sternly*] I speak in the Church's name. [*To the Dauphin*] Do you dare say she shall?

CHARLES [*intimidated but sulky*] Oh, if you make it an excommunication matter, I have nothing more to say, of course. But you havnt read the end of the letter. De Baudricourt says she will raise the siege of Orleans, and beat the English for us.

LA TRÉMOUILLE. Rot!

CHARLES. Well, will you save Orleans for us, with all your bullying?

LA TRÉMOUILLE [*savagely*] Do not throw that in my face again: do you hear? I have done more fighting than you ever did or ever will. But I cannot be everywhere.

THE DAUPHIN. Well, thats something.

BLUEBEARD [*coming between the Archbishop and Charles*] You have Jack Dunois at the head of your troops in Orleans: the brave Dunois, the handsome Dunois, the wonderful invincible Dunois, the darling of all the ladies, the beautiful bastard. Is it likely that the country lass can do what he cannot do?

CHARLES. Why doesnt he raise the siege, then?

LA HIRE. The wind is against him.

BLUEBEARD. How can the wind hurt him at Orleans? It is not on the Channel.

LA HIRE. It is on the river Loire; and the English hold the bridgehead. He must ship his men across the river and upstream, if he is to take them in the rear. Well, he cannot, because there is a devil of a wind blowing the other way. He is tired of paying the priests to pray for a west wind. What he needs is a miracle. You tell me that what the girl did to Foul Mouthed Frank was no miracle. No matter: it finished Frank. If she changes the wind for Dunois, that may not be a miracle either; but it may finish the English. What harm is there in trying?

THE ARCHBISHOP [*who has read the end of the letter and become more thoughtful*] It is true that De Baudricourt seems extraordinarily impressed.

LA HIRE. De Baudricourt is a blazing ass; but he is a soldier; and if he thinks she can beat the English, all the rest of the army will think so too.

LA TRÉMOUILLE [*to the Archbishop, who is hesitating*] Oh, let them have their way. Dunois' men will give up the town in spite of him if somebody does not put some fresh spunk into them.

THE ARCHBISHOP. The Church must examine the girl before anything decisive is done about her. However, since his Highness desires it, let her attend the Court.

LA HIRE. I will find her and tell her. [*He goes out*].

CHARLES. Come with me, Bluebeard; and let us arrange

so that she will not know who I am. You will pretend to be me. [*He goes out through the curtains*].

BLUEBEARD. Pretend to be that thing! Holy Michael! [*He follows the Dauphin*].

LA TRÉMOUILLE. I wonder will she pick him out!

THE ARCHBISHOP. Of course she will.

LA TRÉMOUILLE. Why? How is she to know?

THE ARCHBISHOP. She will know what everybody in Chinon knows: that the Dauphin is the meanest-looking and worst-dressed figure in the Court, and that the man with the blue beard is Gilles de Rais.

LA TRÉMOUILLE. I never thought of that.

THE ARCHBISHOP. You are not so accustomed to miracles as I am. It is part of my profession.

LA TRÉMOUILLE [*puzzled and a little scandalized*] But that would not be a miracle at all.

THE ARCHBISHOP [*calmly*] Why not?

LA TRÉMOUILLE. Well, come! what is a miracle?

THE ARCHBISHOP. A miracle, my friend, is an event which creates faith. That is the purpose and nature of miracles. They may seem very wonderful to the people who witness them, and very simple to those who perform them. That does not matter: if they confirm or create faith they are true miracles.

LA TRÉMOUILLE. Even when they are frauds, do you mean?

THE ARCHBISHOP. Frauds deceive. An event which creates faith does not deceive: therefore it is not a fraud, but a miracle.

LA TRÉMOUILLE [*scratching his neck in his perplexity*] Well, I suppose as you are an archbishop you must be right. It seems a bit fishy to me. But I am no churchman, and dont understand these matters.

THE ARCHBISHOP. You are not a churchman; but you are a diplomatist and a soldier. Could you make our citizens pay war taxes, or our soldiers sacrifice their lives, if they knew what is really happening instead of what seems to them to be happening?

LA TRÉMOUILLE. No, by Saint Dennis: the fat would be in the fire before sundown.

THE ARCHBISHOP. Would it not be quite easy to tell them the truth?

LA TRÉMOUILLE. Man alive, they wouldnt believe it.

THE ARCHBISHOP. Just so. Well, the Church has to rule men for the good of their souls as you have to rule them for the good of their bodies. To do that, the Church must do as you do: nourish their faith by poetry.

LA TRÉMOUILLE. Poetry! I should call it humbug.

THE ARCHBISHOP. You would be wrong, my friend. Parables are not lies because they describe events that have never happened. Miracles are not frauds because they are often—I do not say always—very simple and innocent contrivances by which the priest fortifies the faith of his flock. When this girl picks out the Dauphin among his courtiers, it will not be a miracle for me, because I shall know how it has been done, and my faith will not be increased. But as for the others, if they feel the thrill of the supernatural, and forget their sinful clay in a sudden sense of the glory of God, it will be a miracle and a blessed one. And you will find that the girl herself will be more affected than anyone else. She will forget how she really picked him out. So, perhaps, will you.

LA TRÉMOUILLE. Well, I wish I were clever enough to know how much of you is God's archbishop and how much the most artful fox in Touraine. Come on, or we shall be late for the fun; and I want to see it, miracle or no miracle.

THE ARCHBISHOP [*detaining him a moment*] Do not think that I am a lover of crooked ways. There is a new spirit rising in men: we are at the dawning of a wider epoch. If I were a simple monk, and had not to rule men, I should seek peace for my spirit with Aristotle and Pythagoras rather than with the saints and their miracles.

LA TRÉMOUILLE. And who the deuce was Pythagoras?

THE ARCHBISHOP. A sage who held that the earth is round, and that it moves round the sun.

LA TRÉMOUILLE. What an utter fool! Couldnt he use his eyes?

They go out together through the curtains, which are presently withdrawn, revealing the full depth of the throne-room with the Court assembled. On the right are two Chairs of State on a dais. Bluebeard is standing theatrically on the dais, playing the king, and, like the courtiers, enjoying the joke rather obviously. There is a curtained arch in the wall behind the dais; but the main door, guarded by men-at-arms, is at the other side of the room; and a clear path across is kept and lined by the courtiers. Charles is in this path in the middle of the room. La Hire is on his right. The Archbishop, on his left, has taken his place by the dais: La Trémouille at the other side of it. The Duchess de la Trémouille, pretending to be the Queen, sits in the Consort's chair, with a group of ladies in waiting close by, behind the Archbishop.

The chatter of the courtiers makes such a noise that nobody notices the appearance of the page at the door.

THE PAGE. The Duke of— [*Nobody listens*]. The Duke of—[*The chatter continues. Indignant at his failure to command a hearing, he snatches the halberd of the nearest man-at-arms, and thumps the floor with it. The chatter ceases; and everybody looks at him in silence*]. Attention! [*He restores the halberd to the man-at-arms*]. The Duke of Vendôme presents Joan the Maid to his Majesty.

CHARLES [*putting his finger on his lip*] Ssh! [*He hides behind the nearest courtier, peering out to see what happens*].

BLUEBEARD [*majestically*] Let her approach the throne.

Joan, dressed as a soldier, with her hair bobbed and hanging thickly round her face, is led in by a bashful and speechless nobleman, from whom she detaches herself to stop and look round eagerly for the Dauphin.

THE DUCHESS [*to the nearest lady in waiting*] My dear! Her hair!

All the ladies explode in uncontrollable laughter.

BLUEBEARD [*trying not to laugh, and waving his hand in deprecation of their merriment*] Ssh—ssh! Ladies! Ladies!!

JOAN [*not at all embarrassed*] I wear it like this because

I am a soldier. Where be Dauphin?

A titter runs through the Court as she walks to the dais.

BLUEBEARD [*condescendingly*] You are in the presence of the Dauphin.

Joan looks at him sceptically for a moment, scanning him hard up and down to make sure. Dead silence, all watching her. Fun dawns in her face.

JOAN. Coom, Bluebeard! Thou canst not fool me. Where be Dauphin?

A roar of laughter breaks out as Gilles, with a gesture of surrender, joins in the laugh, and jumps down from the dais beside La Trémouille. Joan, also on the broad grin, turns back, searching along the row of courtiers, and presently makes a dive, and drags out Charles by the arm.

JOAN [*releasing him and bobbing him a little curtsey*] Gentle little Dauphin, I am sent to you to drive the English away from Orleans and from France, and to crown you king in the cathedral at Rheims, where all true kings of France are crowned.

CHARLES [*triumphant, to the Court*] You see, all of you: she knew the blood royal. Who dare say now that I am not my father's son? [*To Joan*] But if you want me to be crowned at Rheims you must talk to the Archbishop, not to me. There he is [*he is standing behind her*]!

JOAN [*turning quickly, overwhelmed with emotion*] Oh, my lord! [*She falls on both knees before him, with bowed head, not daring to look up*] My lord: I am only a poor country girl; and you are filled with the blessedness and glory of God Himself; but you will touch me with your hands, and give me your blessing, wont you?

BLUEBEARD [*whispering to La Trémouille*] The old fox blushes.

LA TRÉMOUILLE. Another miracle!

THE ARCHBISHOP [*touched, putting his hand on her head*] Child: you are in love with religion.

JOAN [*startled: looking up at him*] Am I? I never thought of that. Is there any harm in it?

THE ARCHBISHOP. There is no harm in it, my child. But there is danger.

JOAN [*rising, with a sunflush of reckless happiness irradiating her face*] There is always danger, except in heaven. Oh, my lord, you have given me such strength, such courage. It must be a most wonderful thing to be Archbishop.

The Court smiles broadly: even titters a little.

THE ARCHBISHOP [*drawing himself up sensitively*] Gentlemen: your levity is rebuked by this maid's faith. I am, God help me, all unworthy; but your mirth is a deadly sin.

Their faces fall. Dead silence.

BLUEBEARD. My lord: we were laughing at her, not at you.

THE ARCHBISHOP. What? Not at my unworthiness but at her faith! Gilles de Rais: this maid prophesied that the blasphemer should be drowned in his sin—

JOAN [*distressed*] No!

THE ARCHBISHOP [*silencing her by a gesture*] I prophesy now that you will be hanged in yours if you do not learn when to laugh and when to pray.

BLUEBEARD. My lord: I stand rebuked. I am sorry: I can say no more. But if you prophesy that I shall be hanged, I shall never be able to resist temptation, because I shall always be telling myself that I may as well be hanged for a sheep as a lamb.

The courtiers take heart at this. There is more tittering.

JOAN [*scandalized*] You are an idle fellow, Bluebeard; and you have great impudence to answer the Archbishop.

LA HIRE [*with a huge chuckle*] Well said, lass! Well said!

JOAN [*impatiently to the Archbishop*] Oh, my lord, will you send all these silly folks away so that I may speak to the Dauphin alone?

LA HIRE [*goodhumoredly*] I can take a hint. [*He salutes; turns on his heel; and goes out*].

THE ARCHBISHOP. Come, gentlemen. The Maid comes with God's blessing, and must be obeyed.

The courtiers withdraw, some through the arch, others at the opposite side. The Archbishop marches across to the door, fol-

lowed by the Duchess and La Trémouille. As the Archbishop passes Joan, she falls on her knees, and kisses the hem of his robe fervently. He shakes his head in instinctive remonstrance; gathers the robe from her; and goes out. She is left kneeling directly in the Duchess's way.

THE DUCHESS [*coldly*] Will you allow me to pass, please?

JOAN [*hastily rising, and standing back*] Beg pardon, maam, I am sure.

The Duchess passes on. Joan stares after her; then whispers to the Dauphin.

JOAN. Be that Queen?

CHARLES. No. She thinks she is.

JOAN [*again staring after the Duchess*] Oo-oo-ooh! [*Her awestruck amazement at the figure cut by the magnificently dressed lady is not wholly complimentary*].

LA TRÉMOUILLE [*very surly*] I'll trouble your Highness not to gibe at my wife. [*He goes out. The others have already gone*].

JOAN [*to the Dauphin*] Who be old Gruff-and-Grum?

CHARLES. He is the Duke de la Trémouille.

JOAN. What be his job?

CHARLES. He pretends to command the army. And whenever I find a friend I can care for, he kills him.

JOAN. Why dost let him?

CHARLES [*petulantly moving to the throne side of the room to escape from her magnetic field*] How can I prevent him? He bullies me. They all bully me.

JOAN. Art afraid?

CHARLES. Yes: I am afraid. It's no use preaching to me about it. It's all very well for these big men with their armor that is too heavy for me, and their swords that I can hardly lift, and their muscle and their shouting and their bad tempers. They like fighting: most of them are making fools of themselves all the time they are not fighting; but I am quiet and sensible; and I dont want to kill people: I only want to be left alone to enjoy myself in my own way. I never asked to be a king: it was pushed on me. So if you are going to say

"Son of St Louis: gird on the sword of your ancestors, and lead us to victory" you may spare your breath to cool your porridge; for I cannot do it. I am not built that way; and there is an end of it.

JOAN [*trenchant and masterful*] Blethers! We are all like that to begin with. I shall put courage into thee.

CHARLES. But I dont want to have courage put into me. I want to sleep in a comfortable bed, and not live in continual terror of being killed or wounded. Put courage into the others, and let them have their bellyful of fighting; but let me alone.

JOAN. It's no use, Charlie: thou must face what God puts on thee. If thou fail to make thyself king, thoult be a beggar: what else art fit for? Come! Let me see thee sitting on the throne. I have looked forward to that.

CHARLES. What is the good of sitting on the throne when the other fellows give all the orders? However! [*he sits enthroned, a piteous figure*] here is the king for you! Look your fill at the poor devil.

JOAN. Thourt not king yet, lad: thourt but Dauphin. Be not led away by them around thee. Dressing up dont fill empty noddle. I know the people: the real people that make thy bread for thee; and I tell thee they count no man king of France until the holy oil has been poured on his hair, and himself consecrated and crowned in Rheims Cathedral. And thou needs new clothes, Charlie. Why does not Queen look after thee properly?

CHARLES. We're too poor. She wants all the money we can spare to put on her own back. Besides, I like to see her beautifully dressed; and I dont care what I wear myself: I should look ugly anyhow.

JOAN. There is some good in thee, Charlie; but it is not yet a king's good.

CHARLES. We shall see. I am not such a fool as I look. I have my eyes open; and I can tell you that one good treaty is worth ten good fights. These fighting fellows lose all on the treaties that they gain on the fights. If we can only have a treaty, the English are sure to have the worst of it, because they are better at fighting than at thinking.

JOAN. If the English win, it is they that will make the treaty; and then God help poor France! Thou must fight, Charlie, whether thou will or no. I will go first to hearten thee. We must take our courage in both hands: aye, and pray for it with both hands too.

CHARLES [*descending from his throne and again crossing the room to escape from her dominating urgency*] Oh do stop talking about God and praying. I cant bear people who are always praying. Isnt it bad enough to have to do it at the proper times?

JOAN [*pitying him*] Thou poor child, thou hast never prayed in thy life. I must teach thee from the beginning.

CHARLES. I am not a child: I am a grown man and a father; and I will not be taught any more.

JOAN. Aye, you have a little son. He that will be Louis the Eleventh when you die. Would you not fight for him?

CHARLES. No: a horrid boy. He hates me. He hates everybody, selfish little beast! I dont want to be bothered with children. I dont want to be a father; and I dont want to be a son: especially a son of St Louis. I dont want to be any of these fine things you all have your heads full of: I want to be just what I am. Why cant you mind your own business, and let me mind mine?

JOAN [*again contemptuous*] Minding your own business is like minding your own body: it's the shortest way to make yourself sick. What is my business? Helping mother at home. What is thine? Petting lapdogs and sucking sugar-sticks. I call that muck. I tell thee it is God's business we are here to do: not our own. I have a message to thee from God; and thou must listen to it, though thy heart break with the terror of it.

CHARLES. I dont want a message; but can you tell me any secrets? Can you do any cures? Can you turn lead into gold, or anything of that sort?

JOAN. I can turn thee into a king, in Rheims Cathedral;

and that is a miracle that will take some doing, it seems.

CHARLES. If we go to Rheims, and have a coronation, Anne will want new dresses. We cant afford them. I am all right as I am.

JOAN. As you are! And what is that? Less than my father's poorest shepherd. Thourt not lawful owner of thy own land of France till thou be consecrated.

CHARLES. But I shall not be lawful owner of my own land anyhow. Will the consecration pay off my mortgages? I have pledged my last acre to the Archbishop and that fat bully. I owe money even to Bluebeard.

JOAN [*earnestly*] Charlie: I come from the land, and have gotten my strength working on the land; and I tell thee that the land is thine to rule righteously and keep God's peace in, and not to pledge at the pawnshop as a drunken woman pledges her children's clothes. And I come from God to tell thee to kneel in the cathedral and solemnly give thy kingdom to Him for ever and ever, and become the greatest king in the world as His steward and His bailiff, His soldier and His servant. The very clay of France will become holy: her soldiers will be the soldiers of God: the rebel dukes will be rebels against God: the English will fall on their knees and beg thee let them return to their lawful homes in peace. Wilt be a poor little Judas, and betray me and Him that sent me?

CHARLES [*tempted at last*] Oh, if I only dare!

JOAN. I shall dare, dare, and dare again, in God's name! Art for or against me?

CHARLES [*excited*] I'll risk it. I warn you I shant be able to keep it up; but I'll risk it. You shall see. [*Running to the main door and shouting*] Hallo! Come back, everybody. [*To Joan, as he runs back to the arch opposite*] Mind you stand by and dont let me be bullied. [*Through the arch*] Come along, will you: the whole Court. [*He sits down in the royal chair as they all hurry in to their former places, chattering and wondering*]. Now I'm in for it; but no matter: here goes! [*To the page*] Call for silence, you little beast, will you?

THE PAGE [*snatching a halberd as before and thumping with*

it repeatedly] Silence for His Majesty the King. The King speaks. [*Peremptorily*] Will you be silent there? [*Silence*].

CHARLES [*rising*] I have given the command of the army to The Maid. The Maid is to do as she likes with it. [*He descends from the dais*].

General amazement. La Hire, delighted, slaps his steel thigh-piece with his gauntlet.

LA TRÉMOUILLE [*turning threateningly towards Charles*] What is this? *I* command the army.

Joan quickly puts her hand on Charles's shoulder as he instinctively recoils. Charles, with a grotesque effort culminating in an extravagant gesture, snaps his fingers in the Chamberlain's face.

JOAN. Thourt answered, old Gruff-and-Grum. [*Suddenly flashing out her sword as she divines that her moment has come*] Who is for God and His Maid? Who is for Orleans with me?

LA HIRE [*carried away, drawing also*] For God and His Maid! To Orleans!

ALL THE KNIGHTS [*following his lead with enthusiasm*] To Orleans!

Joan, radiant, falls on her knees in thanksgiving to God. They all kneel, except the Archbishop, who gives his benediction with a sign, and La Trémouille, who collapses, cursing.

SCENE III

ORLEANS, *May 29th,* 1429. *Dunois, aged 26, is pacing up and down a patch of ground on the south bank of the silver Loire, commanding a long view of the river in both directions. He has had his lance stuck up with a pennon, which streams in a strong east wind. His shield with its bend sinister lies beside it. He has his commander's baton in his hand. He is well built, carrying his armor easily. His broad brow and pointed chin give him an equilaterally triangular face, already marked by active service and responsibility, with the expression of a goodnatured and capable man who has no affectations and no foolish illusions. His page is sitting on the ground, elbows on knees, cheeks on fists, idly watching the water. It is evening; and both man and boy are affected by the loveliness of the Loire.*

DUNOIS [*halting for a moment to glance up at the streaming pennon and shake his head wearily before he resumes his pacing*] West wind, west wind, west wind. Strumpet: steadfast when you should be wanton, wanton when you should be steadfast. West wind on the silver Loire: what rhymes to Loire? [*He looks again at the pennon, and shakes his fist at it*] Change, curse you, change, English harlot of a wind, change. West, west, I tell you. [*With a growl he resumes his march in silence, but soon begins again*] West wind, wanton wind, wilful wind, womanish wind, false wind from over the water, will you never blow again?

THE PAGE [*bounding to his feet*] See! There! There she goes!

DUNOIS [*startled from his reverie: eagerly*] Where? Who? The Maid?

THE PAGE. No: the kingfisher. Like blue lightning. She went into that bush.

DUNOIS [*furiously disappointed*] Is that all? You infernal young idiot: I have a mind to pitch you into the river.

THE PAGE [*not afraid, knowing his man*] It looked frightfully jolly, that flash of blue. Look! There goes the other!

DUNOIS [*running eagerly to the river brim*] Where? Where?

THE PAGE [*pointing*] Passing the reeds.

DUNOIS [*delighted*] I see.

They follow the flight till the bird takes cover.

THE PAGE. You blew me up because you were not in time to see them yesterday.

DUNOIS. You knew I was expecting The Maid when you set up your yelping. I will give you something to yelp for next time.

THE PAGE. Arnt they lovely? I wish I could catch them.

DUNOIS. Let me catch you trying to trap them, and I will put you in the iron cage for a month to teach you what a cage feels like. You are an abominable boy.

THE PAGE [*laughs, and squats down as before*]!

DUNOIS [*pacing*] Blue bird, blue bird, since I am friend to thee, change thou the wind for me. No: it does not rhyme. He who has sinned for thee: thats better. No sense in it, though. [*He finds himself close to the page*] You abominable boy! [*He turns away from him*] Mary in the blue snood, kingfisher color: will you grudge me a west wind?

A SENTRY'S VOICE WESTWARD. Halt! Who goes there?

JOAN'S VOICE. The Maid.

DUNOIS. Let her pass. Hither, Maid! To me!

Joan, in splendid armor, rushes in in a blazing rage. The wind drops; and the pennon flaps idly down the lance; but Dunois is too much occupied with Joan to notice it.

JOAN [*bluntly*] Be you Bastard of Orleans?

DUNOIS [*cool and stern, pointing to his shield*] You see the bend sinister. Are you Joan the Maid?

JOAN. Sure.

DUNOIS. Where are your troops?

JOAN. Miles behind. They have cheated me. They have brought me to the wrong side of the river.

DUNOIS. I told them to.

JOAN. Why did you? The English are on the other side!

DUNOIS. The English are on both sides.

JOAN. But Orleans is on the other side. We must fight the English there. How can we cross the river?

DUNOIS [*grimly*] There is a bridge.

JOAN. In God's name, then, let us cross the bridge, and fall on them.

DUNOIS. It seems simple; but it cannot be done.

JOAN. Who says so?

DUNOIS. I say so; and older and wiser heads than mine are of the same opinion.

JOAN [*roundly*] Then your older and wiser heads are fatheads: they have made a fool of you; and now they want to make a fool of me too, bringing me to the wrong side of the river. Do you not know that I bring you better help than ever came to any general or any town?

DUNOIS [*smiling patiently*] Your own?

JOAN. No: the help and counsel of the King of Heaven. Which is the way to the bridge?

DUNOIS. You are impatient, Maid.

JOAN. Is this a time for patience? Our enemy is at our gates; and here we stand doing nothing. Oh, why are you not fighting? Listen to me: I will deliver you from fear. I—

DUNOIS [*laughing heartily, and waving her off*] No, no, my girl: if you delivered me from fear I should be a good knight for a story book, but a very bad commander of the army. Come! let me begin to make a soldier of you. [*He takes her to the water's edge*]. Do you see those two forts at this end of the bridge? the big ones?

JOAN. Yes. Are they ours or the goddams'?

DUNOIS. Be quiet, and listen to me. If I were in either of those forts with only ten men I could hold it against an army. The English have more than ten times ten goddams in those forts to hold them against us.

JOAN. They cannot hold them against God. God did not give them the land under those forts: they stole it from Him. He gave it to us. I will take those forts.

DUNOIS. Single-handed?

JOAN. Our men will take them. I will lead them.

DUNOIS. Not a man will follow you.

JOAN. I will not look back to see whether anyone is

following me.

DUNOIS [*recognizing her mettle, and clapping her heartily on the shoulder*] Good. You have the makings of a soldier in you. You are in love with war.

JOAN [*startled*] Oh! And the Archbishop said I was in love with religion.

DUNOIS. I, God forgive me, am a little in love with war myself, the ugly devil! I am like a man with two wives. Do you want to be like a woman with two husbands?

JOAN [*matter-of-fact*] I will never take a husband. A man in Toul took an action against me for breach of promise; but I never promised him. I am a soldier: I do not want to be thought of as a woman. I will not dress as a woman. I do not care for the things women care for. They dream of lovers, and of money. I dream of leading a charge, and of placing the big guns. You soldiers do not know how to use the big guns: you think you can win battles with a great noise and smoke.

DUNOIS [*with a shrug*] True. Half the time the artillery is more trouble than it is worth.

JOAN. Aye, lad; but you cannot fight stone walls with horses: you must have guns, and much bigger guns too.

DUNOIS [*grinning at her familiarity, and echoing it*] Aye, lass; but a good heart and a stout ladder will get over the stoniest wall.

JOAN. I will be first up the ladder when we reach the fort, Bastard. I dare you to follow me.

DUNOIS. You must not dare a staff officer, Joan: only company officers are allowed to indulge in displays of personal courage. Besides, you must know that I welcome you as a saint, not as a soldier. I have daredevils enough at my call, if they could help me.

JOAN. I am not a daredevil: I am a servant of God. My sword is sacred: I found it behind the altar in the church of St Catherine, where God hid it for me; and I may not strike a blow with it. My heart is full of courage, not of anger. I will lead; and your men will follow: that is all I can do. But I must do it: you shall not stop me.

DUNOIS. All in good time. Our men cannot take those forts by a sally across the bridge. They must come by water, and take the English in the rear on this side.

JOAN [*her military sense asserting itself*] Then make rafts and put big guns on them; and let your men cross to us.

DUNOIS. The rafts are ready; and the men are embarked. But they must wait for God.

JOAN. What do you mean? God is waiting for them.

DUNOIS. Let Him send us a wind then. My boats are downstream: they cannot come up against both wind and current. We must wait until God changes the wind. Come: let me take you to the church.

JOAN. No. I love church; but the English will not yield to prayers: they understand nothing but hard knocks and slashes. I will not go to church until we have beaten them.

DUNOIS. You must: I have business for you there.

JOAN. What business?

DUNOIS. To pray for a west wind. I have prayed; and I have given two silver candlesticks; but my prayers are not answered. Yours may be: you are young and innocent.

JOAN. Oh yes: you are right. I will pray: I will tell St Catherine: she will make God give me a west wind. Quick: shew me the way to the church.

THE PAGE [*sneezes violently*] At-cha!!!

JOAN. God bless you, child! Coom, Bastard.

They go out. The page rises to follow. He picks up the shield, and is taking the spear as well when he notices the pennon, which is now streaming eastward.

THE PAGE [*dropping the shield and calling excitedly after them*] Seigneur! Seigneur! Mademoiselle!

DUNOIS [*running back*] What is it? The kingfisher? [*He looks eagerly for it up the river*].

JOAN. [*joining them*] Oh, a kingfisher! Where?

THE PAGE. No: the wind, the wind, the wind [*pointing to the pennon*]: that is what made me sneeze.

DUNOIS [*looking at the pennon*] The wind has changed.

[*He crosses himself*] God has spoken. [*Kneeling and handing his baton to Joan*] You command the king's army. I am your soldier.

THE PAGE [*looking down the river*] The boats have put off. They are ripping upstream like anything.

DUNOIS [*rising*] Now for the forts. You dared me to follow. Dare you lead?

JOAN [*bursting into tears and flinging her arms round Dunois, kissing him on both cheeks*] Dunois, dear comrade in arms, help me. My eyes are blinded with tears. Set my foot on the ladder, and say "Up, Joan."

DUNOIS [*dragging her out*] Never mind the tears: make for the flash of the guns.

JOAN [*in a blaze of courage*] Ah!

DUNOIS [*dragging her along with him*] For God and Saint Dennis!

THE PAGE [*shrilly*] The Maid! The Maid! God and The Maid! Hurray-ay-ay! [*He snatches up the shield and lance, and capers out after them, mad with excitement*].

SCENE IV

A TENT in the English camp. A bullnecked English chaplain of 50 is sitting on a stool at a table, hard at work writing. At the other side of the table an imposing nobleman, aged 46, is seated in a handsome chair turning over the leaves of an illuminated Book of Hours. The nobleman is enjoying himself: the chaplain is struggling with suppressed wrath. There is an unoccupied leather stool on the nobleman's left. The table is on his right.

THE NOBLEMAN. Now this is what I call workmanship. There is nothing on earth more exquisite than a bonny book, with well-placed columns of rich black writing in beautiful borders, and illuminated pictures cunningly inset. But nowadays, instead of looking at books, people read them. A book might as well be one of those orders for bacon and bran that you are scribbling.

THE CHAPLAIN. I must say, my lord, you take our situation very coolly. Very coolly indeed.

THE NOBLEMAN [*supercilious*] What is the matter?

THE CHAPLAIN. The matter, my lord, is that we English have been defeated.

THE NOBLEMAN. That happens, you know. It is only in history books and ballads that the enemy is always defeated.

THE CHAPLAIN. But we are being defeated over and over again. First, Orleans—

THE NOBLEMAN [*poohpoohing*] Oh, Orleans!

THE CHAPLAIN. I know what you are going to say, my lord: that was a clear case of witchcraft and sorcery. But we are still being defeated. Jargeau, Meung, Beaugency, just like Orleans. And now we have been butchered at Patay, and Sir John Talbot taken prisoner. [*He throws down his pen, almost in tears*] I feel it, my lord: I feel it very deeply. I cannot bear to see my countrymen defeated by a parcel of foreigners.

THE NOBLEMAN. Oh! you are an Englishman, are you?

THE CHAPLAIN. Certainly not, my lord: I am a gentleman. Still, like your lordship, I was born in England; and it makes a difference.

THE NOBLEMAN. You are attached to the soil, eh?

THE CHAPLAIN. It pleases your lordship to be satirical at my expense: your greatness privileges you to be so with impunity. But your lordship knows very well that I am not attached to the soil in a vulgar manner, like a serf. Still, I have a feeling about it; [*with growing agitation*] and I am not ashamed of it; and [*rising wildly*] by God, if this goes on any longer I will fling my cassock to the devil, and take arms myself, and strangle the accursed witch with my own hands.

THE NOBLEMAN [*laughing at him goodnaturedly*] So you shall, chaplain: so you shall, if we can do nothing better. But not yet, not quite yet.

The Chaplain resumes his seat very sulkily.

THE NOBLEMAN [*airily*] I should not care very much about the witch—you see, I have made my pilgrimage to the Holy Land; and the Heavenly Powers, for their own credit, can hardly allow me to be worsted by a village sorceress—but the Bastard of Orleans is a harder nut to crack; and as he has been to the Holy Land too, honors are easy between us as far as that goes.

THE CHAPLAIN. He is only a Frenchman, my lord.

THE NOBLEMAN. A Frenchman! Where did you pick up that expression? Are these Burgundians and Bretons and Picards and Gascons beginning to call themselves Frenchmen, just as our fellows are beginning to call themselves Englishmen? They actually talk of France and England as their countries. Theirs, if you please! What is to become of me and you if that way of thinking comes into fashion?

THE CHAPLAIN. Why, my lord? Can it hurt us?

THE NOBLEMAN. Men cannot serve two masters. If this cant of serving their country once takes hold of them, goodbye to the authority of their feudal lords, and goodbye to the authority of the Church. That is, goodbye to you and me.

THE CHAPLAIN. I hope I am a faithful servant of the Church; and there are only six cousins between me and the barony of Stogumber, which was created by the Conqueror.

But is that any reason why I should stand by and see Englishmen beaten by a French bastard and a witch from Lousy Champagne?

THE NOBLEMAN. Easy, man, easy: we shall burn the witch and beat the bastard all in good time. Indeed I am waiting at present for the Bishop of Beauvais, to arrange the burning with him. He has been turned out of his diocese by her faction.

THE CHAPLAIN. You have first to catch her, my lord.

THE NOBLEMAN. Or buy her. I will offer a king's ransom.

THE CHAPLAIN. A king's ransom! For that slut!

THE NOBLEMAN. One has to leave a margin. Some of Charles's people will sell her to the Burgundians; the Burgundians will sell her to us; and there will probably be three or four middlemen who will expect their little commissions.

THE CHAPLAIN. Monstrous. It is all those scoundrels of Jews: they get in every time money changes hands. I would not leave a Jew alive in Christendom if I had my way.

THE NOBLEMAN. Why not? The Jews generally give value. They make you pay; but they deliver the goods. In my experience the men who want something for nothing are invariably Christians.

A page appears.

THE PAGE. The Right Reverend the Bishop of Beauvais: Monseigneur Cauchon.

Cauchon, aged about 60, *comes in. The page withdraws. The two Englishmen rise.*

THE NOBLEMAN [*with effusive courtesy*] My dear Bishop, how good of you to come! Allow me to introduce myself: Richard de Beauchamp, Earl of Warwick, at your service.

CAUCHON. Your lordship's fame is well known to me.

WARWICK. This reverend cleric is Master John de Stogumber.

THE CHAPLAIN [*glibly*] John Bowyer Spenser Neville de Stogumber, at your service, my lord: Bachelor of Theology, and Keeper of the Private Seal to His Eminence the Cardinal of Winchester.

WARWICK [*to Cauchon*] You call him the Cardinal of England, I believe. Our king's uncle.

CAUCHON. Messire John de Stogumber: I am always the very good friend of His Eminence. [*He extends his hand to the chaplain, who kisses his ring.*]

WARWICK. Do me the honor to be seated. [*He gives Cauchon his chair, placing it at the head of the table*].

Cauchon accepts the place of honor with a grave inclination. Warwick fetches the leather stool carelessly, and sits in his former place. The chaplain goes back to his chair.

Though Warwick has taken second place in calculated deference to the Bishop, he assumes the lead in opening the proceedings as a matter of course. He is still cordial and expansive; but there is a new note in his voice which means that he is coming to business.

WARWICK. Well, my Lord Bishop, you find us in one of our unlucky moments. Charles is to be crowned at Rheims, practically by the young woman from Lorraine; and—I must not deceive you, nor flatter your hopes—we cannot prevent it. I suppose it will make a great difference to Charles's position.

CAUCHON. Undoubtedly. It is a masterstroke of The Maid's.

THE CHAPLAIN [*again agitated*] We were not fairly beaten, my lord. No Englishman is ever fairly beaten.

Cauchon raises his eyebrow slightly, then quickly composes his face.

WARWICK. Our friend here takes the view that the young woman is a sorceress. It would, I presume, be the duty of your reverend lordship to denounce her to the Inquisition, and have her burnt for that offence.

CAUCHON. If she were captured in my diocese: yes.

WARWICK [*feeling that they are getting on capitally*] Just so. Now I suppose there can be no reasonable doubt that she is a sorceress.

THE CHAPLAIN. Not the least. An arrant witch.

WARWICK [*gently reproving the interruption*] We are asking

for the Bishop's opinion, Messire John.

CAUCHON. We shall have to consider not merely our own opinions here, but the opinions—the prejudices, if you like—of a French court.

WARWICK [*correcting*] A Catholic court, my lord.

CAUCHON. Catholic courts are composed of mortal men, like other courts, however sacred their function and inspiration may be. And if the men are Frenchmen, as the modern fashion calls them, I am afraid the bare fact that an English army has been defeated by a French one will not convince them that there is any sorcery in the matter.

THE CHAPLAIN. What! Not when the famous Sir John Talbot himself has been defeated and actually taken prisoner by a drab from the ditches of Lorraine!

CAUCHON. Sir John Talbot, we all know, is a fierce and formidable soldier, Messire; but I have yet to learn that he is an able general. And though it pleases you to say that he has been defeated by this girl, some of us may be disposed to give a little of the credit to Dunois.

THE CHAPLAIN [*contemptuously*] The Bastard of Orleans!

CAUCHON. Let me remind—

WARWICK [*interposing*] I know what you are going to say, my lord. Dunois defeated me at Montargis.

CAUCHON [*bowing*] I take that as evidence that the Seigneur Dunois is a very able commander indeed.

WARWICK. Your lordship is the flower of courtesy. I admit, on our side, that Talbot is a mere fighting animal, and that it probably served him right to be taken at Patay.

THE CHAPLAIN [*chafing*] My lord: at Orleans this woman had her throat pierced by an English arrow, and was seen to cry like a child from the pain of it. It was a death wound; yet she fought all day; and when our men had repulsed all her attacks like true Englishmen, she walked alone to the wall of our fort with a white banner in her hand; and our men were paralyzed, and could neither shoot nor strike whilst the French fell on them and drove them on to the bridge, which immediately burst into flames and crumbled under them, letting them down into the river, where they were drowned in heaps. Was this your bastard's generalship? or were those flames the flames of hell, conjured up by witchcraft?

WARWICK. You will forgive Messire John's vehemence, my lord; but he has put our case. Dunois is a great captain, we admit; but why could he do nothing until the witch came?

CAUCHON. I do not say that there were no supernatural powers on her side. But the names on that white banner were not the names of Satan and Beelzebub, but the blessed names of our Lord and His holy mother. And your commander who was drowned—Clahz-da I think you call him—

WARWICK. Glasdale. Sir William Glasdale.

CAUCHON. Glass-dell, thank you. He was no saint; and many of our people think that he was drowned for his blasphemies against The Maid.

WARWICK [*beginning to look very dubious*] Well, what are we to infer from all this, my lord? Has The Maid converted you?

CAUCHON. If she had, my lord, I should have known better than to have trusted myself here within your grasp.

WARWICK [*blandly deprecating*] Oh! oh! My lord!

CAUCHON. If the devil is making use of this girl—and I believe he is—

WARWICK [*reassured*] Ah! You hear, Messire John? I knew your lordship would not fail us. Pardon my interruption. Proceed.

CAUCHON. If it be so, the devil has longer views than you give him credit for.

WARWICK. Indeed? In what way? Listen to this, Messire John.

CAUCHON. If the devil wanted to damn a country girl, do you think so easy a task would cost him the winning of half a dozen battles? No, my lord: any trumpery imp could do that much if the girl could be damned at all. The Prince of Darkness does not condescend to such cheap drudgery. When he strikes, he strikes at the Catholic Church, whose realm is the whole spiritual world. When he damns, he damns the souls of the entire human race. Against that dreadful design The Church stands ever on guard. And it is as one of the instruments of that design that I see this girl. She is inspired, but diabolically inspired.

THE CHAPLAIN. I told you she was a witch.

CAUCHON [*fiercely*] She is not a witch. She is a heretic.

THE CHAPLAIN. What difference does that make?

CAUCHON. You, a priest, ask me that! You English are strangely blunt in the mind. All these things that you call witchcraft are capable of a natural explanation. The woman's miracles would not impose on a rabbit: she does not claim them as miracles herself. What do her victories prove but that she has a better head on her shoulders than your swearing Glass-dells and mad bull Talbots, and that the courage of faith, even though it be a false faith, will always outstay the courage of wrath?

THE CHAPLAIN [*hardly able to believe his ears*] Does your lordship compare Sir John Talbot, three times Governor of Ireland, to a mad bull? ! ! !

WARWICK. It would not be seemly for you to do so, Messire John, as you are still six removes from a barony. But as I am an earl, and Talbot is only a knight, I may make bold to accept the comparison. [*To the Bishop*] My lord: I wipe the slate as far as the witchcraft goes. None the less, we must burn the woman.

CAUCHON. I cannot burn her. The Church cannot take life. And my first duty is to seek this girl's salvation.

WARWICK. No doubt. But you do burn people occasionally.

CAUCHON. No. When The Church cuts off an obstinate heretic as a dead branch from the tree of life, the heretic is handed over to the secular arm. The Church has no part in what the secular arm may see fit to do.

WARWICK. Precisely. And I shall be the secular arm in

this case. Well, my lord, hand over your dead branch; and I will see that the fire is ready for it. If you will answer for The Church's part, I will answer for the secular part.

CAUCHON [*with smouldering anger*] I can answer for nothing. You great lords are too prone to treat The Church as a mere political convenience.

WARWICK [*smiling and propitiatory*] Not in England, I assure you.

CAUCHON. In England more than anywhere else. No, my lord: the soul of this village girl is of equal value with yours or your king's before the throne of God; and my first duty is to save it. I will not suffer your lordship to smile at me as if I were repeating a meaningless form of words, and it were well understood between us that I should betray the girl to you. I am no mere political bishop: my faith is to me what your honor is to you; and if there be a loophole through which this baptized child of God can creep to her salvation, I shall guide her to it.

THE CHAPLAIN [*rising in a fury*] You are a traitor.

CAUCHON [*springing up*] You lie, priest. [*Trembling with rage*] If you dare do what this woman has done—set your country above the holy Catholic Church—you shall go to the fire with her.

THE CHAPLAIN. My lord: I—I went too far. I— [*he sits down with a submissive gesture*].

WARWICK [*who has risen apprehensively*] My lord: I apologize to you for the word used by Messire John de Stogumber. It does not mean in England what it does in France. In your language traitor means betrayer: one who is perfidious, treacherous, unfaithful, disloyal. In our country it means simply one who is not wholly devoted to our English interests.

CAUCHON. I am sorry: I did not understand. [*He subsides into his chair with dignity*].

WARWICK [*resuming his seat, much relieved*] I must apologize on my own account if I have seemed to take the burning of this poor girl too lightly. When one has seen whole countrysides burnt over and over again as mere items in military routine, one has to grow a very thick skin. Otherwise one might go mad: at all events, I should. May I venture to assume that your lordship also, having to see so many heretics burned from time to time, is compelled to take—shall I say a professional view of what would otherwise be a very horrible incident?

CAUCHON. Yes: it is a painful duty: even, as you say, a horrible one. But in comparison with the horror of heresy it is less than nothing. I am not thinking of this girl's body, which will suffer for a few moments only, and which must in any event die in some more or less painful manner, but of her soul, which may suffer to all eternity.

WARWICK. Just so; and God grant that her soul may be saved! But the practical problem would seem to be how to save her soul without saving her body. For we must face it, my lord: if this cult of The Maid goes on, our cause is lost.

THE CHAPLAIN [*his voice broken like that of a man who has been crying*] May I speak, my lord?

WARWICK. Really, Messire John, I had rather you did not, unless you can keep your temper.

THE CHAPLAIN. It is only this. I speak under correction; but The Maid is full of deceit: she pretends to be devout. Her prayers and confessions are endless. How can she be accused of heresy when she neglects no observance of a faithful daughter of The Church?

CAUCHON [*flaming up*] A faithful daughter of The Church! The Pope himself at his proudest dare not presume as this woman presumes. She acts as if she herself were The Church. She brings the message of God to Charles; and The Church must stand aside. She will crown him in the cathedral of Rheims: she, not The Church! She sends letters to the king of England giving him God's command through her to return to his island on pain of God's vengeance, which she will execute. Let me tell you that the writing of such letters was the practice of the accursed Mahomet, the anti-Christ. Has she ever in all her utterances said one word of The Church? Never. It is always God and herself.

WARWICK. What can you expect? A beggar on horseback! Her head is turned.

CAUCHON. Who has turned it? The devil. And for a mighty purpose. He is spreading this heresy everywhere. The man Hus, burnt only thirteen years ago at Constance, infected all Bohemia with it. A man named WcLeef, himself an anointed priest, spread the pestilence in England; and to your shame you let him die in his bed. We have such people here in France too: I know the breed. It is cancerous: if it be not cut out, stamped out, burnt out, it will not stop until it has brought the whole body of human society into sin and corruption, into waste and ruin. By it an Arab camel driver drove Christ and His Church out of Jerusalem, and ravaged his way west like a wild beast until at last there stood only the Pyrenees and God's mercy between France and damnation. Yet what did the camel driver do at the beginning more than this shepherd girl is doing? He had his voices from the angel Gabriel: she has her voices from St Catherine and St Margaret and the Blessed Michael. He declared himself the messenger of God, and wrote in God's name to the kings of the earth. Her letters to them are going forth daily. It is not the Mother of God now to whom we must look for intercession, but to Joan the Maid. What will the world be like when The Church's accumulated wisdom and knowledge. and experience, its councils of learned, venerable pious men, are thrust into the kennel by every ignorant laborer or dairymaid whom the devil can puff up with the monstrous self-conceit of being directly inspired from heaven? It will be a world of blood, of fury, of devastation, of each man striving for his own hand: in the end a world wrecked back into barbarism. For now you have only Mahomet and his dupes, and the Maid and her dupes; but what will it be when every girl thinks herself a Joan and every man a Mahomet? I shudder to the very marrow of my bones when I think of it. I have fought it all my life; and I will fight it to the end. Let all this woman's sins be forgiven her except only this sin; for it is the sin against the Holy Ghost; and if she does not recant in the dust before the world, and submit herself to the last inch of her soul to her Church, to the fire she shall go if she once falls into my hand.

WARWICK [*unimpressed*] You feel strongly about it, naturally.

CAUCHON. Do not you?

WARWICK. I am a soldier, not a churchman. As a pilgrim I saw something of the Mahometans. They were not so ill-bred as I had been led to believe. In some respects their conduct compared favorably with ours.

CAUCHON [*displeased*] I have noticed this before. Men go to the East to convert the infidels. And the infidels pervert them. The Crusader comes back more than half a Saracen. Not to mention that all Englishmen are born heretics.

THE CHAPLAIN. Englishmen heretics!!! [*Appealing to Warwick*] My lord: must we endure this? His lordship is beside himself. How can what an Englishman believes be heresy? It is a contradiction in terms.

CAUCHON. I absolve you, Messire de Stogumber, on the ground of invincible ignorance. The thick air of your country does not breed theologians.

WARWICK. You would not say so if you heard us quarrelling about religion, my lord! I am sorry you think I must be either a heretic or a blockhead because, as a travelled man, I know that the followers of Mahomet profess great respect for our Lord, and are more ready to forgive St Peter for being a fisherman than your lordship is to forgive Mahomet for being a camel driver. But at least we can proceed in this matter without bigotry.

CAUCHON. When men call the zeal of the Christian Church bigotry I know what to think.

WARWICK. They are only east and west views of the same thing.

CAUCHON [*bitterly ironical*] Only east and west! Cnly!!

WARWICK. Oh, my Lord Bishop, I am not gainsaying you. You will carry The Church with you; but you have to carry the nobles also. To my mind there is a stronger case against The Maid than the one you have so forcibly put. Frankly, I am not afraid of this girl becoming another Mahomet, and superseding The Church by a great heresy. I think you exaggerate that risk. But have you noticed that in these letters of hers, she proposes to all the kings of Europe, as she has already pressed on Charles, a transaction which would wreck the whole social structure of Christendom?

CAUCHON. Wreck The Church. I tell you so.

WARWICK [*whose patience is wearing out*] My lord: pray get The Church out of your head for a moment; and remember that there are temporal institutions in the world as well as spiritual ones. I and my peers represent the feudal aristocracy as you represent The Church. We are the temporal power. Well, do you not see how this girl's idea strikes at us?

CAUCHON. How does her idea strike at you, except as it strikes at all of us, through The Church?

WARWICK. Her idea is that the kings should give their realms to God, and then reign as God's bailiffs.

CAUCHON [*not interested*] Quite sound theologically, my lord. But the king will hardly care, provided he reign. It is an abstract idea: a mere form of words.

WARWICK. By no means. It is a cunning device to supersede the aristocracy, and make the king sole and absolute autocrat. Instead of the king being merely the first among his peers, he becomes their master. That we cannot suffer: we call no man master. Nominally we hold our lands and dignities from the king, because there must be a keystone to the arch of human society; but we hold our lands in our own hands, and defend them with our own swords and those of our own tenants. Now by The Maid's doctrine the king will take our lands—o u r lands!—and make them a present to God; and God will then vest them wholly in the king.

CAUCHON. Need you fear that? You are the makers of kings after all. York or Lancaster in England, Lancaster or Valois in France: they reign according to your pleasure.

WARWICK. Yes; but only as long as the people follow their feudal lords, and know the king only as a travelling show, owning nothing but the highway that belongs to everybody. If the people's thoughts and hearts were turned to the king, and their lords became only the king's servants in their eyes, the king could break us across his knee one by one; and then what should we be but liveried courtiers in his halls?

CAUCHON. Still you need not fear, my lord. Some men are born kings; and some are born statesmen. The two are seldom the same. Where would the king find counsellors to plan and carry out such a policy for him?

WARWICK [*with a not too friendly smile*] Perhaps in the Church, my lord.

Cauchon, with an equally sour smile, shrugs his shoulders, and does not contradict him.

WARWICK. Strike down the barons; and the cardinals will have it all their own way.

CAUCHON [*conciliatory, dropping his polemical tone*] My lord: we shall not defeat The Maid if we strive against one another. I know well that there is a Will to Power in the world. I know that while it lasts there will be a struggle between the Emperor and the Pope, between the dukes and the political cardinals, between the barons and the kings. The devil divides us and governs. I see you are no friend to The Church: you are an earl first and last, as I am a churchman first and last. But can we not sink our differences in the face of a common enemy? I see now that what is in your mind is not that this girl has never once mentioned The Church, and thinks only of God and herself, but that she has never once mentioned the peerage, and thinks only of the king and herself.

WARWICK. Quite so. These two ideas of hers are the same idea at bottom. It goes deep, my lord. It is the protest of the individual soul against the interference of priest or peer between the private man and his God. I should call it Protestantism if I had to find a name for it.

CAUCHON [*looking hard at him*] You understand it wonderfully well, my lord. Scratch an Englishman, and find a Protestant.

WARWICK [*playing the pink of courtesy*] I think you are not entirely void of sympathy with The Maid's secular heresy, my lord. I leave you to find a name for it.

CAUCHON. You mistake me, my lord. I have no sympathy with her political presumptions. But as a priest I have gained a knowledge of the minds of the common people; and there you will find yet another most dangerous idea. I can express it only by such phrases as France for the French, England for the English, Italy for the Italians, Spain for the Spanish, and so forth. It is sometimes so narrow and bitter in country folk that it surprises me that this country girl can rise above the idea of her village for its villagers. But she can. She does. When she threatens to drive the English from the soil of France she is undoubtedly thinking of the whole extent of country in which French is spoken. To her the French-speaking people are what the Holy Scriptures describe as a nation. Call this side of her heresy Nationalism if you will: I can find you no better name for it. I can only tell you that it is essentially anti-Catholic and anti-Christian; for the Catholic Church knows only one realm, and that is the realm of Christ's kingdom. Divide that kingdom into nations, and you dethrone Christ. Dethrone Christ, and who will stand between our throats and the sword? The world will perish in a welter of war.

WARWICK. Well, if you will burn the Protestant, I will burn the Nationalist, though perhaps I shall not carry Messire John with me there. England for the English will appeal to him.

THE CHAPLAIN. Certainly England for the English goes without saying: it is the simple law of nature. But this woman denies to England her legitimate conquests, given her by God because of her peculiar fitness to rule over less civilized races for their own good. I do not understand what your lordships mean by Protestant and Nationalist: you are too learned and subtle for a poor clerk like myself. But I know as a matter of plain commonsense that the woman is a rebel; and that is enough for me. She rebels against Nature by wearing man's clothes, and fighting. She rebels against The Church by usurping the divine authority of the Pope. She rebels against God by her damnable league with Satan and his evil spirits against our army. And all these rebellions are only excuses for her great rebellion against England. That is not to be endured. Let her perish. Let her burn. Let her not infect the whole flock. It is expedient that one woman die for the people.

WARWICK [*rising*] My lord: we seem to be agreed.

CAUCHON [*rising also, but in protest*] I will not imperil my soul. I will uphold the justice of The Church. I will strive to the utmost for this woman's salvation.

WARWICK. I am sorry for the poor girl. I hate these severities. I will spare her if I can.

THE CHAPLAIN [*implacably*] I would burn her with my own hands.

CAUCHON [*blessing him*] Sancta simplicitas!

SCENE V

THE ambulatory in the cathedral of Rheims, near the door of the vestry. A pillar bears one of the stations of the cross. The organ is playing the people out of the nave after the coronation. Joan is kneeling in prayer before the station. She is beautifully dressed, but still in male attire. The organ ceases as Dunois, also splendidly arrayed, comes into the ambulatory from the vestry.

DUNOIS. Come, Joan! you have had enough praying. After that fit of crying you will catch a chill if you stay here any longer. It is all over: the cathedral is empty; and the streets are full. They are calling for The Maid. We have told them you are staying here alone to pray; but they want to see you again.

JOAN. No: let the king have all the glory.

DUNOIS. He only spoils the show, poor devil. No, Joan: you have crowned him; and you must go through with it.

JOAN [*shakes her head reluctantly*].

DUNOIS [*raising her*] Come come! it will be over in a couple of hours. It's better than the bridge at Orleans: eh?

JOAN. Oh, dear Dunois, how I wish it were the bridge at Orleans again! We l i v e d at that bridge.

DUNOIS. Yes, faith, and died too: some of us.

JOAN. Isnt it strange, Jack? I am such a coward: I am frightened beyond words before a battle; but it is so dull afterwards when there is no danger: oh, so dull! dull! dull!

DUNOIS. You must learn to be abstemious in war, just as you are in your food and drink, my little saint.

JOAN. Dear Jack: I think you like me as a soldier likes his comrade.

DUNOIS. You need it, poor innocent child of God. You have not many friends at court.

JOAN. Why do all these courtiers and knights and churchmen hate me? What have I done to them? I have asked nothing for myself except that my village shall not be taxed; for we cannot afford war taxes. I have brought them luck and victory: I have set them right when they were doing all sorts of stupid things: I have crowned Charles and made him a real king; and all the honors he is handing out have gone to them. Then why do they not love me?

DUNOIS [*rallying her*] Sim-ple-ton! Do you expect stupid people to love you for shewing them up? Do blundering old military dug-outs love the successful young captains who supersede them? Do ambitious politicians love the climbers who take the front seats from them? Do archbishops enjoy being played off their own altars, even by saints? Why, I should be jealous of you myself if I were ambitious enough.

JOAN. You are the pick of the basket here, Jack: the only friend I have among all these nobles. I'll wager your mother was from the country. I will go back to the farm when I have taken Paris.

DUNOIS. I am not so sure that they will let you take Paris.

JOAN [*startled*] What!

DUNOIS. I should have taken it myself before this if they had all been sound about it. Some of them would rather Paris took you, I think. So take care.

JOAN. Jack: the world is too wicked for me. If the goddams and the Burgundians do not make an end of me, the French will. Only for my voices I should lose all heart. That is why I had to steal away to pray here alone after the coronation. I'll tell you something, Jack. It is in the bells I hear my voices. Not to-day, when they all rang: that was nothing but jangling. But here in this corner, where the bells come down from heaven, and the echoes linger, or in the fields, where they come from a distance through the quiet of the countryside, my voices are in them. [*The cathedral clock chimes the quarter*] Hark! [*She becomes rapt*] Do you hear? "Dear-child-of-God": just what you said. At the half-hour they will say "Be-brave-go-on." At the three-quarters they will say "I-am-thy-Help." But it is at the hour, when the great bell goes after "God-will-save-France": it is then that St Margaret and St Catherine and sometimes even the blessed Michael will say things that I cannot tell beforehand. Then, oh then—

DUNOIS [*interrupting her kindly but not sympathetically*] Then, Joan, we shall hear whatever we fancy in the booming of the bell. You make me uneasy when you talk about your voices: I should think you were a bit cracked if I hadnt noticed that you give me very sensible reasons for what you do, though I hear you telling others you are only obeying Madame Saint Catherine.

JOAN [*crossly*] Well, I have to find reasons for you, because you do not believe in my voices. But the voices come first; and I find the reasons after: whatever you may choose to believe.

DUNOIS. Are you angry, Joan?

JOAN. Yes. [*Smiling*] No: not with you. I wish you were one of the village babies.

DUNOIS. Why?

JOAN. I could nurse you for awhile.

DUNOIS. You are a bit of a woman after all.

JOAN. No: not a bit: I am a soldier and nothing else. Soldiers always nurse children when they get a chance.

DUNOIS. That is true. [*He laughs*].

King Charles, with Bluebeard on his left and La Hire on his right, comes from the vestry, where he has been disrobing. Joan shrinks away behind the pillar. Dunois is left between Charles and La Hire.

DUNOIS. Well, your Majesty is an anointed king at last. How do you like it?

CHARLES. I would not go through it again to be emperor of the sun and moon. The weight of those robes! I thought I should have dropped when they loaded that crown on to me. And the famous holy oil they talked so much about was rancid: phew! The Archbishop must be nearly dead: his robes must have weighed a ton: they are stripping him still in the vestry.

DUNOIS [*drily*] Your majesty should wear armor oftener. That would accustom you to heavy dressing.

CHARLES. Yes: the old jibe! Well, I am not going to wear armor: fighting is not my job. Where is The Maid?

JOAN [*coming forward between Charles and Bluebeard, and falling on her knee*] Sire: I have made you king: my work is done. I am going back to my father's farm.

CHARLES [*surprised, but relieved*] Oh, are you? Well, that will be very nice.

Joan rises, deeply discouraged.

CHARLES [*continuing heedlessly*] A healthy life, you know.

DUNOIS. But a dull one.

BLUEBEARD. You will find the petticoats tripping you up after leaving them off for so long.

LA HIRE. You will miss the fighting. It's a bad habit, but a grand one, and the hardest of all to break yourself of.

CHARLES [*anxiously*] Still, we dont want you to stay if you would really rather go home.

JOAN [*bitterly*] I know well that none of you will be sorry to see me go. [*She turns her shoulder to Charles and walks past him to the more congenial neighborhood of Dunois and La Hire*].

LA HIRE. Well, I shall be able to swear when I want to. But I shall miss you at times.

JOAN. La Hire: in spite of all your sins and swears we shall meet in heaven; for I love you as I love Pitou, my old sheep dog. Pitou could kill a wolf. You will kill the English wolves until they go back to their country and become good dogs of God, will you not?

LA HIRE. You and I together: yes.

JOAN. No: I shall last only a year from the beginning.

ALL THE OTHERS. What!

JOAN. I know it somehow.

DUNOIS. Nonsense!

JOAN. Jack: do you think you will be able to drive them out?

DUNOIS [*with quiet conviction*] Yes: I shall drive them out. They beat us because we thought battles were tournaments and ransom markets. We played the fool while the goddams took war seriously. But I have learnt my lesson, and taken their measure. They have no roots here. I have beaten them before; and I shall beat them again.

JOAN. You will not be cruel to them, Jack?

DUNOIS. The goddams will not yield to tender handling. We did not begin it.

JOAN [*suddenly*] Jack: before I go home, let us take Paris.

CHARLES [*terrified*] Oh no no. We shall lose everything we have gained. Oh dont let us have any more fighting. We can make a very good treaty with the Duke of Burgundy.

JOAN. Treaty! [*She stamps with impatience*].

CHARLES. Well, why not, now that I am crowned and anointed? Oh, that oil!

The Archbishop comes from the vestry, and joins the group between Charles and Bluebeard.

CHARLES. Archbishop: The Maid wants to start fighting again.

THE ARCHBISHOP. Have we ceased fighting, then? Are we at peace?

CHARLES. No: I suppose not; but let us be content with what we have done. Let us make a treaty. Our luck is too good to last; and now is our chance to stop before it turns.

JOAN. Luck! God has fought for us; and you call it luck! And you would stop while there are still Englishmen on this holy earth of dear France!

THE ARCHBISHOP [*sternly*] Maid: the king addressed himself to me, not to you. You forget yourself. You very often forget yourself.

JOAN [*unabashed, and rather roughly*] Then speak, you; and tell him that it is not God's will that he should take his hand from the plough.

THE ARCHBISHOP. If I am not so glib with the name of God as you are, it is because I interpret His will with the authority of The Church and of my sacred office. When you first came you respected it, and would not have dared to speak as you are now speaking. You came clothed with the virtue of humility; and because God blessed your enterprises accordingly, you have stained yourself with the sin of pride. The old Greek tragedy is rising among us. It is the chastisement of hubris.

CHARLES. Yes: she thinks she knows better than every-one else.

JOAN [*distressed, but naïvely incapable of seeing the effect she is producing*] But I do know better than any of you seem to. And I am not proud: I never speak unless I know I am right.

BLUEBEARD } [*exclaiming together*] { Ha ha!
CHARLES } { Just so.

THE ARCHBISHOP. How do you know you are right?

JOAN. I always know. My voices—

CHARLES. Oh, your voices, your voices. Why dont the voices come to me? I am king, not you.

JOAN. They do come to you; but you do not hear them. You have not sat in the field in the evening listening for them. When the angelus rings you cross yourself and have done with it; but if you prayed from your heart, and listened to the thrilling of the bells in the air after they stop ringing, you would hear the voices as well as I do. [*Turning brusquely from him*] But what voices do you need to tell you what the blacksmith can tell you: that you must strike while the iron is hot? I tell you we must make a dash at Compiégne and relieve it as we relieved Orleans. Then Paris will open its gates; or if not, we will break through them. What is your crown worth without your capital?

LA HIRE. That is what I say too. We shall go through them like a red hot shot through a pound of butter. What do you say, Bastard?

DUNOIS. If our cannon balls were all as hot as your head, and we had enough of them, we should conquer the earth, no doubt. Pluck and impetuosity are good servants in war, but bad masters: they have delivered us into the hands of the English every time we have trusted to them. We never know when we are beaten: that is our great fault.

JOAN. You never know when you are victorious: that is a worse fault. I shall have to make you carry looking-glasses in battle to convince you that the English have not cut off all your noses. You would have been besieged in Orleans still, you and your councils of war, if I had not made you attack. You should always attack; and if you only hold on long enough the enemy will stop first. You dont know how to begin a battle; and you dont know how to use your cannons. And I do.

She squats down on the flags with crossed ankles, pouting.

DUNOIS. I know what you think of us, General Joan.

JOAN. Never mind that, Jack. Tell them what you think of me.

DUNOIS. I think that God was on your side; for I have not forgotten how the wind changed, and how our hearts changed when you came; and by my faith I shall never deny that it was in your sign that we conquered. But I tell you as a soldier that God is no man's daily drudge, and no maid's either. If you are worthy of it he will sometimes snatch you out of the jaws of death and set you on your feet again; but that is all: once on your feet you must fight with all your might and all your craft. For he has to be fair to your enemy too: dont forget that. Well, he set us on our feet through you at Orleans; and the glory of it has carried us through a few good battles here to the coronation. But if we presume on it further, and trust to God to do the work we should do ourselves, we shall be defeated; and serve us right!

JOAN. But—

DUNOIS. Sh! I have not finished. Do not think, any of you, that these victories of ours were won without generalship. King Charles: you have said no word in your proclamations of my part in this campaign; and I make no complaint of that; for the people will run after The Maid and her miracles and not after the Bastard's hard work finding troops for her and feeding them. But I know exactly how much God did for us through The Maid, and how much He left me to do by my own wits; and I tell you that your little hour of miracles is over, and that from this time on he who plays the war game best will win—if the luck is on his side.

JOAN. Ah! if, if, if, if! If ifs and ans were pots and pans there'd be no need of tinkers. [*Rising impetuously*] I tell you, Bastard, your art of war is no use, because your knights are no good for real fighting. War is only a game to them, like tennis and all their other games: they make rules as to what is fair and what is not fair, and heap armor on themselves and on their poor horses to keep out the arrows; and when they fall they cant get up, and have to wait for their squires to come and lift them to arrange about the ransom with the man that has poked them off their horse. Cant you see that all the like of that is gone by and done with? What use is armor against gunpowder? And if it was, do you think men that are fighting for France and for God will stop to bargain about ransoms, as half your knights live by doing? No: they will fight to win; and they will give up their lives out of their own hand into the hand of God when they go into battle, as I do. Common folks understand this. They cannot afford armor and cannot pay ransoms; but they follow me half naked into the moat and up the ladder and over the wall. With them it is my life or thine, and God defend the right! You may shake your head, Jack; and Bluebeard may twirl his billygoat's beard and cock his nose at me; but remember the day your knights and captains refused to follow me to attack the English at Orleans! You locked the gates to keep me in; and it was the townsfolk and the common people that followed me, and forced the gate, and shewed you the way to fight in earnest.

BLUEBEARD [*offended*] Not content with being Pope Joan, you must be Caesar and Alexander as well.

THE ARCHBISHOP. Pride will have a fall, Joan.

JOAN. Oh, never mind whether it is pride or not: is it true? is it commonsense?

LA HIRE. It is true. Half of us are afraid of having our handsome noses broken; and the other half are out for paying off their mortgages. Let her have her way, Dunois: she does not know everything; but she has got hold of the right end of the stick. Fighting is not what it was; and those who know least about it often make the best job of it.

DUNOIS. I know all that. I do not fight in the old way: I have learnt the lesson of Agincourt, of Poitiers and Crecy. I know how many lives any move of mine will cost; and if the move is worth the cost I make it and pay the cost. But Joan never counts the cost at all: she goes ahead and trusts to God: she thinks she has God in her pocket. Up to now she has had the numbers on her side; and she has won. But I know Joan; and I see that some day she will go ahead when she has only ten men to do the work of a hundred. And then she will find that God is on the side of the big battalions. She will be taken by the enemy. And the lucky man that makes the capture will receive sixteen thousand pounds from the Earl of Ouareek.

JOAN [*flattered*] Sixteen thousand pounds! Eh, laddie, have they offered that for me? There cannot be so much money in the world.

DUNOIS. There is, in England. And now tell me, all of you, which of you will lift a finger to save Joan once the English have got her? I speak first, for the army. The day after she has been dragged from her horse by a goddam or a Burgundian, and he is not struck dead: the day after she is locked in a dungeon, and the bars and bolts do not fly open at the touch of St Peter's angel: the day when the enemy finds out that she is as vulnerable as I am and not a bit more invincible, she will not be worth the life of a single soldier to us; and I will not risk that life, much as I cherish her as a companion-in-arms.

JOAN. I dont blame you, Jack: you are right. I am not worth one soldier's life if God lets me be beaten; but France may think me worth my ransom after what God has done for her through me.

CHARLES. I tell you I have no money; and this coronation, which is all your fault, has cost me the last farthing I can borrow.

JOAN. The Church is richer than you. I put my trust in

The Church.

THE ARCHBISHOP. Woman: they will drag you through the streets, and burn you as a witch.

JOAN [*running to him*] Oh, my lord, do not say that. It is impossible. I a witch!

THE ARCHBISHOP. Peter Cauchon knows his business. The University of Paris has burnt a woman for saying that what you have done was well done, and according to God.

JOAN [*bewildered*] But why? What sense is there in it? What I have done is according to God. They could not burn a woman for speaking the truth.

THE ARCHBISHOP. They did.

JOAN. But you know that she was speaking the truth. You would not let them burn me.

THE ARCHBISHOP. How could I prevent them?

JOAN. You would speak in the name of The Church. You are a great prince of The Church. I would go anywhere with your blessing to protect me.

THE ARCHBISHOP. I have no blessing for you while you are proud and disobedient.

JOAN. Oh, why will you go on saying things like that? I am not proud and disobedient. I am a poor girl, and so ignorant that I do not know A from B. How could I be proud? And how can you say that I am disobedient when I always obey my voices, because they come from God.

THE ARCHBISHOP. The voice of God on earth is the voice of the Church Militant; and all the voices that come to you are the echoes of your own wilfulness.

JOAN. It is not true.

THE ARCHBISHOP [*flushing angrily*] You tell the Archbishop in his cathedral that he lies; and yet you say you are not proud and disobedient.

JOAN. I never said you lied. It was you that as good as said my voices lied. When have they ever lied? If you will not believe in them: even if they are only the echoes of my own commonsense, are they not always right? and are not your earthly counsels always wrong?

THE ARCHBISHOP [*indignantly*] It is waste of time admonishing you.

CHARLES. It always comes back to the same thing. She is right; and everyone else is wrong.

THE ARCHBISHOP. Take this as your last warning. If you perish through setting your private judgment above the instructions of your spiritual directors, The Church disowns you, and leaves you to whatever fate your presumption may bring upon you. The Bastard has told you that if you persist in setting up your military conceit above the counsels of your commanders—

DUNOIS [*interposing*] To put it quite exactly, if you attempt to relieve the garrison in Compiègne without the same superiority in numbers you had at Orleans—

THE ARCHBISHOP. The army will disown you, and will not rescue you. And His Majesty the King has told you that the throne has not the means of ransoming you.

CHARLES. Not a penny.

THE ARCHBISHOP. You stand alone: absolutely alone, trusting to your own conceit, your own ignorance, your own headstrong presumption, your own impiety in hiding all these sins under the cloak of a trust in God. When you pass through these doors into the sunlight, the crowd will cheer you. They will bring you their little children and their invalids to heal: they will kiss your hands and feet, and do what they can, poor simple souls, to turn your head, and madden you with the self-confidence that is leading you to your destruction. But you will be none the less alone: they cannot save you. We and we only can stand between you and the stake at which our enemies have burnt that wretched woman in Paris.

JOAN [*her eyes skyward*] I have better friends and better counsel than yours.

THE ARCHBISHOP. I see that I am speaking in vain to a hardened heart. You reject our protection, and are determined to turn us all against you. In future, then, fend for yourself; and if you fail, God have mercy on your soul.

DUNOIS. That is the truth, Joan. Heed it.

JOAN. Where would you all have been now if I had heeded that sort of truth? There is no help, no counsel, in any of you. Yes: I am alone on earth: I have always been alone. My father told my brothers to drown me if I would not stay to mind his sheep while France was bleeding to death: France might perish if only our lambs were safe. I thought France would have friends at the court of the king of France; and I find only wolves fighting for pieces of her poor torn body. I thought God would have friends everywhere, because He is the friend of everyone; and in my innocence I believed that you who now cast me out would be like strong towers to keep harm from me. But I am wiser now; and nobody is any the worse for being wiser. Do not think you can frighten me by telling me that I am alone. France is alone; and God is alone; and what is my loneliness before the loneliness of my country and my God? I see now that the loneliness of God is His strength: what would He be if He listened to your jealous little counsels? Well, my loneliness shall be my strength too: it is better to be alone with God: His friendship will not fail me, nor His counsel, nor His love. In His strength I will dare, and dare, and dare, until I die. I will go out now to the common people, and let the love in their eyes comfort me for the hate in yours. You will all be glad to see me burnt; but if I go through the fire I shall go through it to their hearts for ever and ever. And so, God be with me!

She goes from them. They stare after her in glum silence for a moment. Then Gilles de Rais twirls his beard.

BLUEBEARD. You know, the woman is quite impossible. I dont dislike her, really; but what are you to do with such a character?

DUNOIS. As God is my judge, if she fell into the Loire I would jump in in full armor to fish her out. But if she plays the fool at Compiègne, and gets caught, I must leave her to her doom.

LA HIRE. Then you had better chain me up; for I could

follow her to hell when the spirit rises in her like that.

THE ARCHBISHOP. She disturbs my judgment too: there is a dangerous power in her outbursts. But the pit is open at her feet; and for good or evil we cannot turn her from it.

CHARLES. If only she would keep quiet, or go home!

They follow her dispiritedly.

SCENE VI

ROUEN, *30th May 1431. A great stone hall in the castle, arranged for a trial-at-law, but not a trial-by-jury, the court being the Bishop's court with the Inquisition participating: hence there are two raised chairs side by side for the Bishop and the Inquisitor as judges. Rows of chairs radiating from them at an obtuse angle are for the canons, the doctors of law and theology, and the Dominican monks, who act as assessors. In the angle is a table for the scribes, with stools. There is also a heavy rough wooden stool for the prisoner. All these are at the inner end of the hall. The further end is open to the courtyard through a row of arches. The court is shielded from the weather by screens and curtains.*

Looking down the great hall from the middle of the inner end, the judicial chairs and scribes' table are to the right. The prisoner's stool is to the left. There are arched doors right and left. It is a fine sunshiny May morning.

Warwick comes in through the arched doorway on the judges' side, followed by his page.

THE PAGE [*pertly*] I suppose your lordship is aware that we have no business here. This is an ecclesiastical court; and we are only the secular arm.

WARWICK. I am aware of that fact. Will it please your impudence to find the Bishop of Beauvais for me, and give him a hint that he can have a word with me here before the trial, if he wishes?

THE PAGE [*going*] Yes, my lord.

WARWICK. And mind you behave yourself. Do not address him as Pious Peter.

THE PAGE. No, my lord. I shall be kind to him, because, when The Maid is brought in, Pious Peter will have to pick a peck of pickled pepper.

Cauchon enters through the same door with a Dominican monk and a canon, the latter carrying a brief.

THE PAGE. The Right Reverend his lordship the Bishop of Beauvais. And two other reverend gentlemen.

WARWICK. Get out; and see that we are not interrupted.

THE PAGE. Right, my lord [*he vanishes airily*].

CAUCHON. I wish your lordship good-morrow.

WARWICK. Good-morrow to your lordship. Have I had the pleasure of meeting your friends before? I think not.

CAUCHON [*introducing the monk, who is on his right*] This, my lord, is Brother John Lemaître, of the order of St Dominic. He is acting as deputy for the Chief Inquisitor into the evil of heresy in France. Brother John: the Earl of Warwick.

WARWICK. Your Reverence is most welcome. We have no Inquisitor in England, unfortunately; though we miss him greatly, especially on occasions like the present.

The Inquisitor smiles patiently, and bows. He is a mild elderly gentleman, but has evident reserves of authority and firmness.

CAUCHON [*introducing the Canon, who is on his left*] This gentleman is Canon John D'Estivet, of the Chapter of Bayeux. He is acting as Promoter.

WARWICK. Promoter?

CAUCHON. Prosecutor, you would call him in civil law.

WARWICK. Ah! prosecutor. Quite, quite. I am very glad to make your acquaintance, Canon D'Estivet.

D'Estivet bows. [*He is on the young side of middle age, well mannered, but vulpine beneath his veneer*].

WARWICK. May I ask what stage the proceedings have reached? It is now more than nine months since The Maid was captured at Compiègne by the Burgundians. It is fully four months since I bought her from the Burgundians for a very handsome sum, solely that she might be brought to justice. It is very nearly three months since I delivered her up to you, my Lord Bishop, as a person suspected of heresy. May I suggest that you are taking a rather unconscionable time to make up your minds about a very plain case? Is this trial never going to end?

THE INQUISITOR [*smiling*] It has not yet begun, my lord.

WARWICK. Not yet begun! Why, you have been at it eleven weeks!

CAUCHON. We have not been idle, my lord. We have held fifteen examinations of The Maid: six public and nine private.

THE INQUISITOR [*always patiently smiling*] You see, my lord, I have been present at only two of these examinations. They were proceedings of the Bishop's court solely, and not of the Holy Office. I have only just decided to associate myself—that is, to associate the Holy Inquisition—with the Bishop's court. I did not at first think that this was a case of heresy at all. I regarded it as a political case, and The Maid as a prisoner of war. But having now been present at two of the examinations, I must admit that this seems to be one of the gravest cases of heresy within my experience. Therefore everything is now in order; and we proceed to trial this morning. [*He moves towards the judicial chairs*].

CAUCHON. This moment, if your lordship's convenience allows.

WARWICK [*graciously*] Well, that is good news, gentlemen. I will not attempt to conceal from you that our patience was becoming strained.

CAUCHON. So I gathered from the threats of your soldiers to drown those of our people who favor The Maid.

WARWICK. Dear me! At all events their intentions were friendly to you, my lord.

CAUCHON [*sternly*] I hope not. I am determined that the woman shall have a fair hearing. The justice of The Church is not a mockery, my lord.

THE INQUISITOR [*returning*] Never has there been a fairer examination within my experience, my lord. The Maid needs no lawyers to take her part: she will be tried by her most faithful friends, all ardently desirous to save her soul from perdition.

D'ESTIVET. Sir: I am the Promoter; and it has been my painful duty to present the case against the girl; but believe me, I would throw up my case today and hasten to her defence if I did not know that men far my superiors in learning and piety, in eloquence and persuasiveness, have been sent to reason with her, to explain to her the danger she is running, and the ease with which she may avoid it. [*Suddenly bursting into forensic eloquence, to the disgust of Cauchon and the Inquisitor, who have listened to him so far with patronizing approval*] Men have dared to say that we are acting from hate; but God is our witness that they lie. Have we tortured her? No. Have we ceased to exhort her; to implore her to have pity on herself; to come to the bosom of her Church as an erring but beloved child? Have we—

CAUCHON [*interrupting drily*] Take care, Canon. All that you say is true; but if you make his lordship believe it I will not answer for your life, and hardly for my own.

WARWICK [*deprecating, but by no means denying*] Oh, my lord, you are very hard on us poor English. But we certainly do not share your pious desire to save The Maid: in fact I tell you now plainly that her death is a political necessity which I regret but cannot help. If The Church lets her go—

CAUCHON [*with fierce and menacing pride*] If The Church lets her go, woe to the man, were he the Emperor himself, who dares lay a finger on her! The Church is not subject to political necessity, my lord.

THE INQUISITOR [*interposing smoothly*] You need have no anxiety about the result, my lord. You have an invincible ally in the matter: one who is far more determined than you that she shall burn.

WARWICK. And who is this very convenient partisan, may I ask?

THE INQUISITOR. The Maid herself. Unless you put a gag in her mouth you cannot prevent her from convicting herself ten times over every time she opens it.

D'ESTIVET. That is perfectly true, my lord. My hair bristles on my head when I hear so young a creature utter such blasphemies.

WARWICK. Well, by all means do your best for her if you are quite sure it will be of no avail. [*Looking hard at Cauchon*] I should be sorry to have to act without the blessing of The Church.

CAUCHON [*with a mixture of cynical admiration and contempt*] And yet they say Englishmen are hypocrites! You play for your side, my lord, even at the peril of your soul. I cannot but admire such devotion; but I dare not go so far myself. I fear damnation.

WARWICK. If we feared anything we could never govern England, my lord. Shall I send your people in to you?

CAUCHON. Yes: it will be very good of your lordship to withdraw and allow the court to assemble.

Warwick turns on his heel, and goes out through the courtyard. Cauchon takes one of the judicial seats; and D'Estivet sits at the scribes' table, studying his brief.

CAUCHON [*casually, as he makes himself comfortable*] What scoundrels these English nobles are!

THE INQUISITOR [*taking the other judicial chair on Cauchon's left*] All secular power makes men scoundrels. They are not trained for the work; and they have not the Apostolic Succession. Our own nobles are just as bad.

The Bishop's assessors hurry into the hall, headed by Chaplain de Stogumber and Canon de Courcelles, a young priest of 30. The scribes sit at the table, leaving a chair vacant opposite D'Estivet. Some of the assessors take their seats: others stand chatting, waiting for the proceedings to begin formally. De Stogumber, aggrieved and obstinate, will not take his seat: neither will the Canon, who stands on his right.

CAUCHON. Good morning, Master de Stogumber. [*To the Inquisitor*] Chaplain to the Cardinal of England.

THE CHAPLAIN [*correcting him*] Of Winchester, my lord. I have to make a protest, my lord.

CAUCHON. You make a great many.

THE CHAPLAIN. I am not without support, my lord. Here is Master de Courcelles, Canon of Paris, who associates himself with me in my protest.

CAUCHON. Well, what is the matter?

THE CHAPLAIN [*sulkily*] Speak you, Master de Courcelles, since I do not seem to enjoy his lordship's confidence. [*He sits down in dudgeon next to Cauchon, on his right*].

COURCELLES. My lord: we have been at great pains to draw up an indictment of The Maid on sixtyfour counts. We are now told that they have been reduced, without consulting us.

THE INQUISITOR. Master de Courcelles: I am the culprit. I am overwhelmed with admiration for the zeal displayed in your sixtyfour counts; but in accusing a heretic, as in other things, enough is enough. Also you must remember that all the members of the court are not so subtle and profound as you, and that some of your very great learning might appear to them to be very great nonsense. Therefore I have thought it well to have your sixtyfour articles cut down to twelve—

COURCELLES [*thunderstruck*] Twelve!!!

THE INQUISITOR. Twelve will, believe me, be quite enough for your purpose.

THE CHAPLAIN. But some of the most important points have been reduced almost to nothing. For instance, The Maid has actually declared that the blessed saints Margaret and Catherine, and the holy Archangel Michael, spoke to her in French. That is a vital point.

THE INQUISITOR. You think, doubtless, that they should have spoken in Latin?

CAUCHON. No: he thinks they should have spoken in English.

THE CHAPLAIN. Naturally, my lord.

THE INQUISITOR. Well, as we are all here agreed, I think, that these voices of The Maid are the voices of evil spirits tempting her to her damnation, it would not be very courteous to you, Master de Stogumber, or to the King of England, to assume that English is the devil's native language. So let it pass. The matter is not wholly omitted from the twelve articles. Pray take your places, gentlemen; and let us proceed to business.

All who have not taken their seats, do so.

THE CHAPLAIN. Well, I protest. That is all.

COURCELLES. I think it hard that all our work should go for nothing. It is only another example of the diabolical influence which this woman exercises over the court. [*He takes his chair, which is on the Chaplain's right*].

CAUCHON. Do you suggest that I am under diabolical influence?

COURCELLES. I suggest nothing, my lord. But it seems to me that there is a conspiracy here to hush up the fact that The Maid stole the Bishop of Senlis's horse.

CAUCHON [*keeping his temper with difficulty*] This is not a police court. Are we to waste our time on such rubbish?

COURCELLES [*rising, shocked*] My lord: do you call the Bishop's horse rubbish?

THE INQUISITOR [*blandly*] Master de Courcelles: The Maid alleges that she paid handsomely for the Bishop's horse, and that if he did not get the money the fault was not hers. As that may be true, the point is one on which The Maid may well be acquitted.

COURCELLES. Yes, if it were an ordinary horse. But the Bishop's horse! how can she be acquitted for that? [*He sits down again, bewildered and discouraged*].

THE INQUISITOR. I submit to you, with great respect, that if we persist in trying The Maid on trumpery issues on which we may have to declare her innocent, she may escape us on the great main issue of heresy, on which she seems so far to insist on her own guilt. I will ask you, therefore, to say nothing, when The Maid is brought before us, of these stealings of horses, and dancings round fairy trees with the village children, and prayings at haunted wells, and a dozen other things which you were diligently inquiring into until my arrival. There is not a village girl in France against whom you could not prove such things: they all dance round haunted trees, and pray at magic wells. Some of them would steal the Pope's horse if they got the chance. Heresy, gentlemen, heresy is the charge we have to try. The detection and suppression of heresy is my peculiar business: I am here as an inquisitor, not as an ordinary magistrate. Stick to the heresy, gentlemen; and leave the other matters alone.

CAUCHON. I may say that we have sent to the girl's village

to make inquiries about her; and there is practically nothing serious against her.

THE CHAPLAIN } *[rising and clamoring together]* { Nothing serious, my lord—
COURCELLES. } { What! The fairy tree not—

CAUCHON [*out of patience*] Be silent, gentlemen; or speak one at a time.

Courcelles collapses into his chair, intimidated.

THE CHAPLAIN [*sulkily resuming his seat*] That is what The Maid said to us last Friday.

CAUCHON. I wish you had followed her counsel, sir. When I say nothing serious, I mean nothing that men of sufficiently large mind to conduct an inquiry like this would consider serious. I agree with my colleague the Inquisitor that it is on the count of heresy that we must proceed.

LADVENU [*a young but ascetically fine-drawn Dominican who is sitting next Courcelles, on his right*] But is there any great harm in the girl's heresy? Is it not merely her simplicity? Many saints have said as much as Joan.

THE INQUISITOR [*dropping his blandness and speaking very gravely*] Brother Martin: if you had seen what I have seen of heresy, you would not think it a light thing even in its most apparently harmless and even lovable and pious origins. Heresy begins with people who are to all appearance better than their neighbours. A gentle and pious girl, or a young man who has obeyed the command of our Lord by giving all his riches to the poor, and putting on the garb of poverty, the life of austerity, and the rule of humility and charity, may be the founder of a heresy that will wreck both Church and Empire if not ruthlessly stamped out in time. The records of the holy Inquisition are full of histories we dare not give to the world, because they are beyond the belief of honest men and innocent women; yet they all began with saintly simpletons. I have seen this again and again. Mark what I say: the woman who quarrels with her clothes, and puts on the dress of a man, is like the man who throws off his fur gown and dresses like John the Baptist: they are followed, as surely as the night follows the day, by bands of wild women and men who refuse to wear any clothes at all. When maids will neither marry nor take regular vows, and men reject marriage and exalt their lusts into divine inspirations, then, as surely as the summer follows the spring, they begin with polygamy, and end by incest. Heresy at first seems innocent and even laudable; but it ends in such a monstrous horror of unnatural wickedness that the most tender-hearted among you, if you saw it at work as I have seen it, would clamor against the mercy of The Church in dealing with it. For two hundred years the Holy Office has striven with these diabolical madnesses; and it knows that they begin always by vain and ignorant persons setting up their own judgment against The Church, and taking it upon themselves to be the interpreters of God's will. You must not fall into the common error of mistaking these simpletons for liars and hypocrites. They believe honestly and sincerely that their diabolical inspiration is divine. Therefore you must be on your guard against your natural compassion. You are all, I hope, merciful men: how else could you have devoted your lives to the service of our gentle Savior? You are going to see before you a young girl, pious and chaste; for I must tell you, gentlemen, that the things said of her by our English friends are supported by no evidence, whilst there is abundant testimony that her excesses have been excesses of religion and charity and not of worldliness and wantonness. This girl is not one of those whose hard features are the sign of hard hearts, and whose brazen looks and lewd demeanor condemn them before they are accused. The devilish pride that has led her into her present peril has left no mark on her countenance. Strange as it may seem to you, it has even left no mark on her character outside those special matters in which she is proud; so that you will see a diabolical pride and a natural humility seated side by side in the selfsame soul. Therefore be on your guard. God forbid that I should tell you to harden your hearts; for her punishment if we condemn her will be so cruel that we should forfeit our own hope of divine mercy were there one grain of malice against her in our hearts. But if you hate cruelty—and if any man here does not hate it I command him on his soul's salvation to quit this holy court —I say, if you hate cruelty, remember that nothing is so cruel in its consequences as the toleration of heresy. Remember also that no court of law can be so cruel as the common people are to those whom they suspect of heresy. The heretic in the hands of the Holy Office is safe from violence, is assured of a fair trial, and cannot suffer death, even when guilty, if repentance follows sin. Innumerable lives of heretics have been saved because the Holy Office has taken them out of the hands of the people, and because the people have yielded them up, knowing that the Holy Office would deal with them. Before the Holy Inquisition existed, and even now when its officers are not within reach, the unfortunate wretch suspected of heresy, perhaps quite ignorantly and unjustly, is stoned, torn in pieces, drowned, burned in his house with all his innocent children, without a trial, unshriven, unburied save as a dog is buried: all of them deeds hateful to God and most cruel to man. Gentlemen: I am compassionate by nature as well as by my profession; and though the work I have to do may seem cruel to those who do not know how much more cruel it would be to leave it undone, I would go to the stake myself sooner than do it if I did not know its righteousness, its necessity, its essential mercy. I ask you to address yourself to this trial in that conviction. Anger is a bad counsellor: cast out anger. Pity is sometimes worse: cast out pity. But do not cast out mercy. Remember only that justice comes first. Have you anything to say, my lord, before we proceed to trial?

CAUCHON. You have spoken for me, and spoken better than I could. I do not see how any sane man could disagree with a word that has fallen from you. But this I will add. The crude heresies of which you have told us are horrible; but their horror is like that of the black death: they rage for a while and then die out, because sound and sensible men will not under any incitement be reconciled to nakedness and incest and polygamy and the like. But we are confronted today throughout Europe with a heresy that is spreading among men not weak in mind nor diseased in brain: nay, the stronger the mind, the more obstinate the heretic. It is neither discredited by fantastic extremes nor corrupted by the common lusts of the flesh; but it, too, sets up the private judgment of the single erring mortal against the considered wisdom and experience of The Church. The mighty structure of Catholic Christendom will never be shaken by naked madmen or by the sins of Moab and Ammon. But it may be betrayed from within, and brought to barbarous ruin and desolation, by this arch heresy which the English Commander calls Protestantism.

THE ASSESSORS [*whispering*] Protestantism! What was that? What does the Bishop mean? Is it a new heresy? The English Commander, he said. Did you ever hear of Protestantism? etc., etc.

CAUCHON [*continuing*] And that reminds me. What provision has the Earl of Warwick made for the defence of the secular arm should The Maid prove obdurate, and the people be moved to pity her?

THE CHAPLAIN. Have no fear on that score, my lord. The noble earl has eight hundred men-at-arms at the gates. She will not slip through our English fingers even if the whole city be on her side.

CAUCHON [*revolted*] Will you not add, God grant that she repent and purge her sin?

THE CHAPLAIN. That does not seem to me to be consistent; but of course I agree with your lordship.

CAUCHON [*giving him up with a shrug of contempt*] The court sits.

THE INQUISITOR. Let the accused be brought in.

LADVENU [*calling*] The accused. Let her be brought in.

Joan, chained by the ankles, is brought in through the arched door behind the prisoner's stool by a guard of English soldiers. With them is the Executioner and his assistants. They lead her to the prisoner's stool, and place themselves behind it after taking off her chain. She wears a page's black suit. Her long imprisonment and the strain of the examinations which have preceded the trial have left their mark on her; but her vitality still holds: she confronts the court unabashed, without a trace of the awe which their formal solemnity seems to require for the complete success of its impressiveness.

THE INQUISITOR [*kindly*] Sit down, Joan. [*She sits on the prisoner's stool*]. You look very pale today. Are you not well?

JOAN. Thank you kindly: I am well enough. But the Bishop sent me some carp; and it made me ill.

CAUCHON. I am sorry. I told them to see that it was fresh.

JOAN. You meant to be good to me, I know; but it is a fish that does not agree with me. The English thought you were trying to poison me—

CAUCHON } [*together*] { What!
THE CHAPLAIN } { No, my lord.

JOAN [*continuing*] They are determined that I shall be burnt as a witch; and they sent their doctor to cure me; but he was forbidden to bleed me because the silly people believe that a witch's witchery leaves her if she is bled; so he only called me filthy names. Why do you leave me in the hands of the English? I should be in the hands of The Church. And why must I be chained by the feet to a log of wood? Are you afraid I will fly away?

D'ESTIVET [*harshly*] Woman: it is not for you to question the court: it is for us to question you.

COURCELLES. When you were left unchained, did you not try to escape by jumping from a tower sixty feet high? If you cannot fly like a witch, how is it that you are still alive?

JOAN. I suppose because the tower was not so high then. It has grown higher every day since you began asking me questions about it.

D'ESTIVET. Why did you jump from the tower?

JOAN. How do you know that I jumped?

D'ESTIVET. You were found lying in the moat. Why did you leave the tower?

JOAN. Why would anybody leave a prison if they could get out?

D'ESTIVET. You tried to escape?

JOAN. Of course I did; and not for the first time either. If you leave the door of the cage open the bird will fly out.

D'ESTIVET [*rising*] That is a confession of heresy. I call the attention of the court to it.

JOAN. Heresy, he calls it! Am I a heretic because I try to escape from prison?

D'ESTIVET. Assuredly, if you are in the hands of The Church, and you wilfully take yourself out of its hands, you are deserting The Church; and that is heresy.

JOAN. It is great nonsense. Nobody could be such a fool as to think that.

D'ESTIVET. You hear, my lord, how I am reviled in the execution of my duty by this woman. [*He sits down indignantly*].

CAUCHON. I have warned you before, Joan, that you are doing yourself no good by these pert answers.

JOAN. But you will not talk sense to me. I am reasonable if you will be reasonable.

THE INQUISITOR [*interposing*] This is not yet in order. You forget, Master Promoter, that the proceedings have not been formally opened. The time for questions is after she has sworn on the Gospels to tell us the whole truth.

JOAN. You say this to me every time. I have said again and again that I will tell you all that concerns this trial. But I cannot tell you the whole truth: God does not allow the whole truth to be told. You do not understand it when I tell it. It is an old saying that he who tells too much truth is sure to be hanged. I am weary of this argument: we have been over it nine times already. I have sworn as much as I will swear; and I will swear no more.

COURCELLES. My lord: she should be put to the torture.

THE INQUISITOR. You hear, Joan? That is what happens to the obdurate. Think before you answer. Has she been shewn the instruments?

THE EXECUTIONER. They are ready, my lord. She has seen them.

JOAN. If you tear me limb from limb until you separate my soul from my body you will get nothing out of me beyond what I have told you. What more is there to tell that you could understand? Besides, I cannot bear to be hurt; and if you hurt me I will say anything you like to stop the pain. But I will take it all back afterwards; so what is the use of it?

LADVENU. There is much in that. We should proceed mercifully.

COURCELLES. But the torture is customary.

THE INQUISITOR. It must not be applied wantonly. If the accused will confess voluntarily, then its use cannot be justified.

COURCELLES. But this is unusual and irregular. She refuses to take the oath.

LADVENU [*disgusted*] Do you want to torture the girl for the mere pleasure of it?

COURCELLES [*bewildered*] But it is not a pleasure. It is the law. It is customary. It is always done.

THE INQUISITOR. That is not so, Master, except when the inquiries are carried on by people who do not know their legal business.

COURCELLES. But the woman is a heretic. I assure you it is always done.

CAUCHON [*decisively*] It will not be done today if it is not necessary. Let there be an end of this. I will not have it said that we proceeded on forced confessions. We have sent our best preachers and doctors to this woman to exhort and implore her to save her soul and body from the fire: we shall not now send the executioner to thrust her into it.

COURCELLES. Your lordship is merciful, of course. But it is a great responsibility to depart from the usual practice.

JOAN. Thou art a rare noodle, Master. Do what was done last time is thy rule, eh?

COURCELLES [*rising*] Thou wanton: dost thou dare call

me noodle?

THE INQUISITOR. Patience, Master, patience: I fear you will soon be only too terribly avenged.

COURCELLES [*mutters*] Noodle indeed! [*He sits down, much discontented*].

THE INQUISITOR. Meanwhile, let us not be moved by the rough side of a shepherd lass's tongue.

JOAN. Nay: I am no shepherd lass, though I have helped with the sheep like anyone else. I will do a lady's work in the house—spin or weave—against any woman in Rouen.

THE INQUISITOR. This is not a time for vanity, Joan. You stand in great peril.

JOAN. I know it: have I not been punished for my vanity? If I had not worn my cloth of gold surcoat in battle like a fool, that Burgundian soldier would never have pulled me backwards off my horse; and I should not have been here.

THE CHAPLAIN. If you are so clever at woman's work why do you not stay at home and do it?

JOAN. There are plenty of other women to do it; but there is nobody to do my work.

CAUCHON. Come! we are wasting time on trifles. Joan: I am going to put a most solemn question to you. Take care how you answer; for your life and salvation are at stake on it. Will you for all you have said and done, be it good or bad, accept the judgment of God's Church on earth? More especially as to the acts and words that are imputed to you in this trial by the Promoter here, will you submit your case to the inspired interpretation of the Church Militant?

JOAN. I am a faithful child of The Church. I will obey The Church—

CAUCHON [*hopefully leaning forward*] You will?

JOAN. —provided it does not command anything impossible.

Cauchon sinks back in his chair with a heavy sigh. The Inquisitor purses his lips and frowns. Ladvenu shakes his head pitifully.

D'ESTIVET. She imputes to The Church the error and folly of commanding the impossible.

JOAN. If you command me to declare that all that I have done and said, and all the visions and revelations I have had, were not from God, then that is impossible: I will not declare it for anything in the world. What God made me do I will never go back on; and what He has commanded or shall command I will not fail to do in spite of any man alive. That is what I mean by impossible. And in case The Church should bid me do anything contrary to the command I have from God, I will not consent to it, no matter what it may be.

THE ASSESSORS [*shocked and indignant*] Oh! The Church contrary to God! What do you say now? Flat heresy. This is beyond everything, etc., etc.

D'ESTIVET [*throwing down his brief*] My lord: do you need anything more than this?

CAUCHON. Woman: you have said enough to burn ten heretics. Will you not be warned? Will you not understand?

THE INQUISITOR. If the Church Militant tells you that your revelations and visions are sent by the devil to tempt you to your damnation, will you not believe that The Church is wiser than you?

JOAN. I believe that God is wiser than I; and it is His commands that I will do. All the things that you call my crimes have come to me by the command of God. I say that I have done them by the order of God: it is impossible for me to say anything else. If any Churchman says the contrary I shall not mind him: I shall mind God alone, whose command I always follow.

LADVENU [*pleading with her urgently*] You do not know what you are saying, child. Do you want to kill yourself? Listen. Do you not believe that you are subject to the Church of God on earth?

JOAN. Yes. When have I ever denied it?

LADVENU. Good. That means, does it not, that you are subject to our Lord the Pope, to the cardinals, the archbishops, and the bishops for whom his lordship stands here today?

JOAN. God must be served first.

D'ESTIVET. Then your voices command you not to submit yourself to the Church Militant?

JOAN. My voices do not tell me to disobey The Church; but God must be served first.

CAUCHON. And you, and not The Church, are to be the judge?

JOAN. What other judgment can I judge by but my own?

THE ASSESSORS [*scandalized*] Oh! [*They cannot find words*].

CAUCHON. Out of your own mouth you have condemned yourself. We have striven for your salvation to the verge of sinning ourselves: we have opened the door to you again and again; and you have shut it in our faces and in the face of God. Dare you pretend, after what you have said, that you are in a state of grace?

JOAN. If I am not, may God bring me to it: if I am, may God keep me in it!

LADVENU. That is a very good reply, my lord.

COURCELLES. Were you in a state of grace when you stole the Bishop's horse?

CAUCHON [*rising in a fury*] Oh, devil take the Bishop's horse and you too! We are here to try a case of heresy; and no sooner do we come to the root of the matter than we are thrown back by idiots who understand nothing but horses. [*Trembling with rage, he forces himself to sit down*].

THE INQUISITOR. Gentlemen, gentlemen: in clinging to these small issues you are The Maid's best advocates. I am not surprised that his lordship has lost patience with you. What does the Promoter say? Does he press these trumpery matters?

D'ESTIVET. I am bound by my office to press everything; but when the woman confesses a heresy that must bring upon her the doom of excommunication, of what consequence is it that she has been guilty also of offences which expose her to minor penances? I share the impatience of his lordship as to these minor charges. Only, with great respect, I must emphasize the gravity of two very horrible and blasphemous crimes which she does not deny. First, she has intercourse with evil spirits, and is therefore a sorceress. Second, she wears men's clothes, which is indecent, unnatural, and abominable; and in spite of our most earnest remonstrances and entreaties, she will not change them even to receive the sacrament.

JOAN. Is the blessed St Catherine an evil spirit? Is St Margaret? Is Michael the Archangel?

COURCELLES. How do you know that the spirit which appears to you is an archangel? Does he not appear to you as a naked man?

JOAN. Do you think God cannot afford clothes for him?

The assessors cannot help smiling, especially as the joke is against Courcelles.

LADVENU. Well answered, Joan.

THE INQUISITOR. It is, in effect, well answered. But no evil spirit would be so simple as to appear to a young girl in a guise that would scandalize her when he meant her to take him for a messenger from the Most High. Joan: The Church instructs you that these apparitions are demons seeking your soul's perdition. Do you accept the instruction of The Church?

JOAN. I accept the messenger of God. How could any faithful believer in The Church refuse him?

CAUCHON. Wretched woman: again I ask you, do you know what you are saying?

THE INQUISITOR. You wrestle in vain with the devil for her soul, my lord: she will not be saved. Now as to this matter of the man's dress. For the last time, will you put off that impudent attire, and dress as becomes your sex?

JOAN. I will not.

D'ESTIVET [*pouncing*] The sin of disobedience, my lord.

JOAN [*distressed*] But my voices tell me I must dress as a soldier.

LADVENU. Joan, Joan: does not that prove to you that the voices are the voices of evil spirits? Can you suggest to us one good reason why an angel of God should give you such shameless advice?

JOAN. Why, yes: what can be plainer commonsense? I was a soldier living among soldiers. I am a prisoner guarded by soldiers. If I were to dress as a woman they would think of me as a woman; and then what would become of me? If I dress as a soldier they think of me as a soldier, and I can live with them as I do at home with my brothers. That is why St Catherine tells me I must not dress as a woman until she gives me leave.

COURCELLES. When will she give you leave?

JOAN. When you take me out of the hands of the English soldiers. I have told you that I should be in the hands of The Church, and not left night and day with four soldiers of the Earl of Warwick. Do you want me to live with them in petticoats?

LADVENU. My lord: what she says is, God knows, very wrong and shocking; but there is a grain of worldly sense in it such as might impose on a simple village maiden.

JOAN. If we were as simple in the village as you are in your courts and palaces, there would soon be no wheat to make bread for you.

CAUCHON. That is the thanks you get for trying to save her, Brother Martin.

LADVENU. Joan: we are all trying to save you. His lordship is trying to save you. The Inquisitor could not be more just to you if you were his own daughter. But you are blinded by a terrible pride and self-sufficiency.

JOAN. Why do you say that? I have said nothing wrong. I cannot understand.

THE INQUISITOR. The blessed St Athanasius has laid it down in his creed that those who cannot understand are damned. It is not enough to be simple. It is not enough even to be what simple people call good. The simplicity of a darkened mind is no better than the simplicity of a beast.

JOAN. There is great wisdom in the simplicity of a beast, let me tell you; and sometimes great foolishness in the wisdom of scholars.

LADVENU. We know that, Joan: we are not so foolish as you think us. Try to resist the temptation to make pert replies to us. Do you see that man who stands behind you [*he indicates the Executioner*]?

JOAN [*turning and looking at the man*] Your torturer? But the Bishop said I was not to be tortured.

LADVENU. You are not to be tortured because you have confessed everything that is necessary to your condemnation. That man is not only the torturer: he is also the Executioner. Executioner: let The Maid hear your answers to my questions. Are you prepared for the burning of a heretic this day?

THE EXECUTIONER. Yes, Master.

LADVENU. Is the stake ready?

THE EXECUTIONER. It is. In the market-place. The English have built it too high for me to get near her and make the death easier. It will be a cruel death.

JOAN [*horrified*] But you are not going to burn me now?

THE INQUISITOR. You realize it at last.

LADVENU. There are eight hundred English soldiers waiting to take you to the market-place the moment the sentence of excommunication has passed the lips of your judges. You are within a few short moments of that doom.

JOAN [*looking round desperately for rescue*] Oh God!

LADVENU. Do not despair, Joan. The Church is merciful. You can save yourself.

JOAN [*hopefully*] Yes: my voices promised me I should not be burnt. St Catherine bade me be bold.

CAUCHON. Woman: are you quite mad? Do you not yet see that your voices have deceived you?

JOAN. Oh no: that is impossible.

CAUCHON. Impossible! They have led you straight to your excommunication, and to the stake which is there waiting for you.

LADVENU [*pressing the point hard*] Have they kept a single promise to you since you were taken at Compiègne? The devil has betrayed you. The Church holds out its arms to you.

JOAN [*despairing*] Oh, it is true: it is true: my voices have deceived me. I have been mocked by devils: my faith is broken. I have dared and dared; but only a fool will walk into a fire: God, who gave me my commonsense, cannot will me to do that.

LADVENU. Now God be praised that He has saved you at the eleventh hour! [*He hurries to the vacant seat at the scribes' table, and snatches a sheet of paper, on which he sets to work writing eagerly*].

CAUCHON. Amen!

JOAN. What must I do?

CAUCHON. You must sign a solemn recantation of your heresy.

JOAN. Sign? That means to write my name. I cannot write.

CAUCHON. You have signed many letters before.

JOAN. Yes; but someone held my hand and guided the pen. I can make my mark.

THE CHAPLAIN [*who has been listening with growing alarm and indignation*] My lord: do you mean that you are going to allow this woman to escape us?

THE INQUISITOR. The law must take its course, Master de Stogumber. And you know the law.

THE CHAPLAIN [*rising, purple with fury*] I know that there is no faith in a Frenchman. [*Tumult, which he shouts down*]. I know what my lord the Cardinal of Winchester will say when he hears of this. I know what the Earl of Warwick will do when he learns that you intend to betray him. There are eight hundred men at the gate who will see that this abominable witch is burnt in spite of your teeth.

THE ASSESSORS [*meanwhile*] What is this? What did he say? He accuses us of treachery! This is past bearing. No faith in a Frenchman! Did you hear that? This is an intolerable fellow. Who is he? Is this what English Churchmen are like? he must be mad or drunk, etc., etc.

THE INQUISITOR [*rising*] Silence, pray! Gentlemen: pray silence! Master Chaplain: bethink you a moment of your holy office: of what you are, and where you are. I direct you to sit down.

THE CHAPLAIN [*folding his arms doggedly, his face working convulsively*] I will NOT sit down.

CAUCHON. Master Inquisitor: this man has called me a traitor to my face before now.

THE CHAPLAIN. So you are a traitor. You are all traitors. You have been doing nothing but begging this damnable witch on your knees to recant all through this trial.

THE INQUISITOR [*placidly resuming his seat*] If you will not sit, you must stand: that is all.

THE CHAPLAIN. I will NOT stand [*he flings himself back into his chair*].

LADVENU [*rising with the paper in his hand*] My lord: here is the form of recantation for The Maid to sign.

CAUCHON. Read it to her.

JOAN. Do not trouble. I will sign it.

THE INQUISITOR. Woman: you must know what you are putting your hand to. Read it to her, Brother Martin. And let all be silent.

LADVENU [*reading quietly*] "I, Joan, commonly called The Maid, a miserable sinner, do confess that I have most grievously sinned in the following articles. I have pretended to have revelations from God and the angels and the blessed saints, and perversely rejected The Church's warnings that these were temptations by demons. I have blasphemed abominably by wearing an immodest dress, contrary to the Holy Scripture and the canons of The Church. Also I have clipped my hair in the style of a man, and, against all the duties which have made my sex specially acceptable in heaven, have taken up the sword, even to the shedding of human blood, inciting men to slay each other, invoking evil spirits to delude them, and stubbornly and most blasphemously imputing these sins to Almighty God. I confess to the sin of sedition, to the sin of idolatry, to the sin of disobedience, to the sin of pride, and to the sin of heresy. All of which sins I now renounce and abjure and depart from, humbly thanking you Doctors and Masters who have brought me back to the truth and into the grace of our Lord. And I will never return to my errors, but will remain in communion with our Holy Church and in obedience to our Holy Father the Pope of Rome. All this I swear by God Almighty and the Holy Gospels, in witness whereto I sign my name to this recantation."

THE INQUISITOR. You understand this, Joan?

JOAN [*listless*] It is plain enough, sir.

THE INQUISITOR. And it is true?

JOAN. It may be true. If it were not true, the fire would not be ready for me in the market-place.

LADVENU [*taking up his pen and a book, and going to her quickly lest she should compromise herself again*] Come, child: let me guide your hand. Take the pen. [*She does so; and they begin to write, using the book as a desk*] J.E.H.A.N.E. So. Now make your mark by yourself.

JOAN [*makes her mark, and gives him back the pen, tormented by the rebellion of her soul against her mind and body*] There!

LADVENU [*replacing the pen on the table, and handing the recantation to Cauchon with a reverence*] Praise be to God, my brothers, the lamb has returned to the flock; and the shepherd rejoices in her more than in ninety and nine just persons. [*He returns to his seat*].

THE INQUISITOR [*taking the paper from Cauchon*] We declare thee by this act set free from the danger of excommunication in which thou stoodest. [*He throws the paper down to the table*].

JOAN. I thank you.

THE INQUISITOR. But because thou hast sinned most presumptuously against God and the Holy Church, and that thou mayst repent thy errors in solitary contemplation, and be shielded from all temptation to return to them, we, for the good of thy soul, and for a penance that may wipe out thy sins and bring thee finally unspotted to the throne of grace, do condemn thee to eat the bread of sorrow and drink the water of affliction to the end of thy earthly days in perpetual imprisonment.

JOAN [*rising in consternation and terrible anger*] Perpetual imprisonment! Am I not then to be set free?

LADVENU [*mildly shocked*] Set free, child, after such wickedness as yours! What are you dreaming of?

JOAN. Give me that writing. [*She rushes to the table; snatches up the paper; and tears it into fragments*] Light your fire: do you think I dread it as much as the life of a rat in a hole? My voices were right.

LADVENU. Joan! Joan!

JOAN. Yes: they told me you were fools [*the word gives great offence*], and that I was not to listen to your fine words nor trust to your charity. You promised me my life; but you lied [*indignant exclamations*]. You think that life is nothing but not being stone dead. It is not the bread and water I fear: I can live on bread: when have I asked for more? It is no hardship to drink water if the water be clean. Bread has no sorrow for me, and water no affliction. But to shut me from the light of the sky and the sight of the fields and flowers; to chain my feet so that I can never again ride with the soldiers nor climb the hills; to make me breathe foul damp darkness, and keep from me everything that brings me back to the love of God when your wickedness and foolishness tempt me to hate Him: all this is worse than the furnace in the Bible that was heated seven times. I could do without my warhorse; I could drag about in a skirt; I could let the banners and the trumpets and the knights and soldiers pass me and leave me behind as they leave the other women, if only I could still hear the wind in the trees, the larks in the sunshine, the young lambs crying through the healthy frost, and the blessed blessed church bells that send my angel voices floating to me on the wind. But without these things I cannot live; and by your wanting to take them away from me, or from any human creature, I know that your counsel is of the devil, and that mine is of God.

THE ASSESSORS [*in great commotion*] Blasphemy! blasphemy! She is possessed. She said our counsel was of the devil. And hers of God. Monstrous! The devil is in our midst, etc., etc.

D'ESTIVET [*shouting above the din*] She is a relapsed heretic, obstinate, incorrigible, and altogether unworthy of the mercy we have shewn her. I call for her excommunication.

THE CHAPLAIN [*to the Executioner*] Light your fire, man. To the stake with her.

The Executioner and his assistants hurry out through the courtyard.

LADVENU. You wicked girl: if your counsel were of God would He not deliver you?

JOAN. His ways are not your ways. He wills that I go through the fire to His bosom; for I am His child, and you are not fit that I should live among you. That is my last word to you.

The soldiers seize her.

CAUCHON [*rising*] Not yet.

They wait. There is a dead silence. Cauchon turns to the Inquisitor with an inquiring look. The Inquisitor nods affirmatively. They rise solemnly, and intone the sentence antiphonally.

CAUCHON. We decree that thou art a relapsed heretic.

THE INQUISITOR. Cast out from the unity of the Church.

CAUCHON. Sundered from her body.

THE INQUISITOR. Infected with the leprosy of heresy.

CAUCHON. A member of Satan.

THE INQUISITOR. We declare that thou must be excommunicate.

CAUCHON. And now we do cast thee out, segregate thee, and abandon thee to the secular power.

THE INQUISITOR. Admonishing the same secular power that it moderate its judgment of thee in respect of death and division of the limbs. [*He resumes his seat*].

CAUCHON. And if any true sign of penitence appear in thee, to permit out Brother Martin to administer to thee the sacrament of penance.

THE CHAPLAIN. Into the fire with the witch [*he rushes at her, and helps the soldiers to push her out*].

Joan is taken away through the courtyard. The assessors rise in disorder, and follow the soldiers, except Ladvenu, who has hidden his face in his hands.

CAUCHON [*rising again in the act of sitting down*] No, no: this is irregular. The representative of the secular arm should be here to receive her from us.

THE INQUISITOR [*also on his feet again*] That man is an incorrigible fool.

CAUCHON. Brother Martin: see that everything is done in order.

LADVENU. My place is at her side, my lord. You must exercise your own authority. [*He hurries out*].

CAUCHON. These English are impossible: they will thrust her straight into the fire. Look!

He points to the courtyard, in which the glow and flicker of fire can now be seen reddening the May daylight. Only the Bishop and the Inquisitor are left in the court.

CAUCHON [*turning to go*] We must stop that.

THE INQUISITOR [*calmly*] Yes; but not too fast, my lord.

CAUCHON [*halting*] But there is not a moment to lose.

THE INQUISITOR. We have proceeded in perfect order. If the English choose to put themselves in the wrong, it is not our business to put them in the right. A flaw in the procedure may be useful later on: one never knows. And the sooner it is over, the better for that poor girl.

CAUCHON [*relaxing*] That is true. But I suppose we must see this dreadful thing through.

THE INQUISITOR. One gets used to it. Habit is everything. I am accustomed to the fire: it is soon over. But it is a terrible thing to see a young and innocent creature crushed between these mighty forces, The Church and the Law.

CAUCHON. You call her innocent!

THE INQUISITOR. Oh, quite innocent. What does she know of The Church and the Law? She did not understand a word we were saying. It is the ignorant who suffer. Come, or we shall be late for the end.

CAUCHON [*going with him*] I shall not be sorry if we are: I am not so accustomed as you.

They are going out when Warwick comes in, meeting them.

WARWICK. Oh, I am intruding. I thought it was all over. [*He makes a feint of retiring*].

CAUCHON. Do not go, my lord. It is all over.

THE INQUISITOR. The execution is not in our hands, my lord; but it is desirable that we should witness the end. So by your leave—[*He bows, and goes out through the courtyard*].

CAUCHON. There is some doubt whether your people have observed the forms of law, my lord.

WARWICK. I am told that there is some doubt whether your authority runs in this city, my lord. It is not in your diocese. However, if you will answer for that I will answer for the rest.

CAUCHON. It is to God that we both must answer. Good morning, my lord.

WARWICK. My lord: good morning.

They look at one another for a moment with unconcealed hostility. Then Cauchon follows the Inquisitor out. Warwick looks round. Finding himself alone, he calls for attendance.

WARWICK. Hallo: some attendance here! [*Silence*]. Hallo, there! [*Silence*]. Hallo! Brian, you young blackguard, where are you? [*Silence*]. Guard! [*Silence*]. They have all gone to see the burning: even that child.

The silence is broken by someone frantically howling and sobbing.

WARWICK. What in the devil's name—?

The Chaplain staggers in from the courtyard like a demented creature, his face streaming with tears, making the piteous sounds that Warwick has heard. He stumbles to the prisoner's stool, and throws himself upon it with heartrending sobs.

WARWICK [*going to him and patting him on the shoulder*] What is it, Master John? What is the matter?

THE CHAPLAIN [*clutching at his hands*] My lord, my lord: for Christ's sake pray for my wretched guilty soul.

WARWICK [*soothing him*] Yes, yes: of course I will. Calmly, gently—

THE CHAPLAIN [*blubbering miserably*] I am not a bad man, my lord.

WARWICK. No, no: not at all.

THE CHAPLAIN. I meant no harm. I did not know what it would be like.

WARWICK [*hardening*] Oh! You saw it, then?

THE CHAPLAIN. I did not know what I was doing. I am a hotheaded fool; and I shall be damned to all eternity for it.

WARWICK. Nonsense! Very distressing, no doubt; but it was not your doing.

THE CHAPLAIN [*lamentably*] I let them do it. If I had known, I would have torn her from their hands. You dont know: you havnt seen: it is so easy to talk when you dont know. You madden yourself with words: you damn yourself because it feels grand to throw oil on the flaming hell of your own temper. But when it is brought home to you; when you see the thing you have done; when it is blinding your eyes, stifling your nostrils, tearing your heart, then—then— [*Falling on his knees*] O God, take away this sight from me! O Christ, deliver me from this fire that is consuming me! She cried to Thee in the midst of it: Jesus! Jesus! Jesus! She is in Thy bosom; and I am in hell for evermore.

WARWICK [*summarily hauling him to his feet*] Come come, man! you must pull yourself together. We shall have the whole town talking of this. [*He throws him not too gently into a chair at the table*] If you have not the nerve to see these things, why do you not do as I do, and stay away?

THE CHAPLAIN [*bewildered and submissive*] She asked for a cross. A soldier gave her two sticks tied together. Thank God he was an Englishman! I might have done it; but I did not: I am a coward, a mad dog, a fool. But he was an Englishman too.

WARWICK. The fool! they will burn him too if the priests get hold of him.

THE CHAPLAIN [*shaken with a convulsion*] Some of the

people laughed at her. They would have laughed at Christ. They were French people, my lord: I know they were French.

WARWICK. Hush? someone is coming. Control yourself.

Ladvenu comes back through the courtyard to Warwick's right hand, carrying a bishop's cross which he has taken from a church. He is very grave and composed.

WARWICK. I am informed that it is all over, Brother Martin.

LADVENU [*enigmatically*] We do not know, my lord. It may have only just begun.

WARWICK. What does that mean, exactly?

LADVENU. I took this cross from the church for her that she might see it to the last: she had only two sticks that she put into her bosom. When the fire crept round us, and she saw that if I held the cross before her I should be burnt myself, she warned me to get down and save myself. My lord: a girl who could think of another's danger in such a moment was not inspired by the devil. When I had to snatch the cross from her sight, she looked up to heaven. And I do not believe that the heavens were empty. I firmly believe that her Savior appeared to her then in His tenderest glory. She called to Him and died. This is not the end for her, but the beginning.

WARWICK. I am afraid it will have a bad effect on the people.

LADVENU. It had, my lord, on some of them. I heard laughter. Forgive me for saying that I hope and believe it was English laughter.

THE CHAPLAIN [*rising frantically*] No: it was not. There was only one Englishman there that disgraced his country; and that was the mad dog, de Stogumber. [*He rushes wildly out, shrieking*] Let them torture him. Let them burn him. I will go pray among her ashes. I am no better than Judas: I will hang myself.

WARWICK. Quick, Brother Martin: follow him: he will do himself some mischief. After him, quick.

Ladvenu hurries out, Warwick urging him. The Executioner comes in by the door behind the judges' chairs; and Warwick, returning, finds himself face to face with him.

WARWICK. Well, fellow: who are you?

THE EXECUTIONER [*with dignity*] I am not addressed as fellow, my lord. I am the Master Executioner of Rouen: it is a highly skilled mystery. I am come to tell your lordship that your orders have been obeyed.

WARWICK. I crave your pardon, Master Executioner; and I will see that you lose nothing by having no relics to sell. I have your word, have I, that nothing remains, not a bone, not a nail, not a hair?

THE EXECUTIONER. Her heart would not burn, my lord; but everything that was left is at the bottom of the river. You have heard the last of her.

WARWICK [*with a wry smile, thinking of what Ladvenu said*] The last of her? Hm! I wonder!

EPILOGUE

A RESTLESS fitfully windy night in June 1456, *full of summer lightning after many days of heat. King Charles the Seventh of France, formerly Joan's Dauphin, now Charles the Victorious, aged* 51, *is in bed in one of his royal chateaux. The bed, raised on a dais of two steps, is towards the side of the room so as to avoid blocking a tall lancet window in the middle. Its canopy bears the royal arms in embroidery. Except for the canopy and the huge down pillows there is nothing to distinguish it from a broad settee with bed-clothes and a valance. Thus its occupant is in full view from the foot.*

Charles is not asleep: he is reading in bed, or rather looking at the pictures in Fouquet's Boccaccio with his knees doubled up to make a reading desk. Beside the bed on his left is a little table with a picture of the Virgin, lighted by candles of painted wax. The walls are hung from ceiling to floor with painted curtains which stir at times in the draughts. At first glance the prevailing yellow and red in these hanging pictures is somewhat flamelike when the folds breathe in the wind.

The door is on Charles's left, but in front of him close to the corner farthest from him. A large watchman's rattle, handsomely designed and gaily painted, is in the bed under his hand.

Charles turns a leaf. A distant clock strikes the half-hour softly. Charles shuts the book with a clap; throws it aside; snatches up the rattle; and whirls it energetically, making a deafening clatter. Ladvenu enters, 25 *years older, strange and stark in bearing, and still carrying the cross from Rouen. Charles evidently does not expect him; for he springs out of bed on the farther side from the door.*

CHARLES. Who are you? Where is my gentleman of the bedchamber? What do you want?

LADVENU [*solemnly*] I bring you glad tidings of great joy. Rejoice, O king; for the taint is removed from your blood, and the stain from your crown. Justice, long delayed, is at last triumphant.

CHARLES. What are you talking about? Who are you?

LADVENU. I am Brother Martin.

CHARLES. And who, saving your reverence, may Brother Martin be?

LADVENU. I held this cross when The Maid perished in the fire. Twenty-five years have passed since then: nearly ten thousand days. And on every one of those days I have prayed God to justify His daughter on earth as she is justified in heaven.

CHARLES [*reassured, sitting down on the foot of the bed*] Oh, I remember now. I have heard of you. You have a bee in your bonnet about The Maid. Have you been at the inquiry?

LADVENU. I have given my testimony.

CHARLES. Is it over?

LADVENU. It is over.

CHARLES. Satisfactorily?

LADVENU. The ways of God are very strange.

CHARLES. How so?

LADVENU. At the trial which sent a saint to the stake as a heretic and a sorceress, the truth was told; the law was upheld; mercy was shewn beyond all custom; no wrong was done but the final and dreadful wrong of the lying sentence and the pitiless fire. At this inquiry from which I have just come, there was shameless perjury, courtly corruption, calumny of the dead who did their duty according to their lights, cowardly evasion of the issue, testimony made of idle tales that could not impose on a ploughboy. Yet out of this insult to justice, this defamation of The Church, this orgy of lying and foolishness, the truth is set in the noonday sun on the hilltop; the white robe of innocence is cleansed from the smirch of the burning faggots; the holy life is sanctified; the true heart that lived through the flame is consecrated; a great lie is silenced for ever; and a great wrong is set right before all men.

CHARLES. My friend: provided they can no longer say that I was crowned by a witch and a heretic, I shall not fuss about how the trick has been done. Joan would not have fussed about it if it came all right in the end: she was not that sort: I knew her. Is her rehabilitation complete? I made it pretty clear that there was to be no nonsense about it.

LADVENU. It is solemnly declared that her judges were full of corruption, cozenage, fraud, and malice. Four falsehoods.

CHARLES. Never mind the falsehoods: her judges are dead.

LADVENU. The sentence on her is broken, annulled, annihilated, set aside as non-existent, without value or effect.

CHARLES. Good. Nobody can challenge my consecration now, can they?

LADVENU. Not Charlemagne nor King David himself was more sacredly crowned.

CHARLES [*rising*] Excellent. Think of what that means to me!

LADVENU. I think of what it means to her!

CHARLES. You cannot. None of us ever knew what anything meant to her. She was like nobody else; and she must take care of herself wherever she is; for *I* cannot take care of her; and neither can you, whatever you may think: you are not big enough. But I will tell you this about her. If you could bring her back to life, they would burn her again within six months, for all their present adoration of her. And you would hold up the cross, too, just the same. So [*crossing himself*] let her rest; and let you and I mind our own business, and not meddle with hers.

LADVENU. God forbid that I should have no share in her, nor she in me! [*He turns and strides out as he came, saying*] Henceforth my path will not lie through palaces, nor my conversation be with kings.

CHARLES [*following him towards the door, and shouting after him*] Much good may it do you, holy man! [*He returns to the middle of the chamber, where he halts, and says quizzically to himself*] That was a funny chap. How did he get in? Where are my people? [*He goes impatiently to the bed, and swings the rattle. A rush of wind through the open door sets the walls sway-*

ing agitatedly. The candles go out. He calls in the darkness] Hallo! Someone come and shut the windows: everything is being blown all over the place. [*A flash of summer lightning shews up the lancet window. A figure is seen in silhouette against it*] Who is there? Who is that? Help! Murder! [*Thunder. He jumps into bed, and hides under the clothes*].

JOAN'S VOICE. Easy, Charlie, easy. What art making all that noise for? No one can hear thee. Thourt asleep. [*She is dimly seen in a pallid greenish light by the bedside*].

CHARLES [*peeping out*] Joan! Are you a ghost, Joan?

JOAN. Hardly even that, lad. Can a poor burnt-up lass have a ghost? I am but a dream that thourt dreaming. [*The light increases: they become plainly visible as he sits up*] Thou looks older, lad.

CHARLES. I am older. Am I really asleep?

JOAN. Fallen asleep over thy silly book.

CHARLES. That's funny.

JOAN. Not so funny as that I am dead, is it?

CHARLES. Are you really dead?

JOAN. As dead as anybody ever is, laddie. I am out of the body.

CHARLES. Just fancy! Did it hurt much?

JOAN. Did what hurt much?

CHARLES. Being burnt.

JOAN. Oh, that! I cannot remember very well. I think it did at first; but then it all got mixed up; and I was not in my right mind until I was free of the body. But do not thou go handling fire and thinking it will not hurt thee. How hast been ever since?

CHARLES. Oh, not so bad. Do you know, I actually lead my army out and win battles? Down into the moat up to my waist in mud and blood. Up the ladders with the stones and hot pitch raining down. Like you.

JOAN. No! Did I make a man of thee after all, Charlie?

CHARLES. I am Charles the Victorious now. I had to be brave because you were. Agnes put a little pluck into me too.

JOAN. Agnes! Who was Agnes?

CHARLES. Agnes Sorel. A woman I fell in love with. I dream of her often. I never dreamed of you before.

JOAN. Is she dead, like me?

CHARLES. Yes. But she was not like you. She was very beautiful.

JOAN [*laughing heartily*] Ha ha! I was no beauty: I was always a rough one: a regular soldier. I might almost as well have been a man. Pity I wasnt: I should not have bothered you all so much then. But my head was in the skies; and the glory of God was upon me; and, man or woman, I should have bothered you as long as your noses were in the mud. Now tell me what has happened since you wise men knew no better than to make a heap of cinders of me?

CHARLES. Your mother and brothers have sued the courts to have your case tried over again. And the courts have declared that your judges were full of corruption and cozenage, fraud and malice.

JOAN. Not they. They were as honest a lot of poor fools as ever burned their betters.

CHARLES. The sentence on you is broken, annihilated, annulled: null, non-existent, without value or effect.

JOAN. I was burned, all the same. Can they unburn me?

CHARLES. If they could, they would think twice before they did it. But they have decreed that a beautiful cross be placed where the stake stood, for your perpetual memory and for your salvation.

JOAN. It is the memory and the salvation that sanctify the cross, not the cross that sanctifies the memory and the salvation. [*She turns away, forgetting him*] I shall outlast that cross. I shall be remembered when men will have forgotten where Rouen stood.

CHARLES. There you go with your self-conceit, the same as ever! I think you might say a word of thanks to me for having had justice done at last.

CAUCHON [*appearing at the window between them*] Liar!

CHARLES. Thank you.

JOAN. Why, if it isnt Peter Cauchon! How are you,

Peter? What luck have you had since you burned me?

CAUCHON. None. I arraign the justice of Man. It is not the justice of God.

JOAN. Still dreaming of justice, Peter? See what justice came to with me! But what has happened to thee? Art dead or alive?

CAUCHON. Dead. Dishonored. They pursued me beyond the grave. They excommunicated my dead body: they dug it up and flung it into the common sewer.

JOAN. Your dead body did not feel the spade and the sewer as my live body felt the fire.

CAUCHON. But this thing that they have done against me hurts justice; destroys faith; saps the foundation of the Church. The solid earth sways like the treacherous sea beneath the feet of men and spirits alike when the innocent are slain in the name of law, and their wrongs are undone by slandering the pure of heart.

JOAN. Well, well, Peter, I hope men will be the better for remembering me; and they would not remember me so well if you had not burned me.

CAUCHON. They will be the worse for remembering me: they will see in me evil triumphing over good, falsehood over truth, cruelty over mercy, hell over heaven. Their courage will rise as they think of you, only to faint as they think of me. Yet God is my witness I was just: I was merciful: I was faithful to my light: I could do no other than I did.

CHARLES [*scrambling out of the sheets and enthroning himself on the side of the bed*] Yes: it is always you good men that do the big mischiefs. Look at me! I am not Charles the Good, nor Charles the Wise, nor Charles the Bold. Joan's worshippers may even call me Charles the Coward because I did not pull her out of the fire. But I have done less harm than any of you. You people with your heads in the sky spend all your time trying to turn the world upside down; but I take the world as it is, and say that top-side-up is right-side-up; and I keep my nose pretty close to the ground. And I ask you, what king of France has done better, or been a better fellow in his little way?

JOAN. Art really king of France, Charlie? Be the English gone?

DUNOIS [*coming through the tapestry on Joan's left, the candles relighting themselves at the same moment, and illuminating his armour and surcoat cheerfully*] I have kept my word: the English are gone.

JOAN. Praised be God! now is fair France a province in heaven. Tell me all about the fighting, Jack. Was it thou that led them? Wert thou God's captain to thy death?

DUNOIS. I am not dead. My body is very comfortably asleep in my bed at Chateaudun; but my spirit is called here by yours.

JOAN. And you fought them my way, Jack: eh? Not the old way, chaffering for ransoms; but The Maid's way: staking life against death, with the heart high and humble and void of malice, and nothing counting under God but France free and French. Was it my way, Jack?

DUNOIS. Faith, it was any way that would win. But the way that won was always your way. I give you best, lassie. I wrote a fine letter to set you right at the new trial. Perhaps I should never have let the priests burn you; but I was busy fighting; and it was The Church's business, not mine. There was no use in both of us being burned, was there?

CAUCHON. Ay! put the blame on the priests. But I, who am beyond praise and blame, tell you that the world is saved neither by its priests nor its soldiers, but by God and His Saints. The Church Militant sent this woman to the fire; but even as she burned, the flames whitened into the radiance of the Church Triumphant.

The clock strikes the third quarter. A rough male voice is heard trolling an improvised tune.

Rum tum trumpledum,
Bacon fat and rumpledum,

Old Saint mumpledum,
Pull his tail and stumpledum
O my Ma—ry Ann!

A ruffianly English soldier comes through the curtains and marches between Dunois and Joan.

DUNOIS. What villainous troubadour taught you that doggrel?

THE SOLDIER. No troubadour. We made it up ourselves as we marched. We were not gentlefolks and troubadours. Music straight out of the heart of the people, as you might say. Rum tum trumpledum, Bacon fat and rumpledum, Old Saint mumpledum, Pull his tail and stumpledum: that dont mean anything, you know; but it keeps you marching. Your servant, ladies and gentlemen. Who asked for a saint?

JOAN. Be you a saint?

THE SOLDIER. Yes, lady, straight from hell.

DUNOIS. A saint, and from hell!

THE SOLDIER. Yes, noble captain: I have a day off. Every year, you know. Thats my allowance for my one good action.

CAUCHON. Wretch! In all the years of your life did you do only one good action?

THE SOLDIER. I never thought about it: it came natural like. But they scored it up for me.

CHARLES. What was it?

THE SOLDIER. Why, the silliest thing you ever heard of. I—

JOAN [*interrupting him by strolling across to the bed, where she sits beside Charles*] He tied two sticks together, and gave them to a poor lass that was going to be burned.

THE SOLDIER. Right. Who told you that?

JOAN. Never mind. Would you know her if you saw her again?

THE SOLDIER. Not I. There are so many girls! and they all expect you to remember them as if there was only one in the world. This one must have been a prime sort; for I have a day off every year for her; and so, until twelve o'clock punctually, I am a saint, at your service, noble lords and lovely ladies.

CHARLES. And after twelve?

THE SOLDIER. After twelve, back to the only place fit for the likes of me.

JOAN [*rising*] Back there! You! that gave the lass the cross!

THE SOLDIER [*excusing his unsoldierly conduct*] Well, she asked for it; and they were going to burn her. She had as good a right to a cross as they had; and they had dozens of them. It was her funeral, not theirs. Where was the harm in it?

JOAN. Man: I am not reproaching you. But I cannot bear to think of you in torment.

THE SOLDIER [*cheerfully*] No great torment, lady. You see I was used to worse.

CHARLES. What! worse than hell?

THE SOLDIER. Fifteen years' service in the French wars. Hell was a treat after that.

Joan throws up her arms, and takes refuge from despair of humanity before the picture of the Virgin.

THE SOLDIER [*continuing*]—Suits me somehow. The day off was dull at first, like a wet Sunday. I dont mind it so much now. They tell me I can have as many as I like as soon as I want them.

CHARLES. What is hell like?

THE SOLDIER. You wont find it so bad, sir. Jolly. Like as if you were always drunk without the trouble and expense of drinking. Tip top company too: emperors and popes and kings and all sorts. They chip me about giving that young judy the cross; but I dont care: I stand up to them proper, and tell them that if she hadnt a better right to it than they, she'd be where they are. That dumbfounds them, that does. All they can do is gnash their teeth, hell fashion; and I just laugh, and go off singing the old chanty: Rum tum trumple —Hullo! Who's that knocking at the door?

They listen. A long gentle knocking is heard.

CHARLES. Come in.

The door opens; and an old priest, white-haired, bent, with a silly but benevolent smile, comes in and trots over to Joan.

THE NEWCOMER. Excuse me, gentle lords and ladies. Do not let me disturb you. Only a poor old harmless English rector. Formerly chaplain to the cardinal: to my lord of Winchester. John de Stogumber, at your service. [*He looks at them inquiringly*] Did you say anything? I am a little deaf, unfortunately. Also a little—well, not always in my right mind, perhaps; but still, it is a small village with a few simple people. I suffice: I suffice: they love me there; and I am able to do a little good. I am well connected, you see; and they indulge me.

JOAN. Poor old John! What brought thee to this state?

DE STOGUMBER. I tell my folks they must be very careful. I say to them, "If you only saw what you think about you would think quite differently about it. It would give you a great shock. Oh, a great shock." And they all say "Yes, parson: we all know you are a kind man, and would not harm a fly." That is a great comfort to me. For I am not cruel by nature, you know.

THE SOLDIER. Who said you were?

DE STOGUMBER. Well, you see, I did a very cruel thing once because I did not know what cruelty was like. I had not seen it, you know. That is the great thing: you must see it. And then you are redeemed and saved.

CAUCHON. Were not the sufferings of our Lord Christ enough for you?

DE STOGUMBER. No. Oh no: not at all. I had seen them in pictures, and read of them in books, and been greatly moved by them, as I thought. But it was no use: it was not our Lord that redeemed me, but a young woman whom I saw actually burned to death. It was dreadful: oh, most dreadful. But it saved me. I have been a different man ever since, though a little astray in my wits sometimes.

CAUCHON. Must then a Christ perish in torment in every age to save those that have no imagination?

JOAN. Well, if I saved all those he would have been cruel to if he had not been cruel to me, I was not burnt for nothing, was I?

DE STOGUMBER. Oh no; it was not you. My sight is bad: I cannot distinguish your features: but you are not she: oh no: she was burned to a cinder: dead and gone, dead and gone.

THE EXECUTIONER [*stepping from behind the bed curtains on Charles's right, the bed being between them*] She is more alive than you, old man. Her heart would not burn; and it would not drown. I was a master at my craft: better than the master of Paris, better than the master of Toulouse; but I could not kill The Maid. She is up and alive everywhere.

THE EARL OF WARWICK [*sallying from the bed curtains on the other side, and coming to Joan's left hand*] Madam: my congratulations on your rehabilitation. I feel that I owe you an apology.

JOAN. Oh, please dont mention it.

WARWICK [*pleasantly*] The burning was purely political. There was no personal feeling against you, I assure you.

JOAN. I bear no malice, my lord.

WARWICK. Just so. Very kind of you to meet me in that way: a touch of true breeding. But I must insist on apologizing very amply. The truth is, these political necessities sometimes turn out to be political mistakes; and this one was a veritable howler; for your spirit conquered us, madam, in spite of our faggots. History will remember me for your sake, though the incidents of the connection were perhaps a little unfortunate.

JOAN. Ay, perhaps just a little, you funny man.

WARWICK. Still, when they make you a saint, you will owe your halo to me, just as this lucky monarch owes his crown to you.

JOAN [*turning from him*] I shall owe nothing to any man: I owe everything to the spirit of God that was within me. But fancy me a saint! What would St Catherine and St Margaret say if the farm girl was cocked up beside them!

A clerical-looking gentleman in black frockcoat and trousers, and tall hat, in the fashion of the year 1920, *suddenly appears before them in the corner on their right. They all stare at him. Then they burst into uncontrollable laughter.*

THE GENTLEMAN. Why this mirth, gentlemen?

WARWICK. I congratulate you on having invented a most extraordinarily comic dress.

THE GENTLEMAN. I do not understand. You are all in fancy dress: I am properly dressed.

DUNOIS. All dress is fancy dress, is it not, except our natural skins?

THE GENTLEMAN. Pardon me: I am here on serious business, and cannot engage in frivolous discussions. [*He takes out a paper, and assumes a dry official manner*]. I am sent to announce to you that Joan of Arc, formerly known as The Maid, having been the subject of an inquiry instituted by the Bishop of Orleans—

JOAN [*interrupting*] Ah! They remember me still in Orleans.

THE GENTLEMAN [*emphatically, to mark his indignation at the interruption*]—by the Bishop of Orleans into the claim of the said Joan of Arc to be canonized as a saint—

JOAN [*again interrupting*] But I never made any such claim.

THE GENTLEMAN [*as before*]—The Church has examined the claim exhaustively in the usual course, and, having admitted the said Joan successively to the ranks of Venerable and Blessed,—

JOAN [*chuckling*] Me venerable!

THE GENTLEMAN. —has finally declared her to have been endowed with heroic virtues and favored with private revelations, and calls the said Venerable and Blessed Joan to the communion of the Church Triumphant as Saint Joan.

JOAN [*rapt*] Saint Joan!

THE GENTLEMAN. On every thirtieth day of May, being the anniversary of the death of the said most blessed daughter of God, there shall in every Catholic church to the end of time be celebrated a special office in commemoration of her; and it shall be lawful to dedicate a special chapel to her, and to place her image on its altar in every such church. And it shall be lawful and laudable for the faithful to kneel and address their prayers through her to the Mercy Seat.

JOAN. Oh no. It is for the saint to kneel. [*She falls on her knees, still rapt*].

THE GENTLEMAN [*putting up his paper, and retiring beside the Executioner*] In Basilica Vaticana, the sixteenth day of May, nineteen hundred and twenty.

DUNOIS [*raising Joan*] Half an hour to burn you, dear Saint; and four centuries to find out the truth about you!

DE STOGUMBER. Sir: I was chaplain to the Cardinal of Winchester once. They always would call him the Cardinal of England. It would be a great comfort to me and to my master to see a fair statue to The Maid in Winchester Cathedral. Will they put one there, do you think?

THE GENTLEMAN. As the building is temporarily in the hands of the Anglican heresy, I cannot answer for that.

A vision of the statue in Winchester Cathedral is seen through the window.

DE STOGUMBER. Oh look! look! that is Winchester.

JOAN. Is that meant to be me? I was stiffer on my feet.

The vision fades.

THE GENTLEMAN. I have been requested by the temporal authorities of France to mention that the multiplication of public statues to The Maid threatens to become an obstruction to traffic. I do so as a matter of courtesy to the said authorities, but must point out on behalf of The Church that The Maid's horse is no greater obstruction to traffic than any other horse.

JOAN. Eh! I am glad they have not forgotten my horse.

A vision of the statue before Rheims Cathedral appears.

JOAN. Is that funny little thing me too?

CHARLES. That is Rheims Cathedral where you had me crowned. It must be you.

JOAN. Who has broken my sword? My sword was never

broken. It is the sword of France.

DUNOIS. Never mind. Swords can be mended. Your soul is unbroken; and you are the soul of France.

The vision fades. The Archbishop and the Inquisitor are now seen on the right and left of Cauchon.

JOAN. My sword shall conquer yet: the sword that never struck a blow. Though men destroyed my body, yet in my soul I have seen God.

CAUCHON [*kneeling to her*] The girls in the field praise thee; for thou hast raised their eyes; and they see that there is nothing between them and heaven.

DUNOIS [*kneeling to her*] The dying soldiers praise thee, because thou art a shield of glory between them and the judgment.

THE ARCHBISHOP [*kneeling to her*] The princes of The Church praise thee, because thou hast redeemed the faith their worldlinesses have dragged through the mire.

WARWICK [*kneeling to her*] The cunning counsellors praise thee, because thou hast cut the knots in which they have tied their own souls.

DE STOGUMBER [*kneeling to her*] The foolish old men on their deathbeds praise thee, because their sins against thee are turned into blessings.

THE INQUISITOR [*kneeling to her*] The judges in the blindness and bondage of the law praise thee, because thou hast vindicated the vision and the freedom of the living soul.

THE SOLDIER [*kneeling to her*] The wicked out of hell praise thee, because thou hast shewn them that the fire that is not quenched is a holy fire.

THE EXECUTIONER [*kneeling to her*] The tormentors and executioners praise thee, because thou hast shewn that their hands are guiltless of the death of the soul.

CHARLES [*kneeling to her*] The unpretending praise thee, because thou hast taken upon thyself the heroic burdens that are too heavy for them.

JOAN. Woe unto me when all men praise me! I bid you remember that I am a saint, and that saints can work miracles. And now tell me: shall I rise from the dead, and come back to you a living woman?

A sudden darkness blots out the walls of the room as they all spring to their feet in consternation. Only the figures and the bed remain visible.

JOAN. What! Must I burn again? Are none of you ready to receive me?

CAUCHON. The heretic is always better dead. And mortal eyes cannot distinguish the saint from the heretic. Spare them. [*He goes out as he came*].

DUNOIS. Forgive us, Joan: we are not yet good enough for you. I shall go back to my bed. [*He also goes*].

WARWICK. We sincerely regret our little mistake; but political necessities, though occasionally erroneous, are still imperative; so if you will be good enough to excuse me— [*He steals discreetly away*].

THE ARCHBISHOP. Your return would not make me the man you once thought me. The utmost I can say is that though I dare not bless you, I hope I may one day enter into your blessedness. Meanwhile, however— [*He goes*].

THE INQUISITOR. I who am of the dead, testified that day that you were innocent. But I do not see how The Inquisition could possibly be dispensed with under existing circumstances. Therefore— [*He goes*].

DE STOGUMBER. Oh, do not come back: you must not come back. I must die in peace. Give us peace in our time, O Lord! [*He goes*].

THE GENTLEMAN. The possibility of your resurrection was not contemplated in the recent proceedings for your canonization. I must return to Rome for fresh instructions. [*He bows formally, and withdraws*].

THE EXECUTIONER. As a master in my profession I have to consider its interests. And, after all, my first duty is to my wife and children. I must have time to think over this. [*He goes*].

CHARLES. Poor old Joan! They have all run away from you except this blackguard who has to go back to hell at twelve o'clock. And what can I do but follow Jack Dunois' example, and go back to bed too? [*He does so*].

JOAN [*sadly*] Goodnight, Charlie.

CHARLES [*mumbling in his pillows*] Goo ni. [*He sleeps. The darkness envelops the bed*].

JOAN [*to the soldier*] And you, my one faithful? What comfort have you for Saint Joan?

THE SOLDIER. Well, what do they all amount to, these kings and captains and bishops and lawyers and such like? They just leave you in the ditch to bleed to death; and the next thing is, you meet them down there, for all the airs they give themselves. What I say is, you have as good a right to your notions as they have to theirs, and perhaps better. [*Settling himself for a lecture on the subject*] You see, it's like this. If— [*the first stroke of midnight is heard softly from a distant bell*]. Excuse me: a pressing appointment— [*He goes on tiptoe*].

The last remaining rays of light gather into a white radiance descending on Joan. The hour continues to strike.

JOAN. O God that madest this beautiful earth, when will it be ready to receive Thy saints? How long, O Lord, how long?

THE SIMPLETON OF THE UNEXPECTED ISLES

Shaw was nearly eighty when he wrote *The Simpleton of the Unexpected Isles* during a voyage to New Zealand. Because of his age, the fantastic situation of the play, the apparent looseness of its structure, some critics were led into overhasty condemnation. For anyone who had followed Shaw's artistic development, *The Simpleton* was a natural consequence of all that had preceded it: a dramatic parable that found its own theatrical form. As a result of the critical attacks, Shaw found himself at the end of his career, as at the beginning, forced to point out that it was not his purpose, or his concept of the function of the artist, to gratify his audience's expectations, merely. He tartly defended his work in a program note for its first English performance, incidentally presenting what might serve as an epigraph for a study of his dramatic career:

"If the playgoer is to keep up his (or her) power of enjoyment he must not stick in the same groove all his life. He must be prepared to come across from time to time a sort of play which quite upsets his notions of what a play should be. He may not like it at first, but if it takes a grip of the stage, he must go on enduring it until he does like it, or else give up going to the theatre and be derided by the young as a back number. When a play . . . is disagreeable at first sight, it is a mistake to run away from it, and revile its author for ever after. Of course, if there is nothing new in it, and its disagreeableness is due to mere folly and incompetence on the part of its maker, there is nothing more to be said. But if he is evidently a capable and skilled workman, and therefore must have made his work what it is on purpose and actually liked it, the chances are that you will like it too when you get used to it. . . . Plays of my own, popular enough now, were forbidden by the censorship for many years; and even today, when I am 79, the New York critics can see nothing in my latest play but the antics of a monkey. But they will get used to it in time. . . ."

The Simpleton was first performed by the Theatre Guild

in New York, February 18, 1935, with McKay Morris as Pra, Alla Nazimova as Prola, and Romney Brent as The Clergyman. Its first English performance took place July 29, 1935, at the Malvern Festival, of which Shaw was "patron-in-chief" and to whom its annual repertory performances were dedicated.

THE SIMPLETON OF THE UNEXPECTED ISLES

PROLOGUE

THE emigration office at a tropical port in the British Empire. The office is an annex of the harbor and customs sheds on one side and of the railway station on the other. Placards direct passengers TO THE CUSTOMS and TO THE TRAINS through the open doors right and left respectively. The emigration officer, an unsatisfactory young man of unhealthy habits, is sitting writing at his table in the middle of the room. His clerk is at a standing desk against the wall on the customs side. The officer wears tropical clothes, neither too tidy nor too clean. The clerk is in a shabby dark lounge suit.

THE E. O. [*finishing his writing*] Is that the lot?

CLERK. It's the lot from the French ship; but there is that case standing over from the Liverpool one.

THE E. O. [*exasperated*] Now look here, Wilks. Are you the emigration officer here or am I? Did I tell you that that girl was to be sent back or did I not?

WILKS. Well, I thought—

THE E. O. What business had you to think? I told you she was to go back. I suppose she tipped you to let her come here and make a scene on the chance of getting round me.

WILKS [*hotly*] Youll either take that back or prove it.

THE E. O. I will neither take it back nor prove it until you explain why you are letting this girl bother me again, though she has no papers, no passports, and is in excess of the quota without any excuse for it.

WILKS. Who's letting her bother you again? She told the High Commissioner that you had turned her down; and he told her she had better see you again.

THE E. O. And why the devil didnt you tell me that at first, instead of blithering about her as if she was a common case?

WILKS. The High Commissioner's daughter was on the ship coming back from school. He came down to meet her.

This girl had made friends with her or taken care of her or something.

THE E. O. Thats no good. We cant let her through on that.

WILKS. Well, will you see her?

THE E. O. Is she waiting to see me?

WILKS. She says she's waiting to see what will happen to her.

THE E. O. Same thing, isnt it?

WILKS. I suppose so. But she put it as if there was a difference. I think she's a bit mad. But the Medical Officer says she passes all his tests of sanity, though I could see that he has his doubts.

THE E. O. Oh, shut up. You need a medical test yourself, I think. Fetch her in.

Wilks goes out sulkily through the customs door and returns with a young woman. He leads her to the table and then goes back to his desk.

THE Y. W. Good morning, sir. You dont look as well as you did yesterday. Did you stay up too late?

THE E. O. [*nonplussed for the moment*] I— er— [*Collecting himself*] Look here, young lady. You have to answer questions here, not to ask them.

THE Y. W. You have been drinking.

THE E. O. [*springing up*] What the hell do you mean?

THE Y. W. You have. I smell it.

THE E. O. Very well. Back you go by the next boat, my lady.

THE Y. W. [*unmoved*] At this hour of the morning too! Dont you know you shouldnt?

THE E. O. [*to Wilks*] Take her away, you. [*To the young woman*] Out you go.

THE Y. W. I ought to speak to somebody about it. And look at the state the office is in! Whose business is it to see that it's properly dusted? Let me talk to them for you.

THE E. O. What concern is it of yours?

THE Y. W. I hate to see dust lying about. Look! You

could write your name in it. And it's just awful to see a young man drinking before eleven in the morning.

WILKS [*propitiatory*] Dont say anything about it, Miss: I will see to the dust. Everybody starts the day with a drink here. Dont go talking, Miss, will you?

THE E. O. [*suddenly breaking down in tears*] You can go and tell who you damn well please. For two pins I'd chuck myself into the harbor and have done with it. This climate is hell: you cant stand it unless you drink till you see blue monkeys.

WILKS. Never mind him, Miss: he has nerves. We all have them here sooner or later, off and on. Here! I'll give you a landing ticket; and you just clear off and say nothing. [*He takes a ticket from the table and gives it to her*].

THE E. O. [*weeping*] A man's a slave here worse than a nigger. Spied on, reported on, checked and told off til he's afraid to have a pound note in his pocket or take a glass in his hand for fear of being had up for bribery or drinking. I'm fed up with it. Go and report me and be damned to you: what do I care? [*He sniffs and blows his nose, relieved by his outburst*].

WILKS. Would you have the kindness to clear out, Miss. We're busy. Youre passed all right: nothing to do but shew the ticket. You wont have to go back: we was only joking.

THE Y. W. But I want to go back. If this place is what he says, it is no place for me. And I did so enjoy the voyage out: I ask nothing better than to begin it all over again.

THE E. O. [*with the calm of despair*] Let her have her own way, Wilks. Shew her the way to the ship and shew her the way to the dock gate. She can take which she pleases. But get her out of this or I shall commit suicide.

THE Y. W. Why? Arnt you happy? It's not natural not to be happy. I'd be ashamed not to be happy.

THE E. O. What is there to make a man happy here?

THE Y. W. But you dont need to be made happy. You

ought to be happy from the inside. Then you wouldnt need things to make you happy.

THE E. O. My inside! Oh Lord!

THE Y. W. Well, you can make your inside all right if you eat properly and stop drinking and keep the office dusted and your nice white clothes clean and tidy. You two are a disgrace.

THE E. O. [*roaring with rage*] Chuck that woman out.

WILKS. Chuck her yourself. What can *I* do? [*Imploringly to her*] If youd only have the goodness to go, Miss. We're so busy this morning.

THE Y. W. But I am a stranger here: I have nobody else to talk to. And you have nothing to do until the next boat comes in.

THE E. O. The next boat is due the day after tomorrow at five in the afternoon. Do you expect us to sit here talking to you until then?

THE Y. W. Well, it's I who have to do most of the talking, isnt it? Couldnt you shew me round the town? I'll pay for the taxi.

THE E. O. [*feebly rebellious*] Look here: you cant go on like this, you know.

THE Y. W. What were you going to do with yourself this morning if I hadnt come?

THE E. O. I—I— Whats that to you?

THE Y. W. I see you hadnt made up your mind. Let me make it up for you. Put on your hat and come along and shew me round. I seem to spend my life making up other people's minds for them.

THE E. O. [*helplessly*] All right, all right, all right. You neednt make a ballyhoo about it. But I ask myself—

THE Y. W. Dont ask yourself anything, my child. Let life come to you. March.

THE E. O. [*at the railway door, to Wilks, in a last effort to assert himself*] Carry on, you. [*He goes*].

THE Y. W. Wouldnt you like to come too?

WILKS. Yes, Miss; but somebody must stay in the

office; and it had better be me than him. I am indispensable.

THE Y. W. What a word! Dispensables and indispensables: there you have the whole world. I wonder am I a dispensable or an indispensable. [*She goes out through the railway door*].

WILKS [*alone*] Let life come to you. Sounds all right, that. Let life come to you. Aye; but suppose life doesnt come to you! Look at me! What am I? An empire builder: thats what I am by nature. Cecil Rhodes: thats me. Why am I a clerk with only two shirts to my back, with that young waster wiping his dirty boots on me for doing the work he cant do himself, though he gets all the praise and all the pudding? Because life never came to me like it came to Rhodes. Found his backyard full of diamonds, he did; and nothing to do but wash the clay off them and be a millionaire. I had Rhodes's idea all right. Let the whole earth be England, I said to the school teacher; and let Englishmen govern it. Nobody put that into my head: it came of itself. But what did I find in my backyard? Next door's dead cat. Could I make myself head of a Chartered Company with a dead cat? And when I threw it back over the wall my mother said "You have thrown away your luck, my boy" she says "you shouldnt have thrown it back: you should have passed it on, like a chain letter. Now you will never have no more luck in this world." And no more I have. I says to her "I'll be in the papers yet some day" I says "like Cecil Rhodes: you see if I'm not." "Not you, my lad" she says. "Everything what comes to you you throw it back." Well, so I do. Look at this girl here. "Come with me" she says. And I threw the cat back again. "Somebody must be left in the office" I says. "I am indispensable" I says. And all the time I knew that nobody neednt be in the office, and that any Jew boy could do all I do here and do it better. But I promised my mother I'd get into the papers; and I will. I have that much of the Rhodes touch in me. [*He sits at the table and writes on a luggage label; then reads what he has written*] "Here lies a man who might have been Cecil Rhodes if he had had Rhodes's luck. Mother, farewell: your son has kept his word." [*He ties the label to the lapel of his coat*] Wheres that fool's gun? [*He opens a drawer and takes out a brandy flask and an automatic pistol, which he throws on the table*]. I'll damned well shew em whether I'm an empire builder or not. That lassie shant say that I didnt leave the place tidy either, though she can write in the dust of it with her finger. [*He shuts the drawer, and places the chair trimly at the table. Then he goes to his desk and takes out a duster, with which he wipes first the desk and then the table. He replaces the duster in the desk, and takes out a comb and a hand mirror. He tidies his hair; replaces the comb and glass in the desk; closes it and sets the stool in its place before it. He then returns to the table, and empties the flask at a draught*]. Now for it. The back of the head: thats the Russian touch. [*He takes the pistol and presents it over his shoulder to his occiput*]. Let the whole earth be England; and let Englishmen rule it. [*Singing*] Rule Britannia: Britannia rules the wa—

He blows his brains out and falls dead. The Station Master enters.

THE STATION MASTER. Here! Who's been shooting here? [*He sees the body*] Wilks!! Dear! dear! dear! What a climate! The fifth this month. [*He goes to the door*]. Hallo there, Jo. Bring along the stretcher and two or three with you. Mr. Wilks has shot himself.

JO. [*without, cheerfully*] Right you are, sir.

THE STATION MASTER. What a climate! Poor old Wilks!

SCENE II

A grassy cliff top overhanging the sea. A seat for promenaders. The young woman and the emigration officer stand on the brink.

THE Y. W. Pity theres no beach. We could bathe.

THE E. O. Not us. Not likely. Theres sharks there. And killer whales, worse than any sharks.

THE Y. W. It looks pretty deep.

THE E. O. I should think it is. The biggest liners can get close up. Like Plymouth. Like Lulworth Cove. Dont stand so close. Theres a sort of fascination in it; and you might get giddy.

They come away from the edge and sit on the seat together: she on his left, he nearest the sea.

THE Y. W. It's lovely here. Better than the town.

THE E. O. Dont deceive yourself. It's a horrible place. The climate is something terrible. Do you know that if you hadnt come in this morning I'd have done myself in.

THE Y. W. Dont talk nonsense. Why should you do yourself in?

THE E. O. Yes I should. I had the gun ready in the drawer of that table. I'd have shot Wilks and then shot myself.

THE Y. W. Why should you shoot poor Wilks? What has he done?

THE E. O. I hate him. He hates me. Everybody here hates everybody else. And the fellow is so confoundedly smug and happy and satisfied: it drives me mad when I can hardly bear my own life. No fear of him shooting himself: not much. So I thought I'd save him the trouble.

THE Y. W. But that would be murder.

THE E. O. Not if I shot myself after. That would make us quits.

THE Y. W. Well, I am surprised to hear a young man like you, in the prime of life as you might say, talking like that. Why dont you get married?

THE E. O. My salary's too small for a white woman.

Theyre all snobs; and they want a husband only to take them home out of this.

THE Y. W. Why, it's an earthly paradise.

THE E. O. Tell them so; and see what theyll say to you.

THE Y. W. Well, why not marry a colored woman?

THE E. O. You dont know what youre talking about. Ive tried. But now theyre all educated they wont look at a white man. They tell me I'm ignorant and that I smell bad.

THE Y. W. Well, so you do. You smell of drink and indigestion and sweaty clothes. You were quite disgusting when you tried to make up to me in the taxi. Thats why I got out, and made for the sea air.

THE E. O. [*rising hurriedly*] I cant stand any more of this. [*He takes a wallet of papers from his breast pocket and throws them on the seat*]. Hand them in at the office, will you: theyll be wanted there. I am going over.

He makes for the edge of the cliff. But there is a path down the cliff face, invisible from the seat. A native priest, a handsome man in the prime of life, beautifully dressed, rises into view by this path and bars his way.

PRIEST. Pardon, son of empire. This cliff contains the temple of the goddess who is beyond naming, the eternal mother, the seed and the sun, the resurrection and the life. You must not die here. I will send an acolyte to guide you to the cliff of death, which contains the temple of the goddess's brother, the weeder of the garden, the sacred scavenger, the last friend on earth, the prolonger of sleep and the giver of rest. It is not far off: life and death dwell close together: you need prolong your unhappiness only a bare five minutes. The priest there will attend to your remains and see they are disposed of with all becoming rites.

THE E. O. [*to the young woman*] Is he real; or is it the drink?

THE Y. W. He's real. And, my word! isnt he jolly good looking? [*To the priest*] You'll excuse this young man, sir, wont you? He's been drinking pretty hard.

THE PRIEST [*advancing between them*] Blame him not, sweet one. He comes from a strange mad country where the young are taught languages that are dead and histories that are lies, but are never told how to eat and drink and clothe themselves and reproduce their species. They worship strange ancient gods; and they play games with balls marvellously well; but of the great game of life they are ignorant. Here, where they are in the midst of life and loveliness, they die by their own hands to escape what they call the horrors. We do not encourage them to live. The empire is for those who can live in it, not for those who can only die in it. Take your friend to the cliff of death; and bid him farewell tenderly; for he is very unhappy.

THE E. O. Look here: I am an Englishman; and I shall commit suicide where I please. No nigger alive shall dictate to me.

THE PRIEST. It is forbidden.

THE E. O. Who's to stop me? Will you?

The priest shakes his head and makes way for him.

THE Y. W. Oh, you are not going to let him do it, are you?

THE PRIEST. [*holding her back*] We never offer violence to the unhappy. Do not interfere with his destiny.

THE E. O. [*planting himself on the edge and facing the abyss*] I am going to do it: see? Nobody shall say that I lived a dog's life because I was afraid to make an end of it. [*He bends his knees to spring, but cannot*]. I WILL. [*He makes another effort, bending almost to his haunches, but again fails to make the spring-up a spring-over*].

THE PRIEST. Poor fellow! Let me assist you. [*He shoots his foot against the E. O.'s posterior and sends him over the cliff*].

THE E. O. [*in a tone of the strongest remonstrance as he is catapulted into the void*] Oh! [*A prodigious splash*].

THE Y. W. Murderer!

THE PRIEST. Not quite. There are nets below, and a palisade to keep out the sharks. The shock will do him good.

THE Y. W. Well, I never!

THE PRIEST. Come, young rose blossom, and feast with us in the temple.

THE Y. W. Not so much rose blossom, young man. Are there any priestesses down there?

THE PRIEST. Of course. How can men feast without women?

THE Y. W. Well, let life come to you I always say; and dont cry out until youre hurt. After you, sir.

They descend.

SCENE III

A shelf of rock half way down the cliff forms an esplanade between the sea and a series of gigantic images of oriental deities in shallow alcoves cut in the face of the wall of rock. A feast of fruit and bread and soft drinks is spread on the ground. The young woman is sitting at it between the priest on her right nearest the sea and a very handsome young native priestess in robes of dusky yellow silk on her left nearest the images.

THE Y. W. You know, to me this is a funny sort of lunch. You begin with the dessert. We begin with the entrées. I suppose it's all right; but I have eaten so much fruit and bread and stuff that I dont feel I want any meat.

THE PRIEST. We shall not offer you any. We dont eat it.

THE Y. W. Then how do you keep up your strength?

THE PRIEST. It keeps itself up.

THE Y. W. Oh, how could that be? [*To the priestess*] You wouldnt like a husband that didnt eat plenty of meat, would you? But then youre a priestess; so I suppose it doesnt matter to you, as you cant marry.

THE PRIESTESS. I am married.

THE Y. W. Oh! And you a priestess!

THE PRIESTESS. I could not be a priestess if I were not married. How could I presume to teach others without a completed human experience? How could I deal with children if I were not a mother?

THE Y. W. But that isn't right. My sister was a teacher; but when she married they took her job away from her and wouldnt let her teach any more.

THE PRIESTESS. The rulers of your country must be mad.

THE Y. W. Oh no. Theyre all right: just like other people. [*To the priest*] I say, reverend. What about the poor lad you kicked over the cliff? Is he really safe? I dont feel easy about him.

THE PRIEST. His clothes are drying in the sun. They will lend him some clothes and send him up here as soon as he has recovered from his ducking.

An English lady tourist, Baedeker in hand, has wandered in, trying to identify the images with the aid of her book. She now comes behind the seated group and accosts the priest.

THE L. T. Excuse me; but can you tell me which of these figures is the principal god?

THE PRIEST [*rising courteously*] The principal one? I do not understand.

THE L. T. I get lost among all these different gods: it is so difficult to know which is which.

THE PRIEST. They are not different gods. They are all god.

THE L. T. But how can that be? The figures are different.

THE PRIEST. God has many aspects.

THE L. T. But all these names in the guide book?

THE PRIEST. God has many names.

THE L. T. Not with us, you know.

THE PRIEST. Yes: even with you. The Father, the Son, the Spirit, the Immaculate Mother—

THE L. T. Excuse me. We are not Catholics.

THE PRIESTESS [*sharply*] Are your temples then labelled "For men only"?

THE L. T. [*shocked*] Oh, really! So sorry to have troubled you. [*She hurries away*].

THE PRIEST [*resuming his seat*] You should not be rude to the poor lady. She is English, and doesnt understand.

THE PRIESTESS. I find these heathen idolaters very trying. Is it really kind to treat them according to their folly instead of to our wisdom?

THE Y. W. Here! Steady on, you. Who are you calling heathen idolaters? Look at all those images. I should say, if you ask me, that the boot is on the other leg.

THE PRIEST. Those images are not idols: they are personifications of the forces of nature by which we all live. But of course to an idolater they are idols.

THE Y. W. You talk a lot about religion here. Cant you think of something livelier? I always say let life come to you; and dont bother about religion.

THE PRIESTESS. An excellent rule. But the more you let life come to you, the more you will find yourself bothering about religion.

The Emigration Officer rises into view in a spotless white robe. He is clean and rather pale, but looks regenerated.

THE Y. W. Oh boy, you do look the better for your dip. Why, he's an angel, a lamb. What have you done to him?

THE E. O. [*seating himself at the end of the table with his back to the sea*] Well, if you want to know, this blighter kicked me into the sea; and when I'd swallowed a ton or two of your best salt water they fished me out in a net and emptied me out. I brought up my immortal soul. They gave me what I thought was a nice cup of their tea to settle my stomach; but it made me ten times as sick as I was before. Theres nothing of the man you met this morning left except his skin and bones. You may regard me as to all intents and purposes born again.

THE PRIEST. Do you still wish to kill yourself?

THE E. O. When you have been through what I have been through since they fished me out of the water you wont worry about trifles as I used to, old man.

THE Y. W. Thats right. Let life come to you, I always say.

THE E. O. Yes, let life come. The premises are quite empty.

THE LADY TOURIST [*returning and addressing the priest*] Excuse me; but I have been thinking so much about you since you spoke to me. Would you mind accepting and reading this little tract?

THE PRIEST [*rising and coming forward to her, mean-*

while reading the title with a polite show of interest] "Where will you spend eternity?"

THE L. T. [*strangely moved*] I have been haunted by your face. I could not bear to think of your spending eternity in torment. I feel sure it is a Christian face.

THE PRIEST. It is very kind of you. I will read the tract with the greatest attention. Thank you.

The lady, having no excuse for staying, moves away reluctantly towards the images.

THE PRIESTESS [*calling after her imperiously*] Where have you spent eternity so far, may I ask? That which has no end can have no beginning?

THE L. T. Excuse me: I have no desire to speak to you.

THE Y. W. [*indicating the priest*] Fallen in love with him, have you? Well, let yourself rip. Let life come to you.

THE L. T. Oh! How dare you? Really! Really!! [*She goes out indignantly*].

THE PRIESTESS. Another conquest, Pra?

THE Y. W. Is his name Pra?

THE PRIESTESS. He has many names; but he answers to Pra when you call him.

THE Y. W. Oh, what a way to put it! The man isn't a dog, is he?

THE PRIESTESS. He inspires a doglike devotion in women. He once did in me; so I know.

THE PRIEST. Dont be vindictive, Prola. I dont do it on purpose. [*He sits down again, this time next her on her left*].

THE PRIESTESS. No: you do it by instinct. That, also, is rather doglike.

THE PRIEST. No matter: I shall soon get the poor lady beyond the doglike stage.

THE E. O. [*who has been unable to take his eyes off the priestess*] Is your name Prola?

THE PRIEST. She has many names: some of them terrible ones; but she answers to Prola when you call her.

THE PRIESTESS. Young man: are my eyes like the fishpools of Heshbon?

THE E. O. Well, I have never seen the fishpools of Heshbon; but your eyes make me feel like that.

THE Y. W. Seems to me theres some sort of magic about this old cave thats dangerous. If you dont mind, I'll bid you all good morning. I always say let life come to you; but here it's coming a bit too thick for me. [*She rises*].

THE PRIESTESS. Wait. We can share him.

THE Y. W. Well I never! [*She flops back into her seat, flabbergasted*].

THE PRIESTESS. Hush. Look.

The Lady Tourist returns and again goes to the priest.

THE L. T. Excuse me; but could I have a word with you alone?

THE PRIEST [*rising*] Certainly. Come with me.

They go into the caves together.

THE E. O. What about a word with me alone, Prola?

THE Y. W. [*with redoubled emphasis*] Well I NEVER!!

THE PRIESTESS [*to the Officer*] You are not yet sufficiently regenerated. But you may hope.

THE Y. W. You take care, boy. I think youve got a touch of the sun. You cant be too careful in the tropics.

An English male tourist enters from among the images. He is on the young side of middle age, with pleasant aristocratic appearance and manners.

THE M. T. Excuse me: I have mislaid my wife. English lady with a guide book. Wears glasses. Bi-focals.

THE Y. W. Her husband! Oh, I say!

THE E. O. [*rising deferentially*] Just left us, Sir Charles.

THE M. T. Hallo! Weve met before, I think, havnt we?

THE E. O. When you landed, Sir Charles. I am the emigration officer.

SIR CHARLES. Ah, of course: yes. You know Lady Farwaters by sight. Which way did she go?

THE E. O. I am sorry: I didnt notice.

SIR CHARLES [*worried*] I wonder what she can be doing.

THE Y. W. So do I.

SIR CHARLES. I beg your pardon?

THE Y. W. Granted.

THE PRIESTESS [*rising and coming to him*] May I shew you round the temple, Sir Charles? We shall probably find her there.

SIR CHARLES [*who has not yet hitherto looked particularly at her*] No thank you, no, no.

THE PRIESTESS. It is interesting. I am not a professional guide: I am a priestess; and I will see that you are not asked for anything. You had better come with me.

SIR CHARLES. No: I— [*he looks at her. His tone changes instantly*]. Well, yes, if you will be so good. Certainly. Thank you.

They go into the alcoves together.

THE Y. W. [*leaving the table*] Oh boy, what do you think of this abode of love? Lady Farwaters, as white as Canterbury veal, has fallen for a brown bishop; and her husband, the whitest English west-end white, has been carried off to her den by an amber colored snake charmer. Lets get out of it while we're safe.

THE E. O. I feel quite safe, thank you. I have been cleaned up. You havnt.

THE Y. W. What do you mean, I havnt?

THE E. O. I mean that you were quite right to object to me half an hour ago. Your offensive personal remarks were fully justified. But now the tables are turned. I havnt gone through the fire; but Ive gone through the water. And the water has gone through me. It is for me now to object and to make personal remarks.

THE Y. W. Make as much as one; and you will get your face smacked.

THE E. O. [*seizing her by the wrist and the back of*

her collar] Go and get cleaned up, you disgusting little devil. [*He rushes her to the edge*].

THE Y. W. [*screaming*] No.

THE E. O. Yes. [*He hurls her over*].

A scream cut short by a splash. The E. O. sits down at the table and attacks the remains of the feast ravenously.

THE PROLOGUE ENDS

ACT I

The lawn of a stately house on the north coast of a tropical island in the Pacific commands a fine view of the ocean and of a breakwater enclosing a harbor, large enough to accommodate a fleet, but at present shipless. The western face of the house is reached by a terrace and a flight of steps. The steps lead down to a crescent formed by two curved stone seats separated by a patch of sward surrounding a circular well with a low marble parapet. This parapet, like the stone seats, has silk cushions scattered about it.

Behind the crescent the lawn is banked to a higher level and becomes a flower garden, sheltered from the wind by shrubberies. To the west of the flower garden the lawn falls away to the sea, but not to sea level, all that is visible of the port being the top of the lighthouse. There are trees enough in all directions to provide shade everywhere.

However, the raised flower garden is the centre of interest; for in it are four shrines marking the corners of a square. In the two foremost shrines two girl-goddesses sit crosslegged. In the two further ones two youthful gods are sitting in the same fashion. The ages of the four appear to be between 17 *and* 20. *They are magically beautiful in their Indian dresses, softly brilliant, making the tropical flowers of the garden seem almost crude beside them. Their expressions are intent, grave, and inscrutable. They face south with their backs to the sea. The goddess to the east has raven black hair, a swarthy skin, and robes of a thousand shades of deep carnation, in contrast to the younger one on her right, who is a ravishing blonde in a diaphanous white and gold sari. There is a parallel contrast between the two youths, the one on the west being the younger and more delicate, and the one on his left older and more powerfully framed.*

The four figures give the garden a hieratic aspect which has its effect on a young English clergyman, who wan-

ders into the grounds at the north west corner, looking curiously and apprehensively about him with the air of a stranger who is trespassing. When he catches sight of the four figures he starts nervously and whips off his hat; then approaches them on tiptoe. He has a baby complexion, and a childish expression, credulous and disarmingly propitiatory. His age is at most 24.

Down the steps at this moment comes Pra, about twenty years older than when we saw him last, but splendidly preserved. His approach is dignified and even courteous, though not warmly so. He evidently wants to know what the stranger is doing in his garden.

THE CLERGYMAN [*nervously, hat in hand*] I beg your pardon. I fear I am trespassing. I am a stranger here; and I could not find a road up from the beach. I thought I might cut across through your grounds. [*Indicating the figures*] But I assure you I had no idea I was intruding on consecrated ground.

PRA. You are not on consecrated ground, except in so far as all ground is consecrated.

THE CLERGYMAN. Oh, excuse me. I thought—those idols—

PRA. Idols!

THE CLERGYMAN. No, of course not idols. I meant those gods and goddesses—

PRA. They are very beautiful, are they not? [*He speaks without awe or enthusiasm, with a touch of pity for the parson and weariness on his own part*].

THE CLERGYMAN. They are most beautiful. Quite marvellous even to me, an English clergyman. I can hardly wonder at your worshipping them, though of course you shouldnt.

PRA. Beauty is worshipful, within limits. When you have worshipped your fill may I shew you the shortest way out? It is through the house. Where do you wish to go, by the way?

THE CLERGYMAN. I dont know. I am lost.

PRA. Lost?

THE CLERGYMAN. Yes, quite lost. I dont know where I am. I mean I dont even know what country I am in.

PRA. You are in the Unexpected Isles, a Crown Colony of the British Empire.

THE CLERGYMAN. Do you mean the isles that came up out of the sea when I was a baby.

PRA. Yes. [*Pointing to the breakwater*] That is the harbor of the port of Good Adventure.

THE CLERGYMAN. They put me on shore there.

PRA. Who put you on shore?

THE CLERGYMAN. The pirates.

PRA. Pirates!

THE CLERGYMAN. Yes. I was their chaplain.

PRA. You were their—! [*He turns to the house and calls*] Prola. Prola.

PROLA'S VOICE. Yes. What is it?

PRA. Come out here.

Prola comes down the steps. She, like Pra, is twenty years older; but the years have only made her beauty more impressive.

THE CLERGYMAN [*gaping at her in undisguised awe and admiration*] Oh dear! Is this the lady of the house?

PROLA [*coming past Pra to the Clergyman*] Who is this gentleman?

PRA. He does not seem to know. I think he has escaped from the asylum.

THE CLERGYMAN [*distressed*] Oh, dear beautiful lady, I am not mad. Everybody thinks I am. Nobody believes what I say, though it is the simple truth. I know it is very hard to believe.

PROLA. In the Unexpected Isles nothing is unbelievable. How did you get in here?

THE CLERGYMAN. I lost my way trying to find a short cut up from the beach. I climbed the fence. I am so sorry.

PROLA. Really sorry?

THE CLERGYMAN. I did not mean to intrude. I apologize most sincerely.

PROLA. I did not ask you to apologize: you are quite welcome. I asked were you really sorry. Do you regret finding yourself in this garden?

THE CLERGYMAN. Oh no. It's like the Garden of Eden: I should like to stay here forever. [*Suddenly breaking down to the verge of tears*] I have nowhere to go.

PROLA. Perhaps he is weak with hunger.

THE CLERGYMAN. No: it's not that. I have been under a great strain for a long time; and now that I have escaped—and the beauty of those four—and your lovely awfulness—and—oh [*collapsing on the stone seat*] I am making a fool of myself. I always make a fool of myself. Dont mind me.

PRA. He thinks he has been chaplain in a pirate ship.

THE CLERGYMAN [*rising in desperate protest*] But I have. I have. They kidnapped me at Weston Super Mare where I was doing locum tenens for the Rector of Saint Biddulphs. It was on a Sunday afternoon: I had my clerical clothes on after taking the afternoon service. "You look so innocent and respectable" they said. "Just what we want!" They took me all over the world, where I couldnt speak the language and couldnt explain.

PRA. And they wanted you to minister to them spiritually?

THE CLERGYMAN. No no: that was what was so dreadful. They were crooks, racketeers, smugglers, pirates, anything that paid them. They used me to make people believe that they were respectable. They were often so bored that they made me hold a service and preach; but it was only to make themselves ill laughing at me. Though perhaps I shouldnt say that. Some of them were such dear nice fellows: they assured me it did them no end of good. But they got tired of me and put me ashore here. [*He again resorts to the stone seat, clasping his temples distractedly*] Oh dear! oh dear! nothing ever happens to me that happens to other people. And all because I was not a natural baby. I was a nitrogen baby.

PROLA. A nitrogen baby!

PRA [*to Prola*] Steady. There may be something in this. [*He goes to the clergyman and sits down beside him*] What do you mean by a nitrogen baby?

THE CLERGYMAN. You see, my father is a famous biological chemist.

PROLA. I do not see. Your father may be a biological chemist; but biological chemists' children are like other people's children.

THE CLERGYMAN. No. No, I assure you. Not my father's children. You dont know my father. Even my Christian name is Phosphor.

PRA. Is what?

THE CLERGYMAN. Phosphor. [*He spells it*] P.H.O.S. P.H.O.R. The name of the morning star. Phosphorus, you know. The stuff they make matches with. Such a name to baptize a boy by! Please dont call me by it.

PRA. Come come! Neither your father nor your godfathers and godmothers could change your human nature by giving you an unusual name in baptism.

THE CLERGYMAN. But it wasnt only the name. My father fed our cows on nitrogen grass.

PRA. Nitrogen gas, you mean.

THE CLERGYMAN. No: nitrogen grass. Some sort of grass that came up when he sprinkled our fields with chemicals. The cows ate it; and their butter was very yellow and awfully rich. So was the milk. I was fed on that sort of milk and butter. And the wheat in my bread was grown from special nitrates that my father made.

PRA [*to Prola*] I believe he is not mad after all.

THE CLERGYMAN. I assure you I am not. I am weak-minded; but I am not mad.

PRA. I have read some very interesting articles about this by an English chemist named Hammingtap.

THE CLERGYMAN. Thats my father. My name is Hammingtap. The old family name is Hummingtop; but my grandfather changed it when he was at Oxford.

PRA. Prola: our young friend here may really be a new sort of man. Shall we go in and tell the others about him? We might take him into the family for a while, as an experiment.

THE CLERGYMAN [*alarmed*] Oh please, no. Why does everyone want to make an experiment of me?

PROLA. All men and women are experiments. What is your religion?

THE CLERGYMAN. The Christian religion, of course. I am a clergyman.

PROLA. What is the Christian religion?

THE CLERGYMAN. Well, it is—well, I suppose it is the Christian religion. I thought everybody knew. But then of course you are a heathen.

PROLA. What does the Christian religion mean to you?

THE CLERGYMAN. Oh, to me it means everything that is good and lovely and kind and holy. I dont profess to go any further than that.

PROLA. You need not. You had better not. Wait here until we return. We may find some use for you. Come, Pra.

She goes up the steps into the house, followed by Pra. The Clergyman, left with the four figures, looks at them, looks round to make sure that nobody is watching. Then he steals up to the fair goddess.

THE CLERGYMAN. Oh, how lovely you are! How I wish you were alive and I could kiss your living lips instead of the paint on a hard wooden image. I wonder is it idolatry to adore you? St Peter in Rome is only a bronze image; but his feet have been worn away by the kisses of Christian pilgrims. You make me feel as I have never felt before. I must kiss you. [*He does so and finds that she is alive. She smiles as her eyes turn bewitchingly towards him*]. Oh!!! [*He stands gasping, palpitating*].

THE ELDER YOUTH. Beware.

THE YOUNGER. On guard.

THE FAIR GIRL. Let him worship. His lips are sweet and pure.

THE DARK ONE. "For he on honey dew hath fed"—

THE FAIR ONE.—"and drunk the milk of paradise."

THE DARK ONE. I, Vashti, can see his aura. It is violet.

THE FAIR ONE. I, Maya, can see his halo. It is silvery.

VASHTI. Blessed are the shining ones!

MAYA. Blessed are the simple ones!

THE ELDER YOUTH. Beware. I, Janga, warn thee.

THE YOUNGER YOUTH. On guard. I, Kanchin, shew thee the red light.

JANGA. Their eyebrows are drawn bows.

KANCHIN. Their arrows feel sweet in the heart—

JANGA. —but are deadly.

KANCHIN. The ground within reach of their arms is enchanted.

JANGA. Vashti is lovely even to her brothers.

KANCHIN. Little children would die for Maya.

JANGA. Beware.

KANCHIN. On guard.

JANGA. Trust them not.

KANCHIN. They will break thy spear.

JANGA. They will pierce thy shield.

VASHTI. Fear not, beginner: I will strengthen thee.

MAYA. Strive not, beloved: I will keep thy soul for thee.

THE 2 YOUTHS [*together, fortissimo*] Beware.

The two girl-goddesses suddenly and simultaneously spring from their shrines and march down upon him, Vashti to his left, Maya to his right.

VASHTI. Dare you tread the plains of heaven with us, young pilgrim?

MAYA. We are waves of life in a sea of bliss. Dare you breast them, young swimmer?

THE CLERGYMAN. Oh, I dont know whether you are gods and goddesses or real people. I only know that you fill my heart with inexpressible longings.

MAYA. We are the awakening.

VASHTI. We are the way.

MAYA. We are the life.

VASHTI. I am the light. Look at me. [*She throws her arm round him and turns his face to hers*].

MAYA. I am the fire. Feel how it glows [*She also throws her arm round him*].

LADY FARWATERS *comes from the house, and pauses at the top of the steps to take in what is going on.*

THE CLERGYMAN. Oh, one at a time, please.

VASHTI. Perfect love casteth out choice.

MAYA. In love there is neither division nor measure.

LADY FARWATERS [*rushing to him and dragging him away from them*] Stop it, children: you are driving the man mad. Go away, all of you.

The two youths spring from their pedestals and whirl the girls away through the shrubberies.

VASHTI [*invisible, calling*] I will return in dreams.

MAYA [*similarly*] I leave my arrow in your heart.

LADY FARWATERS. You mustnt mind them.

Prola and Pra come down the steps, followed by Sir Charles Farwaters and by Hugo Hyering C.B. and Mrs Hyering. Hyering is the former emigration officer, now an elderly and very different man, disciplined, responsible and well groomed. His wife is the emigrant girl twenty years older and better drilled socially, but still very much her old self. Lady Farwaters, once a gaunt and affected tourist visiting cave temples and distributing tracts to the heathen, is now a bland and attractive matron.

PRA. Mr Hammingtap: let me introduce you to the Governor of the Unexpected Isles, Sir Charles Farwaters.

SIR CHARLES [*offering his hand*] How do you do, Mr Hammingtap?

THE CLERGYMAN [*jerkily nervous*] Very pleased. [*They shake hands*].

Sir Charles sits down in the middle of the stone seat nearest the steps.

PRA. Lady Farwaters.

LADY FARWATERS [*smiles and proffers her hand*]!

THE CLERGYMAN. Most kind— er. [*He shakes*].

Lady Farwaters sits down in the middle of the other stone seat.

PRA. This is Mr Hugo Hyering, political secretary to the Isles.

THE CLERGYMAN. How do you do, Sir Hugo?

HYERING [*shaking hands*] Not Sir Hugo. [*Introducing*] Mrs Hyering.

MRS HYERING [*shaking hands*] C.B., in case you are addressing a letter. [*She sits down on Sir Charles's left*].

THE CLERGYMAN. Oh, I am so sorry.

HYERING. Not at all. [*He sits on Lady Farwaters' right*].

PRA [*indicating the parapet of the well*] You had better sit here.

THE CLERGYMAN [*sitting down as directed*] Thank you.

Prola sits down on Sir Charles's left, and Pra on Lady Farwaters' left.

LADY FARWATERS. You have made the acquaintance of our four children, Mr Hammingtap?

THE CLERGYMAN. I couldnt help it. I mean—

PROLA. We know what you mean. You need not explain.

THE CLERGYMAN. But I assure you I—that is—

MRS HYERING. Dont apologize, Mr Hammingtap. We know quite well what our daughters are capable of when they are attracted by a young stranger.

THE CLERGYMAN. I did not understand. They are so sunburnt, and their dresses are so eastern: I thought they were orientals.

SIR CHARLES. They are half orientals. You see, the family is a mixed one. This lady, whom you may address as Prola, and this gentleman, known as Pra, are both entirely oriental, and very dominant personalities at that; so that naturally our children would have a strong oriental strain, would they not?

THE CLERGYMAN [*hastily*] Oh, of course. Quite. Certainly. [*He looks piteously at their gracious unconcerned faces, which tell him nothing*]. I beg your pardon. I am frightfully sorry; but my nerves are in rags; and I cannot follow what you are saying.

HYERING. Oh yes you can. It's all right: you have understood perfectly.

MRS HYERING. Buck up, Mr Hammingtap. Let life come to you.

LADY FARWATERS. Our family arrangements are not those usual in England. We are making a little domestic experiment—

THE CLERGYMAN. Oh, not an experiment, I hope. Chemical experiments are bad enough: I am one myself; but they are scientific. I dont think I could countenance a domestic experiment. And in spite of what you say I am not sure that I am not going mad.

SIR CHARLES. We are distracting you. Let us change the subject. Would you like to be a bishop?

THE CLERGYMAN. Oh dear! Can you make me one?

SIR CHARLES. Well, my recommendation would probably be decisive. A bishop is needed here: a bishop in partibus infidelium. Providence seems to have thrown you on this shore for the purpose, like Jonah. Will you undertake it?

THE CLERGYMAN. I should like to have a bishop's salary, certainly. But unfortunately I am weakminded.

SIR CHARLES. Many bishops are; and they are the best sort. A strongminded bishop is a horror.

THE CLERGYMAN. I am too young.

SIR CHARLES. You will not remain so. Most bishops are too old.

THE CLERGYMAN [*tempted*] It would be rather a lark, wouldnt it?

MRS HYERING. Thats right, Mr Hammingtap: let life come to you.

PRA. What objection have you to be a bishop?

THE CLERGYMAN. Oh, none, I assure you. Of course no clergyman could object to be a bishop. But why do you want to make me one?

SIR CHARLES. I will be quite frank with you, Mr Hammingtap. Twenty years ago my wife and I, with Mr and Mrs Hyering, joined this eastern gentleman and his colleague in a eugenic experiment. Its object was to try out the result of a biological blend of the flesh and spirit of the west with the flesh and spirit of the east. We formed a family of six parents.

THE CLERGYMAN. Six?

SIR CHARLES. Yes, six. The result has been a little disappointing from the point of view of numbers; but we have produced four children, two of each sex, and educated them in the most enlightened manner we were capable of. They have now grown up; consequently the time has arrived when the family group must be extended by young persons of their own age, so that the group may produce a second generation. Now sooner or later this extension of the family group will set people talking.

THE CLERGYMAN. It would strike my people dumb, if I grasp your meaning rightly.

SIR CHARLES. You do. I mean exactly what I say. There will be a struggle with public opinion in the empire. We shall not shirk it: it is part of our plan to open people's minds on the subject of eugenics and the need for mixing not only western and eastern culture but eastern and western blood. Still, we do not want to be stopped, as the Mormons were, or as the Oneida Community would have been if it had not voluntarily broken up. We want to set the intelligent people talking, and to strike the stupid people dumb. And we think we could do both by adding a bishop to the family.

MRS HYERING. And that is where you come in, young man.

PRA. There is another consideration that weighs with us: at least with me. I am convinced that there is something lacking in the constitution of the children. It may be a deficiency of nitrogen. It certainly is a deficiency of something that is essential to a complete social human being.

THE CLERGYMAN. Oh, I cannot believe that. They seemed to me to be quite perfect. I cannot imagine anyone more perfect than Maya.

PRA. Well, what did you think of Maya's conscience, for example?

THE CLERGYMAN [*bewildered*] Her conscience? I suppose—I dont know—I—

PRA. Precisely. You dont know Well, we do know. Our four wonderful children have all sorts of talents, all sorts of accomplishments, all sorts of charms. And we are heartily tired of all their attractions because, though they have artistic consciences, and would die rather than do anything ugly or vulgar or common, they have not between the whole four of them a scrap of moral conscience. They have been very carefully fed: all the vitamins that the biological chemists have discovered are provided in their diet. All their glands are scientifically nourished. Their physical health is perfect. Unfortunately the biological chemists have not yet discovered either the gland that produces and regulates the moral conscience or the vitamins that nourish it. Have you a conscience, Mr Hammingtap?

THE CLERGYMAN. Oh yes: I wish I hadnt. It tortures me. You know, I should have enjoyed being a pirate's chaplain sometimes if it hadnt been for my terrible conscience. It has made my life one long remorse; for I have never had the strength of mind to act up to it.

PRA. That suggests very strongly that the conscientious man is, chemically speaking, the nitrogenic man. Here, then, we have four young adults, insufficiently nitrogenized, and therefore deficient in conscience. Here also we have a young adult saturated with nitrogen from his cradle, and suffering from a morbid excess of conscience. A union between him and our girls is clearly indicated.

THE CLERGYMAN. You mean that I ought to marry one

of them?

PRA. Not at all. They would regard that as an invidious proceeding.

THE CLERGYMAN. Invidious! I dont understand.

LADY FARWATERS [*goodnaturedly*] Let me try to break it to you, Mr Hammingtap. The two girls attract you very much, dont they?

THE CLERGYMAN. How can one help being attracted, Lady Farwaters? Theyre quite beautiful.

LADY FARWATERS. Both of them?

THE CLERGYMAN. Oh, as a clergyman I could not be attracted by more than one at a time. Still, somehow, I seem to love them all in an inexpressible sort of way. Only, if there were any question of marriage, I should have to choose.

PROLA. And which would you choose?

THE CLERGYMAN. Oh, I should choose Maya.

PROLA. Maya would at once reject you.

THE CLERGYMAN [*much dejected*] I suppose so. I know I am no catch for Maya. Still, she was very kind to me. In fact—but perhaps I oughtnt to tell you this—she kissed me.

SIR CHARLES. Indeed? That shews that she contemplates a union with you.

LADY FARWATERS. You must not think she would reject you on the ground of any personal unworthiness on your part.

THE CLERGYMAN. Then on what ground? Oh, I shouldnt have kissed her.

MRS HYERING. Oho! You said it was she who kissed you.

THE CLERGYMAN. Yes: I know I should have explained that. But she let me kiss her.

MRS HYERING. That must have been a thrill, Mr Hammingtap. Life came to you that time, didnt it?

THE CLERGYMAN. Oh please, I cant speak of it. But why should she reject me if I make her an honorable proposal?

LADY FARWATERS. Because she will consider your honorable proposal dishonorable, Mr Hammingtap, unless it includes all the ladies of the family. You will not be allowed to pick and choose and make distinctions. You marry all or none.

THE CLERGYMAN. Oh dear! My poor little brain is giving way. I cant make sense of what you are saying. I know that your meaning must be perfectly right and respectable, Lady Farwaters; but it sounds like a dreadful sort of wickedness.

LADY FARWATERS. May I try to explain?

THE CLERGYMAN. Please do, Lady Farwaters. But I wish you wouldnt call me Mr Hammingtap. I am accustomed to be called Iddy among friends.

MRS HYERING. What does Iddy stand for?

THE CLERGYMAN. Well, in our home I was known as the idiot.

MRS HYERING. Oh! I am sorry: I didnt know.

THE CLERGYMAN. Not at all. My sister was the Kiddy; so I became the Iddy. Do please call me that. And be kind to me. I am weakminded and lose my head very easily; and I can see that you are all wonderfully clever and strongminded. That is why I could be so happy here. I can take in anything if you will only tell it to me in a gentle hushabyebaby sort of way and call me Iddy. Now go on, Lady Farwaters. Excuse me for interrupting you so long.

LADY FARWATERS. You see, Iddy—

IDDY. Oh, thanks!

LADY FARWATERS [*continuing*] —our four children are not like European children and not like Asiatic children. They have the east in their brains and the west in their blood. And at the same time they have the east in their blood and the west in their brains. Well, from the time when as tiny tots they could speak, they invented fairy stories. I thought it silly and dangerous, and wanted to stop them; but Prola would not let me: she taught them a game called the heavenly parliament in which all of them told tales and added them to the general stock until a fairyland was built up, with laws and religious rituals, and finally a great institution which they called the Superfamily. It began by my telling them in my old conventional English way to love oneanother; but they would not have that at all: they said it was vulgar nonsense and made them interfere with oneanother and hate oneanother. Then they hit out for themselves the idea that they were not to love oneanother, but that they were to be oneanother.

IDDY. To be oneanother! I dont understand.

SIR CHARLES. Neither do I. Pra and Prola think they understand it; but Lady Farwaters and I dont; and we dont pretend to. We are too English. But the practical side of it—the side that concerns you—is that Vashti and Maya are now grown up. They must have children. The boys will need a young wife.

IDDY. You mean two wives.

LADY FARWATERS. Oh, a dozen, if so many of the right sort can be found.

IDDY. But—but—but that would be polygamy.

PROLA. You are in the east, Mr Iddy. The east is polygamous. Try to remember that polygamists form an enormous majority of the subjects of the British Empire, and that you are not now in Clapham.

IDDY. How dreadful! I never thought of that.

LADY FARWATERS. And the girls will need a young husband.

IDDY [*imploringly*] Two young husbands, Lady Farwaters. Oh please, two.

LADY FARWATERS. I think not, at first.

IDDY. Oh! But I am not an oriental. I am a clergyman of the Church of England.

HYERING. That means nothing to Vashti.

PRA. And still less to Maya.

IDDY. But—but—oh dear! dont you understand? I want to marry Maya. And if I marry Maya I cannot marry

Vashti. An English clergyman could not marry two women.

LADY FARWATERS. From their point of view they are not two women: they are one. Vashti is Maya; and Maya is Vashti.

IDDY. But even if such a thing were possible how could I be faithful to Vashti without being unfaithful to Maya? I couldnt bear to be unfaithful to Maya.

LADY FARWATERS. Maya would regard the slightest unfaithfulness to Vashti as a betrayal of herself and a breach of your marriage vow.

IDDY. But thats nonsense: utter nonsense. Please dont put such things into my head. I am trying so hard to keep sane; but you are terrifying me. If only I could bring myself never to see Maya again I should rush out of this garden and make for home. But it would be like rushing out of heaven. I am most unhappy; and yet I am dreadfully happy. I think I am under some sort of enchantment.

MRS HYERING. Well, stick to the enchantment while it lasts. Let life come to you.

PRA. May I remind you that not only Vashti and Maya, but all the ladies here, are included in the superfamily compact.

IDDY. Oh, how nice and comfortable that would be! They would be mothers to me.

PROLA [*rebuking Pra*] Let him alone, Pra. There is such a thing as calf love. Vashti and Maya are quite enough for him to begin with. Maya has already driven him half mad. There is no need for us old people to drive him quite out of his senses. [*She rises*] This has gone far enough. Wait here alone, Mr Hammingtap, to collect your thoughts. Look at the flowers; breathe the air; open your soul to the infinite space of the sky. Nature always helps.

IDDY [*rising*] Thank you, Lady Prola. Yes: that will be a great help.

PROLA. Come. [*She goes up the steps and into the house*].

They all rise and follow her, each bestowing a word of counsel or comfort on the distracted clergyman.

PRA. Relax. Take a full breath and then relax. Do not strangle yourself with useless anxieties. [*He goes*].

LADY FARWATERS. Cast out fear, Iddy. Warm heart. Clear mind. Think of having a thousand friends, a thousand wives, a thousand mothers. [*She pats him on the shoulder and goes*].

SIR CHARLES. Stand up to it, my boy. The world is changing. Stand up to it. [*He goes*].

MRS HYERING. Dont let that conscience of yours worry you. Let life come to you. [*She goes*].

HYERING. Try to sleep a little. The morning has been too much for you. [*He goes*].

IDDY. Sleep! I will not sleep. They want me to disgrace my cloth; but I wont. I wont relax: I wont disobey my conscience: I wont smell those flowers: I wont look at the sky. Nature is not good for me here. Nature is eastern here: it's poison to an Englishman. I will think of England and tighten myself up and pull myself together. England! The Malverns! the Severn plain! the Welsh border! the three cathedrals! England that is me: I that am England! Damn and blast all these tropical paradises: I am an English clergyman; and my place is in England. Floreat Etona! Back to England and all that England means to an Englishman! In this sign I shall conquer. [*He turns resolutely to go out as he came in, and finds himself face to face with Maya, who has stolen in and listened gravely and intently to his exhortation*].

IDDY [*collapsing in despair on the parapet of the well*] Oh, Maya, let me go, let me go.

MAYA [*sinking beside him with her arm round his neck*] Speak to me from your soul, and not with words that you have picked up in the street.

IDDY. Respect my cloth, Miss Farwaters.

MAYA. Maya. Maya is my name. I am the veil of the temple. Rend me in twain.

IDDY. I wont. I will go home and marry some honest English girl named Polly Perkins. [*Shuddering in her embrace*] Oh, Maya, darling: speak to me like a human being.

MAYA. That is how I speak to you; but you do not recognize human speech when you hear it: you crave for slang and small talk, and for readymade phrases that mean nothing. Speak from your soul; and tell me: do you love Vashti? Would you die for Vashti?

IDDY. No.

MAYA [*with a flash of rage, springing up*] Wretch! [*Calmly and conclusively*] You are free. Farewell [*She points his way through the house*].

IDDY [*clutching at her robe*] No, no. Do not leave me. I love you—you. I would die for you. That sounds like a word picked up in the street; but it is true. I would die for you ten times over.

MAYA. It is not true. Words, words, words out of the gutter. Vashti and Maya are one: you cannot love me if you do not love Vashti: you cannot die for me without dying for Vashti.

IDDY. Oh, I assure you I can.

MAYA. Lies, lies. If you can feel one heart throb for me that is not a throb for Vashti: if for even an instant there are two women in your thoughts instead of one, then you do not know what love can be.

IDDY. But it's just the contrary. I—

VASHTI [*who has entered silently, sits beside him and throws an arm round his shoulders*] Do you not love me? Would you not die for me?

IDDY [*mesmerized by her eyes*] Oh DEAR!!! Yes: your eyes make my heart melt: your voice opens heaven to me: I love you. I would die a thousand times for you.

VASHTI. And Maya? You love Maya. You would die a million times for Maya?

IDDY. Yes, yes. I would die for either, for both: for one, for the other—

MAYA. For Vashti Maya?

IDDY. For Vashti Maya, for Maya Vashti.

VASHTI. Your lives and ours are one life.

MAYA [*sitting down beside him*] And this is the Kingdom of love.

The three embrace with interlaced arms and vanish in black darkness.

ACT II

A fine forenoon some years later. The garden is unchanged; but inside the distant breakwater the harbor is crowded with cruisers; and on the lawn near the steps is a writing table littered with papers and furnished with a wireless telephone. Sir Charles is sitting at the end of it with his back to the house. Seated near him is Pra. Both are busy writing. Hyering enters.

SIR CHARLES. Morning, Hyering.

HYERING. Morning. [*He sits at the other end of the table after waving an acknowledgment of Pra's indication of a salaam*]. Anything fresh?

SIR CHARLES [*pointing to the roadstead*] Look! Five more cruisers in last night. The papers say it is the first time the fleets of the British Empire have ever assembled in one place.

HYERING. I hope it will never happen again. If we dont get rid of them quickly there will be the biggest naval battle on record. They are quarrelling already like Kilkenny cats.

SIR CHARLES. What about?

HYERING. Oh, about everything. About moorings, about firing salutes: which has the right to fire first? about flags, about shore parties, about nothing. We shall never be able to keep the peace between them. The Quebec has got alongside the Belfast. The Quebec has announced Mass at eleven on All Saints Day; and the Belfast has announced firing practice at the same hour. Do you see that sloop that came in last night?

SIR CHARLES. What is it?

HYERING. The Pitcairn Island fleet. They are Seventh Day Adventists, and are quite sure the Judgment Day is fixed for five o'clock this afternoon. They propose to do nothing until then but sing hymns. The Irish Free State admiral threatens to sink them if they dont stop. How am I to keep them quiet?

PRA. Dont keep them quiet. Their squabbles will make

them forget what they were sent here for.

HYERING. Forget! not they. I have six ultimatums from their admirals, all expiring at noon today. Look. [*He takes a batch of letters from his pocket and throws them on the table*].

SIR CHARLES [*pointing to the letters on the table*] Look at these!

PRA. All about Iddy.

SIR CHARLES. Iddy has got into the headlines at home. The cables are humming with Iddy. Iddy has convulsed the Empire, confound him!

HYERING. Anything fresh from London or Delhi?

SIR CHARLES. The same old songs. The Church of England wont tolerate polygamy on any terms, and insists on our prosecuting Iddy if we cannot whitewash him. Delhi declares that any attempt to persecute polygamy would be an insult to the religions of India.

PRA. The Cultural Minister at Delhi adds a postscript to say that as he has been married two hundred and thirty-four times, and could not have lived on his salary without the dowries, the protest of the Church of England shews a great want of consideration for his position. He has a hundred and seventeen children surviving.

SIR CHARLES. Then there's a chap I never heard of, calling himself the Caliph of British Islam. He demands that Iddy shall put away all his wives except four.

HYERING. What does the Foreign Office say to that?

PRA. The Foreign Office hails it as a happy solution of a difficulty that threatened to be very serious.

HYERING. What do you think about it all yourself, Pra?

PRA. Think! Thought has no place in such discussions. Each of them must learn that its ideas are not everybody's ideas. Here is a cablegram from the League of British Imperial Womanhood, Vancouver and Pretoria. "Burn him alive and his hussies with him." Do you expect me to think about such people?

HYERING. Nobody has made any practical suggestion,

I suppose?

PRA. The United States intervene with a friendly suggestion that the parties should be divorced. But the Irish Free State will not hear of divorce, and points out that if the parties become Catholics their marriages can be annulled with the greatest ease.

HYERING. Oh, the west! the west! the west!

PRA. Oh, the east! the east! the east! I tried to reconcile them; and I had only two successes: you and Lady Farwaters.

HYERING. You kicked me into the sea.

SIR CHARLES. You made love to Lady Farwaters.

PRA. I had to use that method with very crude novices; and Lady Farwaters, with her English ladylike bringing-up, was so crude that she really could not understand any purely intellectual appeal. Your own mind, thanks to your public school and university, was in an even worse condition; and Prola had to convert you by the same elementary method. Well, it has worked, up to a point. The insight you obtained into eastern modes of thought has enabled you to govern the eastern crown colonies with extraordinary success. Downing Street hated you; but Delhi supported you; and since India won Dominion status Delhi has been the centre of the British Empire. You, Hyering, have had the same diplomatic success in the east for the same reason. But beyond this we have been unable to advance a step. Our dream of founding a millennial world culture: the dream which united Prola and Pra as you first knew them, and then united us all six, has ended in a single little household with four children, wonderful and beautiful, but sterile. When we had to find a husband for the blossoming girls, only one man was found capable of merging himself in the unity of the family: a man fed on air from his childhood. And how has this paragon turned out? An impotent simpleton. It would be impossible to conceive a human being of less consequence in the world. And yet, look! There is the Imperial Armada, in which every petty province insists on its separate fleet, every trumpery islet its battleship, its cruiser, or at least its sloop or gunboat! Why are they here, armed to the teeth, threatening what they call their sanctions? a word that once meant the approval of the gods, and now means bombs full of poison gas. Solely on account of the simpleton. To reform his morals, half of them want to rain destruction on this little household of ours, and the other half is determined to sink them if they attempt it.

HYERING. They darent use their bombs, you know.

PRA. True; but what is to prevent them from taking to their fists and coming ashore to fight it out on the beach with sticks and bottles and stones, or with their fists? What do the ultimatums say, Hyering?

HYERING [*reading them*] Number one from the English admiral. "If the polygamist-adulterer Hammingtap is not handed over by noon tomorrow" that is today "I shall be obliged to open fire on Government House." Number two, from the commander of the Bombay Squadron. "Unless an unequivocal guarantee of the safety and liberty of Mr Hammingtap be in my hands by noon today" that came this morning "I shall land a shore party equipped with machine guns and tear gas bombs to assist the local police in the protection of his person." Number three: "I have repeatedly informed you that the imperial province of Holy Island demands the immediate and exemplary combustion of the abominable libertine and damnable apostate known as Phosfor Hammingtap. The patience of the Holy Island fleet will be exhausted at noon on the 13th" today "and the capital of the Unexpected Islands must take the consequences." Number four—

SIR CHARLES. Oh, bother number four! They are all the same: not one of them has originality enough to fix half-past-eleven or a quarter-to-one.

HYERING. By the way, Pra, have you taken any steps? I havnt.

PRA. Yes I have. Dont worry. I have sent a message.

SIR CHARLES. What message?

PRA. The Mayor of the Port earnestly begs the commanders of the imperial fleet to suspend action for another day, as his attention is urgently occupied by a serious outbreak of smallpox in the harbor district.

SIR CHARLES. Good. [*The boom of a cannon interrupts him*] There goes the noonday cannon!

HYERING. I hope they got the message in time.

The garden and its occupants vanish. When they reappear, the harbor is empty: not a ship is visible. The writing table, with its chairs and papers, has been removed and replaced by a small tea-table. Tea is ready. The wireless telephone is still there.

Vashti and Maya are in their shrines. Lady Farwaters is sitting on the western stone seat, with Mrs Hyering beside her on her right. Prola is sitting on the eastern seat. All five ladies are taking tea.

Pra comes from the house with Sir Charles and Hyering. They help themselves to tea. Pra abstains.

SIR CHARLES. Not a blessed ship left in the harbor! Your message certainly did the trick, Pra. [*He sits down beside Prola, on her left*].

PRA [*sitting down between the two British ladies*] They may come back.

HYERING [*sitting beside Prola, on her right*] Not a bit of it. By the time the fleet realizes that it has been humbugged the Empire will be tired of Iddy.

VASHTI. The world is tired of Iddy.

MAYA. *I* am tired of Iddy.

VASHTI. Iddy is a pestilence.

MAYA. Iddy is a bore.

VASHTI. Let us throw ourselves into the sea to escape from Iddy.

MAYA. Let us throw Iddy into the sea that he may escape from himself.

VASHTI. You are wise, Prola. Tell us how to get rid of Iddy.

MAYA. We cannot endure Iddy for ever, Prola.

PROLA. You two chose him, not I.

MAYA. We were young: we did not know.

VASHTI. Help us, Pra. You have lost faith in us; but your wits are still keen.

MAYA. Pra: we beseech thee. Abolish the incubus.

VASHTI. Give him peace that we may have rest.

MAYA. Give him rest that we may have peace.

VASHTI. Let him be as he was before we knew him.

MAYA. When we were happy.

VASHTI. When he was innocent.

PRA. You raised this strange spirit. I cannot exorcise him.

VASHTI. Rather than endure him I will empty the heavens of their rain and dew.

MAYA. Silence him, O ye stars.

Iddy comes from the house in a condition of lazy self-complacence. He is received in dead silence. Nobody looks at him. He pours himself out a cup of tea. The silence becomes grim. He sits down on the grass at Prola's feet, and sips his tea. The silence continues.

IDDY [*at last*] I am a futile creature.

They all turn as if stung and look at him. Then they resume their attitudes of deadly endurance.

IDDY. It is a terrible thing to be loved. I dont suppose any man has ever been loved as I have been loved, or loved as I have loved. But there's not so much in it as people say. I am writing a sermon about it. It is a sermon on Eternity.

They look at him as before.

IDDY. The line I am going to take is this. We have never been able to imagine eternity properly. St John of Patmos started the notion of playing harps and singing praises for ever and ever. But the organist tells me that composers have to use the harp very sparingly because, though it makes a very pretty effect at first, you get tired of it so soon. You couldnt go on playing the harp for ever; and if you sang "Worthy is the Lamb" for ever you would drive the Lamb mad. The notion is that you cant have too much of a good thing; but you can: you can bear hardship much longer than you could bear heaven. Love is like music. Music is very nice: the organist says that when the wickedness of mankind tempts him to despair he comforts himself by remembering that the human race produced Mozart; but a woman who plays the piano all day is a curse. A woman who makes love to you all day is much worse; and yet nothing is lovelier than love, up to a point. We all love one another here in a wonderful way: I love Vashti, I love Maya, I love Prola; and they all love me so wonderfully that their three loves are only one love. But it is my belief that some day we'll have to try something else. If we dont we'll come to hate one another.

VASHTI. If it is any consolation to you, Iddy, I can assure you that I already hate you so intensely that if it were in my nature to kill anything I should kill you.

IDDY. There now! I ought to be wounded and horrified; but I'm not: I feel as if youd given me a strawberry ice. Thank you, dear Vashti, thank you. You give me hope that even Maya will get tired of me someday.

MAYA. I have been on the point of beating you to a jelly for ever so long past; but just as my fists were clenched to do it you always managed to come out with some stroke of idiocy that was either so funny or so piteous that I have kissed you instead.

IDDY. You make me happier than I have been for months. But, you know, that does not settle my difficulties. I dont know whether other people are like me or not—

LADY FARWATERS. No, Iddy: you are unique.

IDDY. Anyhow, I have made a discovery as regards myself.

VASHTI. Enough is known already.

MAYA. Seek no further: there is nothing there.

VASHTI. There never has been anything.

IDDY. Shut up, you two. This is something really interesting. I am writing a second sermon.

ALL THE REST [*gasp*]!!!!!!!

PRA. Was eternity not long enough for one sermon?

IDDY. This one is on love.

VASHTI [*springing up*] I will cast myself down from a precipice.

MAYA [*springing up*] I will gas myself.

IDDY. Oh, not until you have heard my sermon, please.

PROLA. Listen to him, children. Respect the wisdom of the fool.

VASHTI. [*resuming her goddess-in-a-shrine attitude*] The oracles of the wise are unheeded. Silence for the King of Idiots.

MAYA [*also enshrining herself*] Speak, Solomon.

IDDY. Well, the discovery I have made is that we were commanded to love our enemies because loving is good for us and dreadfully bad for them. I love you all here intensely; and I enjoy loving you. I love Vashti; I love Maya; and I adore Prola with a passion that grows and deepens from year to year.

PROLA. Dolt! I am too old.

IDDY. You were never young and you will never be old. You are the way and the light for me. But you have never loved me and never will love me. You have never loved anything human: why should you? Nothing human is good enough to be loved. But every decent human creature has some capacity for loving. Look at me! What a little worm I am! My sermons are wretched stuff, except these last two, which I think really have something in them. I cannot bear being loved, because I know that I am a worm, and that nobody could love me unless they were completely deluded as to my merits. But I can love, and delight in loving. I love Vashti for hating me, because she is quite right to hate me: her hatred is a proof of her beautiful clear judgment. I love Maya for being out of all patience with me, because I know that I am enough to drive anybody mad, and she is wise enough to know how worthless I am. I love Prola because she is far above loving or hating me; and there is something about her dark beauty that—

PROLA [*kicking him*] Silence, simpleton. Let the unspeakable remain unspoken.

IDDY. I dont mind your kicking me, Prola: you understand; and that is enough for me. And now you see what a jolly fine sermon it will be, and why I shall be so happy here with you from this day on. For I have the joy of loving you all without the burden of being loved in return, or the falsehood of being idolized.

MAYA. Solomon has spoken.

VASHTI. Stupendous.

LADY FARWATERS. Do not mock, darlings. There is something in what he says.

MAYA [*desperately*] But how are we to get rid of him? He is settling down with us for life.

VASHTI. We have brought him on ourselves.

MAYA. We cannot make him hate us.

VASHTI. He will go with us to heaven.

MAYA. In the depths of hell he will find us.

Kanchin and Janga enter processionally, reading newspapers.

KANCHIN. News!

JANGA. News!

They sit enshrined, foursquare with their sisters.

KANCHIN. By wireless.

JANGA. Tomorrow's three o'clock edition.

KANCHIN. The land that brought forth Iddy begins the Apocalypse.

HYERING. What do you mean? Has anything happened in England?

KANCHIN. England has broken loose.

SIR CHARLES. What do you mean? broken loose. Read the news, man. Out with it.

KANCHIN [*reading the headlines*] Dissolution of the British Empire.

JANGA [*reading*] Withdrawal of England from the Empire.

KANCHIN. England strikes for independence.

JANGA. Downing Street declares for a right little tight little island.

KANCHIN. The British Prime Minister cuts the cable and gives the new slogan.

JANGA. Back to Elizabeth's England; and to hell with the empire!

KANCHIN. Ireland to the rescue!

JANGA. Free State President declares Ireland cannot permit England to break the unity of the Empire. Ireland will lead the attack on treason and disruption.

KANCHIN. The Prime Minister's reply to the President suppressed as unprintable.

JANGA. Canada claims position of premier Dominion left vacant by the secession of England.

KANCHIN. Australia counterclaims as metropolitan dominion.

JANGA. New Zealand proclaims a butter blockade until its claim to precedence is recognized by Australia.

KANCHIN. South Africa renames Capetown Empire City, and gives notice to all Britishers to clear out of Africa within ten days.

JANGA. His Holiness the Pope calls on all Christendom to celebrate the passing away of the last vain dream of earthly empire, and the unity of all living souls in the Catholic Kingdom of God and his Church.

LADY FARWATERS. That sounds like the voice of a grown-up man through the whooping of a pack of schoolboys.

JANGA [*prosaically*] So far, there have been no disturbances and little popular interest.

KANCHIN. The various international Boards are carrying on as usual.

JANGA. Today's football—

PROLA. No, Janga: certainly not.

SIR CHARLES. But what becomes of our jobs as Governor and political secretary, Hyering? Will this affect our salaries?

HYERING. They will stop: that is all. We had better proclaim the Unexpected Isles an independent republic and secure the new jobs for ourselves.

VASHTI. The world is tired of republics and their jobberies. Proclaim a kingdom.

MAYA. Or a queendom.

IDDY. Oh yes: let us make Prola queen. And I shall be her chaplain.

PRA. By all means, as far as I am concerned. Prola has always been the real ruler here.

VASHTI. Prola is she who decides.

MAYA. Prola is she who unites.

VASHTI. Prola is she who knows.

MAYA. No one can withstand Prola.

PROLA. Be quiet, you two. You shall not make an idol of me.

KANCHIN. We shall make you Empress of the Isles.

JANGA. Prola the First.

VASHTI. Homage, Prola.

MAYA. Love, Prola.

KANCHIN. Obedience, Prola.

JANGA. Absolute rule, Prola.

PROLA. All your burdens on me. Lazy idle children.

KANCHIN. Hurrah! All burdens on Prola.

JANGA. The burden of thought.

VASHTI. The burden of knowledge.

MAYA. The burden of righteousness.

VASHTI. The burden of justice.

MAYA. The burden of mercy.

PROLA. Cease, cease: these are not burdens to me: they are the air I breathe. I shall rule you as I have always done because you are too lazy to rule yourselves.

HYERING. You can rule us, Prola. But will the public ever understand you?

PRA. They will obey her. They would not do that if they understood.

IDDY. I have just been thinking—

MAYA. Solomon has been thinking.

VASHTI. Thoughts without brains.

IDDY. Will the Antiphonal Quartet, if it wants to give another concert, kindly remove itself out of hearing.

KANCHIN. Silence for the Prophet.

JANGA. Mum!

VASHTI. Dumb.

MAYA. Tiddy iddy um. Carry on, darling.

IDDY. Prola can rule this house because she knows what is happening in it. But how is she to be an Empress if she doesnt know what is happening everywhere?

MRS HYERING. She can read the newspapers, cant she, silly?

IDDY. Yes; but fifteen years later, when the statesmen write their memoirs and autobiographies and publish them, we shall find that it never happened at all and what really happened was quite different. We dont know the truth about any of our statesmen until they are dead and cant take libel actions. Nobody knows the sort of people we really are. The papers have been full of us for weeks past; and not a single word they say about us is true. They think I am a sort of Mahdi or Mad Mullah, and that Prola and Vashti and Maya are a troop of immoral dancing girls, and that Sir Charles is a voluptuous sultan and Hyering a co-respondent. They dont live in a world of truth: they live in a world of their own ideas, which have nothing to do with our ideas. Consequently—Therefore—er—er— What was I going to say, Pra? My brain is not strong enough to keep the thread of my remarks. I ought to have written it down.

PRA. What you have arrived at is that we cannot live in a world of political facts, because we shall not know the political facts for years to come. We must therefore live in a world of original ideas, created by ourselves out of our own nature.

IDDY. Yes. We mustnt pretend to be omniscient. Even

God would not be omniscient if He read the newspapers. We must have an ideal of a beautiful and good world. We must believe that to establish that beautiful and good world on earth is the best thing we can do, and the only sort of religion and politics that is worth bothering about.

PROLA. What about the people who have no original ideas, Iddy?

PRA. The great majority of mankind?

IDDY. Theyll be only too glad to do what you tell them, Prola, if you can make them feel that it's right.

PROLA. And if they are incapable of feeling it?

JANGA. Kill.

KANCHIN. Kill.

VASHTI. Kill.

MAYA. Kill.

PROLA. They can do that as easily as I. Any fool can. And there are more of them.

JANGA. Set them to kill one another; and rule.

KANCHIN. Divide and govern.

VASHTI. Feed them on splendid words.

MAYA. Dazzle them with our beauty.

MRS HYERING. Well I never!

IDDY [*rising*] Excuse me. I'm going into the house to get the field glass. [*He goes up the steps*].

MRS HYERING. Whatever do you want the field glass for?

IDDY [*pointing to the sky*] There's a strange bird flying about there. I think it's an albatross. [*He goes into the house*].

VASHTI, MAYA, KANCHIN, JANGA [*hissing after him*] Liar. Baby. Dastard. Hypocrite.

SIR CHARLES [*laughing*] An albatross! Now would anybody in the world, over the age of six, except Iddy, invent such a ridiculous excuse for going to his room to indulge in his poor little secret vice of cigaret smoking?

MAYA. Faugh! The unkissable.

VASHTI. The air poisoner.

KANCHIN. The albatrocity.

MAYA. VASHTI. JANGA [*shocked by the pun*] Oh!!

LADY FARWATERS. Cant you four darlings do something useful instead of sitting there deafening us with your slogans?

KANCHIN [*springing erect*] Yes, action. Action!

JANGA [*rising similarly*] No more of this endless talk! talk! talk!

VASHTI. Yes, action! daring! Let us rob.

MAYA. Let us shoot.

KANCHIN. Let us die for something.

JANGA. For our flag and for our Empress.

VASHTI. For our country, right or wrong.

MAYA. Let there be sex appeal. Let the women make the men brave.

KANCHIN. We must defend our homes.

JANGA. Our women.

VASHTI. Our native soil.

MAYA. It is sweet to die for one's country.

VASHTI. It is glorious to outface death.

ALL FOUR. Yes. Death! death! Glory! glory!

PROLA. Hold your tongues, you young whelps. Is this what we have brought you up for?

PRA. Stop screaming about nothing, will you. Use your minds.

MAYA. We have no minds.

VASHTI. We have imaginations.

KANCHIN. We have made this house a temple.

JANGA. We have made Prola its goddess.

MAYA. We have made it a palace.

VASHTI. A palace for Queen Prola.

KANCHIN. She shall reign.

JANGA. For ever and ever.

VASHTI AND MAYA [*in unison*] Hail, Prola, our goddess!

KANCHIN AND JANGA [*in unison*] Hail, Prola, our empress!

ALL FOUR [*rushing down to the lawn and throwing themselves on their knees before her*] Hail!

PROLA. Will you provoke me to box your ears, you abominable idolaters. Get up this instant. Go and scrub the floors. Do anything that is dirty and grubby and smelly enough to shew that you live in a real world and not in a fool's paradise. If I catch you grovelling to me, a creature of the same clay as yourselves, but fortunately for you with a little more common sense, I will beat the slavishness out of your bones.

MAYA. Oh, what ecstasy to be beaten by Prola!

VASHTI. To feel her rule in the last extremity of pain!

KANCHIN. To suffer for her!

JANGA. To die for her!

PROLA. Get out, all four. My empire is not of such as you. Begone.

MAYA. How lovely is obedience! [*She makes an obeisance and runs away through the garden*].

VASHTI. Obedience is freedom from the intolerable fatigue of thought. [*She makes her obeisance and sails away, disappearing between the garden and the house*].

KANCHIN. You speak as an empress should speak. [*He salaams and bounds off after Maya*].

JANGA. The voice of authority gives us strength and unity. Command us always thus: it is what we need and love. [*He strides away in Vashti's footsteps*].

PROLA. An excuse for leaving everything to me. Lazy, lazy, lazy! Someday Heaven will get tired of lazy people; and the Pitcairn Islanders will see their Day of Judgment at last.

A distant fusillade of shotguns answers her.

SIR CHARLES. Shooting! What can the matter be?

They all rise and listen anxiously.

A trumpet call rings out from the sky.

HYERING. Where on earth did that come from? There is not such a thing as a trumpet in the island.

The four come rushing back into the garden, wildly excited.

KANCHIN. Look, look, quick! The albatross.

PRA. [*rising*] The albatross!!

MAYA. Yes: Iddy's albatross. Look!

JANGA. Flying all over the town.

VASHTI [*Pointing*] There it goes. See.

A second fusillade of shotguns, much nearer.

MAYA. Oh, theyre all trying to shoot it. Brutes!

KANCHIN. They havnt hit it. Here it comes.

MAYA. It's flying this way.

VASHTI. It's swooping down.

Iddy comes from the house and trots down the steps with a field glass in his hand.

IDDY. Ive been looking at it through the window for the last five minutes. It isnt an albatross. Look at it through this. [*He hands the glass to Pra*].

KANCHIN. Then what is it?

IDDY. I think it's an angel.

JANGA. Oh get out, you silly idiot.

PRA [*looking through the glass*] That is no bird.

An angel flies down into the middle of the garden. General stupefaction. He shakes himself. Quantities of bullets and small shot fall from his wings and clothes.

THE ANGEL. Really, your people ought to know better than to shoot at an angel.

MAYA. Are you an angel?

THE ANGEL. Well, what do you suppose I am?

VASHTI. Of course he is an angel. Look at his wings.

THE ANGEL. Attention, please! Have you not heard the trumpet? This is the Judgment Day.

ALL THE REST. The what???!!!

THE ANGEL. The Judgment Day. The Day of Judgment.

SIR CHARLES. Well I'll be damned!

THE ANGEL. Very possibly.

HYERING. Do you mean that the Pitcairn Islanders were right after all?!

THE ANGEL. Yes. You are all now under judgment, in common with the rest of the English speaking peoples. Dont gape at me as if you had never seen an angel before.

PROLA. But we never have.

THE ANGEL [*relaxing*] True. Ha ha ha! Well, you thoroughly understand, dont you, that your records are now being looked into with a view to deciding whether you are worth your salt or not.

PRA. And suppose it is decided that we are not worth our salt?

THE ANGEL [*reassuring them in a pleasantly offhanded manner*] Then you will simply disappear: that is all. You will no longer exist. Dont let me keep you all standing. Sit down if you like. Never mind me: sitting and standing are all alike to an angel. However—[*he sits down on the parapet of the well*].

They sit as before, the four superchildren enshrining themselves as usual.

The telephone rings. Hyering rises and takes it.

HYERING [*to the angel*] Excuse me. [*To the telephone*] Yes? Hyering speaking. . . . Somebody what? . . . . Oh! Somebody fooling on the wireless. Well, theyre not fooling: an angel has just landed here to tell us the same thing. . . . An angel. A for arrowroot, N for nitrogen, G for—thats it: an angel. . . . Well, after all, the Judgment Day had to come some day, hadnt it? Why not this day as well an another? . . . . I'll ask the angel about it and ring you later. Goodbye. [*He rings off*]. Look here, angel. The wireless has been on all over Europe. London reports the Judgment Day in full swing; but Paris knows nothing about it; Hilversum knows nothing about it; Berlin, Rome, Madrid, and Geneva know nothing about it; and Moscow says the British bourgeoisie has been driven mad by its superstitions. How do you account for that? If it is the Judgment Day in England it must be the Judgment Day everywhere.

THE ANGEL. Why?

HYERING [*sitting down*] Well, it stands to reason.

THE ANGEL. Does it? Would it be reasonable to try cases in hundreds of different lands and languages and creeds and colors on the same day in the same place? Of course not. The whole business will last longer than what you call a year. We gave the English speaking folk the first turn in compliment to one of your big guns—a dean—name of Inge, I think. I announced it to him last night in a dream, and asked him whether the English would appreciate the compliment. He said he thought they would prefer to put it off as long as possible, but that they needed it badly and he was ready. The other languages will follow. The United States of America will be tried tomorrow, Australasia next day, Scotland next, then Ireland—

LADY FARWATERS. But excuse me: they do not speak different languages.

THE ANGEL. They sound different to us.

SIR CHARLES. I wonder how they are taking it in England.

THE ANGEL. I am afraid most of them are incapable of understanding the ways of heaven. They go motoring or golfing on Sundays instead of going to church; and they never open a Bible. When you mention Adam and Eve, or Cain and Abel, to say nothing of the Day of Judgment, they dont know what you are talking about. The others—the pious ones—think we have come to dig up all the skeletons and put them through one of their shocking criminal trials. They actually expect us to make angels of them for ever and ever.

MRS HYERING. See here, angel. This isnt a proper sort of Judgment Day. It's a fine day. It's like Bank Holiday.

THE ANGEL. And pray why should the Day of Judgment not be a fine day?

MRS HYERING. Well, it's hardly what we were led to expect, you know.

JANGA. "The heavens shall pass away with a great noise."

KANCHIN. "The elements shall melt with fervent heat."

JANGA. "The earth also and the works that are therein shall be burnt up."

VASHTI. The stars are fixed in their courses. They have not fallen to the earth.

MAYA. The heavens are silent. Where are the seven thunders?

VASHTI. The seven vials full of the wrath of God?

JANGA. The four horses?

KANCHIN. The two witnesses?

THE ANGEL. My good people, if you want these things you must provide them for yourselves. If you want a great noise, you have your cannons. If you want a fervent heat to burn up the earth you have your high explosives. If you want vials of wrath to rain down on you, they are ready in your arsenals, full of poison gases. Some years ago you had them all in full play, burning up the earth and spreading death, famine, and pestilence. But the spring came and created life faster than you could destroy it. The birds sang over your trenches; and their promise of summer was fulfilled. The sun that shone undisturbed on your pitiful Day of Wrath shines today over Heaven's Day of Judgment. It will continue to light us and warm us; and there will be no noise nor wrath nor fire nor thunder nor destruction nor plagues nor terrors of any sort. I am afraid you will find it very dull.

LADY FARWATERS [*politely*] Not at all. Pray dont think that.

MRS HYERING. Well, a little good manners never does any harm; but I tell you straight, Mister Angel, I cant feel as if there was anything particular happening, in spite of you and your wings. Ive only just had my tea; and I cant feel a bit serious without any preparation or even an organ playing.

THE ANGEL. You will feel serious enough presently when things begin to happen.

MRS HYERING. Yes; but what things?

THE ANGEL. What was foretold to you. "His angels shall gather together his elect. Then shall two be in the field: the one shall be taken and the other left. Two women shall be grinding at the mill. The one shall be taken and the other left."

MRS HYERING. But which? Thats what I want to know.

PROLA. There is nothing new in this taking of the one and leaving the other: natural death has always been doing it.

THE ANGEL. Natural death does it senselessly, like a blind child throwing stones. We angels are executing a judgment. The lives which have no use, no meaning, no purpose, will fade out. You will have to justify your existence or perish. Only the elect shall survive.

MRS HYERING. But where does the end of the world come in?

THE ANGEL. The Day of Judgment is not the end of the world, but the end of its childhood and the beginning of its responsible maturity. So now you know; and my business with you is ended. [*He rises*]. Is there any way of getting out on the roof of this house?

SIR CHARLES [*rising*] Certainly: it is a flat roof where we often sit. [*He leads the way to the house*].

KANCHIN. In theory.

JANGA. In fact we never sit there.

THE ANGEL. That does not matter. All I want is a parapet to take off from. Like the albatross, I cannot rise from the ground without great difficulty. An angel is far from being the perfect organism you imagine. There is always something better.

VASHTI. Excelsior.

ALL FOUR [*rising and singing vociferously*] Eck-cel-see-orr! Eck-cel-see-or!

THE ANGEL [*putting his fingers in his ears*] Please, no. In heaven we are tired of singing. It is not done now. [*He follows Sir Charles out*].

KANCHIN. Lets see him take off.

The four rush up the garden and look up at the roof. The others rise and watch.

JANGA [*calling up*] Start into the wind, old man. Spring off hard, from the ball of the foot. Dont fall on us.

KANCHIN. Oopsh! Off he goes.

The beating of the angel's wings is heard.

VASHTI. He makes a noise like a vacuum cleaner.

MAYA [*wafting kisses*] Goodbye, silly old Excelsior.

The noise stops.

JANGA. His wings have stopped beating. He is soaring up the wind.

KANCHIN. He is getting smaller and smaller. His speed must be terrific.

MAYA. He is too small for an albatross.

VASHTI. He is smaller than a canary.

KANCHIN. He is out of sight.

MAYA. There! One last glint of the sun on his wings. He is gone.

The four troop back and resume their seats. The others sit as before, except that Iddy deserts Prola and sits on the well parapet. Sir Charles returns from the house with a batch of wireless messages in his hand.

SIR CHARLES [*sitting in his former place*] Well, my dears: the Judgment Day is over, it seems.

IDDY. I cant believe it was really the Judgment Day.

PRA. Why?

IDDY. Well, I thought some special notice would have

been taken of the clergy. Reserved seats or something like that. But he treated me as if I were only the organ blower.

SIR CHARLES. There are such a lot of priests in the world, Iddy. It would be impossible to reserve seats for them all.

IDDY. Oh, I meant only the clergy of the Church of England, of course.

MRS HYERING. What I cant get over is their sending along just one angel to judge us, as if we didnt matter.

LADY FARWATERS. He actually went away and forgot to judge us.

PRA. I am not so sure of that.

IDDY. Well, are we sheep or goats? tell me that.

MAYA. You are a sheep, Iddy, my sweet: there can be no doubt about that.

IDDY [*bursting into tears*] I love you, Maya; and you always say unkind things to me. [*He rushes away through the garden, sobbing*].

MAYA. Oh, poor Iddy! I'll go and soothe him with a thousand kisses. [*She runs after him*].

HYERING [*to Sir Charles*] What have you got there? Any news from London?

SIR CHARLES. Yes: Exchange Telegraph and Reuters. Copyright reserved.

HYERING. Lets have it.

SIR CHARLES [*reading*] "Judgment Day. Widespread incredulity as to anything having really happened. Reported appearance of angels in several quarters generally disbelieved. Several witnesses are qualifying or withdrawing their statements in deference to the prevailing scepticism."

HYERING. We shall have to be careful too, Charles. Who will believe us if we tell this yarn of an angel flying down into the garden?

SIR CHARLES. I suppose so. .I never thought of it in that way. Still, listen to this. [*Reading*] "Policeman who attempted to arrest angel in Leicester Square removed to mental hospital. Church Assembly at Lambeth Palace decides by a large majority that there has been a Visitation. Dissenting minority, led by the Bishop of Edgbaston, denounces the reports as nonsense that would not impose even on the Society for Psychical Research. His Holiness the Pope warns Christendom that supernatural communications reaching the earth otherwise than through the Church are contrary to the Catholic faith, and, if authentic, must be regarded as demoniacal. Cabinet hastily summoned to discuss the situation. Prime Minister, speaking in emergency meeting at the Mansion House, declares that reports of utterances by angels are hopelessly contradictory, and that alleged verbatim reports by shorthand writers contain vulgar expressions. The Government could not in any case allow the British Empire to be placed in the position of being judged by a commission of a few angels instead of by direct divine authority. Such a slight to the flag would never be tolerated by Englishmen; and the Cabinet was unanimous in refusing to believe that such an outrage had occurred. The Prime Minister's speech was received with thunderous applause, the audience rising spontaneously to sing the National Anthem."

PRA. They would.

SIR CHARLES [*looking at another paper*] Hallo! Whats this? [*Reading*] "Later. During the singing of the second verse of the National Anthem at the Mansion House the proceedings were interrupted by the appearance of an angel with a flaming sword who demanded truculently what they meant by ordering God about to do their dirty political work. He was accompanied by unruly cherubim who floated about tweaking the Lord Mayor's nose, pouring ink into the Prime Minister's hat, and singing derisively Con-Found Their Poll-It-Ticks. Part of the audience fell to their knees, repeating the Confession. Others rushed frantically to the doors. Two Salvation lasses stemmed the rush, at great personal danger to themselves, by standing in the doorway and singing Let Angels Prostrate Fall. Order was restored by the Prime Minister, who offered the angel an unreserved apology and an undertaking that the offending verse should not be sung again. A new one is to be provided by the Poet Laureate. The Premier's last words were lost through the misconduct of a cherub who butted him violently in the solar plexus. A wave of the angel's sword and a terrible thunderclap then threw the entire audience prone to the floor. When they rose to their feet the angel and the cherubs had disappeared."

HYERING. Oh, an invention. We cant swallow those cherubs, really.

SIR CHARLES [*taking up a third paper*] This sounds a little more plausible. "A representative of the Fascist Press has called at the War Office to ask whether any steps are being taken to defend the right of public meeting, and to deal with the angelic peril. The Commander-in-Chief, whilst denying that there is any such thing as a right of public meeting by undisciplined and irresponsible persons, declared that the Mansion House incident was quite incomprehensible to him, as he could not conceive how the only really practical part of the National Anthem could give any offence. Any suggestion that it was not the plain duty of the Ruler of the Universe to confound England's enemies could only lead to widespread atheism. The First Lord of the Admiralty, interviewed last night, said that he could not make head or tail of the reports, but that he could assure the public that whatever had really happened, the British Navy would not take it lying down. Later. A Hyde Park orator was thrown into the Serpentine for saying that the British Empire was not the only pebble on the beach. He has been fined thirty shillings for being in unlawful possession of a life buoy, the property of the Royal Humane Society. There can be no doubt that the disparaging remarks and assumed superiority of the angels has started a wave of patriotism throughout the country which is bound to lead to action of some sort."

PRA. Which means, if it means anything, that England's next war will be a war with heaven.

PROLA. Nothing new in that. England has been at war with heaven for many a long year.

VASHTI [*inspired*] The most splendid of all her wars!

KANCHIN. The last conquest left to her to achieve!

VASHTI. To overcome the angels!

JANGA. To plant the flag of England on the ramparts of Heaven itself! that is the final glory.

PROLA. Oh go away, children: go away. Now that Maya has gone to kiss somebody, there is nothing left for you to glorify but suicide.

VASHTI [*rising*] I rebel.

JANGA [*rising*] We rebel against Prola, the goddess empress.

KANCHIN [*rising*] Prola has turned back from the forlorn hope.

VASHTI. Prola is a coward. She fears defeat and death.

KANCHIN. Without death there can be no heroism.

JANGA. Without faith unto death there can be no faith.

VASHTI. Prola has failed us in the great Day of Judgment.

KANCHIN. Our souls have been called to their final account.

ALL THREE [*marching away through the garden*] Guilty, Prola: guilty. Adieu, Prola!

PROLA. Oh, adieu until you all want your tea.

PRA. We have taught them everything except common sense.

LADY FARWATERS. We have taught them everything except how to work for their daily bread instead of praying for it.

PROLA. It is dangerous to educate fools.

PRA. It is still more dangerous to leave them uneducated.

MRS HYERING. There just shouldnt be any fools. They wernt born fools: we made fools of them.

PRA. We must stop making fools.

Iddy returns alone. Something strange has happened to him. He stares at them and tries to speak; but no sound comes from his lips.

LADY FARWATERS. What on earth is the matter with you, Iddy? Have you been drinking?

IDDY [*in a ghastly voice*] Maya.

PROLA. What has happened to Maya?

IDDY. Heaven and earth shall pass away; but I shall not pass away. That is what she said. And then there was nothing in my arms. Nothing. Nothing in my arms. Heaven and earth would pass away; but the love of Maya would never pass away. And there was nothing. [*He collapses on the well parapet, overcome, not in tears but in a profound awe*].

PRA. Do you mean that she died in your arms?

IDDY. Died? No. I tell you there was nothing. Dont you understand? Where she had just been there was nothing. There never had been anything.

PROLA. And the others? Quick, Pra: go and find the others.

PRA. What others?

PROLA. The other three: our children. I forget their names.

IDDY. They said "Our names shall live forever." What were their names?

HYERING. They have gone clean out of my head.

SIR CHARLES. Most extraordinary. I cant for the life of me remember. How many of them did you say there were, Prola?

PROLA. Four. Or was it four hundred?

IDDY. There were four. Their names were Love, Pride, Heroism and Empire. Love's pet name was Maya. I loved Maya. I loved them all; but it was through love of Maya that I loved them. I held Maya in my arms. She promised to endure for ever; and suddenly there was nothing in my arms. I have searched for the others; but she and they were one: I found nothing. It is the Judgment.

PROLA. Has she left a great void in your heart, Iddy, that girl who turned to nothing in your arms?

IDDY. No. This is a beautiful climate; and you are beautiful people; but you are not real to me; and the sun here is not what it is in the valley of the Severn. I am glad I am an English clergyman. A village and a cottage: a garden and a church: these things will not turn to nothing. I shall be content with my little black coat and my little white collar and my little treasure of words spoken by my Lord Jesus. Blessed be the name of the Lord: I shall not forget it as I shall forget Maya's. [*He goes out seaward like a man in a trance*].

LADY FARWATERS [*troubled, half rising*] But, Iddy,—

PROLA. Let him go. The pigeon knows its way home.

Lady Farwaters sinks back into her seat. There is a moment of rather solemn silence. Then the telephone rings.

PRA [*taking up the receiver*] Yes? . . . What? . . . Yes: amazing news: we know all about that. What is the latest? . . . Yes: "plot to destroy our most valuable citizens": I got that; but what was the first word? What plot? . . . Oh, Russian plot. Rubbish! havnt you some sensible reports? . . . Special news broadcast just coming in? . . . Good: put me on to it. [*To the others*] Im through to London Regional. Listen: I'll repeat it as it comes. [*He echoes the news*] Extraordinary disappearances. Indescribable panic. Stock Exchange closes: only two members left. House of Commons decimated: only fourteen members to be found: none of Cabinet rank. House of Lords still musters fifty members; but not one of them has ever attended a meeting of the Chamber. Mayfair a desert: six hotels left without a single guest. Fresh disappearances. Crowded intercession service at Westminster Abbey brought to a close by disappearance of the congregation at such a rate that the rest fled leaving the dean preaching to the choir. At the Royal Institution Sir Ruthless

Bonehead, Egregious Professor of Mechanistic Biology to the Rockefeller Foundation, drew a crowded audience to hear his address on "Whither have they gone?" He disappeared as he opened his mouth to speak. Noted Cambridge professor suggests that what is happening is a weeding-out of nonentities. He has been deprived of his Chair; and The Times, in a leading article, points out that the extreme gravity of the situation lies in the fact that not only is it our most important people who are vanishing, but that it is the most unquestionably useful and popular professions that are most heavily attacked, the medical profession having disappeared almost en bloc, whilst the lawyers and clergy are comparatively immune. A situation of terrible suspense has been created everywhere. Happy husbands and fathers disappear from the family dinner with the soup. Several popular leaders of fashion and famous beauties, after ringing their bells for their maids, have been found non-existent when the bells were answered. More than a million persons have disappeared in the act of reading novels. The Morning Post contains an eloquent protest by Lady Gushing, president of the Titled Ladies' League of Social Service, on the inequality of sacrifice as between the west end and the east, where casualties have been comparatively few. Lady Gushing has since disappeared. There is general agreement that our losses are irreparable, though their bad effects are as yet unfelt. But before long—

HYERING. Whats the use of going on, Pra? The angels are weeding the garden. The useless people, the mischievous people, the selfish somebodies and the noisy nobodies, are dissolving into space, which is the simplest form of matter. We here are awaiting our own doom.

MRS HYERING. What was it the angel said?

PROLA. The lives which have no use, no meaning, no purpose, will fade out. We shall have to justify our existences or perish. We shall live under a constant sense of that responsibility. If the angels fail us we shall set up tribunals of our own from which worthless people will not come out alive. When men no longer fear the judgment of God, they must learn to judge themselves.

SIR CHARLES. I seem to remember somebody saying "Judge not, that ye be not judged."

PROLA. That means "Punish not, that ye be not punished." This is not punishment, but judgment.

HYERING. What is judgment?

PRA. Judgment is valuation. Civilizations live by their valuations. If the valuations are false, the civilization perishes as all the ancient ones we know of did. We are not being punished today: we are being valued. That is the Newest Dispensation.

LADY FARWATERS. I feel an absolute conviction that I shall not disappear and that Charles will not disappear. We have done some queer things here in the east perhaps; but at bottom we are comfortable commonsense probable English people; and we shall not do anything so improbable as disappear.

SIR CHARLES [*to his wife*] Do not tempt the angels, my dear. Remember: you used to distribute tracts before you met Pra.

LADY FARWATERS. Ssh-sh-sh! Dont remind the angels of those tracts.

HYERING [*rising*] Look here. I have an uneasy feeling that we'd better get back to our work. I feel pretty sure that we shant disappear as long as we're doing something useful; but if we only sit here talking, either we shall disappear or the people who are listening to us will. What we have learnt here today is that the day of judgment is not the end of the world but the beginning of real human responsibility. Charles and I have still our duties: the Unexpected Islands have to be governed today just as they had to be yesterday. Sally: if you have given your orders for the housework today, go and cook something or sew something or tidy up the books. Come on, Charles. Lets get to work. [*He goes into the house*].

SIR CHARLES [*to his wife, rising*] You might take a turn in the garden, dear: gardening is the only unquestionably useful job. [*He follows Hyering into the house*].

LADY FARWATERS [*rising*] Prola: shall I bring you some knitting to occupy you?

PROLA. No, thank you. I have some thinking to do.

LADY FARWATERS. Well, dear: I hope that will count as work. I shall feel safer with my gardening basket. [*She goes into the house*].

MRS HYERING. J'you think itll be all right if I go and do some crossword puzzles? It cultivates the mind so, dont you think?

PROLA. Does it? Well, do the puzzles and see what will happen. Let life come to you. Goodbye.

MRS HYERING [*alarmed*] Why do you say goodbye? Do you think I am going to disappear?

PROLA. Possibly. Or possibly *I* may.

MRS HYERING. Oh then for heaven's sake dont do it in my presence. Wait til Ive gone.

She scuttles up the steps into the house, leaving Prola and Pra alone together.

PRA. Tell me the truth, Prola. Are you waiting for me to disappear? Do you feel that you can do better without me? Have you always felt that you could do better without me?

PROLA. That is a murderer's thought. Have you ever let yourself think it? How often have you said to yourself "I could do better alone, or with another woman"?

PRA. Fairly often, my dear, when we were younger. But I did not murder you. Thats the answer. And you?

PROLA. All that stuff belongs to the past: to the childhood of our marriage. We have now grown together until we are each of us a part of the other. I no longer think of you as a separate possibility.

PRA. I know. I am part of the furniture of your house. I am a matter of course. But was I always that? Was I that in the childhood of our marriage?

PROLA. You are still young enough and manlike enough to ask mischievous questions.

PRA. No matter: we shall both disappear presently; and I have still some curiosity left. Did you ever really care for me? I know I began as a passion and have ended as a habit, like all husbands; but outside that routine there is a life of the intellect that is quite independent of it. What have I been to you in that life? A help or a hindrance?

PROLA. Pra: I always knew from the very beginning that you were an extraordinarily clever fool.

PRA. Good. That is exactly what I am.

PROLA. But I knew also that nobody but a fool would be frivolous enough to join me in doing all the mad things I wanted to do. And no ordinary fool would have been subtle enough to understand me, nor clever enough to keep off the rocks of social ruin. Ive grown fond enough of you for all practical purposes;—

PRA. Thank you.

PROLA. —but Ive never allowed you or any other man to cut me off my own stem and make me a parasite on his. That sort of love and sacrifice is not the consummation of a capable woman's existence: it is the temptation she must resist at all costs.

PRA. That temptation lies in the man's path too. The worst sacrifices I have seen have been those of men's highest careers to women's vulgarities and follies.

PROLA. Well, we two have no reproaches and no regrets on that score.

PRA. No. We are awaiting judgment here quite simply as a union of a madwoman with a fool.

PROLA. Who thought they had created four wonderful children. And who are now brought to judgment and convicted of having created nothing. We have only repeated the story of Helen and Faust and their beautiful child Euphorion. Euphorion also vanished, in his highest flight.

PRA. Yes; but Helen was a dream. You are not a

dream. The children did not vanish like Euphorion in their infancy. They grew up to bore me more intensely than I have ever been bored by any other set of human creatures. Come, confess: did they not bore you?

PROLA. Have I denied it? Of course they bored me. They must have bored one another terribly in spite of all their dressing up and pretending that their fairyland was real. How they must have envied the gardener's boy his high spirits!

PRA. The coming race will not be like them. Meanwhile we are face to face with the fact that we two have made a precious mess of our job of producing the coming race by a mixture of east and west. We are failures. We shall disappear.

PROLA. I do not feel like that. I feel like the leader of a cavalry charge whose horse has been shot through the head and dropped dead under him. Well, a dead hobby horse is not the end of the world. Remember: we are in the Unexpected Isles; and in the Unexpected Isles all plans fail. So much the better: plans are only jigsaw puzzles: one gets tired of them long before one can piece them together. There are still a million lives beyond all the Utopias and the Millenniums and the rest of the jigsaw puzzles: I am a woman and I know it. Let men despair and become cynics and pessimists because in the Unexpected Isles all their little plans fail: women will never let go their hold on life. We are not here to fulfil prophecies and fit ourselves into puzzles, but to wrestle with life as it comes. And it never comes as we expect it to come.

PRA. It comes like a thief in the night.

PROLA. Or like a lover. Never will Prola go back to the Country of the Expected.

PRA. There is no Country of the Expected. The Unexpected Isles are the whole world.

PROLA. Yes, if our fools only had vision enough to see that. I tell you this is a world of miracles, not of jigsaw puzzles. For me every day must have its miracle, and no child be born like any child that ever was born before. And to witness this miracle of the children I will abide the uttermost evil and carry through it the seed of the uttermost good.

PRA. Then I, Pra, must continue to strive for more knowledge and more power, though the new knowledge always contradicts the old, and the new power is the destruction of the fools who misuse it.

PROLA. We shall plan commonwealths when our empires have brought us to the brink of destruction; but our plans will still lead us to the Unexpected Isles. We shall make wars because only under the strain of war are we capable of changing the world; but the changes our wars will make will never be the changes we intended them to make. We shall clamor for security like frightened children; but in the Unexpected Isles there is no security; and the future is to those who prefer surprise and wonder to security. I, Prola, shall live and grow because surprise and wonder are the very breath of my being, and routine is death to me. Let every day be a day of wonder for me and I shall not fear the Day of Judgment. [*She is interrupted by a roll of thunder*]. Be silent: you cannot frighten Prola with stage thunder. The fountain of life is within me.

PRA. But you have given the key of it to me, the Man.

PROLA. Yes: I need you and you need me. Life needs us both.

PRA. All hail, then, the life to come!

PROLA. All Hail. Let it come.

They pat hands, eastern fashion.

"IN GOOD KING CHARLES'S GOLDEN DAYS"

As his years stretched toward the century mark, Shaw's disciples hopefully reminded him that Sophocles at the end of his long life had produced *Oedipus at Colonus,* one of the masterpieces of classical Greek drama. But instead of an apocalyptical revelation or the solemn testament of the patriarch, Shaw continued to frustrate, if not perversely to insult, his disciples with extravaganza and historical whimsy. Thus, *"In Good King Charles's Golden Days"* (1939) was taken to be an afterthought, a curiosity loosely appended to a career that had long passed its climacteric. Most of the essential elements of a theatrical work seem to be missing: of plot, with its classically required beginning, middle and end, there is none; the conflict is almost entirely intellectual; the physical action erupts in odd moments of farce.

Yet if the career of Bernard Shaw, his development as an artist, stands for anything in the modern theatre, it is hardly proper to try to align his last plays with those of any other highly individual playwright, whether Pinero or Ibsen or Chekhov or, especially, Sophocles. Seen in relation to the whole Shavian repertory, the evolution of *"King Charles"* is as inevitable as the lengthened neck of the giraffe. Shaw had long since willed himself free of the *bienfaitisme* of Pinero, the intricately developed and modishly scientific analyses of Ibsen; he had successfully survived the years of despair that might have led to a tragic statement. The very title of the play announced that the author had not abandoned his comic mask, for any student of history or reader of historical fiction knew that the Restoration was not golden but gilded.

Once again Shaw returned to his familiar position of enlightening the audience by attacking its expectations. *Sweet Nell of Old Drury* and the older *Masks and Faces* had been romances masquerading as histories; their central character was not the King, but Nell Gwyn, the most amusing of his many mistresses. Shaw is not so unrealistic as to omit the ladies, of course; he introduces them, as he said, "to relieve the intellectual tension." But the real concern of the play is expressed by Isaac Newton; while awaiting a visit from King

Charles he hears that George Fox, the Quaker, has been trying to see him. "Those two men ought to meet," he says, and on this principle what action the play possesses is based. *"King Charles,"* then, is not a chronicle play like *Caesar* or *Saint Joan*, exploiting recorded history, but a romance in which certain historical names are made to represent the forces of modernism in art, religion, science, and politics in what the subtitle of the 1945 text calls "a true history that never happened." The original 1939 subtitle, "a history lesson," is perhaps closer to Shaw's intention. Knowing Shaw, the reader will be wise enough to understand that the play is not a lesson *from* history, but a lesson *to* history, to the audience who will decide the history of their own times.

In the mode of the tent scene and the epilogue of *Saint Joan*, Kneller is permitted to anticipate Hogarth ("The line of beauty is a curve") and Newton to anticipate Einstein, for Shaw was still on his cart in Hyde Park, pointing out the path to perfectibility. Let the governed insist that their governors be enlightened enough to choose to hobnob with scientists, artists, philosophers, theologians; and such was Shaw's confidence in the mind, the intuition, the life force, that he saw optimistic romance becoming happy reality. So strong was his conviction, indeed, that he inserted into *"King Charles"* a dramatic image from the play and the playwright that had been his model from the commencement of his dramatic career. The Isaac Newton who is able to wrestle the Duke of York to a fall is, among other things, a colleague of that Master of Philosophy who emerges in tattered triumph after an offstage scuffle to maintain the superiority of his subject over those of the other tutors engaged to turn M. Jourdain into a *Gentilhomme.*

At the Malvern Festival in 1939 the role of Charles was created by Ernest Thesiger, of Queen Catherine by Irene Vanbrugh. Newton was played by Cecil Trouncer, Louise de Keroualle by Yvonne Arnaud, and Fox by Herbert Lomas. In New York the play had an off-Broadway run at the Downtown Theater, beginning on January 24, 1957.

"IN GOOD KING CHARLES'S GOLDEN DAYS"

ACT I

THE library in the house of Isaac Newton in Cambridge in the year 1680. It is a cheerful room overlooking the garden from the first floor through a large window which has an iron balcony outside, with an iron staircase down to the garden level. The division of the window to the left as you look out through it is a glass door leading to these stairs, making the room accessible from the garden. Inside the room the walls are lined with cupboards below and bookshelves above. To the right of the window is a stand-up writing desk. The cupboards are further obstructed by six chairs ranged tidily along them, three to the right of the window and three to the left (as you look out). Between them a table belonging to the set of chairs stands out in the middle with writing materials on it and a prodigious open Bible, made for a church lectern. A comfortable chair for the reader faces away from the window. On the reader's left is a handsome armchair, apparently for the accommodation of distinguished visitors to the philosopher.

Newton's housekeeper, a middle aged woman of very respectable appearance, is standing at the desk working at her accounts.

A serving maid in morning deshabille comes in through the interior door, which is in the side wall to the left of the window (again as you look out through it).

THE MAID. Please, Mrs Basham, a Mr Rowley wants to know when the master will be at home to receive him.

MRS BASHAM. Rowley? I dont know him. This is no hour to call on Mr Newton.

THE MAID. No indeed, maam. And look at me! not dressed to open the door to gentlefolk.

MRS BASHAM. Is he a gentleman? Rowley is not much of a name.

THE MAID. Dressed like a nobleman, maam. Very tall and very dark. And a lot of dogs with him, and a lackey. Not a person you could shut the door in the face of, maam. But very condescending, I must say.

MRS BASHAM. Well, tell him to come back at half past eleven; but I can't promise that Mr Newton will be in. Still, if he likes to come on the chance. And without his dogs, mind. Our Diamond would fight with them.

THE MAID. Yes, maam: I'll tell him [*going*].

MRS BASHAM. Oh, Sally, can you tell me how much is three times seven. You were at school, werent you?

SALLY. Yes, maam; but they taught the boys to read, write, and cipher. Us girls were only taught to sew.

MRS BASHAM. Well, never mind. I will ask Mr Newton. He'll know, if anybody will. Or stop. Ask Jack the fish hawker. He's paunching the rabbit in the kitchen.

SALLY. Yes, maam. [*She goes*].

MRS BASHAM. Three sixpences make one and sixpence and three eightpences make two shillings: they always do. But three sevenpences! I give it up.

Sally returns.

SALLY. Please, maam, another gentleman wants Mr Newton.

MRS BASHAM. Another nobleman?

SALLY. No, maam. He wears leather clothes. Quite out of the common.

MRS BASHAM. Did he give his name?

SALLY. George Fox, he said, maam.

MRS BASHAM. Why, thats the Quaker, the Man in Leather Breeches. He's been in prison. How dare he come here wanting to see Mr Newton? Go and tell him that Mr Newton is not at home to the like of him.

SALLY. Oh, he's not a person I could talk to like that, maam. I dursnt.

MRS BASHAM. Are you frightened of a man that would call a church a steeple house and walk into it without taking off his hat? Go this instant and tell him you will raise the street against him if he doesnt go away. Do you hear. Go and do as I tell you.

SALLY. I'd be afraid he'd raise the street against us. I will do my best to get rid of him without offence. [*She goes*].

MRS BASHAM [*calling after her*] And mind you ask Jack how much three times seven is.

SALLY [*outside*] Yes'm.

Newton, aged 38, *comes in from the garden, hatless, deep in calculation, his fists clenched, tapping his knuckles together to tick off the stages of the equation. He stumbles over the mat.*

MRS BASHAM. Oh, do look where youre going, Mr Newton. Someday youll walk into the river and drown yourself. I thought you were out at the university.

NEWTON. Now dont scold, Mrs Basham, dont scold. I forgot to go out. I thought of a way of making a calculation that has been puzzling me.

MRS BASHAM. And you have been sitting out there forgetting everything else since breakfast. However, since you have one of your calculating fits on I wonder would you mind doing a little sum for me to check the washing bill. How much is three times seven?

NEWTON. Three times seven? Oh, that is quite easy.

MRS BASHAM. I suppose it is to you, sir; but it beats me. At school I got as far as addition and subtraction; but I never could do multiplication or division.

NEWTON. Why, neither could I: I was too lazy. But they are quite unnecessary: addition and subtraction are quite sufficient. You add the logarithms of the numbers; and the antilogarithm of the sum of the two is the answer. Let me see: three times seven? The logarithm of three must be decimal four seven seven or thereabouts. The logarithm of seven is, say, decimal eight four five. That makes one decimal three two two, doesnt it? What's the antilogarithm of one decimal three two two? Well, it must be less than twentytwo and more than twenty. You will be safe if you put it down as—

Sally returns.

SALLY. Please, maam, Jack says it's twentyone.

NEWTON. Extraordinary! Here was I blundering over this simple problem for a whole minute; and this uneducated fish hawker solves it in a flash! He is a better mathematician than I.

MRS BASHAM. This is our new maid from Woolsthorp, Mr Newton. You havnt seen her before.

NEWTON. Havnt I? I didnt notice it. [*To Sally*] Youre from Woolsthorp, are you? So am I. How old are you?

SALLY. Twentyfour, sir.

NEWTON. Twentyfour years. Eight thousand seven hundred and sixty days. Two hundred and ten thousand two hundred and forty hours. Twelve million six hundred and fourteen thousand, four hundred minutes. Seven hundred and fiftysix million eight hundred and sixtyfour thousand seconds. A long long life.

MRS BASHAM. Come now, Mr Newton: you will turn the child's head with your figures. What can one do in a second?

NEWTON. You can do, quite deliberately and intentionally, seven distinct actions in a second. How do you count seconds? Hackertybackertyone, hackertybackertytwo, hackertybackertythree and so on. You pronounce seven syllables in every second. Think of it! This young woman has had time to perform more than five thousand millions of considered and intentional actions in her lifetime. How many of them can you remember, Sally?

SALLY. Oh sir, the only one I can remember was on my sixth birthday. My father gave me sixpence: a penny for every year.

NEWTON. Six from twentyfour is eighteen. He owes you one and sixpence. Remind me to give you one and sevenpence on your next birthday if you are a good girl. Now be off.

SALLY. Oh, thank you, sir. [*She goes out*].

NEWTON. My father, who died before I was born, was a wild, extravagant, weak man: so they tell me. I inherit his wildness, his extravagance, his weakness, in the shape of a craze for figures of which I am most heartily ashamed. There are so many more important things to be worked at: the transmutations of matter, the elixir of life, the magic of light and color, above all, the secret meaning of the Scriptures. And when I should be concentrating my mind on these I find myself wandering off into idle games of speculation about numbers in infinite series, and dividing curves into indivisibly short triangle bases. How silly! What a waste of time, priceless time!

MRS BASHAM. There is a Mr Rowley going to call on you at half past eleven.

NEWTON. Can I never be left alone? Who is Mr Rowley? What is Mr Rowley?

MRS BASHAM. Dressed like a nobleman. Very tall. Very dark. Keeps a lackey. Has a pack of dogs with him.

NEWTON. Oho! So that is who he is! They told me he wanted to see my telescope. Well, Mrs Basham, he is a person whose visit will be counted a great honor to us. But I must warn you that just as I have my terrible weakness for figures Mr Rowley has a very similar weakness for women; so you must keep Sally out of his way.

MRS BASHAM. Indeed! If he tries any of his tricks on Sally I shall see that he marries her.

NEWTON. He is married already. [*He sits at the table*].

MRS BASHAM. Oh! That sort of man! The beast!

NEWTON. Shshsh! Not a word against him, on your life. He is privileged.

MRS BASHAM. He is a beast all the same!

NEWTON [*opening the Bible*] One of the beasts in the Book of Revelation, perhaps. But not a common beast.

MRS BASHAM. Fox the quaker, in his leather breeches, had the impudence to call.

NEWTON [*interested*] George Fox? If he calls again I will see him. Those two men ought to meet.

MRS BASHAM. Those two men indeed! The honor of meeting you ought to be enough for them, I should think.

NEWTON. The honor of meeting me! Dont talk nonsense. They are great men in their very different ranks. I am nobody.

MRS BASHAM. You are the greatest man alive, sir. Mr Halley told me so.

NEWTON. It was very wrong of Mr Halley to tell you anything of the sort. You must not mind what he says. He is always pestering me to publish my methods of calculation and to abandon my serious studies. Numbers! Numbers! Numbers! Sines, cosines, hypotenuses, fluxions, curves small enough to count as straight lines, distances between two points that are in the same place! Are these philosophy? Can they make a man great?

He is interrupted by Sally, who throws open the door and announces visitors.

SALLY. Mr Rowley and Mr Fox.

King Charles the Second, aged 50, *appears at the door, but makes way for George Fox the Quaker, a big man with bright eyes and a powerful voice in reserve, aged* 56. *He is decently dressed; but his garments are made of leather.*

CHARLES. After you, Mr Fox. The spiritual powers before the temporal.

FOX. You are very civil, sir; and you speak very justly. I thank you [*he passes in*].

Sally, intensely impressed by Mr Rowley, goes out.

FOX. Am I addressing the philosopher Isaac Newton?

NEWTON. You are, sir. [*Rising*] Will your noblė friend do me the honor to be seated in my humble dwelling?

Charles bows and takes the armchair with easy grace.

FOX. I must not impose on you by claiming the gentleman as my friend. We met by chance at your door; and his favorite dog was kind enough to take a fancy to me.

CHARLES. She is never mistaken, sir. Her friends are my friends, if so damaged a character as mine can claim any friends.

NEWTON [*taking a chair from the wall and placing it near his table to his left*] Be seated, Mr Fox, pray.

FOX. George Fox at your service, not Mister. But I am very sensible of your civility. [*He sits*].

NEWTON [*resuming his seat at the table*] It seems that it is I who am at your service. In what way can I oblige you?

FOX. As you remind me, I have come here uninvited. My business will keep while you discharge yours with this nobleman—so called.

CHARLES. I also am uninvited, Pastor. I may address you so both truthfully and civilly, may I not?

FOX. You have found the right word. I tended my father's sheep when I was a child. Now I am a pastor of men's souls.

CHARLES. Good. Well, Pastor, I must inform you I have

no business here except to waste our host's invaluable time and to improve my own, if he will be good enough to allow me such a liberty. Proceed then with your business; and take no notice of me. Unless, that is, you would prefer me to withdraw.

FOX. I have no business in this world that all men may not hear: the more the better.

CHARLES. I guessed as much; and confess to an unbounded curiosity to hear what George Fox can have to say to Isaac Newton. It is not altogether an impertinent curiosity. My trade, which is a very unusual one, requires that I should know what Tom, Dick and Harry have to say to oneanother. I find you two gentlemen much more interesting and infinitely more important.

MRS BASHAM [*posted behind Newton's chair*] What is your business, Mr Rowley? Mr Newton has much to do this morning. He has no time for idle conversation.

NEWTON. I had forgotten to make this lady known to you, gentlemen. Mrs Basham: my housekeeper, and the faithful guardian of my hours.

CHARLES. Your servant, Mistress Basham.

FOX. God be with you, woman.

NEWTON. Mr Rowley is a gentleman of great consequence, Mrs Basham. He must not be questioned as if he were Jack the fish hawker. His business is his father's business.

CHARLES. No, no. My father's business is abolished in England: he was executed for practising it. But we keep the old signboard up over the door of the old shop. And I stand at the shop door in my father's apron. Mrs Basham may ask me as many questions as she pleases; for I am far less important now in England than Jack the fish hawker.

MRS BASHAM. But how do you live, sir? That is all I meant to ask.

CHARLES. By my wits, Mistress Basham: by my wits. Come, Pastor: enough of me. You are face to face with Isaac Newton. I long to hear what you have to say to him.

FOX. Isaac Newton: I have friends who belong to the new socalled Royal Society which the King has established, to enquire, it seems, into the nature of the universe. They tell me things that my mind cannot reconcile with the word of God as revealed to us in the Holy Scriptures.

NEWTON. What is your warrant for supposing that revelation ceased when King James's printers finished with the Bible?

FOX. I do not suppose so. I am not one of those priest-ridden churchmen who believe that God went out of business six thousand years ago when he had called the world into existence and written his book about it. We three sitting here together may have a revelation if we open our hearts and minds to it. Yes: even to you, Charles Stuart.

CHARLES. The mind of Charles Stuart is only too open, Pastor.

MRS BASHAM. What did you call the gentleman, Mr Fox?

CHARLES. A slip of the tongue, Mistress Basham. Nowhere in Holy writ, Pastor, will you find any disapproval of Paul when he changed his name from Saul. Need you be more scrupulous than the apostles?

FOX. It is against my sinful nature to disoblige any man; so Mr Rowley you shall be if you so desire. But I owed it to you to let you know that I was not deceived by your new name.

CHARLES. I thank you, Pastor. Your sinful nature makes you the best mannered man in the kingdom. And now, what about the revelations?

FOX. I am troubled. I cannot conceive that God should contradict himself. How must the revelation of today be received if it be contrary to the revelation of yesterday? If what has been revealed to you, Isaac Newton, be true, there is no heaven above us and no hell beneath us. The sun which stood still upon Gibeon and the moon in the Valley of Ajalon had stood still since the creation of the world.

NEWTON. Do not let that trouble you, Pastor. Nothing has ever stood still for an instant since the creation of the world: neither the sun, the moon, the stars, nor the smallest particle of matter, except on two occasions.

CHARLES. Two! I remember only one.

NEWTON. Yes, sir: two. The first was when the sun stood still on Gibeon to give Joshua time to slaughter the Amorites. The second was when the shadow on the dial of Ahaz went ten degrees backward as a sign from God to good King Hezekiah who was dying of a boil until the prophet Isaiah made them put a lump of figs on it.

MRS BASHAM. There is nothing like a poultice of roasted figs to cure a gumboil. And to think that is because it is in the Holy Bible! I never knew it.

NEWTON. On reflection, the sun has stopped three times; for it must have stopped for an infinitesimal moment when it turned back, and again when it resumed its course.

FOX. I thank God that you are not an unbeliever and would not make me one.

NEWTON. My good friend, there is nothing so wonderful that a philosopher cannot believe it. The philosopher sees a hundred miracles a day where the ignorant and thoughtless see nothing but the daily round, the common task. Joshua was an ignorant soldier. Had he been a philosopher he would have known that to stop the nearest speck of dust would have served his turn as well as to stop the sun and moon; for it could not have stopped without stopping the whole machinery of the heavens. By the way, Mrs Basham, the fact that the sun and moon were visible at the same time may help me to fix the day on which the miracle occurred. [*To the others*] Excuse me, gentlemen: I have written a chronological history of the world; and the dates give me some trouble.

CHARLES. Did not the late Archbishop Ussher fix the dates of everything that ever happened?

NEWTON. Unfortunately he did not allow for the precession of the equinoxes. I had to correct some of his results accordingly.

CHARLES. And, saving the pastor's presence, what the divvle is the precession of the equinoxes?

FOX. I am sinful enough to be glad that you are as ignorant as myself. I suffer greatly from shame at my ignorance.

NEWTON. Shame will not help you, Pastor. I spend my

life contemplating the ocean of my ignorance. I once boasted of having picked up a pebble on the endless beach of that ocean. I should have said a grain of sand.

CHARLES. I can well believe it. No man confronted with the enormity of what he does not know can think much of what he does know. But what is the precession of the equinoxes? If I fire off those words at court the entire peerage will be prostrate before the profundity of my learning.

MRS BASHAM. Oh, tell the gentlemen, Mr Newton; or they will be here all day.

NEWTON. It is quite simple: a child can understand it. The two days in the year on which the day and night are of equal duration are the equinoxes. In each successive sidereal year they occur earlier. You will see at once that this involves a retrograde motion of the equinoctial points along the ecliptic. We call that the precession of the equinoxes.

FOX. I thank you, Isaac Newton. I am as wise as I was before.

MRS BASHAM. You ought to be ashamed of yourself, Mr Newton, injuring the poor gentlemen's brains with such outlandish words. You must remember that everybody is not as learned as you are.

NEWTON. But surely it is plain to everybody—

MRS BASHAM. No: it isnt plain to anybody, Mr Newton.

SALLY [*bursting in*] Mr Rowley: theres a lady in a coach at the door wants to know are you ready to take a drive with her.

CHARLES. Any name?

SALLY. No, sir. She said youd know.

CHARLES. A duchess, would you say?

SALLY. Oh no, sir. Spoke to me quite familiar.

CHARLES. Nelly! Mr Newton: would you like to be introduced to Mistress Gwynn, the famous Drury Lane actress?

MRS BASHAM [*turning imperatively to Charles*] Oh, I couldnt allow that, Mr Rowley. I am surprised at you mentioning such a person in my presence.

CHARLES. I apologize. I did not know that you disapproved of the playhouse, Mrs Basham.

MRS BASHAM. I do not disapprove of the playhouse, sir. My grandfather, who is still alive and hearty, was befriended in his youth by Mr William Shakespear, a well-known player and writer of comedies, tragedies, and the like. Mr Shakespear would have died of shame to see a woman on the stage. It is unnatural and wrong. Only the most abandoned females would do such a thing.

CHARLES. Still, the plays are more natural with real women in them, are they not?

MRS BASHAM. Indeed they are not, Mr Rowley. They are not like women at all. They are just like what they are; and they spoil the play for anyone who can remember the old actors in the women's parts. They could make you believe you were listening to real women.

CHARLES. Pastor Fox: have you ever spoken with a female player?

FOX [*shuddering*] I! No, sir: I do not frequent such company.

CHARLES. Why not, Pastor? Is your charity so narrow? Nell is no worse than Mary Magdalen.

MRS BASHAM. I hope Mary Magdalen made a good end and was forgiven; though we are nowhere told so. But I should not have asked her into my house. And at least she was not on the stage. [*She retires behind Newton's chair*].

CHARLES. What do you say, Pastor? Is Nelly not good enough for you?

FOX. Sir: there is nobody who is not good enough for me. Have I not warned our Christian friends who are now captives in Barbary not to forget that the life of God and the power of God are in their heathen masters the Turks and the Moors as well as in themselves? Is it any the less in this player woman than in a Turk or a Moor? I am not afraid of her.

CHARLES. And you, Mr Newton?

NEWTON. Women enter a philosopher's life only to disturb it. They expect too much attention. However, Mistress Gwynn has called to take you away, not to interrupt my work on fluxions. And if you will condescend to go down to her she need not come up to us. [*He rises in dismissal of the King*].

CHARLES [*rising*] I see I must take my leave.

Nelly dashes in. Sally withdraws.

NELLY. Rowley darling: how long more are you going to keep me waiting in the street?

CHARLES. You are known to everyone present, Mistress Gwynn, I think. May I make our host known to you? The eminent philosopher, Mr Newton.

NELLY [*going past Charles to Newton*] I dont know what a philosopher is, Mr Newton; but you look one, every inch. Your servant, sir. [*She curtsies to him*].

NEWTON. Yours, madam. I am ashamed that you should have been kept waiting at the wrong side of my door.

NELLY. It is an honor to be seen at your door, Mr Newton. [*Looking round her*] And who keeps your house so beautifully? I thought philosophers were like Romish priests, not allowed to marry.

NEWTON. Is my house beautifully kept? I have never noticed it. This is Mrs Basham, my housekeeper. [*He sits resignedly*].

NELLY. You never noticed it! You dont deserve such a housekeeper. Your servant, Mrs Basham.

Mrs Basham bows stiffly, trying not to be flattered.

CHARLES. The other gentleman is the famous founder of the sect of Quakers.

FOX. Of Friends, Friend Rowley.

NELLY [*running to Fox*] I know. I know. The man in the leather breeches.

FOX [*stubbornly seated*] I am also known as George Fox.

NELLY [*clapping him on the shoulder*] What of that? Anybody might be George Fox; but there is only one man in the leather breeches. Your servant, George.

FOX. Yours, Nelly.

NELLY. There! Nelly! [*She goes to the wall for a chair and plants it at Fox's left, quite close*]. If I may add you to the list of my beaus I shall be the proudest woman in London.

FOX. I did not found the order of beaus. I founded that

of Friends.

NELLY. Ten times better. Our beaus are our foes: they care for nothing but to steal our honor. Pray for me, Friend Fox: I think you have God by the ear closer than the bishops.

FOX. He is closer to you than you have placed yourself to me. Let no priest come between you.

CHARLES. We must not waste any more of Mr Newton's time, Mistress Gwyn. He is at work on fluxions.

NELLY. On what?

CHARLES. Fluxions I think you said, Mr Newton.

NELLY. What are fluxions?

CHARLES. Mr Newton will tell you. I should be glad to know, myself.

NEWTON. Fluxions, Madam, are the rates of change of continuously varying quantities.

NELLY. I must go home and think about that, Mr Philosopher.

NEWTON [*very seriously*] I shall be much indebted to you, Madam, if you will communicate to me the result of your reflections. The truth is, I am not quite satisfied that my method—or perhaps I had better say the notation of my method—is the easiest that can be devised. On that account I have never cared to publish it.

NELLY. You really think I could teach you something, Mr Newton? What a compliment! Did you hear that, Rowley darling?

NEWTON. In these very simple matters one may learn from anyone. And you, Madam, must have very remarkable mental powers. You repeat long parts from memory in the theatre. I could not do that.

NELLY. Bless me, so I do, Mr Newton. You are the first man I ever met who did not think an actress must be an ignorant ninny—except schoolboys, who think she is a goddess. I declare you are the wisest man in England, and the kindest.

CHARLES. And the busiest, Nelly. Come. He has given us as much of his time as we have any right to ask for.

NELLY. Yes, I know. I am coming. [*She rises and goes to Charles, whose left arm she takes*]. May I come again,

Mr Newton?

NEWTON [*rising*] No no no no no, Madam. I cannot entertain ladies. They do not fit into my way of life. Mr Rowley: you are well known to be as interested in ladies as I am interested in the Scriptures; and I thank you for bringing this very attractive sample for my diversion—

NELLY [*as if tasting a sweet*] Oh!

NEWTON [*continuing*]—but sufficient unto the day is the evil thereof—

NELLY [*in violent protest*] Oh!!!

NEWTON. —and I beg you will bring no more ladies here until I have time to set aside a day of relaxation for their reception.

NELLY. We must go, Rowley darling. He doesnt want us.

CHARLES. You are fortunate, Mr Newton, in suffering nothing worse than Nell. But I promise you your house shall be a monastery henceforth.

As Charles and Nell turn to the door to go out, the Duchess of Cleveland, 39, *formerly Lady Castlemaine, and born Barbara Villiers, bursts into the room and confronts them in a tearing rage.*

BARBARA. Ah! I have caught you, have I, with your trull. This is the scientific business which made it impossible for you to see me this morning.

CHARLES. Be silent for a moment, Barbara, whilst I present you to Mr Newton, the eminent philosopher, in whose house you are an uninvited guest.

BARBARA. A pretty house. A pretty philosopher. A house kept for you to meet your women in.

MRS BASHAM [*coming indignantly to the middle of the room*] Oh! Mr Newton: either this female leaves the house this instant or I do.

BARBARA. Do you know, woman, that you are speaking of the Duchess of Cleveland?

MRS BASHAM. I do not care who I am speaking of. If you are the Duchess of Cleveland and this house were what you said it was you would be only too much at home in it. The house being what it is you are out of place in it. You go or I go.

BARBARA. You insolent slut, I will have you taken to the Bridewell and whipped.

CHARLES. You shall not, Barbara. If you do not come down with me to your carriage without another word, I will throw you downstairs.

BARBARA. Do. Kill me; and be happy with that low stage player. You have been unfaithful to me with her a thousand times.

NEWTON. Patience, patience, patience. Mrs Basham: the lady is not in a state of reason: I will prove to you that what she says has no sense and need not distress us. [*To Barbara*] Your Grace alleges that Mr Rowley has been unfaithful to you a thousand times.

BARBARA. A hundred thousand times.

NEWTON. For each unfaithfulness allow a day—or shall I say a night? Now one hundred thousand nights are almost two hundred and seventyfour years. To be precise, 273 years 287 days, allowing 68 days for Leap Year every four years. Now Mr Rowley is not 300 years old: he is only fifty, from which you must deduct at least fifteen years for his childhood.

BARBARA. Fourteen.

NEWTON. Let us say fourteen. Probably your Grace was also precocious. How many years shall we strike off your age for the days of your innocence?

NELL. Five at most.

BARBARA. Be silent, you.

NEWTON. Say twelve. That makes you in effect about twentyeight.

BARBARA. Have I denied it?

NELL. Flatterer!

NEWTON. Twentyeight to Mr Rowley's thirtysix. Your Grace has been available since, say, the year 1652, twenty-eight years ago. My calculation is therefore correct.

BARBARA. May I ask what you mean by available?

NEWTON. I mean that the number of occasions on which

Mr Rowley could possibly be unfaithful to you is ten thousand two hundred and twenty plus seven for leap years. Yet you allege one hundred thousand occasions, and claim to have lived for nearly three centuries. As that is impossible, it is clear that you have been misinformed about Mistress Gwynn.

Nell claps vigorously.

BARBARA [*to Newton*] Are you mocking me, sir?

NEWTON. Figures cannot mock, because they cannot feel. That is their great quality, and their great fault. [*He goes to the door*]. And now may I have the honor of conducting your Grace to your coach—or is it one of those new fangled sedan chairs? Or would your Grace prefer to be thrown down my humble staircase by Mr Rowley? It has twenty-four steps, in two flights.

BARBARA. I will not leave this house until that player woman has gone first. [*She strides past them and plants herself in Newton's chair*].

NELL. After all, dear, it's Mr Newton's house and not ours. He was in the act of putting me out when you burst in. I stayed only because I wanted to see you in one of those tantrums of yours that Rowley so often tells me about. I might copy them on the stage.

BARBARA. He dares talk to you about me!!

NELL. He talks to me about everything, dear, because I let him get in a word occasionally, which is more than you do.

BARBARA [*to Charles*] Will you stand there and let me be insulted by this woman?

CHARLES [*with conviction*] Barbara: I am tired of your tantrums. I made you a duchess: you behave like a streetwalker. I pensioned you and packed you off to Paris; you have no business to be here. Pastor: what have you to say to all this? You are the oldest and wisest person present, are you not?

FOX. Fiftysix. And still a child in wisdom.

BARBARA [*contemptuously, noticing Fox for the first time*] What does this person know about women?

FOX. Only what the woman in myself teaches me.

NELL. Good for leather breeches! What do you think of her, George?

FOX. She prates overmuch about unfaithfulness. The man Rowley cannot be unfaithful to her because he has pledged no faith to her. To his wife only can he be unfaithful.

CHARLES. Wrong, Pastor. You do not know my wife. To her only I can never be unfaithful.

NELL. Yes: you are kind to us; but we are nothing to you. [*Sighing*] I would change places with her.

BARBARA. Will you order this common player to be silent in my presence?

NELL. It is not fair of her to keep mentioning my profession when I cannot decently mention hers.

With a scream of rage the duchess rises to fly at Nell, but is seized by Fox, who drags down her raised fists and throws her back into the chair.

FOX [*sternly*] Woman: behave yourself. In any decent English village you would go to the ducking stool to teach you good manners and gentle speech. You must control yourself—

He is interrupted by the clangor of a church bell, which has a terrible effect on him.

FOX [*in a thundering voice, forgetting all about the duchess*] Ha! I am called: I must go.

He makes for the door but is stopped by Charles, who, releasing Nell, shuts it quickly and posts himself with his back to it.

CHARLES. Stop. You are going to brawl in church. You will be thrown into prison; and I shall not be able to save you.

FOX. The bell, the bell. It strikes upon my life. I am called. Earthly kings cannot stay me. Let me pass.

CHARLES. Stand back, Mr Fox. My person is sacred.

NEWTON. What is the matter?

CHARLES. The church bell: it drives him mad. Someone send and stop it.

The bell stops.

FOX. God has stopped it. [*He falls on his knees and col-*

lapses, shivering like a man recovering from a fit.

Charles and Newton help him to his feet and lead him back to his chair.

FOX [*to Charles*] Another stroke, and I should not have answered for your life.

BARBARA. You must control yourself, preacher. In any decent English village you would be put in the stocks to teach you good manners.

FOX. Woman: I have been put in the stocks; and I shall be put there again. But I will continue to testify against the steeple house and the brazen clangor of its belfries.

MRS BASHAM. Now Mr Fox. You must not say such things here.

FOX. I tell you that from the moment you allow this manmade monster called a Church to enter your mind your inner light is like an extinguished candle; and your soul is plunged in darkness and damned. There is no atheist like the Church atheist. I have converted many a poor atheist who would have been burnt or hanged if God had not sent him into my hands; but I have never converted a churchman: his answer to everything is not his God, but the Church, the Church, the Church. They burn each other, these churchmen: they persecute: they do wickednesses of which no friend of God would be capable.

MRS BASHAM. The Popish Church, not the Protestant one, Mr Fox.

FOX. All, all, all of them. They are all snares of the devil. They stand between Man and his Maker, and take on themselves divine powers when they lack divine attributes. Am I to hold my peace in the face of this iniquity? When the bell rings to announce some pitiful rascal twaddling in his pulpit, or some fellow in a cassock pretending to bind and loose, I hear an Almighty Voice call "George Fox, George Fox: rise up: testify: unmask these impostors: drag them down from their pulpits and their altars; and let it be known that what the world needs to bring it back to God is not Churchmen but Friends, Friends of God, Friends of man, friendliness and sincerity everywhere, superstition and pulpit playacting nowhere."

CHARLES. Pastor: it is not given to every man as it has been to you to make a religion for himself. A readymade Church is an indispensable convenience for most of us. The inner light must express itself in music, in noble architecture, in eloquence: in a word, in beauty, before it can pass into the minds of common men. I grant you the clergy are mostly dull dogs; but with a little disguise and ritual they will pass as holy men with the ignorant. And there are great mysteries that must be symbolized, because though we feel them we do not know them, Mr Newton having not yet discovered their nature, in spite of all his mathematics. And this reminds me that we are making a most unwarrantable intrusion on our host's valuable time. Mr Newton: on my honor I had no part in bringing upon you this invasion of womanhood. I hasten to take them away, and will wait upon you at some happier moment. Come, ladies: we must leave Mr Newton to his mathematics. [*He is about to go to the door. Barbara rises to accompany him*].

NEWTON [*stopping him*] I must correct that misunderstanding, sir. I would not have you believe that I could be so inhospitable as to drive away my guests merely to indulge in the trifling pursuit of mathematical calculation, which leads finally nowhere. But I have more serious business in hand this morning. I am engaged in a study of the prophecies in the book of Daniel. [*He indicates the Bible*]. It may prove of the greatest importance to the world. I beg you to allow me to proceed with it in the necessary solitude. The ladies have not wasted my time: I have to thank her Grace of Cleveland for some lights on the Book of Revelation suggested to me by her proceedings. But solitude—solitude absolutely free from the pleasant disturbance of ladies' society—is now necessary to me; and I must beg you to withdraw.

Sally, now dressed in her best, throws the door open from without, and proudly announces—

SALLY. Her Grace the Duchess of Portsmouth.

Louise de Kéroualle, a Frenchwoman who at 30 *retains her famous babyish beauty, appears on the threshold.*

NEWTON [*beside himself*] Another woman! Take her

away. Take them all away. [*He flings himself into his chair at the table and buries his face in his hands*].

CHARLES. Louise: it is unlike you to pursue me. We are unwelcome here.

LOUISE [*coming over to him*] Pursue you! But I have never been so surprised in my life as to find you here. And Nelly! And her Grace of Cleveland back from Paris! What are you all doing here? I came to consult Mr Newton, the alchemist. [*Newton straightens up and stares*]. My business with him is private: it is with him, not with you, chéri. I did not know he was holding a reception.

CHARLES. Mr Newton is not an alchemist.

LOUISE. Pardon me: he is.

CHARLES. Mr Newton: are you an alchemist?

NEWTON. My meditations on the ultimate constitution of matter have convinced me that the transmutation of metals, and indeed of all substances, must be possible. It is occurring every day. I understand that you, Mr Rowley, have a private laboratory at Whitehall, in which you are attempting the fixation of mercury.

CHARLES. Without success, Mr Newton. I shall give it up and try for the philosopher's stone instead.

FOX. Would you endanger your souls by dabbling in magic? The scripture says "Thou shalt not suffer a witch to live." Do you think that God is fonder of sorcerers and wizards than of witches? If you count the wrath of God as nothing, and are above the law by your rank, are you not ashamed to believe such old wives' tales as the changing of lead into gold by the philosopher's stone?

NEWTON. Pastor Fox: I thank you for your wellmeant warning. Now let me warn you. The man who begins by doubting the possibility of the philosopher's stone soon finds himself beginning to doubt the immortality of the soul. He ends by doubting the existence of the soul. There is no witchcraft about these things. I am as certain of them as I am of the fact that the world was created four thousand and four years before the birth of our Lord.

FOX. And what warrant have you for that? The Holy

Bible says nothing of your four thousand and four. It tells us that the world was created "in the beginning": a mighty word. "In the beginning"! Think of it if you have any imagination. And because some fool in a steeplehouse, dressed up like a stage player in robes and mitre, dares to measure the days of the Almighty by his kitchen clock, you take his word before the word of God! Shame on you, Isaac Newton, for making an idol of an archbishop! There is no credulity like the credulity of philosophers.

NEWTON. But the archbishop has counted the years! My own chronology of the world has been founded on his calculation. Do you mean to tell me that all the labor I have bestowed on that book has been wasted?

FOX. Sinfully wasted.

NEWTON. George Fox: you are an infidel. Leave my house.

FOX [*rising*] Your philosophy has led you to the conclusion that George Fox is an infidel. So much the worse for your philosophy! The Lord does not love men that count numbers. Read second Samuel, chapter twentyfour: the book is before you. Good morning; and God bless you and enlighten you. [*He turns to go*].

CHARLES. Stay, Pastor. [*He makes Fox sit down again and goes to Newton, laying a hand on his shoulder*]. Mr Newton: the word infidel is not one to be used hastily between us three. Old Tom Hobbes, my tutor, who was to me what Aristotle was to Alexander the Great, was called an infidel. You yourself, in spite of your interest in the book of Daniel, have been suspected of doubting whether the apple falls from the tree by the act of God or by a purely physical attraction. Even I, the head of the Church, the Defender of the Faith, stand between the Whigs who suspect me of being a Papist and the Tories who suspect me of being an atheist. Now the one thing that is true of all three of us is that if the common people knew our real minds they would hang us and bury us in unconsecrated ground. We must stand together, gentlemen. What does it matter to us whether the world is four thousand years old, or, as I should guess, ten thousand?

NEWTON. The world ten thousand years old! Sir: you are mad.

NELL [*shocked*] Rowley darling: you mustnt say such things.

BARBARA. What business is it of yours, pray? He has always defied God and betrayed women. He does not know the meaning of the word religion. He laughed at it in France. He hated it in Scotland. In England he believes nothing. He loves nothing. He fears nothing except having to go on his travels again, as he calls it. What are ten thousand years to him, or ten million?

FOX. Are ten million years beyond the competence of Almighty God? They are but a moment in His eyes. Four thousand years seem an eternity to a mayfly, or a mouse, or a mitred fool called an archbishop. Are we mayflies? Are we mice? Are we archbishops?

MRS BASHAM. Mr Fox: I have listened to too much blasphemy this morning. But to call an archbishop a mitred fool and compare him to a mouse is beyond endurance. I cannot believe that God will ever pardon you for that. Have you no fear of hell?

FOX. How shall I root out the sin of idolatry from this land? Worship your God, woman, not a dressed-up priest.

MRS BASHAM. The archbishop is not a graven image. And when he is officiating he is not in the likeness of anything in the heavens above or on the earth beneath. I am afraid you do not know your catechism, Mr Fox.

CHARLES [*laughing*] Excellent, Mrs Basham. Pastor: she has gravelled you with the second commandment. And she has put us to shame for quarrelling over a matter of which we know nothing. By the way, where were we when we began to quarrel? I have clean forgotten.

LOUISE. It was my business with Mr Newton, I think. Nellie: will you take our sovereign lord away and leave me to speak with the alchemist in private?

CHARLES. Mr Newton: not for worlds would I deprive you of a *tête-à-tête* with her Grace of Portsmouth. Pastor: you will accompany us. Nellie: you will come with the pastor. But first I must throw the Duchess of Cleveland downstairs [*moving towards her*].

BARBARA [*screaming and making for the door*] Coward! Help! Murder! [*She rushes out*].

CHARLES. Your servant, Mrs Basham.

Mrs Basham curtsies. Charles salutes her and goes out.

NELL [*beckoning to Fox*] Come on, leather breeches.

FOX [*rising and going towards the door*] Well, what you are, God made you. I am bound to be your friend.

NELL [*taking his arm as he passes*] I am proud of your friendship, George.

They go out arm in arm.

Louise, being now the person of highest rank present, follows them as far as the armchair, in which she seats herself with distinguished elegance.

LOUISE [*to Mrs Basham*] Madam: may I have a moment alone with the alchemist?

NEWTON. You certainly may not, your Grace. I will not have Mr Locke and his friends accuse me of having relations with women. If your business cannot be discussed before Mrs Basham it cannot be discussed with me. And you will please not speak of me as "the alchemist" as you might speak of the apothecary or the chimney sweep. I am by profession—if it can be called a profession—a philosopher.

LOUISE. Pardon: I am not habituated to your English manners. It is strange to me that a philosopher should need a chaperon. In France it is I who should need one.

NEWTON. You are quite safe with me and Mrs Basham, madam. What is your business?

LOUISE. I want a love charm.

NEWTON. A what?

LOUISE. A love charm. Something that will make my lover faithful to me if I drop it into his tay. And mind! it must make him love me, and not love everybody. He is far too amorous already of every pretty woman he meets. I make no secret of who he is: all the world knows it. The love charm must not do him any harm; for if we poison the king we shall be executed in the most horrible manner. It must be something that will be good for him.

NEWTON. And peculiar to yourself? Not to Mistress Gwynn?

LOUISE. I do not mind Nellie: she is a dear, and so helpful when there is any trouble or illness. He picked her up out of the gutter; but the good God sometimes drops a jewel there: my nurse, a peasant woman, was worth a thousand duchesses. Yes: he may have Nellie: a change is sometimes good for men.

MRS BASHAM [*fearfully shocked*] Oh! Mr Newton: I must go. I cannot stay and listen to this French lady's talk. [*She goes out with dignity*].

LOUISE. I shall never understand the things that Englishwomen are prudish about. And they are so extraordinarily coarse in other things. May I stay, now that your chaperon has gone?

NEWTON. You will not want to stay when I tell you that I do not deal in love potions. Ask the nearest apothecary for an aphrodisiac.

LOUISE. But I cannot trust a common apothecary: it would be all over the town tomorrow. Nobody will suspect you. I will pay any price you like.

NEWTON. I tell you, madam, I know nothing about such things. If I wished to make you fall in love with me—which God forbid!—I should not know how to set about it. I should learn to play some musical instrument, or buy a new wig.

LOUISE. But you are an alchemist: you must know.

NEWTON. Then I am not an alchemist. But the changing of Bodies into Light and Light into Bodies is very conformable to the Course of Nature, which seems delighted with Transmutations.

LOUISE. I do not understand. What are transmutations?

NEWTON. Never mind, madam. I have other things to do than to peddle love charms to the King's ladies.

LOUISE [*ironically*] Yes: to entertain the Duchess of Cleveland and Mistress Gwynn, and hire a mad preacher to amuse them! What else have you to do that is more important than my business with you?

NEWTON. Many other things. For instance, to ascertain

the exact distance of the sun from the earth.

LOUISE. But what a waste of time! What can it possibly matter whether the sun is twenty miles away or twentyfive?

NEWTON. Twenty or twentyfive!!! The sun is millions and millions of miles from the earth.

LOUISE. Oh! Oh!! Oh!!! You are quite mad, Monsieur Nieuton. At such a distance you could not see it. You could not feel its heat. Well, you cannot see it so plainly here as in France, nor so often; but you can see it quite plainly sometimes. And you can feel its heat. It burns your skin, and freckles you if you are sandy-haired. And then comes a little cloud over it and you shiver with cold. Could that happen if it were a thousand miles away?

NEWTON. It is very very large, madam. It is one million three hundred thousand times heavier than the earth.

LOUISE. My good Monsieur Nieuton: do not be so fanciful. [*Indicating the window*] Look at it. Look at it. It is much smaller than the earth. If I hold up a sou—what you call a ha-pen-ny—before my eye, it covers the sun and blots it out. Let me teach you something, Monsieur Nieuton. A great French philosopher, Blaise Pascal, teached me this. You must never let your imagination run away with you. When you think of grandiose things—hundreds of millions and things like that—you must continually come down to earth to keep sane. You must see: you must feel: you must measure.

NEWTON. That is very true, madam. Above all, you must measure. And when you measure you find that many things are bigger than they look. The sun is one of them.

LOUISE [*rising and going to the table to coax him*] Ah! You are impossible. But you will make me a love potion, will you not?

NEWTON. I will write you a prescription, madam.

He takes a sheet of paper and writes the prescription. Louise watches as he writes.

LOUISE. Aqua? But aqua is only water, monsieur.

NEWTON. Water with a cabalistic sign after it, madam.

LOUISE. Ah, parfaitement. And this long magical word, what is it? Mee-kah-pah-nees. What is that?

NEWTON. Mycapaynis, madam. A very powerful life-giving substance.

LOUISE. It sounds wonderful. Is it harmless?

NEWTON. The most harmless substance in the world, madam, and the most precious.

LOUISE. Truly you are a great man, Monsieur Nieuton, in spite of your millions of miles. And this last word here?

NEWTON. Only sugar, to sweeten the micapanis, but with the cabalistic sign after it. Here is your love charm, madam. But it is not a potion: the apothecary will make it into pills for you.

LOUISE [*taking the paper and tucking it into the bosom of her dress*] Good. That is better, much better. It is so much easier to make men take pills than drink potions. And now, one thing more. You must swear to give this prescription to no other woman of the court. It is for me alone.

NEWTON. You have my word of honor, madam.

LOUISE. But a word of honor must be a gentleman's word of honor. You, monsieur, are a bourgeois. You must swear on your Bible.

NEWTON. My word is my word, madam. And the Bible must not be mixed up with the magic of micapanis.

LOUISE. Not black magic, is it? I could not touch that.

NEWTON. Neither black nor white, madam. Shall we say grey? But quite harmless, I assure you.

LOUISE. Good. And now I must make you a little present for your pills. How much shall it be?

NEWTON. Keep your money for the apothecary, madam: he will be amply satisfied with five shillings. I am sufficiently rewarded by the sound scientific advice you have given me from your friend Blaise Pascal. He was anticipated by an Englishman named Bacon, who was, however, no mathematician. You owe me nothing.

LOUISE. Shall I give one of the new golden guineas to the lady I shocked if I meet her on the stairs?

NEWTON. No. She would not take it.

LOUISE. How little you know the world, Monsieur! Nobody refuses a golden guinea.

NEWTON. You can try the experiment, madam. That

would be the advice of your friend Pascal. [*He goes to the door, and opens it for her*].

LOUISE. Perhaps I had better make it two guineas. She will never refuse that.

NEWTON [*at the door, calling*] Sally!

LOUISE [*with a gracious inclination of her head*] Monsieur—

NEWTON. I wish your Grace good morning.

SALLY [*at the door*] Yes, sir?

NEWTON. Shew her Grace the Duchess of Portsmouth to her chair or whatever it is.

LOUISE. Au plaisir de vous revoir, Monsieur le philosophe.

The Duchess goes out, Sally making her a rustic curtsey as she passes, and following her out, leaving Newton alone.

NEWTON [*greatly relieved*] Ouf!

He returns to his place at the table and to his Bible, which, helped by a marker, he opens at the last two chapters of the book of Daniel. He props his head on his elbows.

NEWTON. Twelve hundred and ninety days. And in the very next verse thirteen hundred and thirtyfive days. Five months difference! And the king's daughter of the south: who was she? And the king of the south? And he that cometh against him? And the vile person who obtains the kingdom by flatteries? And Michael? Who was Michael? [*He considers this a moment; then suddenly snatches a sheet of paper and writes furiously*].

SALLY [*throwing open the door, bursting with pride*] His Royal Highness the Duke of York.

The Duke, afterwards James II, comes in precipitately.

JAMES [*imperiously*] Where is his Majesty the King?

NEWTON [*rising in ungovernable wrath*] Sir: I neither know nor care where the King is. This is my house; and I demand to be left in peace in it. I am engaged in researches of the most sacred importance; and for them I require solitude. Do you hear, sir? solitude!

JAMES. Sir: I am the Duke of York, the King's brother.

NEWTON. I am Isaac Newton, the philosopher. I am also an Englishman; and my house is my castle. At least it was until this morning, when the whole court came here uninvited. Are there not palaces for you and the court to resort to? Go away.

JAMES. I know you. You are a follower of the arch infidel Galileo!

NEWTON. Take care, sir. In my house the great Galileo shall not be called an infidel by any Popish blockhead, prince or no prince, Galileo had more brains in his boots than you have in your whole body.

JAMES. Had he more brains in his boots than the Catholic Church? Than the Pope and all his cardinals, the greatest scholars of his day? Is there more learning in your head than in the libraries of the Vatican?

NEWTON. Popes and cardinals are abolished in the Church of England. Only a fool would set up these superstitious idolaters against the Royal Society, founded by your royal brother for the advancement of British science?

JAMES. A club of damnable heretics. I shall know how to deal with them.

NEWTON [*rising in a fury and facing him menacingly*] Will you leave my house, or shall I throw you out through the window?

JAMES. You throw me out! Come on, you scum of a grammar school.

They rush at one another, and in the scuffle fall on the floor, Newton uppermost. Charles comes in at his moment.

CHARLES. Odsfish, Mr Newton, whats this? A wrestling match?

Newton hastily rolls off James. The two combatants remain sitting on the floor, staring up at Charles.

CHARLES. And what the divvle are you doing here, Jamie? Why arnt you in Holland?

JAMES. I am here where I have been thrown by your friend and protégé, the infidel philosopher Newton.

CHARLES. Get up, man: dont play the fool. Mr Newton: your privilege with me does not run to the length of knocking my brother down. It is a serious matter to lay hands on a royal personage.

NEWTON. Sir: I had no intention of knocking your royal

brother down. He fell and dragged me down. My intention was only to throw him out of the window.

CHARLES. He could have left by the door, Mr Newton.

NEWTON. He could; but he would not, in spite of my repeated requests. He stayed here to heap insults on the immortal Galileo, whose shoe latchet he is unworthy to unloose.

He rises and confronts the King with dignity.

CHARLES. Will you get up, Jamie, and not sit on the floor grinning like a Jackanapes. Get up, I tell you.

JAMES [*rising*] You see what comes of frequenting the houses of your inferiors. They forget themselves and take liberties. And you encourage heretics. I do not.

CHARLES. Mr Newton: we are in your house and at your orders. Will you allow my brother and myself to have this room to ourselves awhile?

NEWTON. My house is yours, sir. I am a resolute supporter of the Exclusion Bill because I hope to prove that the Romish Church is the little horn of the fourth beast mentioned by the prophet Daniel. But the great day of wrath is not yet come. Your brother is welcome here as long as you desire it.

Newton goes out. Charles takes the armchair. When he is seated James takes Newton's chair at the table.

JAMES. That fellow is crazy. He called me a Popish blockhead. You see what comes of encouraging these Protestants. If you had a pennorth of spunk in you you would burn the lot.

CHARLES. What I want to know is what you are doing here when you should be in Holland. I am doing what I can to stop this Exclusion Bill and secure the crown for you when I die. I sent you to Holland so that your talent for making yourself unpopular might be exercised there and not here. Your life is in danger in London. You had no business to come back. Why have you done it?

JAMES. Charles: I am a prince.

CHARLES. Oh, do I not know it, God help you!

JAMES. Our father lost his head by compromising with Protestants, Republicans, Levellers and Atheists. What did he gain by it? They beheaded him. I am not going to share his fate by repeating that mistake. I am a Catholic; and I am civil to none but Catholics, however unpopular it may make me. When I am king—as I shall be, in my own right, and not by the leave of any Protestant parliamentary gang—I shall restore the Church and restore the monarchy: yes, the monarchy, Charles; for there has been no real Restoration: you are no king, cleverly as you play with these Whigs and Tories. That is because you have no faith, no principles: you dont believe in anything; and a man who doesnt believe in anything is afraid of everything. Youre a damned coward, Charles. I am not. When I am king I shall reign: these fellows shall find what a king's will is when he reigns by divine right. They will get it straight in the teeth then; and Europe will see them crumble up like moths in a candle flame.

CHARLES. It is a funny thing, Jamie, that you, who are clever enough to see that the monarchy is gone and that I keep the crown by my wits, are foolish enough to believe that you have only to stretch out your clenched fist and take it back again. I sometimes ask myself whether it would not be far kinder of me to push the Exclusion Bill through and save you from the fate of our father. They will have your head off inside of five years unless you jump into the nearest fishing smack and land in France.

JAMES. And leave themselves without a king again! Not they: they had enough of that under old Noll's Major-Generals. Noll knew how to rule: I will say that for him; and I thank him for the lesson. But when he died they had to send for us. When they bully you you give in to them and say that you dont want to go on your travels again. But by God, if they try to bully me I will threaten to go on my travels and leave them without a king. That is the way to bring them down on their marrowbones.

CHARLES. You could not leave them without a king. Protestant kings—Stuart kings—are six a penny in Europe today. The Dutch lad's grandfather-in-law was our grandfather. Your daughter Mary is married to him. The Elector of Hanover has the same hook on to grandfather James.

Both of them are rank Protestants and hardened soldiers, caring for nothing but fighting the French. Besides Mary there is her sister Anne, Church of England to the backbone. With the Protestants you do not succeed by divine right: they take their choice and send for you, just as they sent for me.

JAMES. Yes, if you look at it in that way and let them do it. Charles: you havnt the spirit of a king: that is what is the matter with you. As long as they let you have your women, and your dogs, and your pictures, and your music, and your chemical laboratory, you let them do as they like. The merry monarch: thats what you are.

CHARLES. Something new in monarchs, eh?

JAMES. Psha! A merry monarch is no monarch at all.

CHARLES. All the same, I must pack you off to Scotland. I cannot have you here until I prorogue parliament to get rid of the Exclusion Bill. And you will have to find a Protestant husband for Anne: remember that.

JAMES. You pretend you are packing me off to save me from my Catholic unpopularity. The truth is you are jealous of my popularity.

CHARLES. No, Jamie: I can beat you at that game. I am an agreeable sort of fellow: old Newcastle knocked that into me when I was a boy. Living at the Hague on two hundred and forty pounds a year finished my education in that respect. Now you, Jamie, became that very disagreeable character a man of principle. The people, who have all sorts of principles which they havnt gathered out of your basket, will never take to you until you go about shouting No Popery. And you will die rather than do that: wont you?

JAMES. Certainly I shall; and so, I trust, would you. Promise me you will die a Catholic, Charles.

CHARLES. I shall take care not to die in an upstart sect like the Church of England, and perhaps lose my place in Westminster Abbey when you are king. Your principles might oblige you to throw my carcase to the dogs. Meanwhile, however popular you may think yourself, you must go and be popular in Scotland.

JAMES. I am popular everywhere: thats what you dont

understand because you are not a fighting man; and I am. In the British Isles, Charles, nothing is more popular than the navy; and nobody is more popular than the admiral who has won a great naval victory. Thats what I have done, and you havnt. And that puts me ahead of you with the British people every time.

CHARLES. No doubt; but the British people do not make kings in England. The crown is in the hands of the damned Whig squirearchy who got rich by robbing the Church, and chopped off father's head, crown and all. They care no more for your naval victory than for a bunch of groundsel. They would not pay for the navy if we called it ship money, and let them know what they are paying for.

JAMES. I shall make them pay. I shall not be their puppet as you are. Do you think I will be in the pay of the king of France, whose bitter bread we had to eat in our childhood, and who left our mother without firewood in the freezing winter? And all this because these rebellious dogs will not disgorge enough of their stolen wealth to cover the cost of governing them! If you will not teach them their lesson they shall learn it from me.

CHARLES. You will have to take your money where you can get it, Jamie, as I do. French money is as good as English. King Louis gets little enough for it: I take care of that.

JAMES. Then you cheat him. How can you stoop?

CHARLES. I must. And I know that I must. To play the king as you would have me I should need old Noll's army; and they took good care I should not have that. They grudge me even the guards.

JAMES. Well, what old Noll could do I can do; and so could you if you had the pluck. I will have an army too.

CHARLES. Of Protestants?

JAMES. The officers will be Catholics. The rank and file will be what they are ordered to be.

CHARLES. Where will you get the money to pay them? Old Noll had the city of London and its money at his back.

JAMES. The army will collect the taxes. How does King Louis do it? He keeps the biggest army in Europe; and he keeps you into the bargain. He hardly knows what a parliament is. He dragoons the Protestants out of France into Spitalfields. I shall dragoon them out of Spitalfields.

CHARLES. Where to?

JAMES. To hell, or to the American plantations, whichever they prefer.

CHARLES. So you are going to be the English Louis, the British Roi Soleil, the sun king. This is a deuced foggy climate for sun kings, Jamie.

JAMES. So you think, Charles. But the British climate has nothing to do with it. What is it that nerves Louis to do all these things? The climate of the Catholic Church. His foot is on the rock of Saint Peter; and that makes him a rock himself.

CHARLES. Your son-in-law Dutch Billy is not afraid of him. And Billy's house is built, not on a rock, not even on the sands, but in the mud of the North Sea. Keep your eye on the Orangeman, Jamie.

JAMES. I shall keep my eye on your Protestant bastard Monmouth. Why do you make a pet of that worthless fellow? Know you not he is longing for your death so that he may have a try for the crown while this rascally Popish plot is setting the people against me?

CHARLES. For my death! What a thought! I grant you he has not the makings of a king in him: I am not blind to his weaknesses. But surely he is not heartless.

JAMES. Psha! there is not a plot in the kingdom to murder either of us that he is not at the bottom of.

CHARLES. He is not deep enough to be at the bottom of anything, Jamie.

JAMES. Then he is at the top. I forgive him for wanting to make an end of me: I am no friend of his. But to plot against you, his father! you, who have petted him and spoilt him and forgiven him treason after treason! for that I shall not forgive him, as he shall find if ever he falls into my hand.

CHARLES. Jamie: this is a dreadful suspicion to put into my mind. I thought the lad had abused my affection until it was exhausted; but it still can hurt. Heaven keep him out of your hand! that is all I can say. Absalom! O Absalom:

my son, my son!

JAMES. I am sorry, Charles; but this is what comes of bringing up your bastards as Protestants and making dukes of them.

CHARLES. Let me tell you a secret, Jamie: a king's secret. Peter the fisherman did not know everything. Neither did Martin Luther.

JAMES. Neither do you.

CHARLES. No; but I must do the best I can with what I know, and not with what Peter and Martin knew. Anyhow, the long and the short of it is that you must start for Scotland this very day, and stay there until I send you word that it is safe for you to come back.

JAMES. Safe! What are you afraid of, man? If you darent face these Protestant blackguards, is that any reason why I should run away from them?

CHARLES. You were talking just now about your popularity. Do you know who is the most popular man in England at present?

JAMES. Shaftesbury, I suppose. He is the Protestant hero just as Nelly is the Protestant whoor. I tell you Shaftesbury will turn his coat as often as you crack your whip. Why dont you crack it?

CHARLES. I am not thinking of Shaftesbury.

JAMES. Then who?

CHARLES. Oates.

JAMES. Titus Oates! A navy chaplain kicked out of the service for the sins of Sodom and Gomorrah! Are you afraid of him?

CHARLES. Yes. At present he is the most popular man in the kingdom. He is lodged in my palace at Whitehall with a pension of four hundred pounds a year.

JAMES. What!!!

CHARLES. And I, who am called a king, cannot get rid of him. This house is Isaac Newton's; and he can order you out and throw you out of the window if you dont go. But my house must harbor the vilest scoundrel in Europe while he parades in lawn sleeves through the street with his No Popery mob at his heels, and murders our best Catholic families with his brazen perjuries and his silly Popish plot that should not impose on a rabbit. No man with eyes in his head could look at the creature for an instant without seeing that he is only half human.

JAMES. Flog him through the town. Flog him to death. They can if they lay on hard enough and long enough. The same mob that now takes him for a saint will crowd to see the spectacle and revel in his roarings.

CHARLES. That will come, Jamie. I am hunting out his record; and your man Jeffries will see to it that the poor divvle shall have no mercy. But just now it is not Oates that we have to kill: the people would say that he was murdered by the Catholics and run madder than ever. They blame the Catholics now for the Great Fire of London and the plague. We must kill the Popish Plot first. When we have done that, God help Titus Oates! Meanwhile, away with you to Scotland and try your cat-o-ninetails on the Covenanters there.

JAMES. Well, I suppose I must, since England is governed by its mob instead of by its king. But I tell you, Charles, when I am king there shall be no such nonsense. You jeer at me and say that I am the protector of your life, because nobody will kill you to make me king; but I take that as the highest compliment you could pay me. This mob that your Protestant Republicans and Presbyterians and Levellers call the people of England will have to choose between King James the Second and King Titus Oates. And James and the Church—and there is only one real Church of God—will see to it that their choice will be Hobson's choice.

CHARLES. The people of England will have nothing to do with it. The real Levellers today, Jamie, are the lords and the rich squires—Cromwell's sort—and the moneyed men of the city. They will keep the people's noses to the grindstone no matter what happens. And their choice will be not between you and Titus Oates, but between your daughter Mary's Protestant husband and you.

JAMES. He will have to cross the seas to get here. And I, as Lord High Admiral of England, will meet him on the seas and sink him there. He is no great general on land: on water he is nothing. I have never been beaten at sea.

CHARLES. Jamie, Jamie: nothing frightens me so much as your simple stupid pluck, and your faith in Rome. You think you will have the Pope at your back because you are a Catholic. You are wrong: in politics the Pope is always a Whig, because every earthly monarch's court is a rival to the Vatican.

JAMES. Do you suppose that if Orange Billy, the head of the Protestant heresy in Europe, the anti-Pope you might call him, dared to interfere with me, a Catholic king, the Pope could take his part against me in the face of all Europe! How can you talk such nonsense? Do you think Mary would share the crown if he tore it from her father's head? Rochester called you the king that never said a foolish thing and never did a wise one; but it seems to me that you talk silly-clever nonsense all day, though you are too wise: that is, too big a coward, ever to risk a fight with the squirearchy. What are they in France? Lackeys round the throne at Versailles: not one of them dare look King Louis straight in the face. But in France there is a real king.

CHARLES. He has a real army and real generals. And taxes galore. Old Noll went one better than Louis: he was a general himself. And what a general! Preston, Dunbar, Worcester: we could do nothing against him though we had everything on our side, except him. I have been looking for his like ever since we came back. I sometimes wonder whether Jack Churchill has any military stuff in him.

JAMES. What! That henpecked booby! I suppose you know that he got his start in life as your Barbara's kept man?

CHARLES. I know that the poor lad risked breaking his bones by jumping out of Barbara's window when she was seducing him and I came along unexpectedly. I have always liked him for that.

JAMES. It was worth his while. She gave him five thousand pounds for it.

CHARLES. Yes: I had to find the money. I was tremendously flattered when I heard of it. I had no idea that Barbara put so high a price on my belief in her faithfulness, in which, by the way, I did not believe. Poor Barbara was never alone with a pretty fellow for five minutes without finding out how much of a man he was. I threw Churchill in her way purposely to keep her in good humor. What struck me most in the affair was that Jack bought an annuity with the money instead of squandering it as any other man of his age would have done. That was a sign of solid ability. He may be henpecked: what married man is not? But he is no booby.

JAMES. Meanness. Pure meanness. The Churchills never had a penny to bless themselves with. Jack got no more education than my groom.

CHARLES. Latin grammar is not much use on the battlefield, as we found out. Turenne found Jack useful enough in Spain; and Turenne was supposed to be France's greatest general. Your crown may depend on Jack: by the time I die he will be as old a soldier as Oliver was at Dunbar.

JAMES. Never fear. I shall buy him if he's worth it.

CHARLES. Or if you are worth it. Jack is a good judge of a winner.

JAMES. He has his price all the same.

CHARLES. All intelligent men have, Jamie.

JAMES. Psha! Dont waste your witticisms on me: they butter no parsnips. If he can pick a winner he had better pick me.

CHARLES. There are only two horses in the race now: the Protestant and the Catholic. I have to ride both at once.

JAMES. That was what Father tried to do. See what he got by it!

CHARLES. See what I get by it! Not much, perhaps; but I keep my head on my shoulders. It takes a man of brains to do that. Our father unfortunately tried his hand at being also a man of blood, as Noll called him. We Stuarts are no good at that game: Noll beat us at it every time. I hate blood and battles: I have seen too much of them to have any dreams of glory about them. I am, as you say, no king. To be what you call a king I lack military ambition; and I lack cruelty. I have to manage Protestants who are so frightfully cruel that I dare not interfere with Protestant judges who are merciless. The penalty for high treason is so abominable that only a divvle could have invented it, and a nation of divvles crowd to see it done. The only time I risked my crown was when I stopped them after they had butchered ten of the regicides: I could bear no more. They were not satisfied: they dug up the body of old Noll, and butchered it rather than have their horrible sport cut short.

JAMES. Serve the rascals right! A good lesson for them and their like. Dont be such a mollycoddle, Charles. What you need is a bit of my sea training to knock the nonsense out of you.

CHARLES. So you will try your luck as a man of blood, will you?

JAMES. I will do what is necessary. I will fight my enemies if they put me to it. I will take care that those who put me to it shall not die easy deaths.

CHARLES. Well, that will seem very natural to the mob. You will find plenty of willing tools. But I would not light the fires of Smithfield again if I were you. Your pet Jeffries would do it for you and enjoy it; but Protestants do not like being burnt alive.

JAMES. They will have to lump it if they fly in the face of God.

CHARLES. Oh, go to Scotland: go to Jericho. You sicken me. Go.

JAMES. Charles! We must not part like this. You know you always stand by me as far as you dare. I ought not to talk to you about government and kingcraft: you dont understand these matters and never will; and I do understand them. I have resolved again and again not to mention them to you; for after all we are brothers; and I love you in spite of all the times you have let me down with the Protestants. It is not your fault that you have no head for politics and no knowledge of human nature. You need not be anxious about me. I will leave for Scotland tomorrow. But I have business in London tonight that I will not postpone for fifty thousand Titus Oateses.

CHARLES. Business in London tonight! The one redeeming point in your character, Jamie, is that you are not a man of principle in the matter of women.

JAMES. You are quite wrong there: I am in all things a

man of principle and a good Catholic, thank God. But being human I am also a man of sin. I confess it; and I do my penances!

CHARLES. The women themselves are worse penances than any priest dare inflict on you. Try Barbara: a week with her is worse than a month in hell. But I have given up all that now. Nelly is a good little soul who amuses me. Louise manages my French affairs. She has French brains and manners, and is always a lady. But they are now my friends only: affectionate friends, family friends, nothing else. And they alone are faithful to the elderly king. I am fifty, Jamie, fifty: dont forget that. And women got hold of me when I was fourteen, thirtysix years ago. Do you suppose I have learnt nothing about women and what you call love in that time? You still have love affairs: I have none. However, I am not reproaching you: I am congratulating you on being still young and green enough to come all the way from Holland for a night in London.

Mrs Basham returns, much perturbed.

MRS BASHAM. Mr Rowley: I must tell you that I cannot receive any more of your guests. I have not knives nor plates nor glasses enough. I have had to borrow chairs from next door. Your valet, Mr Chiffinch, tells who ever has any business with you this morning to come on here. Mr Godfrey Kneller, the new Dutch painter, with a load of implements connected with his trade, had got in in spite of me: he heard the noise your people were making. There are the two ladies and the player woman, and yourself and your royal brother and Mr Fox and the painter. That makes seven; and Mr Newton makes eight and I make nine. I have nothing to offer them but half a decanter of sherry that was opened last Easter, and the remains of a mouldy cake. I have sent Sally out with orders that will run away with a fortnight's housekeeping money; and that wont be half what theyll expect. I thought they were all going away when they came downstairs; but the French lady wanted to look through Mr Newton's telescope; and the jealous lady wouldnt leave until the French lady left; and the player woman is as curious as a magpie and makes herself as much at home as if she lived here. It has ended in their all staying. And now Mr Newton is explaining everything and shewing off his telescope and never thinking what I am to do with them! How am I to feed them?

CHARLES. Dont feed them, Mrs Basham. Starve them out.

MRS BASHAM. Oh no: I cant do that. What would they think of us? Mr Newton has his position to keep up.

CHARLES. It is the judgment of heaven on you for turning away my pretty spaniels from your door this morning.

MRS BASHAM. There were twelve of them, sir.

CHARLES. You would have found them much better company than nine human beings. But never mind. Sally will tell all the tradesmen that Mr Newton is entertaining me and my brother. They will call themselves Purveyors to his Majesty the King. Credit will be unlimited.

JAMES. Remember that this is Friday: a fast day. All I need is three or four different kinds of fish.

MRS BASHAM. No, sir: in this house you will have to be content with a Protestant dinner. Jack the fish hawker is gone. But he left us a nice piece of cod; and thats all youll get, sir.

CHARLES. Jamie: we must clear out and take the others with us. It seems we cannot visit anyone without ruining them.

JAMES. Pooh! What can a few pounds more or less matter to anybody?

CHARLES. I can remember when they meant a divvle of a lot to me, and to you too. Let us get back to Newmarket.

MRS BASHAM. No, sir: Mr Newton would not like that: he knows his duties as your host. And if you will excuse me saying so, sir: you all look as if a plain wholesome dinner would do you no harm for once in a way. By your leave I will go to look after it. I must turn them all out of the laboratory and send them up here while I lay the table there.

She goes out.

JAMES. "A nice piece of cod!" Among nine people!

CHARLES. "Isnt that a dainty dish to set before a king?"

Your fast will be a real fast, Jamie, for the first time in your life.

JAMES. You lie. My penances are all real.

CHARLES. Well, a hunk of bread, a lump of cheese, and a bottle of ale are enough for me or for any man at this hour.

All the rest come back except Mrs Basham, Barbara, and Newton. Fox comes first.

FOX. I have made eight new friends. But has the Lord sent them to me? Such friends! [*He takes his old seat, much perplexed*].

NELL [*coming in*] Oh, Rowley darling, they want me to recite my big speech from The Indian Emperor. But I cant do that without proper drapery: its classical. [*Going to the Duke*] And what is my Jamie doing here?

LOUISE [*taking a chair from the wall and planting it at Charles's right, familiarly close*] Why not give us a prologue? Your prologues are your best things. [*She sits*].

CHARLES and JAMES. Yes, yes: a prologue.

All are now seated, except Nell.

NELL. But I cant do a prologue unless I am in breeches.

FOX [*rising*] No. Eleanor Gwyn: how much more must I endure from you? I will not listen to a prologue that can be spoken only by a woman in breeches. And I warn you that when I raise my voice to heaven against mummery, whether in playhouse or steeplehouse, I can drown and dumb the loudest ribald ranter.

CHARLES. Pastor: Mistress Gwyn is neither a ribald nor a ranter. The plays and prologues in which she is famous are the works of the greatest poet of the age: the poet Laureate, John Dryden.

FOX. If he has given to the playhouse talents that were given to him for the service of God, his guilt is the deeper.

CHARLES. Have you considered, Pastor, that the playhouse is a place where two or three are gathered together?

NELL. Not when I am playing, Rowley darling. Two or three hundred, more likely.

FOX [*resuming his seat in the deepest perplexity*] Sir:

you are upsetting my mind. You have forced me to make friends with this player woman; and now you would persuade me that the playhouse is as divine as my meeting house. I find your company agreeable to me, but very unsettling.

CHARLES. The settled mind stagnates, Pastor. Come! Shall I give you a sample of Mr Dryden at his best?

NELL. Oh yes, Rowley darling: give us your pet speech from Aurengzebe.

LOUISE. Yes yes. He speaks it beautifully. He is almost as good an actor as King Louis; and he has really more of the grand air.

CHARLES. Thank you, Louise. Next time leave out the almost. My part is more difficult than that of Louis.

JAMES. Pray silence for his Majesty the King, who is going to make a fool of himself to please the Quaker.

CHARLES. Forgive Jamie, ladies and gentlemen. He will give you his own favorite recitation presently; but the King comes first. Now listen. [*He rises. They all rise, except Fox*]. No, pray. My audience must be seated. [*They sit down again*].

Charles recites the pessimistic speech from Aurengzebe as follows:

When I consider life, 'tis all a cheat;
Yet, fooled with hope, men favor the deceit;
Trust on, and think tomorrow will repay:
Tomorrow's falser than the former day;
Lies worse; and, while it says we shall be blest
With some new choice, cuts off what we possessed.
Strange cozenage! None would live past years again;
Yet all hope pleasure in what yet remain;
And from the dregs of life think to receive
What the first sprightly running could not give.
I'm tired of waiting for this chemic gold
Which fools us young, and beggars us when old.

Nell and Louise applaud vigorously.

CHARLES. What do you think of that, Pastor? [*He sits*].

FOX. It is the cry of a lost soul from the bottomless blackness of its despair. Never have I heard anything so terrible. This man has never lived. I must seek him out and shew him the light and the truth.

NELL. Tut tut, George! The man in the play is going to be killed. To console himself he cries Sour Grapes: that is all. And now what shall I give you?

JAMES. Something oldfashioned. Give him a bit of Shakespear.

NELL. What! That author the old actors used to talk about. Kynaston played women in his plays. I dont know any. We cannot afford them nowadays. They require several actors of the first quality; and—would you believe it, George?—those laddies will not play now for less than fifteen shillings a week.

FOX [*starting up again*] Fifteen shillings a week to a player when the servants of God can scarce maintain themselves alive by working at mechanical trades! Such wickedness will bring a black judgment on the nation. Charles Stuart: have you no regard for your soul that you suffer such things to be done?

CHARLES. You would not grudge these poor fellows their fifteen shillings if you knew what women cost.

FOX. What manner of world is this that I have come into? Is virtue unknown here, or is it despised? [*He gives it up, and relapses into his seat*].

JAMES. Mr Dryden has an answer for that. [*He recites, seated*].

How vain is virtue which directs our ways
Through certain danger to uncertain praise!
The world is made for the bold impious man
Who stops at nothing, seizes all he can.
Justice to merit does weak aid afford;
She trusts her balance, and ignores her sword.
Virtue is slow to take whats not her own,
And, while she long consults, the prize is gone.

FOX. I take no exception to this. I have too good reason to know that it is true. But beware how you let these bold impious fellows extinguish hope in you. Their day is short; but the inner light is eternal.

JAMES. I am safe in the bosom of my Church, Pastor.

LOUISE. Take the gentleman's mind off his inner light, Nell. Give us a speech.

NELL. They dont want a speech from me. Rowley began talking about speeches because he wanted to do one himself. And now His Highness the Duke of York must have his turn.

JAMES. Are we poor devils of princes not to have any of the good things, nor do any of the pleasant things, because we are Royal Highnesses? Were you not freer and happier when you sold oranges in Drury Lane than you are now as a court lady?

FOX. Did you sell oranges in Drury Lane?

NELL. They say I did. The people like to believe I did. They love me for it. I say nothing.

CHARLES. Come! Give us one of Cydara's speeches from The Indian Emperor. It was in that that you burst on the world as the ambitious orange girl.

NELL. A wretched part: I had to stand mum on the stage for hours while the others were spouting. Mr Dryden does not understand how hard that is. Just listen to this, the longest speech I had.

May I believe my eyes! What do I see?
Is this her hate to him? her love to me?
'Tis in my breast she sheathes her dagger now.
False man: is this thy faith? Is this thy vow?

Then somebody says something.

CHARLES.

What words, dear saint, are these I hear you use?
What faith? what voice? are those which you accuse?

NELL. "Those which you accuse": thats my cue.

More cruel than the tiger o'er his spile
And falser than the weeping crocodile
Can you add vanity to guilt, and take
A pride to hear the conquests which you make?
Go: publish your renown: let it be said
The woman that you love you have betrayed—

Rowley darling: I cannot go on if you keep laughing at me. If only Mr Dryden had given me some really great lines, like the ones he gave to Montezuma. Listen.

Still less and less my boiling spirits flow
And I grow stiff, as cooling metals do.
Farewell, Almira.

FOX. Now do you tell me that living men and women, created by God in His likeness and not in that of gibbering apes, can be bribed to utter such trash, and that others will pay to hear them do it when they will not enter a meeting house for a penny in the plate to hear the words of God Himself? What society is this I am in? I must be dreaming that I am in hell.

NELL. George: you are forgetting yourself. You should have applauded me. I will recite no more for you. [*She takes a chair from the wall and seats herself beside Louise, on her right*].

CHARLES. He does not understand, Nell. Tell him the story of the play, and why Montezuma says such extravagant things.

NELL. But how can I, Rowley darling? I dont know what it is all about: I know only my part and my cue. All I can say is that when Montezuma speaks those lines he drops dead.

FOX. Can you wonder that he does so? I should drop dead myself if I heard such fustian pass my lips.

JAMES. Is it worse than the fustian that passes the lips of the ranters in your conventicles?

FOX. I cannot deny it: the preachers are a greater danger than the players. I had not thought of this before. Again you unsettle my mind. There is one Jeremy Collier who swears he will write such a book on the profaneness and immorality of the stage as will either kill the theatre or shame it into decency; but these lines just uttered by Eleanor Gwyn are not profane and immoral: they are mad and foolish.

LOUISE. All the less harmful, monsieur. They are not meant to be taken seriously; and no one takes them so. But your Huguenot ranters pretend to be inspired; and foolish people are deluded by them. And what sort of world would they make for us if they got the upper hand? Can you name a single pleasure that they would leave us to make life worth living?

FOX. It is not pleasure that makes life worth living. It is life that makes pleasure worth having. And what pleasure is better than the pleasure of holy living?

JAMES. I have been in Geneva, blasphemously called the City of God under that detestable Frenchman Calvin, who, thank God, has by now spent a century in hell. And I can testify that he left the wretched citizens only one worldly pleasure.

CHARLES. Which one was that?

JAMES. Moneymaking.

CHARLES. Odsfish! that was clever of him. It is a very satisfying pleasure, and one that lasts til death.

LOUISE. It does not satisfy me.

CHARLES. You have never experienced it, Louise. You spend money: you do not make it. You spend ten times as much as Nelly; but you are not ten times as happy. If you made ten times as much as she, you would never tire of it and never ask for anything better.

LOUISE. Charles: if I spent one week making money or even thinking about it instead of throwing it away with both hands all my charm would be gone. I should become that dull thing, a plain woman. My face would be full of brains instead of beauty. And you would send me back to France by the next ship, as you sent Barbara.

CHARLES. What if I did? You will soon be tired of me; for I am an ugly old fellow. But you would never tire of moneymaking.

NELL. Now the Lord be praised, my trade is one in which I can make money without losing my good looks!

LOUISE [*to Charles*] If you believe what you say, why do you not make money yourself instead of running after women?

CHARLES. Because there is a more amusing occupation for me.

LOUISE. I have not seen you practise it, Charles. What is it?

CHARLES. Kingcraft.

JAMES. Of which you have not the faintest conception.

CHARLES. Like Louise, you have not seen me practise it. But I am King of England; and my head is still on my shoulders.

NELL. Rowley darling: you must learn to keep King Charles's head out of your conversation. You talk too much of him.

CHARLES. Why is it that we always talk of my father's head and never of my great grandmother's? She was by all accounts a pretty woman; but the Protestants chopped her head off in spite of Elizabeth. They had Strafford's head off in spite of my father. And then they had his own off. I am not a bit like him; but I have more than a touch in me of my famous grandfather Henry the Fourth of France. And he died with a Protestant's dagger in his heart: the deadliest sort of Protestant: a Catholic Protestant. There are such living paradoxes. They burnt the poor wretch's hand off with the dagger in it, and then tore him to pieces with galloping horses. But Henry lay dead all the same. The Protestants will have you, Jamie, by hook or crook: I foresee that: they are the real men of blood. But they shall not have me. I shall die in my bed, and die King of England in spite of them.

FOX. This is not kingcraft: it is chicanery. Protestantism gives the lie to itself: it overthrows the Roman Church and immediately builds itself another nearer home and makes you the head of it, though it is now plain to me that your cleverness acknowledges no Church at all. You are right there: Churches are snares of the divvle. But why not follow the inner light that has saved you from the Churches? Be neither Catholic nor Protestant, Whig nor Tory: throw your crown into the gutter and be a Friend: then all the rest shall be added to you.

They all laugh at him except Charles.

CHARLES. A crown is not so easy to get rid of as you think, Pastor. Besides, I have had enough of the gutter: I prefer Whitehall.

JAMES [*to Fox*] You would like to have a king for your follower, eh?

FOX. I desire Friends, not followers. I am simple in my

tastes. I am not schooled and learned as you two princes are.

CHARLES. Thank your stars for that, Pastor: you have nothing to unlearn.

FOX. That is well said. Too often have I found that a scholar is one whose mind is choked with rubbish that should never have been put there. But how do you come to know this? Things come to my knowledge by the grace of God; yet the same things have come to you who live a most profane life and have no sign of grace at all.

CHARLES. You and I are mortal men, Pastor. It is not possible for us to differ very greatly. You have to wear leather breeches lest you be mistaken for me.

Barbara storms in with a sheet of drawing paper in her hand.

BARBARA [*thrusting the paper under Charles's nose*] Do you see this?

CHARLES [*scrutinizing it admiringly*] Splendid! Has Mr Kneller done this? Nobody can catch a likeness as he can.

BARBARA. Likeness! You have bribed him to insult me. It makes me look a hundred.

CHARLES. Nonsense, dear. It is you to the life. What do you say, Jamie? [*He hands the drawing to James*].

JAMES. It's you, duchess. He has got you, wrinkle for wrinkle.

BARBARA. You say this to my face! You, who have seen my portrait by Lilly!

NELL. You were younger then, darling.

BARBARA. Who asked you for your opinion, you jealous cat?

CHARLES. Sit down; and dont be silly, Barbara. A woman's face does not begin to be interesting until she is our age.

BARBARA. Our age! You old wreck, do you dare pretend that you are as young as I am?

CHARLES. I am only fifty, Barbara. But we are both getting on.

BARBARA. Oh! [*With a scream of rage she tears the drawing to fragments and stamps on them*].

CHARLES. Ah, that was wicked of you: you have destroyed a fine piece of work. Go back to France. I tell you I am tired of your tantrums.

Barbara, intimidated, but with a defiant final stamp on the drawing, flings away behind James to one of the chairs against the cupboards, and sits there sulking.

Newton comes in from the garden, followed by Godfrey Kneller, a Dutchman of 34, *well dressed and arrogant. They are both almost as angry as Barbara.*

NEWTON. Mr Kneller: I will dispute with you no more. You do not understand what you are talking about.

KNELLER. Sir: I must tell you in the presence of His Majesty you are a most overweening, a most audacious man. You presume to teach me my profession.

CHARLES. What is the matter, Mr Newton?

NEWTON. Let it pass, Mr Rowley. This painter has one kind of understanding: I have another. There is only one course open to us both; and that is silence. [*Finding his chair occupied by the Duke of York he takes another from beside Barbara and seats himself at the side of the table on the Duke's left*].

CHARLES. Mr Newton is our host, Mr Kneller; and he is a very eminent philosopher. Will you not paint his picture for me? That can be done in silence.

KNELLER. I will paint his picture if your Majesty so desires. He has an interesting head: I should have drawn it this morning had not Her Grace of Cleveland insisted on my drawing her instead. But how can an interesting head contain no brain: that is the question.

CHARLES. Odsfish, man, he has the greatest brain in England.

KNELLER. Then he is blinded by his monstrous conceit. You shall judge between us, sir. Am I or am I not the greatest draughtsman in Europe?

CHARLES. You are certainly a very skilful draughtsman, Mr Kneller.

KNELLER. Can anyone here draw a line better than I?

CHARLES. Nobody here can draw a line at all, except the Duchess of Cleveland, who draws a line at nothing.

BARBARA. Charles—

CHARLES. Be quiet, Barbara. Do you presume to contradict your King.

KNELLER. If there is a science of lines, do I not understand it better than anyone?

CHARLES. Granted, Mr Kneller. What then?

KNELLER. This man here, this crazy and conceited philosopher, dares to assert in contradiction of me, of ME! that a right line is a straight line, and that everything that moves moves in a straight line unless some almighty force bends it from its path. This, he says, is the first law of motion. He lies.

CHARLES. And what do you say, Mr Kneller?

KNELLER. Sir: I do not say: I know. The right line, the line of beauty, is a curve. My hand will not draw a straight line: I have to stretch a chalked string on my canvas and pluck it. Will you deny that your duchess here is as famous for her beauty as the Psyche of the divine Raphael? Well, there is not a straight line in her body: she is all curves.

BARBARA [*outraged, rising*] Decency, fellow! How dare you?

CHARLES. It is true, Barbara. I can testify to it.

BARBARA. Charles: you are obscene. The impudence! [*She sits*].

KNELLER. The beauty, madam. Clear your mind of filth. There is not a line drawn by the hand of the Almighty, from the rainbow in the skies to the house the snail carries on his back, that is not a curve, and a curve of beauty. Your apple fell in a curve.

NEWTON. I explained that.

KNELLER. You mistake explanations for facts: all you science-mongers do. The path of the world curves, as you yourself have shewn; and as it whirls on its way it would leave your apple behind if the apple fell in a straight line. Motion in a curve is the law of nature; and the law of nature is the law of God. Go out into your garden and throw a stone straight if you can. Shoot an arrow from a bow, a bullet from a pistol, a cannon ball from the mightiest cannon the King can lend you, and though you had the strength of

Hercules, and gunpowder more powerful than the steam which hurls the stones from Etna in eruption, yet cannot you make your arrow or your bullet fly straight to its mark.

NEWTON [*terribly perturbed*] This man does not know what he is saying. Take him away; and leave me in peace.

CHARLES. What he says calls for an answer, Mr Newton.

JAMES. The painter is right. A cannon ball flies across the sea in curves like the arches of a bridge, hop, hop, hop. But what does it matter whether it flies straight or crooked provided it hits between wind and water?

NEWTON. To you, admiral, it matters nothing. To me it makes the difference between reason and madness.

JAMES. How so?

NEWTON. Sir: if what this man believes be true, then not only is the path of the cannon ball curved, but space is curved; time is curved; the universe is curved.

KNELLER. Of course it is. Why not?

NEWTON. Why not! Only my life's work turned to waste, vanity, folly. This comes of admitting strangers to break into my holy solitude with their diabolical suggestions. But I am rightly rebuked for this vice of mine that led me to believe that I could construct a universe with empty figures. In future I shall do nothing but my proper work of interpreting the scriptures. Leave me to that work and to my solitude. [*Desperately, clutching his temples*] Begone, all of you. You have done mischief enough for one morning.

CHARLES. But, Mr Newton, may we not know what we have done to move you thus? What diabolical suggestions have we made? What mischief have we done?

NEWTON. Sir: you began it, you and this infidel quaker. I have devoted months of my life to the writing of a book—a chronology of the world—which would have cost any other man than Isaac Newton twenty years hard labor.

CHARLES. I have seen that book, and been astounded at the mental power displayed in every page of it.

NEWTON. You may well have been, Mr Rowley. And now what have you and Mr Fox done to that book? Reduced it to a monument of the folly of Archbishop Ussher, who dated the creation of the world at four thousand and four, B.C., and of my stupidity in assuming that he had proved his case. My book is nonsense from beginning to end. How could I, who have calculated that God deals in millions of miles of infinite space, be such an utter fool as to limit eternity, which has neither beginning nor end, to a few thousand years? But this man Fox, without education, without calculation, without even a schoolboy's algebra, knew this when I, who was born one of the greatest mathematicians in the world, drudged over my silly book for months, and could not see what was staring me in the face.

JAMES. Well, why howl about it? Bring out another edition and confess that your Protestant mathematics are a delusion and a snare, and your Protestant archbishops impostors.

NEWTON. You do not know the worst, sir. I have another book in hand: one which should place me in line with Kepler, Copernicus, and Galileo as a master astronomer, and as the completer of their celestial systems. Can you tell me why the heavenly bodies in their eternal motion do not move in straight lines, but always in ellipses?

CHARLES. I understand that this is an unsolved problem of science. I certainly cannot solve it.

NEWTON. I have solved it by the discovery of a force in nature which I call gravitation. I have accounted for all the celestial movements by it. And now comes this painter, this ignorant dauber who, were it to save his soul—if he has a soul—could not work out the simplest equation, or as much as conceive an infinite series of numbers! this fellow substitutes for my first law of motion—straight line motion—motion in a curve.

JAMES. So bang goes your second volume of Protestant philosophy! Squashed under Barbara's outlines.

BARBARA. I will not have my outlines discussed by men. I am not a heathen goddess: I am a Christian lady. Charles always encourages infidels and libertines to blaspheme. And now he encourages them to insult me. I will not bear it.

CHARLES. Do not be an idiot, Barbara: Mr Kneller is paying you the greatest compliment in taking you for a model of the universe. The choice would seem to be between a universe of Barbara's curves and a universe of straight lines seduced from their straightness by some purely mathematical attraction. The facts seem to be on the side of the painter. But in a matter of this kind can I, as founder of the Royal Society, rank the painter as a higher authority than the philosopher?

KNELLER. Your Majesty: the world must learn from its artists because God made the world as an artist. Your philosophers steal all their boasted discoveries from the artists; and then pretend they have deduced them from figures which they call equations, invented for that dishonest purpose. This man talks of Copernicus, who pretended to discover that the earth goes round the sun instead of the sun going round the earth. Sir: Copernicus was a painter before he became an astronomer. He found astronomy easier. But his discovery was made by the great Italian painter Leonardo, born twentyone years before him, who told all his intimates that the earth is a moon of the sun.

NEWTON. Did he prove it?

KNELLER. Man: artists do not prove things. They do not need to. They KNOW them.

NEWTON. This is false. Your notion of a spherical universe is borrowed from the heathen Ptolemy, from all the magicians who believed that the only perfect figure is the circle.

KNELLER. Just what such blockheads would believe. The circle is a dead thing like a straight line: no living hand can draw it: you make it by twirling a pair of dividers. Take a sugar loaf and cut it slantwise, and you will get hyperbolas and parabolas, ellipses and ovals, which Leonardo himself could not draw, but which any fool can make with a knife and a lump of sugar. I believe in none of these mechanical forms. The line drawn by the artist's hand, the line that flows, that strikes, that speaks, that reveals! that is the line that shews the divine handiwork.

CHARLES. So you, too, are a philosopher, Mr Kneller!

KNELLER. Sir: when a man has the gift of a painter, that qualification is so magical that you cannot think of him as anything else. Who thinks of Leonardo as an engineer? of Michael Angelo as an inventor or a sonneteer? of me as a scholar and a philosopher? These things are all in our day's work: they come to us without thinking. They are trifles beside our great labor of creation and interpretation.

JAMES. I had a boatswain once in my flagship who thought he knew everything.

FOX. Perhaps he did. Divine grace takes many strange forms. I smell it in this painter. I have met it in common sailors like your boatswain. The cobbler thinks there is nothing like leather—

NELL. Not when you make it into breeches instead of boots, George.

BARBARA. Be decent, woman. One does not mention such garments in well-bred society.

NELL. Orange girls and players and such like poor folk think nothing of mentioning them. They have to mend them, and sometimes to make them; so they have an honest knowledge of them, and are not ashamed like fine ladies who have only a dishonest knowledge of them.

CHARLES. Be quiet, Nelly: you are making Barbara blush.

NELL. Thats more than you have ever been able to do, Rowley darling.

BARBARA. It is well for you that you have all these men to protect you, mistress. Someday when I catch you alone I'll make you wish you had ten pairs of leather breeches on you.

CHARLES. Come come! no quarrelling.

NELL. She began it, Rowley darling.

CHARLES. No matter who began it, no quarrelling, I command.

LOUISE. Charles: the men have been quarrelling all the morning. Does your command apply to them too?

CHARLES. Their quarrels are interesting, Louise.

NELL. Are they? They bore me to distraction.

CHARLES. Much blood has been shed for them; and much more will be after we are gone.

BARBARA. Oh, do not preach, Charles. Leave that to this person who is dressed partly in leather. It is his profession:

it is not yours.

CHARLES. The Protestants will not let me do anything else, my dear. But come! Mr Newton has asked us to leave his house many times. And we must not forget that he never asked us to come into it. But I have a duty to fulfil before we go. I must reconcile him with Mr Kneller, who must paint his portrait to hang in the rooms of the Royal Society.

KNELLER. It is natural that your Majesty should desire a work of mine for the Society. And this man's head is unusual, as one would expect from his being a philosopher: that is, half an idiot. I trust your Majesty was pleased with my sketch of Her Grace of Cleveland.

BARBARA. Your filthy caricature of Her Grace of Cleveland is under your feet. You are walking on it.

KNELLER [*picking up a fragment and turning it over to identify it*] Has the King torn up a work of mine? I leave the country this afternoon.

CHARLES. I would much sooner have torn up Magna Carta. Her Grace tore it up herself.

KNELLER. It is a strange fact, your Majesty, that no living man or woman can endure his or her portrait if it tells all the truth about them.

BARBARA. You lie, you miserable dauber. When our dear Peter Lilly, who has just died, painted me as I really am, did I destroy his portrait? But he was a great painter; and you are fit only to whitewash unmentionable places.

CHARLES. Her Grace's beauty is still so famous that we are all tired of it. She is the handsomest woman in England. She is also the stupidest. Nelly is the wittiest: she is also the kindest. Louise is the loveliest and cleverest. She is also a lady. I should like to have portraits of all three as they are now, not as Lilly painted them.

LOUISE. No, Charles: I do not want to have the whole truth about me handed down to posterity.

NELL. Same here. I prefer the orange girl.

KNELLER. I see I shall not succeed in England as a painter. My master Rembrandt did not think a woman worth painting until she was seventy.

NELL. Well, you shall paint me when I am seventy. In

the theatre the young ones are beginning to call me Auntie! When they call me Old Mar Gwyn I shall be ready for you; and I shall look my very best then.

CHARLES. What about your portrait, Mr Fox? You have been silent too long.

FOX. I am dumbfounded by this strange and ungodly talk. To you it may seem mere gossip; but to me it is plain that this painter claims that his hand is the hand of God.

KNELLER. And whose hand is it if not the hand of God? You need hands to scratch your heads and carry food to your mouths. That is all your hands mean to you. But the hand that can draw the images of God and reveal the soul in them, and is inspired to do this and nothing else even if he starves and is cast off by his father and all his family for it: is not his hand the hand used by God, who, being a spirit without body, parts or passions, has no hands?

FOX. So the men of the steeplehouse say; but they lie. Has not God a passion for creation? Is He not all passion of that divine nature?

KNELLER. Sir: I do not know who you are; but I will paint your portrait.

CHARLES. Bravo! We are getting on. How about your portrait, Mr Newton?

NEWTON. Not by a man who lives in a curved universe. He would distort my features.

LOUISE. Perhaps gravitation would distort them equally, Mr Newton.

CHARLES. That is very intelligent of you, Louise.

BARBARA. It takes some intelligence to be both a French spy and a bluestocking. I thank heaven for my stupidity, as you call it.

CHARLES. Barbara: must I throw you downstairs?

LOUISE. In France they call me the English spy. But this is the first time I have been called a bluestocking. All I meant was that Mr Kneller and Mr Newton seem to mean exactly the same thing; only one calls it beauty and the other gravitation; so they need not quarrel. The portrait will be the same both ways.

NEWTON. Can he measure beauty?

KNELLER. No. I can paint a woman's beauty; but I cannot measure it in a pint pot. Beauty is immeasurable.

NEWTON. I can measure gravitation. Nothing exists until it is measured. Fine words are nothing. Do you expect me to go to the Royal Society and tell them that the orbits of a planet are curved because painters think them prettier so? How much are they curved? This man cannot tell you. I can. Where will they be six months hence? He cannot tell you. I can. All he has to say is that the earth is a moon of the sun and that the line of beauty is a curve. Can he measure the path of the moon? Can he draw the curve?

KNELLER. I can draw your portrait. Can you draw mine?

NEWTON. Yes, with a camera obscura; and if I could find a chemical salt sensitive to light I could fix it. Some day portraits will be made at the street corners for sixpence apiece.

KNELLER. A looking glass will make your portrait for nothing. It makes the duchess's portrait fifty times a day.

BARBARA. It does not. I dont look at myself in the glass fifty times a day. Charles never passes one without looking at himself. I have watched him.

CHARLES. It rebukes my vanity every time, Barbara. I am an ugly fellow; yet I always think of myself as an Adonis.

LOUISE. You are not so ugly as you think, Charles. You were an ugly baby; and your wicked mother told you so. You have never got over it. But when I was sent to England to captivate you with my baby face, it was you who captivated me with your seventy inches and your good looks.

BARBARA. Ay, flatter him, flatter him: he loves it.

CHARLES. I cannot bear this. The subject is to be dropped.

LOUISE. But, Charles—

CHARLES. No, no, No. Not a word more. The King commands it.

Dead silence. They sit as if in church, except Fox, who chafes at the silence.

FOX. In the presence of this earthly king all you great nobles become dumb flunkeys. What will you be when the

King of Kings calls you from your graves to answer for your lives?

NELL. Trust you, George, to put in a cheerful word. Rowley darling: may we all stop being dumb flunkeys and be human beings again?

CHARLES. Mr Rowley apologizes for his lapse into royalty. Only, the King's person is not to be discussed.

LOUISE. But, Charles, I love you when you put on your royalty. My king, Louis Quatorze, le grand monarque, le roi soleil, never puts off his royalty for a moment even in the most ridiculous circumstances.

BARBARA. Yes; and he looks like a well-to-do grocer, and will never look like anything else.

LOUISE. You would not dare to say so at Versailles, or even to think so. He is always great; and his greatness makes us great also. But it is true that he is not six feet high, and that the grand manner is not quite natural to him. Charles can do it so much better when he chooses. Charles: why dont you choose?

CHARLES. I prefer to keep the crown and the grand manner up my sleeve until I need them. Louis and I played together when we were boys. We know each other too well to be pleasant company; so I take care to keep out of his way. Besides, Louise, when I make you all great you become terrible bores. I like Nelly because nothing can make a courtier of her. Do you know why?

BARBARA. Because the orange girl has the gutter in her blood.

CHARLES. Not at all. Tell her the reason, Nell.

NELL. I dont know it, Rowley darling. I never was an orange girl; but I have the gutter in my blood all right. I think I have everything in my blood; for when I am on the stage I can be anything you please, orange girl or queen. Or even a man. But I dont know the reason why. So you can tell it to her, Rowley darling, if you know it.

CHARLES. It is because in the theatre you are a queen. I tell you the world is full of kings and queens and their little courts. Here is Pastor Fox, a king in his meeting house, though his meetings are against the law. Here is Mr Newton, a king in the new Royal Society. Here is Godfrey Kneller: a king among painters. I can make you duchesses and your sons dukes; but who would be mere dukes or duchesses if they could be kings and queens?

NELL. Dukes will be six a penny if you make all Barbara's sons dukes.

BARBARA. Oh! My sons have gentle blood in their veins, not gutter dirt.

CHARLES. For shame, Nelly! It was illbred of you to reproach her Grace for the most amiable side of her character.

NELL. I beg pardon. God forgive me, I am no better myself.

BARBARA. No better! You impudent slut.

NELL. Well, no worse, if you like. One little duke is enough for me.

LOUISE. Change the subject, Charles. What you were saying about little kings and queens being everywhere was very true. You are very spiritual.

BARBARA. Ha ha! Ha ha ha! He spiritual!

LOUISE. Clever, you call it. I am always in trouble with my English. And Charles is too lazy to learn French properly, though he lived in France so long.

BARBARA. If you mean clever, he is as clever as fifty foxes.

FOX. He may be fifty times as clever as I; but so are many of the blackest villains. Value him rather for his flashes of the inner light? Did he not stop the butchering of the regicides on the ground that if he punished them they could never punish themselves? That was what made me his loyal subject.

BARBARA. I did not mean fifty of you: I meant real foxes. He is so clever that he can always make me seem stupid when it suits him: that is, when I want anything he wont give me. He is as stingy as a miser.

CHARLES. You are like a dairymaid: you think there is no end to a king's money. Here is my Nelly, who is more careful of my money than she is of her own. Well, when I am dying, and all the rest of you are forgotten, my last thought will be of Nelly.

NELL. Rowley darling: dont make me cry. I am not the only one. Louise is very thoughtful about money.

BARBARA. Yes: she knows exactly how much he has: she gets it for him from the King of France.

LOUISE. This subject of conversation is in the worst possible taste. Charles: be a king again; and forbid it.

CHARLES. Nobody but Barbara would have introduced it. I forbid it absolutely.

Mrs Basham returns.

MRS BASHAM. Mr Newton: dinner is served.

BARBARA. You should address yourself to His Majesty. Where are your manners, woman?

MRS BASHAM. In this house Mr Newton comes first. Come along quick, all of you; or your victuals will be cold.

NEWTON [*rising*] Mr Kneller: will you take her Grace of Cleveland, as you are interested in her curves?

BARBARA [*violently*] No. I am the senior duchess: it is my right to be taken in by the King.

CHARLES [*rising and resignedly giving her his arm*] The Duke of York will follow with the junior duchess. Happy man!

All rise, except Fox.

BARBARA. Brute! [*She tries to disengage herself*].

CHARLES [*holding her fast*] You are on the King's arm. Behave yourself. [*He takes her out forcibly*].

MRS BASHAM. Now, your Highness. Now, Madam Carwell.

JAMES [*taking Louise*] You have remembered, I hope, that Madam Carwell is a Catholic?

MRS BASHAM. Yes: there will be enough cod for the two of you.

LOUISE. Provided Charles does not get at it first. Let us hurry. [*She hurries James out*].

MRS BASHAM. Will you take the player woman, Mr Kneller?

NELL. No no. The player woman goes with her dear old Fox. [*She swoops on the Quaker and drags him along*] George: today you will dine with publicans and sinners. You will say grace for them.

FOX. You remind me that where my Master went I must follow. [*They go out*].

MRS BASHAM. There is no one left for you to take in, Mr Kneller. Mr Newton must take me in and come last.

KNELLER. I will go home. I cannot eat in this house of straight lines.

MRS BASHAM. You will do nothing of the sort, Mr Kneller. There is a cover laid for you; and the King expects you.

NEWTON. The lines are not straight, Mr Kneller. Gravitation bends them. And at bottom I know no more about gravitation than you do about beauty.

KNELLER. To you the universe is nothing but a clock that an almighty clockmaker has wound up and set going for all eternity.

NEWTON. Shall I tell you a secret, Mr Beautymonger? The clock does not keep time. If it did there would be no further need for the Clockmaker. He is wiser than to leave us to our foolish selves in that fashion. When He made a confusion of tongues to prevent the Tower of Babel from reaching to heaven He also contrived a confusion of time to prevent us from doing wholly without Him. The sidereal clock, the clock of the universe, goes wrong. He has to correct it from time to time. Can you, who know everything because you and God are both artists, tell me what is amiss with the perihelion of Mercury?

KNELLER. The what?

NEWTON. The perihelion of Mercury.

KNELLER. I do not know what it is.

NEWTON. I do. But I do not know what is amiss with it. Not until the world finds this out can it do without the Clockmaker in the heavens who can set the hands back or forward, and move the stars with a touch of His almighty finger as He watches over us in the heavens.

KNELLER. In the heavens! In your universe there is no heaven. You have abolished the sky.

NEWTON. Ignoramus: there may be stars beyond our vision bigger than the whole solar system. When I have perfected my telescope it will give you your choice of a hundred heavens.

MRS BASHAM. Mr Kneller: your dinner will be cold; and you will be late for grace. I cannot have any more of this ungodly talk. Down with you to your dinner at once.

KNELLER. In this house, you said, Mr Newton comes first. But you take good care that he comes last. The mistress of this and every other house is she who cooks the dinner. [*He goes out*].

MRS BASHAM [*taking Newton out*] Thats a funny fellow, sir. But you really should not begin talking about the stars to people just as they are going away quietly. It is a habit that is growing on you. What do they know or care about the perry healing of Mercury that interests you so much? We shall never get these people out of the house if— [*They pass out of hearing*].

There is peace in the deserted room.

ACT II

THE boudoir of Catherine of Braganza, Charles's queen, in his not too palatial quarters in Newmarket late in the afternoon on the same day. A prie-dieu, and the pictures, which are all devotional, are signs of the queen's piety. Charles, in slippers and breeches, shirt and cravat, wrapped in an Indian silk dressing gown, is asleep on a couch. His coat and boots are on the carpet where he has thrown them. His hat and wig are on a chair with his tall walking stick. The door, opening on a staircase landing, is near the head of the couch, between it and the prie-dieu. There is a clock in the room.

Catherine, aged 42, enters. She contemplates her husband and the untidiness he has made. With a Portuguese shake of the head (about six times) she sets to work to put the room in order by taking up the boots and putting them tidily at the foot of the couch. She then takes out the coat and hangs it on the rail of the landing. Returning, she purposely closes the door with a bang sufficient to wake Charles.

CHARLES. How long have I been asleep?

CATHERINE. I not know. Why leave you your things about all over my room? I have to put them away like a chambermaid.

CHARLES. Why not send for Chiffinch? It is his business to look after my clothes.

CATHERINE. I not wish to be troubled with Chiffinch when we are alone.

CHARLES [*rising*] Belovéd: you should make me put away my clothes myself. Why should you do chambermaid's work for me? [*His "beloved" always has three syllables*].

CATHERINE. I not like to see you without your wig. But I am your wife and must put up with it.

CHARLES [*getting up*] I am your husband; and I count it a great privilege. [*He kisses her*].

CATHERINE. Yes yes; but why choose you my boudoir for your siesta?

CHARLES. Here in our Newmarket lodging it is the only place where the women cannot come after me.

CATHERINE. A wife is some use then, after all.

CHARLES. There is nobody like a wife.

CATHERINE. I hear that Cleveland has come back from Paris. Did you send for her?

CHARLES. Send for her! I had as soon send for the divvle. I finished with Barbara long ago.

CATHERINE. How often have you told me that you are finished with all women! Yet Portsmouth keeps her hold on you, and Nellie the player. And now Cleveland comes back.

CHARLES. Beloved: you do not understand. These women do not keep their hold on me: I keep my hold on them. I have a bit of news for you about Louise. What do you think I caught her at this morning?

CATHERINE. I had rather not guess.

CHARLES. Buying a love potion. That was for me. I do not make love to her enough, it seems. I hold her because she is intelligent and ladylike and keeps me in touch with France and the French court, to say nothing of the money I have to extract from Louis through her.

CATHERINE. And Nelly? She can play the fine lady; but is she one?

CHARLES. Nelly is a good creature; and she amuses me. You know, beloved, one gets tired of court ladies and their conversation, always the same.

CATHERINE. And you really did not send for Cleveland to come back?

CHARLES. Beloved: when I was young I thought that there was only one unbearable sort of woman: the one that could think of nothing but her soul and its salvation. But in Barbara I found something worse: a woman who thought of nothing but her body and its satisfaction, which meant men and money. For both, Barbara is insatiable. Grab, grab, grab. When one is done with Barbara's body—a very fine body, I admit—what is there left?

CATHERINE. And you are done with Barbara's body?

CHARLES. Beloved: I am done with all bodies. They are all alike: all cats are grey in the dark. It is the souls and the brains that are different. In the end one learns to leave the body out. And then Barbara is packed off to Paris, and is not asked back by me, though I have no doubt there is some man in the case.

CATHERINE. Why spend you so much time with me here—so much more than you used to?

CHARLES. Beloved: do I plague you? I am off.

He makes for the door: she runs to it and bars his egress.

CATHERINE. No: that is not what I meant. Go back and sit down.

Charles obediently goes back to the couch, where they sit side by side.

CHARLES. And what did you mean, beloved?

CATHERINE. You spend too much time away from court. Your brother is stealing the court away from you. When he is here his rooms are crowded: yours are empty.

CHARLES. I thank heaven for it. The older I grow, the less I can endure that most tiresome of all animals, the courtier. Even a dissolute court, as they say mine is—I suppose they mean a court where bawdy stories are told out loud instead of whispered—is more tedious than a respectable one. They repeat themselves and repeat themselves endlessly. And I am just as bad with my old stories about my flight after the battle of Worcester. I told the same one twice over within an hour last Tuesday. This morning Barbara called me an old wreck.

CATHERINE [*flaming up*] She dared! Send her to the Tower and let her rot there.

CHARLES. She is not so important as that, beloved. Nor am I. And we must forgive our enemies when we can afford to.

CATHERINE. I forgive my enemies, as you well know, Charles. It is my duty as a Catholic and a Christian. But it is not my duty to forgive your enemies. And you never forgive mine.

CHARLES. An excellent family arrangement for a royal pair. We can exchange our revenges and remain good Christians. But Barbara may be right. When a king is shunned, and his heir is courted, his death is not far off.

CATHERINE. You must not say things like that: I not can bear it. You are stronger in your mind than ever; and nobody can keep up with you walking.

CHARLES. Nevertheless, beloved, I shall drop before you do. What will happen to you then? that is what troubles me. When I am dead you must go back to Portugal, where your brother the king will take care of you. You will never be safe here, because you are a Catholic queen.

CATHERINE. I not think I shall care what becomes of me when you are gone. But James is a Catholic. When he is king what have I to fear? Or do you believe your son Monmouth will prevent him from succeeding you and become a Protestant king?

CHARLES. No. He will try, poor boy; but Jamie will kill him. He is his mother's son; and his mother was nothing. Then the Protestants will kill Jamie; and the Dutch lad will see his chance and take it. He will be king: a Protestant king. So you must make for Portugal.

CATHERINE. But such things not could happen. Why are you, who are afraid of nothing else, so afraid of the Protestants?

CHARLES. They killed my great grandmother. They killed my father. They would kill you if I were not a little too clever for them: they are trying hard enough, damn them! They are great killers, these Protestants. Jamie has just one chance. They may call in Orange Billy before they kill him; and then it will hardly be decent for Billy to kill his wife's father. But they will get rid of Jamie somehow; so you must make for home the moment I have kissed you goodbye for the last time.

CATHERINE [*almost in tears*] you not must talk of it— [*She breaks down*].

CHARLES [*caressing her*] Beloved: you will only lose the worst of husbands.

CATHERINE. That is a lie: if anyone else said it I would kill her. You are the very best husband that ever lived.

CHARLES [*laughing*] Oh! Oh! Oh! The merry monarch! Beloved: can anything I can ever do make up to you for my unfaithfulness?

CATHERINE. People think of nothing but that, as if that were the whole of life. What care I about your women? your concubines? your handmaidens? the servants of your common pleasures? They have set me free to be something more to you than they are or can ever be. You have never been really unfaithful to me.

CHARLES. Yes, once, with the woman whose image as Britannia is on every British penny, and will perhaps stay there to all eternity. And on my honor nothing came of that: I never touched her. But she had some magic that scattered my wits: she made me listen for a moment to those who were always pressing me to divorce my patient wife and take a Protestant queen. But I could never have done it, though I was furious when she ran away from me and married Richmond.

CATHERINE. Oh, I know, I know: it was the only time I ever was jealous. Well, I forgive you: why should a great man like you be satisfied with a little thing like me?

CHARLES. Stop. I cannot bear that. I am not a great man; and neither are you a little woman. You have more brains and character than all the rest of the court put together.

CATHERINE. I am nothing except what you have made me. What did I know when I came here? Only what the nuns teach a Portuguese princess in their convent.

CHARLES. And what more had I to teach you except what I learnt when I was running away from the battle of Worcester? And when I had learnt that much there was an end of me as a king. I knew too much.

CATHERINE. With what you have taught me I shall govern Portugal if I return to it?

CHARLES. I have no doubt of it, beloved; but whether that will make you any happier I have my doubts. I wish you could govern the English for me.

CATHERINE. No one can govern the English: that is why they will never come to any good. In Portugal there is the holy Church: we know what we believe; and we all believe the same things. But here the Church itself is a heresy; and there are a thousand other heresies: almost as many heresies as there are people. And if you ask any of them what his sect believes he does not know: all he can say is that the men of the other sects should be hanged and their women whipped through the town at the cart's tail. But they are all against the true Church. I do not understand the English; and I do not want to govern them.

CHARLES. You are Portuguese. I am Italian, French, Scottish, hardly at all English. When I want to know how the great lump of my subjects will take anything I tell it to Barbara. Then I tell it to Chiffinch. Then I tell it to Jamie. When I have the responses of Barbara, Chiffinch, and Jamie, I know how Tom, Dick and Harry will take it. And it is never as I take it.

CATHERINE. In Portugal we not have this strange notion that Tom, Dick and Harry matter. What do they know about government?

CHARLES. Nothing; but they hate it. And nobody teaches them how necessary it is. Instead, when we teach them anything we teach them grammar and dead languages. What is the result? Protestantism and parliaments instead of citizenship.

CATHERINE. In Portugal, God be praised, there are no Protestants and no parliaments.

CHARLES. Parliaments are the very divvle. Old Noll began by thinking the world of parliaments. Well, he tried every sort of parliament, finishing with a veritable reign of the saints. And in the end he had to turn them all out of doors, neck and crop, and govern through his major-generals. And when Noll died they went back to their parliament and made such a mess of it that they had to send for me.

CATHERINE. Suppose there had been no you?

CHARLES. There is always somebody. In every nation there must be the makings of a capable council and a capable king three or four times over, if only we knew how to pick them. Nobody has found out how to do it: that is why the world is so vilely governed.

CATHERINE. But if the rulers are of noble birth—

CHARLES. You mean if they are the sons of their fathers. What good is that?

CATHERINE. You are king because you are the son of your father. And you are the best of kings.

CHARLES. Thank you. And your brother Alfonso was king of Portugal because he was the son of his father. Was he also the best of kings?

CATHERINE. Oh, he was dreadful. He was barely fit to be a stable boy; but my brother Pedro took his crown and locked him up; and Pedro also is my father's son.

CHARLES. Just so: six of one and half a dozen of the other. Heredity is no use. Learning Latin is no use: Jack Churchill, who is an ignoramus, is worth fifty scholars. If Orange Billy dies and one of my nieces succeeds him Jack will be King of England.

CATHERINE. Perhaps the Church should select the king—or the queen.

CHARLES. The Church has failed over and over again to select a decent Pope. Alexander Borgia was a jolly fellow; and I am the last man alive to throw stones at him; but he was not a model Pope.

CATHERINE. My father was a great king. He fought the Spaniards and set Portugal free from their yoke. And it was the people who chose him and made him do it. I have sometimes wondered whether the people should not choose their king.

CHARLES. Not the English people. They would choose Titus Oates. No, beloved: the riddle of how to choose a ruler is still unanswered; and it is the riddle of civilization. I tell you again there are in England, or in any other country, the makings of half a dozen decent kings and councils; but they are mostly in prison. If we only knew how to pick them out and label them, then the people could have their choice out of the half dozen. It may end that way, but not until we have learnt how to pick the people who are fit to be chosen before they are chosen. And even then the picked ones will be just those whom the people will not choose. Who is it that said that no nation can bear being well governed for more than three years? Old Noll found that out. Why am I a popular king? Because I am a lazy fellow. I enjoy myself and let the people see me doing it, and leave things as they are, though things as they are will not bear thinking of by those who know what they are. That is what the people like. It is what they would do if they were kings.

CATHERINE. You are not lazy: I wish you were: I should see more of you. You take a great deal too much exercise: you walk and walk and nobody can keep up with you; you are always gardening or sailing or building and talking to gardeners and sailors and shipwrights and bricklayers and masons and people like that, neglecting the court. That is how your brother gathers the court round him and takes it away from you.

CHARLES. Let him. There is nothing to be learnt at court except that a courtier's life is not a happy one. The gardeners and the watermen, the shipwrights and bricklayers and carpenters and masons, are happier and far far more contented. It is the worst of luck to be born a king. Give me a skilled trade and eight or ten shillings a week, and you and I, beloved, would pig along more happily than we have ever been able to do as our majesties.

CATHERINE. I not want to pig along. I was born to rule; and if the worst comes to the worst and I have to go back to my own country I shall shew the world that I can rule, and that I am not the ninny I am made to look like here.

CHARLES. Why dont you do it, beloved? I am not worth staying with.

CATHERINE. I am torn ten different ways. I know that I should make you divorce me and marry a young Protestant wife who would bring you a son to inherit the crown and save all this killing of Monmouth and James and the handing over of your kingdom to the Hollander. I am tempted to do it because then I should return to my own beautiful country and smell the Tagus instead of the dirty Thames, and rule Portugal as my mother used to rule over the head of my worthless brother. I should be somebody then. But I cannot bring myself to leave you: not for all the thrones in the world. And my religion forbids me to put a Protestant on the throne of England when the rightful heir to it is a good Catholic.

CHARLES. You shall not, beloved. I will have no other widow but you.

CATHERINE. Ah! you can coax me so easily.

CHARLES. I treated you very badly when I was a young man because young men have low tastes and think only of themselves. Besides, odsfish! we could not talk to one-another. The English they taught you in Portugal was a tongue that never was spoke on land or sea; and my Portuguese made you laugh. We must forget our foolish youth: we are grown-up now.

CATHERINE. Happy man! You forget so easily. But think of the difference in our fortunes! All your hopes of being a king were cut off: you were an exile, an outcast, a fugitive. Yet your kingdom dropped into your mouth at last; and you have been a king since you were old enough to use your power. But I! My mother was determined from my birth that I should be a queen: a great queen: Queen of England. Well, she had her way: we were married; and they call me queen. But have I ever reigned? Am I not as much an exile and an outcast as ever you were? I am not Catherine of England: I am Catherine of Bragança: a foreign woman with a funny name that they cannot pronounce. Yet I have the blood of rulers in my veins and the brains of rulers in my head.

CHARLES. They are no use here: the English will not be ruled; and there is nothing they hate like brains. For brains and religion you must go to Scotland; and Scotland is the most damnable country on earth: never shall I forget the life they led me there with their brains and their religion when they made me their boy king to spite Old Noll. I sometimes think religion and brains are the curse of the world. No, beloved, England for me, with all its absurdities!

CATHERINE. There can be only one true religion; and England has fifty.

CHARLES. Well, the more the merrier, if only they could let one another live. But they will not do even that.

CATHERINE. Have you no conscience?

CHARLES. I have; and a very troublesome one too. I would give a dukedom to any doctor that would cure me of it. But somehow it is not a conscience of the standard British pattern.

CATHERINE. That is only your witty nonsense. Our consciences, which come from God, must be all the same.

CHARLES. They are not. Do you think God so stupid that he could invent only one sort of conscience?

CATHERINE [*shocked*] What a dreadful thing to say! I must not listen to you.

CHARLES. No two consciences are the same. No two love affairs are the same. No two marriages are the same. No two illnesses are the same. No two children are the same. No two human beings are the same. What is right for one is wrong for the other. Yet they cannot live together without laws; and a law is something that obliges them all to do the same thing.

CATHERINE. It may be so in England. But in Portugal the Holy Church makes all Catholics the same. My mother ruled them though she was a Spaniard. Why should I not do what my mother did?

CHARLES. Why not, indeed? I daresay you will do it very well, beloved. The Portuguese can believe in a Church and obey a king. The English robbed the Church and destroyed it: if a priest celebrates Mass anywhere in England outside your private chapel he is hanged for it. My great grandmother was a Catholic queen: rather than let her succeed to the throne they chopped her head off. My father was a Protestant king: they chopped his head off for trying to govern them and asking the Midlands to pay for the navy. While the Portuguese were fighting the Spaniards the English were fighting oneanother. You can do nothing with the English. How often have I told you that I am no real king: that the utmost I can do is to keep my crown on my head and my head on my shoulders. How often have you asked me to do some big thing like joining your Church, or some little thing like pardoning a priest or a Quaker condemned to some cruel punishment! And you have found that outside the court, where my smiles and my frowns count for everything, I have no power. The perjured scoundrel, Titus Oates, steeped in unmentionable vices, is lodged in my palace with a pension. If I could have my way he would be lodged on the gallows. There is a preacher named Bunyan who has written a book about the Christian life that is being read, they tell me, all the world over; and I could not release him from Bedford Gaol, where he rotted for years. The world will remember Oates and Bunyan; and I shall be The Merry Monarch. No: give me English birds and English trees, English dogs and Irish horses, English rivers and English ships; but English men! No, NO, NO.

CATHERINE. And Englishwomen?

CHARLES. Ah! there you have me, beloved. One cannot do without women: at least I cannot. But having to manage rascals like Buckingham and Shaftesbury, and dodgers like Halifax, is far worse than having to manage Barbara and Louise.

CATHERINE. Is there really any difference? Shaftesbury is trying to have me beheaded on Tower Hill on a charge of plotting to poison you sworn to by Titus Oates. Barbara is quite ready to support him in that.

CHARLES. No, beloved. The object of having you beheaded is to enable me to marry a Protestant wife and have a Protestant heir. I have pointed out to Barbara that the Protestant wife would not be so kind to her as you are, and would have her out of the kingdom before she could say Jack Robinson. So now she has thrown over Shaftesbury; and when I have thrown him over, as I shall know how to do presently, there will be an end of him. But he will be succeeded by some stupider rascal, or, worse still, some stupid fellow who is not a rascal. The clever rascals are all for sale; but the honest dunderheads are the very divvle.

CATHERINE. I wish you were not so clever.

CHARLES. Beloved: you could not do without my cleverness. That is why you must go back to Portugal when I am gone.

CATHERINE. But it makes your mind twist about so. You are so clever that you think you can do without religion. If only I could win you to the Church I should die perfectly happy; and so would you.

CHARLES. Well, I promise you I will not die a Protestant. You must see to that when the hour strikes for me: the last hour. So my very belovedest will die happy; and that is all I care about. [*Caressing her*] Does that satisfy you?

CATHERINE. If only I could believe it.

CHARLES. You mean I am the king whose word no man relies on.

CATHERINE. No: you are not that sort of king for me. But will it be a real conversion? I think you would turn Turk to please me.

CHARLES. Faith I believe I would. But there is more in it than that. It is not that I have too little religion in me for the Church: I have too much, like a queer fellow I talked with this morning. [*The clock strikes five*]. Odsfish! I have a Council meeting. I must go. [*He throws off his dressing gown*]. My boots! What has become of my boots?

CATHERINE. There are your boots. And wait until I make you decent.

Whilst he pulls his boots on, she fetches his coat and valets him into it. He snatches up his hat and stick and puts the hat on.

CATHERINE. No no: you have forgotten your wig. [*She takes his hat off and fetches the wig*]. Fancy your going into the Council Chamber like that! Nobody would take you for King Charles the Second without that wig. Now. [*She puts the wig on him; then the hat. A few final pats and pulls complete his toilet*]. Now you look every inch a king. [*Making him a formal curtsey*] Your Majesty's visit has made me very happy. Long live the King!

CHARLES. May the Queen live for ever!

He throws up his arm in a gallant salute and stalks out. She rises and throws herself on her knees at her prie-dieu.

APPENDIX

THE CENCI

Shaw's first successful career in the eyes of the world was that of critic and journalist. Most of his earliest criticism was given over to contemporary painting and music, but occasionally it glanced at the theatre. One such early dramatic criticism reviewed a belated first performance of Shelley's The Cenci, *and is particularly significant for what it tells us about Shaw's early attitude (six years before he completed his first play) toward the literary five-act tragedy in blank verse, the orthodox nineteenth-century vehicle for dramatic high-seriousness. The review appeared in "Art Corner," Shaw's department in Mrs. Annie Besant's liberal journal* Our Corner, *in June, 1886.*

The most remarkable event of last month with which I have any concern in this Corner is the performance of Shelley's tragedy, "The Cenci", for the first time during the sixty-seven years which have elapsed since it was published in 1819. The Censor forbade the representation; and the Shelley Society could therefore do no more than engage a large theatre—the Grand at Islington—and have their play in strict technical privacy, which in this case meant in the presence of a crowded audience who were only distinguished from other audiences by the fact that they had not paid for their seats at the doors in the usual way. That tickets may, nevertheless, have changed hands for money is quite possible: I am myself a member of the Shelley Society; I received applications from people desirous of purchasing my tickets; and it was certainly not any sentiment of loyalty to the Lord Chamberlain that restrained me from meeting their wishes. The official licence was withheld on the ground that the performance of such a play would deprave the public. Yet the play has been performed; its attractions have been supplemented by the presence of a number of celebrated persons in the auditorium; and as many people as the theatre could hold have been not only admitted for nothing, but invited and personally welcomed. So far, the anticipated depravation of the public seems not to have come off; for the conduct of the nation has not perceptibly altered for the worse since the afternoon of Friday, the 7th of May, 1886; whilst the attempt to drive theatre-goers from the performances of the Shelley Society to such licensed alternatives as the Criterion Theatre, for example, has so accentuated the anomaly, folly, and hypocrisy of the censorship as to strengthen the hope that the institution may soon be as extinct as the Star Chamber, to which, in point of obnoxiousness to all accredited political principle, it is exactly similar.

A performance of "The Cenci" must have come sooner or later, because Shelley, although he rushed into print before he was ripe for it, and often disgraced himself by doing very ordinary literary jobs in an unworkmanlike way, is yet, with the exception—under certain limitations—of Shakspere, the greatest of English poets; and "The Cenci" is the only work which he wrote with a view to actual representation on the stage. In indulging his whim to produce something in the obsolete and absurd form which Shakspere had done so much with, Shelley no doubt believed that he was engaged upon a solid and permanent composition. In reality he was only experimenting to find a suitable form for his efforts to "teach the human heart, through its sympathies and antipathies, the knowledge of itself; in proportion to the possession of which knowledge, every human being is wise, just, sincere, tolerant, and kind". This, he says, is the purpose of "the highest species of drama"; and it seems to me that such purpose makes all the difference between the writer of fiction and the ordinary imaginative liar. However that may be, Shelley, groping for the scientific drama which is yet in the future, and which alone could have reconciled his philosophic craving for truth to the unrealities of the stage, certainly got hold of the wrong vehicle when he chose the five-act tragedy in blank verse which had sufficed for Otway and Nicholas Rowe. The obligations imposed on him by this form and its traditions were that he should imitate Shakspere in an un-Shaksperean fashion by attempting to write constantly as Shakspere only wrote at the extreme emotional crises in his plays; that his hero should have a dash of Richard III. in him; that the tragedy should be raised to "the dignity of history" by the arbitrary introduction of incidents (mostly fictitious) mentioned in recondite historical manuscripts; and that the whole should be made sufficiently stagey to appear natural and suitable to actors and frequenters of the theatre, and outrageous and impossible to everyone else. Shelley, with the modesty of a novice, complied with these conditions. He produced a villain worse than Richard III., Macbeth, Iago, Antiochus, and Ireland's Vortigern all rolled into one. He expanded Othello's "Put out the light; and then put out the light" into a whole scene. He wrote a father's curse compared to which Lear's on Goneril appears a mere petulance. He put Lady Macbeth's famous "Give me the daggers" into the mouth of a heroine urging her father's murder. He gave her a sad song to sing before her death, like Desdemona. Long tirades, thunder and lightening, a banquet, a castle, murders, tortures, and executions were not spared. The inevitable historical document was duly translated from the Italian original. And he wrote a preface in which he scrupulously stated that an idea in one of the speeches was suggested by a passage in Calderon's "El Purgatorio de San Patricio". This, he said, was the only plagiarism he had intentionally committed in the whole piece; a declaration which proves how unconsciously he had been guilty of all the second-hand Shakspere. The result furnishes an artistic parallel to Wagner's "Rienzi". It is a strenuous but futile and never-to-be-repeated attempt to bottle the new wine in the old skins.

The Cenci, then, is a failure in the sense in which we call an experiment with a negative result a failure. But the powers called forth by it were so extraordinary that many generations of audiences will probably submit to have the experiment repeated on them, in spite of the incidental tedium. And if the play be ever adequately acted, the experiment will not be even temporarily fatiguing to witness, though it perhaps may prove at one or two points unendurably horrible. For Count Cenci, mere stage puppet, striking figure in Italian history, tragedy villain and so forth, as he is supposed to be, is really a personification of the Almighty Fiend of "Queen Mab", the God whose attributes convicted the average evangelical Briton in Shelley's eyes of being a devil worshipper. Cenci is ruthless, powerful, and malignant; and, above all, there is no appeal and no relief from his injustice. He identifies his cause with that of his God by the appalling preface to his valediction against Beatrice:

"The world's Father
Must grant a parent's prayer against his child."

Beatrice, too, banishes all mere stage heroinism from our minds when she absolutely despairs, and, without losing her self-possession, dies in her despair. She withstands physical torture; but she succumbs, as she tells her torturer

"——with considering all the wretched life
Which I have lived, and its now wretched end,
And the small justice shown by Heaven and Earth
To me or mine; and what a tyrant thou art,
And what slaves these; and what a world we make,
The oppressor and the oppressed."

Those who have witnessed the agony and death of any innocent creature upon whom Nature has wantonly fastened a dreadful malady, will recognize here a tragedy truer and deeper than that of any conventional heroine whose lover dies in the fifth act. Shelley and Shakspere are the only dramatists who have dealt in despair of this quality; and Shelley alone has shown it driven into the heart of a girl. The devil-god, incarnate in a wicked human tyrant, is characteristically Shelleyan. He is of course as pure a superstition as the benevolent *deus ex machina* of optimistic religious playwrights; but both represent a real aspect of nature; and the one is therefore as terribly real and effective as the other is delightfully pleasant and useful. . . .

Mr. Herman Vezin did what he could with the part of Cenci, and did it very well considering the impossibility of such an impersonation to an actor who happily cannot make a monster of himself. Mr. Leonard Outram had the most important of the really feasible parts—that of Orsino; and his treatment of it confirmed the high estimate of his ability which his performance as Valence, in "Colombe's Birthday", caused the Browning Society and their guests to form last year at St. George's Hall. Miss Maude Brennan's appearance was surprisingly in accordance with the description of Lucretia in Shelley's historical document; but the effect was not quite satisfactory from the artistic point of view. Mr. de Cordova and Mr. Foss came off with credit as Giacomo and Marzio; and Mr. Mark Ambient's earnestness helped him through the self-sacrifice of playing the tragic boy Bernardo Cenci. A prologue by Mr. John Todhunter, in which Mr. Browning, who was present, was pointedly apostrophized, was recited by Mr. Outram. A rough-and-ready orchestra played the most sublime pieces in their repertory—the overture to "Masaniello", "The Lost Chord", the march from "The Prophet", selections from "Lucrezia Borgia", and the like, with the best intentions.

NYDIA

From 1888 to 1894, Shaw was staff music critic, first for The Star, *a new liberal newspaper, then for* The World, *a fashionable weekly. His instructions at* The Star *were to "for God's sake, not write about Bach in B Minor"—to make music criticism readable. The result was some of the acutest and liveliest music criticism ever written. In* The Star *Shaw signed himself Corno di Bassetto, or "basset horn," an instrument distin-*

guished, he was later appalled to discover, by its "peculiar watery melancholy . . . just the thing for a funeral." Shaw's review of George Fox's Nydia *appeared in* The World *on May 18, 1892. Fox was an operatic baritone of some note, and Shaw combines the occasion of a "singer's opera" with the recent publication of Frank Archer's book,* How to Write a Good Play, *to dissect the clichés of opera and to ridicule the opera or play which is no more than a hopeful reshuffling of established conventions.*

The other day an actor published a book of directions for making a good play. His plan was a simple one. Take all the devices which bring down the house in existing plays; make a new one by stringing them all together; and there you are. If that book succeeds, I am prepared to write a similar treatise on opera composition. I know quite a lot of things that would be of great use to any young composer. For instance, when two lovers are on the stage together, be sure you make them catch sight of the moon or stars and gaze up rapturously whilst the violins discourse ravishing strains with their mutes on. Mutes are also useful for spinning-wheel business and for fires, as in Marta and Die Walküre.

For dreamy effects, tonic pedals as patented by Gounod and Bizet are useful. When large orchestras are available, broad melodies on the fourth string of the violins may be relied on for a strong and popular impression. When the heroine is alone on the stage, a rapid, agitated movement, expressive of her anticipation of the arrival of her lover, and culminating in a vigorous instrumental and vocal outburst as he rushes on the stage and proceeds without an instant's loss of time to embrace her ardently, never fails to leave the public breathless. The harmonic treatment of this situation is so simple that nobody can fail to master it in a few lessons. The lady must first sing the gentleman's name on the notes belonging to the chord of the dominant seventh in some highly unexpected key; the gentleman then vociferates the lady's name a peg higher on the notes of a more extreme discord; and, finally, the twain explode simultaneously upon a brilliant six-four chord, leading, either directly through the dominant chord, or after some pretty interruption of the cadence, to a flowing melody in which the gentleman either protests his passion or repeatedly calls attention to the fact that at last they meet again.

The whole situation should be repeated in the last act, with the difference that this time it is the gentleman who must be alone at the beginning. Furthermore, he must be in a gloomy dungeon, not larger at the outside than the stage of Covent Garden Theatre; and he must be condemned to die next morning. The reason for putting the gentleman, rather than the lady, in this situation is to be found in the exclusion of women from politics, whereby they are deprived of the privilege of being condemned to death, without any reflection on their personal characters, for heading patriotic rebellions. The difficulty has nevertheless been successfully got over by making the lady go mad in the fourth act, and kill somebody, preferably her own child. Under these circumstances she may sing almost anything she pleases of a florid nature in her distraction, and may take the gentleman's place in the prison-cell in the next act without forfeiting the moral approval of the audience. Florid mad scenes, though they are very pretty when the lady's affliction is made to take the playful turn of a trial of skill with the first flute, which should partly imitate the voice and partly accompany it in thirds, is now out of fashion; and it is far better, in dramatic opera, to be entirely modern in style.

. . . .

But I am neglecting my week's work. Although I repeat that "How to compose a good opera" might be written as easily as "How to write a good play," I must not set about writing it myself in this column, although the above sample will shew every learned musician how thoroughly I am qualified for the task. The fact is, I had been reading the reviews of Mr Frank Archer's book; and it set me thinking of what are called actors' plays, meaning plays which are not plays at all, but compilations consisting of a series of stage effects devised *ad hoc*. Indeed, stage effects is too wide a term: actors' effects would be more accurate. I thought of how hopelessly bad all such works are, even when, as in the case of Cibber's Richard III and Garrick's Katharine and Petruchio, they are saved from instant perdition by a mutilated mass of poetry and drama stolen from some genuine playwright.

And then I fell to considering which would be the worst thing to have to sit out in a theatre—an actor's play or a singer's opera. Before I could settle the point the clock struck; and I suddenly realized that if I lost another moment I should miss the one-fifty-five train to the Crystal Palace, where I was due at two-forty-five to witness the performance of Mr George Fox's new opera, Nydia. And when I sat down just now to write an account of Nydia, it naturally reminded me of Mr Frank Archer, and led to the above tremendous disgression on the subject of operatic composition in general.

Nydia is founded on Bulwer Lytton's Last Days of Pompeii, a novel which I read when a boy. I remember nothing of it except the name Arbaces, and the Roman sentinel, and Pliny—though, indeed, I am not sure that I did not get the last two out of Chambers's Miscellany. At all events, I found the libretto of Nydia as new to me as it is in the nature of any libretto to be to a musical critic of my age. It began with a bustling crowd, singing:

> Water melons, rich and rare,
> None excel them we declare;
> Olives, figs, and honey sweet,
> You will find them hard to beat;
> Here is game, wild mountain boar,
> Oysters too from Britain's shore,
> Come and buy, come and buy.

This was out of Carmen, tune and all, except the oysters; and even their freshness must have been severely tried by hawking them in the full blaze of an Italian sun.

Then we had a blind girl with a Leitmotif, also rather like the jealousy motive in Carmen, with a heroine, lover, and villain, in due course. The villain, a Pompeian archbishop, held a service in a temple on the lines of the one in Aida; and the lover came in and dashed him down the steps of the altar, for which exploit he was haled away to prison—very properly, as I thought—in spite of the entreaties of the heroine. In prison he shared his cell with a Nazarene, who strove hard, not without some partial success, to make him see the beauty of being eaten by a lion in the arena. Next came the amphitheatre, with a gladiator fight which only needed a gallery full of shrieking vestals with their thumbs turned down to be perfectly *à la* Gérome. Then the hero, kept up to the mark by the Nazarene, was thrown to the lion, whereupon Vesuvius emitted clouds of spangles and red fire. A scene of terror and confusion in the streets followed, the crowd standing stock-still, with its eyes on the conductor, and the villain falling, slain by lightning, and then creeping off on all-fours behind the calves of the multitude.

Finally the clouds parted; and we had a pretty pictorial composition of the hero and heroine at sea in a galley with the blind girl, who presently took a deliberate header into the waves, to the intense astonishment of everybody except the hero, who, without making the smallest attempt to save her, set up a thundering Salve eternum just as I was expecting him to break into

Rosy lips above the water,
Blowing bubbles soft and fine;
As for me, I was no swimmer,
So I lost my Clementine.

THE SECOND MRS. TANQUERAY

In January, 1895, Shaw became the regular dramatic critic of The Saturday Review. *By this time he had already completed four plays of his own, and two of them,* Widowers' Houses *and* Arms and the Man, *had been produced and had become the subjects of critical controversies. A third play,* Mrs. Warren's Profession, *had been refused a license by the official dramatic censor. In his columns in* The Saturday Review, *Shaw took an early opportunity to write about a play whose immense success had immediately preceded the writing of* Mrs. Warren's Profession. *This was Arthur Wing Pinero's* The Second Mrs. Tanqueray, *a "well-made play" about a woman who had once been an elegant courtesan. In his criticism of February 23, 1895, Shaw reflects on the play's construction and subject matter. Both of these embodied conventions of current dramatic types to which* Mrs. Warren's Profession *was Shaw's officially-gagged dramatic refutation.*

I am indebted to Mr Heinemann for a copy of The Second Mrs Tanqueray, which he has just published in a five-shilling volume, with an excellent photographic portrait of the author by Mr Hollyer. Those who did not see the play at the St James's Theatre can now examine the literary basis of the work that so immoderately fascinated playgoing London in 1893. But they must not expect the play to be as imposing in the library as it was on the stage. Its merit there was relative to the culture of the playgoing public. Paula Tanqueray is an astonishingly well-drawn figure as stage figures go nowadays, even allowing for the fact that there is no cheaper subject for the character draughtsman than the ill-tempered sensual woman seen from the point of view of the conventional man. But off the stage her distinction vanishes. The novels of Anthony Trollope, Charles Lever, Bulwer Lytton, Charles Reade, and many other novelists, whom nobody praised thirty years ago in the terms in which Mr Pinero is praised now, are full of feats of character-drawing in no way inferior—to say the least—to Mr Pinero's. The theatre was not ready for that class of work then: it is now; and accordingly Mr Pinero, who in literature is a humble and somewhat belated follower of the novelists of the middle of the nineteenth century, and who has never written a line from which it could be guessed that he is a contemporary of Ibsen, Tolstoi, Meredith, or Sarah Grand, finds himself at the dawn of the twentieth hailed as a man of new ideas, of daring originality, of supreme literary distinction, and even—which is perhaps oddest—of consummate stage craft. Stage craft, after all, is very narrowly limited by the physical conditions of stage representation; but when one turns over the pages of The Second Mrs Tanqueray, and notes the naïve machinery of the exposition in the first act, in which two whole actors are wasted on sham parts, and the hero, at his own dinner party, is compelled to get up and go ignominiously into the next room "to write some letters" when something has to be said behind his back; when one follows Cayley Drummle, the confidant to whom both Paula and her husband explain themselves for the benefit of the audience; when one counts the number of doors which Mr Pinero needs to get his characters on and off the stage, and how they have finally to be supplemented by the inevitable "French windows" (two of them); and when the activity of the postman is taken into consideration, it is impossible to avoid the conclusion that what most of our critics mean by mastery of stage craft is recklessness in the substitution of dead machinery and lay figures for vital action and real characters. I do not deny that an author may be driven by his own limitations to ingenuities which Shakespear had no occasion to cultivate, just as a painter without hands or feet learns to surprass Michael Angelo in the art of drawing with the brush held in the mouth; but I regard such ingenuity as an extremity to be deplored, not as an art to be admired. In the Second Mrs Tanqueray I find little except a scaffold for the situation of a step-daughter and step-mother finding themselves in the positions respectively of affianced wife and discarded mistress to the same man. Obviously, the only necessary conditions of this situation are that the persons concerned shall be respectable enough to be shocked by it, and that the step-mother shall be an improper person. Mr Pinero has not got above this minimum. He is, of course, sufficiently skilled in fiction to give Ellean, Mrs Cortelyon, Ardale, Tanqueray, and Cayley Drummle a passable air of being human beings. He has even touched up Cayley into a Thackerayan *flâneur* in order to secure toleration of his intrusiveness. But who will pretend that any of these figures are more than the barest accessories to the main situation? To compare them with the characters in Robertson's Caste would be almost as ridiculous as to compare Caste with A Doll's House. The two vulgar characters produce the requisite jar—a pitilessly disagreeable jar—and that is all. Still, all the seven seem good as far as they go; and that very little way may suggest that Mr Pinero might have done good creative work if he had carried them further. Unfortunately for this surmise, he has carried Paula further; and with what result? The moment the point is reached at which the comparatively common gift of "an eye for character" has to be supplemented by the higher dramatic gift of sympathy with character—of the power of seeing the world from the point of view of others instead of merely describing or judging them from one's own point of view in terms of the conventional systems of morals, Mr Pinero breaks down. I remember that when I saw the play acted I sat up very attentively when Tanqueray said to Paula, "I know what you were at Ellean's age. You hadnt a thought that wasnt a wholesome one; you hadnt an impulse that didnt tend towards good; you never harbored a notion you couldnt have gossiped about to a parcel of children. And this was a very few years back, etc. etc." On the reply to that fatuous but not unnatural speech depended the whole question of Mr Pinero's rank as a dramatist. One can imagine how, in a play by a master-hand, Paula's reply would have opened

Tanqueray's foolish eyes to the fact that a woman of that sort is already the same at three as she is at thirty-three, and that however she may have found by experience that her nature is in conflict with the ideals of differently constituted people, she remains perfectly valid to herself, and despises herself, if she sincerely does so at all, for the hypocrisy that the world forces on her instead of for being what she is. What reply does Mr Pinero put into her mouth? Here it is, with the stage directions: "A few—years ago! (*She walks slowly towards the door, then suddenly drops upon the ottoman in a paroxysm of weeping.*) O God! A few years ago!" That is to say, she makes her reply from the Tanqueray-Ellean-Pinero point of view, and thus betrays the fact that she is a work of prejudiced observation instead of comprehension, and that the other characters only owe their faint humanity to the fact that they are projections of Mr Pinero's own personal amiabilities and beliefs and conventions. Mr Pinero, then, is no interpreter of character, but simply an adroit describer of people as the ordinary man sees and judges them. Add to this a clear head, a love of the stage, and a fair talent for fiction, all highly cultivated by hard and honorable work as a writer of effective stage plays for the modern commercial theatre; and you have him on his real level. On that level he is entitled to all the praise The Second Mrs Tanqueray has won him; and I very heartily regret that the glamor which Mrs Patrick Campbell cast round the play has forced me to examine pretensions which Mr Pinero himself never put forward rather than to acknowledge the merits with which his work is so concisely packed.

TWO BAD PLAYS

On April 20, 1895, Shaw reviewed "Two Bad Plays," both imports, but both very much at home with different segments of the London audience. One was a military melodrama by the Americans Franklin Fyles and David Belasco; the other, a "well-made play" by the leading French playwright Victorien Sardou. Shaw profits from the occasion to moralize on the nature of the theatre audience, to sketch a poetics of melodrama, and to make invidious comparisons between popular melodrama and the fashionable well-made play, much to the detriment of the latter. In Arms and the Man, *Shaw had pointedly held up to scorn the military and romantic conventions of the whole breed of bad melodramas like Fyles and Belasco's* The Girl I Left Behind Me. *At the same time, Shaw's appreciation of melodrama at its best was more than theoretical; and melodrama contributes to his playmaking, most notably in* The Devil's Disciple *and* Captain Brassbound's Conversion, *but also in* Mrs. Warren's Profession, Arms and the Man, Caesar and Cleopatra, *and* Androcles and the Lion.

Last Saturday was made memorable to me by my first visit to the Adelphi Theatre. My frequent allusions to Adelphi melodrama were all founded on a knowledge so perfect that there was no need to verify it experimentally; and now that the experiment has been imposed on me in the course of my professional duty, it has confirmed my deductions to the minutest particular.

Should anyone rush to the conclusion hereupon that my attitude towards the Adelphi Theatre is that of a superior person, he will be quite right. It is precisely because I am able to visit all theatres as a superior person that I am entrusted with my present critical function. As a superior person, then, I hold Adelphi melodrama in high consideration. A really good Adelphi melodrama is of first-rate literary importance, because it only needs elaboration to become a masterpiece. Molière's Festin de Pierre and Mozart's Don Juan are elaborations of Punch and Judy, just as Hamlet, Faust, and Peer Gynt are elaborations of popular stories. Unfortunately, a really good Adelphi melodrama is very hard to get. It should be a simple and sincere drama of action and feeling, kept well within that vast tract of passion and motive which is common to the philosopher and the laborer, relieved by plenty of fun, and depending for variety of human character, not on the high comedy idiosyncrasies which individualize people in spite of the closest similarity of age, sex, and circumstances, but on broad contrasts between types of youth and age, sympathy and selfishness, the masculine and the feminine, the serious and the frivolous, the sublime and the ridiculous, and so on. The whole character of the piece must be allegorical, idealistic, full of generalizations and moral lessons; and it must represent conduct as producing swiftly and certainly on the individual the results which in actual life it only produces on the race in the course of many centuries. All of which, obviously, requires for its accomplishment rather greater heads and surer hands than we commonly find in the service of the playhouse.

The latest Adelphi melodrama, The Girl I Left Behind Me, is a very bad one. The only stroke in it that comes home is at the close of the second act, where the heroine sends her soldier lover, who has been accused of cowardice, off on a dangerous duty, and tells him that she loves him. The authors, I need hardly say, did not invent this situation, nor did they freshen it or add anything to it; but they at least brought it off without bungling it, and so saved the piece from the hostility of that sceptical spirit which is now growing among first-night audiences in a very marked degree. This is an inevitable reaction against the artificialities, insincerities, and impossibilities which form about three-fourths of the stock-in-trade of those playwrights who seek safety and success in the assumption that it is impossible to underrate the taste and intelligence of the British public. But there is a profound error in this policy. It is true that the public consists largely of people who are incapable of fully appreciating the best sort of artistic work. It is even true that in every audience, especially on first nights, there is an appreciable number of persons whose condition is such that—to turn Tennyson's shallow claptrap into a terrible truth—they needs must hate the highest when they see it. But why should we credit these unhappy persons with that attribute of the highest character, the power of liking what pleases them, of believing in it, of standing by those who give it to them? For the most part they never enjoy anything; they are always craving for stimulants, whereas the essence of art is recreation; let their flatterer slip, as he always does sooner or later, and they are at his throat mercilessly before he can recover himself. But if you speak in their hearing as the great men speak (which is easy enough if you happen to be a great man), then you will find that their speciality is self-torture, and that they are always hankering, in spite of themselves, after their own boredom and bewilderment, driven, probably, by some sort of uneasy hope that Ibsen or Wagner or some other gigantic bore may exorcise the devils which rend them. The fact is, there is nothing the public despises so much as an attempt to please it. Torment is its natural element: it is only the saint who has any capacity for happiness. There is no greater mistake in theology than to suppose that it is necessary to lock people into hell or out of heaven. You might as well suppose that it is necessary to lock a professional tramp into a public-house or out of a Monday popular concert, on the ground that the concert is the better and cheaper place of the two. The artist's rule must be Cromwell's: "Not what they want, but what is good for them." That rule, carried out in a kindly and sociable way, is the secret to success in the long run at the theatre as elsewhere.

My strong propensity for preaching is, I fear, leading me to deal with The Girl I Left Behind Me in rather too abstract a fashion. But it is only in its abstract bearings that the play provides interesting material to the critic. Instead of being natural and sincere, it is artificial and sanctimonious. The language, which should be vividly vernacular, is ineptly literary. Its fun runs too much on the underclothing of the ladies, which they tear up to make bandages for wounds, or offer, without detachment, to be used by gentlemen at a loss for towels after washing. The characters, instead of being consistent and typical, are patched and rickety, the author's grip constantly slipping from them. The villain and coward of the piece punches the hero's head with pluck and promptitude in the first act, lapses into abject poltroonery in the second, and in the third faces without concern a military emergency which drives all the rest into hysterical desperation. The hero, assaulted as aforesaid, ingloriously brings down the curtain with a stage villain's retort, "You shall rrepent—thiss—bblow," and subsequently becomes the sport of circumstances, which turn out happily for him without much aid from himself. As to Kennion, the sympathetic general, I cannot believe that even in the army so incapable a man could rise to high command. It is, of course, usual on the stage for all army commanders to be superseded at critical moments by their daughters; but still there is no good reason why they should not have moments of efficiency when nothing but routine business is in hand. Private Jones, who is cordially received by his officer when he describes, with an air of conscious merit, how he has just run away on being actually fired at by the enemy, and who calmly quits his post as sentry (at a stockade which may be surprised at any moment) to sit down beside his sleeping lady love, and is supported in that proceeding by the general against a not unnatural remonstrance from his lieutenant—Private Jones is certainly consistent; but what he is consistent with is not himself—for as an individual human being he has no credible existence—but the trained incapacity of the Adelphi audience to understand true military valor. Instead of being, as he should be in a popular melodrama, a typically good soldier, he is a mere folly of the ignorant civil imagination. There is also a medical man, an army surgeon, who makes love to a girl of sixteen by way of comic relief. He relaxed the tension of the third act very happily by a slight but astonishingly effective alteration of a single syllable in the author's text. In the agony of the siege, when all hope was gone, he sat down with heroic calmness to write two documents: one a prescription which there was no apparent means of getting compounded, and the other a farewell—I did not quite catch to whom—probably to his mother. The last touching words of this communication were prefaced by the author with the sentence, "I will add a postscript." The doctor, however, adroitly substituted, "I will add a postcard," and sent the audience, just at the moment when their feelings could bear no further harrowing, into shrieks of refreshing laughter.

The third act, by the way, is an adaptation of the Relief of Lucknow, which, as a dramatic situation, is so strong and familiar that it is hardly possible to spoil it, though the authors have done their best. The main difficulty is the foreknowledge of the hopelessly sophisticated audience that Mr Terriss will rush in at the last moment, sword in hand, and rescue everybody. The authors' business was to carry us on from incident to incident so convincingly and interestingly as to preoccupy us with the illusion of the situation sufficiently to put Mr Terriss out of our heads. Messrs Fyles and Belasco have not been equal to this. They have lamely staved off Mr Terriss for the necessary time by a flabbily commonplace treatment of the question of killing the women to save them from the Indians, and by bringing in the Indian chief's daughter to die in the stockade at the instant when the sound of her voice would have won quarter for the garrison. This is ill contrived, and only passes because the explanation is deferred until the last act, which is so transcendently imbecile that an absurdity more or less does not matter. As to the heroine, who had to kneel in the middle of the stage and rave her way through the burial service whilst her father, the general, hopped about, pulling horrible faces, and trying to make up his mind to shoot her, she was so completely out of the question from any rational human point of view, that I think the effort to impersonate her temporarily unhinged Miss Millward's reason; for when the rescue came, and she had to wave the American flag instead of expressing her feelings naturally, she all but impaled the general on it in a frightful manner. Miss Millward and Mr Terriss and the rest of the company must bear with my irreverent way of describing the performance. I quite appreciate their skill, which is perhaps more indispensable for nonsense of this kind than for plays good enough to be comparatively "actor-proof"; but the better the skill, the more annoying it is to see it nine-tenths wasted.

All the same, the evening was not a dull one. The play is not good drama, nor good melodrama; but it is tolerable pastime. I have spun out my criticism of it in order to leave as little room as possible for another play which was not tolerable even as pastime. When Mr Comyns Carr came before the curtain at the end of Sardou's Delia Harding at the Comedy Theatre on Wednesday, I found myself instinctively repeating the words of Sam Weller, "You raytber want somebody to look arter you, sir, ven your judgment goes out a wisitin'." Delia Harding is the worst play I ever saw. Taking it as a work bearing the same relation to the tastes of the upper middle class as the Adelphi drama to those of the lower middle class, I declare enthusiastically in favor of the Adelphi. Sardou's plan of playwriting is first to invent the action of his piece, and then to carefully keep it off the stage and have it announced merely by letters and telegrams. The people open the letters and read them, whether they are addressed to them or not; and then they talk either about what the letters announce as having occurred already or about what they intend to do tomorrow in consequence of receiving them. When the news is not brought by post, the characters are pressed into the service. Delia Harding, for instance, consists largely of the fashionable intelligence in Bellagio. As thus: "Stanley French arrived in Bellagio this morning," "Mr Harding will arrive in Bellagio tomorrow afternoon," "Miss Harding lives in that villa on the lake," "Sir

Christopher Carstairs will remain here for another month at least," "This is my brother, Sir Arthur Studley," "Janet: we shall pack up and leave tomorrow morning," etc. etc., the person addressed invariably echoing with subdued horror, "This morning!" "Tomorrow afternoon!" "In *that* villa!" and so on. The whole business was so stale, so obviously factitious, so barrenly inept, that at last the gallery broke out into open derision, almost as if they were listening to a particularly touching and delicate passage in a really good play. As for me, I felt ashamed and remorseful. The time has now come for pity rather than vengeance on the poor old "well made play." Fifteen years ago I was almost alone in my contempt for these clumsy booby traps. Nowadays an actor cannot open a letter or toss off somebody else's glass of poison without having to face a brutal outburst of jeering.

DUSE AND BERNHARDT

A charge that modern critics paid no attention to acting had been answered by William Archer, Shaw's fellow critic, with the complaint that the moderns had no opportunity to compare ambitious actors rivaling each other in famous parts. With the simultaneous visit to London of Eleonora Duse, the great Italian actress, and Sarah Bernhardt, the famous French star, such an opportunity occurred; and Shaw conscientiously seized it. Shaw wrote two successive analyses of Duse's art. The second, the comparison with Bernhardt, appeared June 15, 1895.

This week began with the relapse of Sarah Bernhardt into her old profession of serious actress. She played Magda in Sudermann's Heimat, and was promptly challenged by Duse in the same part at Drury Lane on Wednesday. The contrast between the two Magdas is as extreme as any contrast could possibly be between artists who have finished their twenty years apprenticeship to the same profession under closely similar conditions. Madame Bernhardt has the charm of a jolly maturity, rather spoilt and petulant, perhaps, but always ready with a sunshine-through-the-clouds smile if only she is made much of. Her dresses and diamonds, if not exactly splendid, are at least splendacious; her figure, far too scantily upholstered in the old days, is at its best; and her complexion shews that she has not studied modern art in vain. Those charming roseate effects which French painters produce by giving flesh the pretty color of strawberries and cream, and painting the shadows pink and crimson, are cunningly reproduced by Madame Bernhardt in the living picture. She paints her ears crimson and allows them to peep enchantingly through a few loose braids of her auburn hair. Every dimple has its dab of pink; and her finger-tips are so delicately incarnadined that you fancy they are transparent like her ears, and that the light is shining through their delicate blood-vessels. Her lips are like a newly painted pillar box; her cheeks, right up to the languid lashes, have the bloom and surface of a peach; she is beautiful with the beauty of her school, and entirely inhuman and incredible. But the incredibility is pardonable, because, though it is all the greatest nonsense, nobody believing in it, the actress herself least of all, it is so artful, so clever, so well recognized a part of the business, and carried off with such a genial air, that it is impossible not to accept it with good-humor. One feels, when the heroine bursts on the scene, a dazzling vision of beauty, that instead of imposing on you, she adds to her own piquancy by looking you straight in the face, and saying, in effect: "Now who would ever suppose that I am a grandmother?" That, of course, is irresistible; and one is not sorry to have been coaxed to relax one's notions of the dignity of art when she gets to serious business and shews how ably she does her work. The coaxing suits well with the childishly egotistical character of her acting, which is not the art of making you think more highly or feel more deeply, but the art of making you admire her, pity her, champion her, weep with her, laugh at her jokes, follow her fortunes breathlessly, and applaud her wildly when the curtain falls. It is the art of finding out all your weaknesses and practising on them—cajoling you, harrowing you, exciting you—on the whole, fooling you. And it is always Sarah Bernhardt in her own capacity who does this to you. The dress, the title of the play, the order of the words may vary; but the woman is always the same. She does not enter into the leading character: she substitutes herself for it.

All this is precisely what does not happen in the case of Duse, whose every part is a separate creation. When she comes on the stage, you are quite welcome to take your opera-glass and count whatever lines time and care have so far traced on her. They are the credentials of her humanity; and she knows better than to obliterate that significant handwriting beneath a layer of peach-bloom from the chemist's. The shadows on her face are grey, not crimson; her lips are sometimes nearly grey also; there are neither dabs nor dimples; her charm could never be imitated by a barmaid with unlimited pin money and a row of footlights before her instead of the handles of a beer-engine. The result is not so discouraging as the patrons of the bar might suppose. Wilkes, who squinted atrociously, boasted that he was only quarter of an hour behind the handsomest man in Europe: Duse is not in action five minutes before she is quarter of a century ahead of the handsomest woman in the world. I grant that Sarah's elaborate Monna Lisa smile, with the conscious droop of the eyelashes and the long carmined lips coyly disclosing the brilliant row of teeth, is effective of its kind—that it not only appeals to your susceptibilities, but positively jogs them. And it lasts quite a minute, sometimes longer. But Duse, with a tremor of the lip which you feel rather than see, and which lasts half an instant, touches you straight on the very heart; and there is not a line in the face, or a cold tone in the grey shadow that does not give poignancy to that tremor. As to youth and age, who can associate purity and delicacy of emotion, and simplicity of expression, with the sordid craft that repels us in age; or voluptuous appeal and egotistical self-insistence with the candor and generosity that attract us in youth? Who ever thinks of Potiphar's wife as a young woman, or St Elizabeth of Hungary as an old one? These associations are horribly unjust to age, and undeserved by youth: they belong of right to differences of character, not of years; but they rule our imaginations; and the great artist profits by them to appear eternally young. However, it would be a critical blunder as well as a personal folly on my part to suggest that Duse, any more than Sarah Bernhardt, neglects any art that could heighten the effect of her acting when she is impersonating young and pretty women. The truth is that in the art of being beautiful, Madame Bernhardt is a child beside her. The French artist's stock of attitudes and facial effects could be catalogued as easily as her stock of dramatic ideas: the counting would hardly go beyond the fingers of both hands. Duse produces the illusion of being infinite in variety of beautiful pose and motion. Every idea, every shade of thought and mood, expresses itself delicately but vividly to the eye; and yet, in an apparent million of changes and inflexions, it is impossible to catch any line at an awkward angle, or any strain interfering with the perfect abandonment of all the limbs to what appears to be their natural gravitation towards the finest grace. She is ambidextrous and supple, like a gymnast or a panther; only the multitude of ideas which find physical expression in her movements are all of that high quality which marks off humanity from the animals, and, I fear I must add, from a good many gymnasts. When it is remembered that the majority of tragic actors excel only in explosions of those passions which are common to man and brute, there will be no difficulty in understanding the indescribable distinction which Duse's acting acquires from the fact that behind every stroke of it is a distinctively human idea. In nothing is this more apparent than in the vigilance in her of that high human instinct which seeks to awaken the deepest responsive feeling without giving pain. In La Dame aux Camélias, for instance, it is easy for an intense actress to harrow us with her sorrows and paroxysms of phthisis, leaving us with a liberal pennyworth of sensation, not fundamentally distinguishable from that offered by a public execution, or any other evil in which we still take a hideous delight. As different from this as light from darkness is the method of the actress who shews us how human sorrow can express itself only in its appeal for the sympathy it needs, whilst striving by strong endurance to shield others from the infection of its torment. That is the charm of Duse's interpretation of the stage poem of Marguerite Gauthier. It is unspeakably touching because it is exquisitely considerate: that is, exquisitely sympathetic. No physical charm is noble as well as beautiful unless it is the expression of a moral charm; and it is because Duse's range includes these moral high notes, if I may so express myself, that her compass, extending from the depths of a mere predatory creature like Claude's wife up to Marguerite Gauthier at her kindest or Magda at her bravest, so immeasurably dwarfs the poor little octave and a half on which Sarah Bernhardt plays such pretty canzonets and stirring marches.

Obvious as the disparity of the two famous artists has been to many of us since we first saw Duse, I doubt whether any of us realized, after Madame Bernhardt's very clever performance as Magda on Monday night, that there was room in the nature of things for its annihilation within forty-eight hours by so comparatively quiet a talent as Duse's. And yet annihilation is the only word for it. Sarah was very charming, very jolly when the sun shone, very petulant when the clouds covered it, and positively angry when they wanted to take her child away from her. And she did not trouble us with any fuss about the main theme of Sudermann's play, the revolt of the modern woman against that ideal of home which exacts the sacrifice of her whole life to its care, not by her grace, and as its own sole help and refuge, but as a right which it has to the services of all females as abject slaves. In fact, there is not the slightest reason to suspect Madame Bernhardt of having discovered any such theme in the play; though Duse, with one look at Schwartze, the father, nailed it to the stage as the subject of the impending dramatic struggle before she had been five minutes on the scene. Before long, there came a stroke of acting which will probably never be forgotten by those who saw it, and which explained at once why those artifices of the dressing-table which help Madame Bernhardt would hinder Duse almost as much as a screen placed in front of her. I should explain, first, that the real name of the play is not Magda but Home. Magda is a daughter who has been turned out of doors for defying her father, one of those outrageous persons who mistake their desire to have everything their own way in the house for a sacred principle of home life. She has a hard time of it, but at last makes a success as an opera singer, though not until her lonely struggles have thrown her for sympathy on a fellow student, who in due time goes his way, and leaves her to face motherhood as best she can. In the fullness of her fame she returns to her native town, and in an attack of homesickness makes advances to her father, who consents to receive her again. No sooner is she installed in the house than she finds that one of the most intimate friends of the family is the father of her child. In the third act of the play she is on the stage when he is announced as a visitor. It must be admitted that Sarah Bernhardt played this scene very lightly and pleasantly: there was genuine good fellowship in the way in which she reassured the embarrassed gallant and made him understand that she was not going to play off the sorrows of Gretchen on him after all those years, and that she felt that she owed him the priceless experience of maternity, even if she did not particularly respect him for it. Her self-possession at this point was immense: the peach-bloom never altered by a shade. Not so with Duse. The moment she read the card handed her by the servant, you realized what it was to have to face a meeting with the man. It was interesting to watch how she got through it when he came in, and how, on the whole, she got through it pretty well. He paid his compliments and offered his flowers; they sat down; and she evidently felt that she had got it safely over and might allow herself to think at her ease, and to look at him to see how much he had altered. Then a terrible thing happened to her. She began to blush; and in another moment she was conscious of it, and the blush was slowly spreading and deepening until, after a few vain efforts to avert her face or to obstruct his view of it without seeming to do so, she gave up and hid the blush in her hands. After that feat of acting I did not need to be told why Duse does not paint an inch thick. I could detect no trick in it: it seemed to me a perfectly genuine effect of the dramatic imagination. In the third act of La Dame aux Camélias, where she produces a touching effect by throwing herself down, and presently rises with her face changed and flushed with weeping, the flush is secured by the preliminary plunge to a stooping attitude, imagination or no imagination; but Magda's blush did not admit of that explanation; and I must confess to an intense professional curiosity as to whether it always comes spontaneously.

I shall make no attempt to describe the rest of that unforgettable act. To say that it left the house not only frantically applauding, but actually roaring, is to say nothing; for had we not applauded Sarah as Gismonda and roared at Mrs Patrick Campbell as Fedora? But there really was something to roar at this time. There was a real play, and an actress who understood the author and was a greater artist than he. And for me, at least, there was a confirmation of my sometimes flagging faith that a dramatic critic is really the servant of a high art, and not a mere advertiser of entertainments of questionable respectability of motive.

THE SIGN OF THE CROSS

On January 11, 1896, Shaw reviewed a spectacular melodrama of Christians and pagans in the days of Nero, written by the actor Wilson Barrett. Barrett played a Roman aristocrat who attempts to seduce a beautiful Christian maiden until the maiden converts him instead and he joins her in martyrdom. The play was attacked by freethinkers (and others) as a profanation of sacred things, and defended by clergymen as a pious spectacle. In his review, Shaw pretends to take the play's sentimental pieties as scathing ironies, pretends to find in Barrett another Ibsen. When Androcles and the Lion *appeared in 1913, several critics noted its inverted similarity to* The Sign of the Cross *and the genre which Barrett's play had made endlessly popular.*

Mr Wilson Barrett has given me such unbounded delight by his feat of persuading the London critics that several of the most characteristic passages in his Sign of the Cross are quotations from the Bible that I have nothing but praise for him. Sterne's "tempering the wind to the shorn lamb" need never again be quoted as the champion instance of scripturization. It is true that Mr Wilson Barrett, following the universal law of art development, has founded his Sermon on the Mount to some extent on the original one; but I can assure the public that the text of The Sign of the Cross is essentially original; and if Mr Wilson Barrett writes to the papers to assure us, in the usual terms, that so far from his having taken his play from the Bible, he has never even read that volume, I am quite prepared to believe him. His literary style is altogether different. The play is a monument of sacred and profane history. The influence of Ibsen is apparent throughout, the Norwegian keynote being struck by Mr Barrett himself in the words: "How many crimes are committed under the cloak of duty!" With scathing, searching irony, and with resolute courage in the face of the prejudiced British public, he has drawn a terrible contrast between the Romans ("Pagans, I regret to say," as Mr Pecksniff remarked of the sirens), with their straightforward sensuality, and the strange, perverted voluptuousness of the Christians, with their shuddering exaltations of longing for the whip, the rack, the stake, and the lions. The whole drama lies in the spectacle of the hardy Roman prefect, a robust soldier and able general, gradually falling under the spell of a pale Christian girl, white and worn with spiritual ecstasy, and beautiful as Mary Anderson. As she gradually throws upon him the fascination of suffering and martyrdom, he loses his taste for wine; the courtezans at his orgies disgust him; heavenly visions obsess him; undreamt-of raptures of sacrifice, agony, and escape from the world to indescribable holiness and bliss tempt him; and finally he is seen, calm and noble, but stark mad, following the girl to her frightfully voluptuous death. It is a tremendous moral lesson; and though I am pagan enough to dislike most intensely the flogging and racking and screaming on the stage (I really am such a bloodless creature that I take no delight in torture), yet no doubt it helps to drive the irony of the theme home.

On the intellectual side, Christianity hardly receives justice from Mr Wilson Barrett. "Christianity is not in itself a crime," says Marcus to Nero. "Marcus argues strongly, Cæsar," is Poppea's comment. I must say I think Poppea is rather too easily satisfied. But, after all, we do not want to hear the case argued at this time of day. What we enjoy is being so familiarly in Rome that it sounds quite natural when such directions to wayfarers as "Fourth on the right from the statue of Hercules" are given by the lictors. We come into the presence of Nero, and hear him ordering a set of living torches for that evening, and boasting of what an artist he is. We see the Roman ladies at home sticking pins into their slaves, and the Roman diner-out exhausted by his second vomit. We hear the thunder of the chariot race, and see the gladiator enter the arena. And we have, as aforesaid, whips and racks, chains and dungeons, uplifted crosses and Christian martyrs, not to mention plenty of music well handled by Mr Edward Jones, with hymns for the Christians, waltzes for the Romans, and Sullivan's Thou'rt passing hence, my brother, and Gounod's Nazareth on the cornet and sackbut between the acts.

The mounting is handsome, and the stage management good and unselfish, all the parts being played with quite extraordinary spirit, and in no way sacrificed to the actor-manager's. I have never seen better work got out of a company. Mr Wilson Barrett has honestly sunk the actor in the author, and done his best for the play, instead of for himself personally. Indeed, the one conspicuous and laughable oversight is in Mr Barrett's own make-up. Instead of wearing the proper cropped Roman wig, he wears his own hair in his old familiar feminine fashion, with the result that when he first steps on the stage he presents such an amazing resemblance to Miss Victor that, instead of applauding him, I stared with a shocked conviction that I had that lady before me in the costume of a Roman warrior. The effect is amusing; but it spoils an otherwise manly picture.

HAMLET

Some of Shaw's most notable irreverences were committed against the great actor Henry Irving, whose management had made the Lyceum Theatre into something of a national shrine. On October 2, 1897, Shaw used the occasion of another actor's production of Hamlet *to deplore the cut and altered versions, radical re-creations, and unwieldy productions characteristic of the Lyceum, and indeed of the whole tradition of Shakespeare in the theatre. Shaw also suggests a reading of* Hamlet *in consonance with the "classical" acting of the title part by Johnston Forbes-Robertson. Forbes-Robertson, Shaw later declared, was "the only actor on the English stage then capable of playing a classical part in the grand manner without losing the charm and lightness of an accomplished comedian." It was specifically for Forbes-Robertson that Shaw wrote* Caesar and Cleopatra*—"because he is the classic actor of our day." Some of the traits Shaw found in Forbes-Robertson's Hamlet appear again in Julius Caesar.*

The Forbes Robertson Hamlet at the Lyceum is, very unexpectedly at that address, really not at all unlike Shakespear's play of the same name. I am quite certain I saw Reynaldo in it for a moment; and possibly I may have seen Voltimand and Cornelius; but just as the time for their scene arrived, my eye fell on the word "Fortinbras" in the program, which so amazed me that I hardly know what I saw for the next ten minutes. Ophelia, instead of being a strenuously earnest and self-possessed young lady giving a concert and recitation for all she was worth, was mad—actually mad. The story of the play was perfectly intelligible, and quite took the attention of the audience off the principal actor at moments. What is the Lyceum coming to? Is it for this that Sir Henry Irving has invented a whole series of original romantic dramas, and given the credit of them without a murmur to the immortal bard whose profundity (as exemplified in the remark that good and evil are mingled in our natures) he has just been pointing out to the inhabitants of Cardiff, and whose works have been no more to him than the word-quarry from which he has hewn and blasted the lines and titles of masterpieces which are really all his own? And now, when he has created by these means a reputation for Shakespear, he no sooner turns his back for a moment on London than Mr Forbes Robertson competes with him on the boards of his own theatre by actually playing off against him the authentic Swan of Avon. Now if the result had been the utter exposure and collapse of that impostor, poetic justice must have proclaimed that it served Mr Forbes Robertson right. But alas! the wily William, by literary tricks which our simple Sir Henry has never quite understood, has played into Mr Forbes Robertson's hands so artfully that the scheme is a prodigious success. The effect of this success, coming after that of Mr Alexander's experiment with a Shakespearean version of As You Like It, makes it almost probable that we shall presently find managers vying with each other in offering the public as much of the original Shakespearean stuff as possible, instead of, as heretofore, doing their utmost to reassure us that everything that the most modern resources can do to relieve the irreducible minimum of tedium inseparable from even the most heavily cut acting version will be lavished on their revivals. It is true that Mr Beerbohm Tree still holds to the old scepticism, and calmly proposes to insult us by offering us Garrick's puerile and horribly caddish knockabout farce of Katharine and Petruchio for Shakespear's Taming of the Shrew; but Mr Tree, like all romantic actors, is incorrigible on the subject of Shakespear.

Mr Forbes Robertson is essentially a classical actor, the only one, with the exception of Mr Alexander, now established in London management. What I mean by classical is that he can present a dramatic hero as a man whose passions are those which have produced the philosophy, the poetry, the art, and the statecraft of the world, and not merely those which have produced its weddings, coroners' inquests, and executions. And that is just the sort of actor that Hamlet requires. A Hamlet who only understands his love for Ophelia, his grief for his father, his vindictive hatred of his uncle, his fear of ghosts, his impulse to snub Rosencrantz and Guildenstern, and the sportsman's excitement with which he lays the "mousetrap" for Claudius, can, with sufficient force or virtuosity of execution, get a great reputation in the part, even though the very intensity of his obsession by these sentiments (which are common not only to all men but to many animals) shews that the characteristic side of Hamlet, the side that differentiates him from Fortinbras, is absolutely outside the actor's consciousness. Such a reputation is the actor's, not Hamlet's.

Hamlet is not a man in whom "common humanity" is raised by great vital energy to a heroic pitch, like Coriolanus or Othello. On the contrary, he is a man in whom the common personal passions are so superseded by wider and rarer interests, and so discouraged by a degree of critical self-consciousness which makes the practical efficiency of the instinctive man on the lower plane impossible to him, that he finds the duties dictated by conventional revenge and ambition as disagreeable a burden as commerce is to a poet. Even his instinctive sexual impulses offend his intellect; so that when he meets the woman who excites them he invites her to join him in a bitter and scornful criticism of their joint absurdity, demanding "What should such fellows as I do crawling between heaven and earth?" "Why wouldst thou be a breeder of sinners?" and so forth, all of which is so completely beyond the poor girl that she naturally thinks him mad. And, indeed, there is a sense in which Hamlet is insane; for he trips over the mistake which lies on the threshold of intellectual self-consciousness: that of bringing life to utilitarian or Hedonistic tests, thus treating it as a means instead of an end. Because Polonius is "a foolish prating knave," because Rosencrantz and Guildenstern are snobs, he kills them as remorselessly as he might kill a flea, shewing that he has no real belief in the superstitious reason which he gives for not killing himself, and in fact anticipating exactly the whole course of the intellectual history of Western Europe until Schopenhauer found the clue that Shakespear missed. But to call Hamlet mad because he did not anticipate Schopenhauer is like calling Marcellus mad because he did not refer the Ghost to the Psychical Society. It is in fact not possible for any actor to represent Hamlet as mad. He may (and generally does) combine some notion of his own of a man who is the creature of affectionate sentiment with the figure drawn by the lines of Shakespear; but the result is not a madman, but simply one of those monsters produced by the imaginary combination of two normal species, such as sphinxes, mermaids, or centaurs. And this is the invariable resource of the instinctive, imaginative, romantic actor. You will see him weeping bucketsful of tears over Ophelia, and treating the players, the gravedigger, Horatio, Rosencrantz, and Guildenstern as if they were mutes at his own funeral. But go and watch Mr Forbes Robertson's Hamlet seizing delightedly on every opportunity for a bit of philosophic discussion or artistic recreation to escape from the "cursed spite" of revenge and love and other common troubles; see how he brightens up when the players come; how he tries to talk philosophy with Rosencrantz and Guildenstern the moment they come into the room; how he stops on his country walk with Horatio to lean over the churchyard wall and draw out the gravedigger whom he sees singing at his trade; how even his fits of excitement find expression in declaiming scraps of poetry; how the shock of Ophelia's death relieves itself in the fiercest intellectual contempt for Laertes's ranting, whilst an hour afterwards, when Laertes stabs him, he bears no malice for that at all, but embraces him gallantly and comradely; and how he dies as we forgive everything to Charles II for dying, and makes "the rest is silence" a touchingly humorous apology for not being able to finish his business. See all that; and you have seen a true classical Hamlet. Nothing half so charming has been seen by this generation. It will bear seeing again and again.

And please observe that this is not a cold Hamlet. He is none of your logicians who reason their way through the world because they cannot feel their way through it: his intellect is the organ of his passion: his eternal self-criticism is as alive and thrilling as it can possibly be. The great soliloquy—no: I do NOT mean "To be or not to be": I mean the dramatic one, "O what a rogue and peasant slave am I!"—is as passionate in its scorn of brute passion as the most bull-necked affirmation or sentimental dilution of it could be. It comes out so without violence: Mr Forbes Robertson takes the part quite easily and spontaneously.

There is none of that strange Lyceum intensity which comes from the perpetual struggle between Sir Henry Irving and Shakespear. The lines help Mr Forbes Robertson instead of getting in his way at every turn, because he wants to play Hamlet, and not to slip into his inky cloak a changeling of quite another race. We may miss the craft, the skill double-distilled by constant peril, the subtlety, the dark rays of heat generated by intense friction, the relentless parental tenacity and cunning with which Sir Henry nurses his own pet creations on Shakespearean food like a fox rearing its litter in the den of a lioness; but we get light, freedom, naturalness, credibility, and Shakespear.

THE TECHNICAL NOVELTY IN IBSEN'S PLAYS

In 1890, Shaw delivered a lecture on Ibsen and his ideas to the Fabian society, a lecture he later turned into an expository treatise and published as The Quintessence of Ibsenism *(1891). In 1913, he completed the analysis of the plays to the death of Ibsen and added several new chapters, including one called "The Technical Novelty in Ibsen's Plays." This last turned out to be a historical and formal account of the dramatic discussion, and a defense of the discursive techniques for which critics had taken Shaw to task. In the few years prior to 1913 Shaw had written several plays, notably* Major Barbara, Getting Married, *and* Misalliance, *subtitled "A Discussion," "A Conversation," "A Debate in One Sitting." And in 1913 he began* Heartbreak House.

It is a striking and melancholy example of the preoccupation of critics with phrases and formulas to which they have given life by taking them into the tissue of their own living minds, and which therefore seem and feel vital and important to them whilst they are to everybody else the deadest and dreariest rubbish (this is the great secret of academic dryasdust), that to this day they remain blind to a new technical factor in the art of popular stage-play making which every considerable playwright has been thrusting under their noses night after night for a whole generation. This technical factor in the play is the discussion. Formerly you had in what was called a well made play an exposition in the first act, a situation in the second, and unravelling in the third. Now you have exposition, situation, and discussion; and the discussion is the test of the playwright. The critics protest in vain. They declare that discussions are not dramatic, and that art should not be didactic. Neither the playwrights nor the public take the smallest notice of them. The discussion conquered Europe in Ibsen's Doll's House; and now the serious playwright recognizes in the discussion not only the main test of his highest powers, but also the real centre of his play's interest. Sometimes he even takes every possible step to assure the public beforehand that his play will be fitted with that newest improvement.

This was inevitable if the drama was ever again to be raised above the childish demand for fables without morals. Children have a settled arbitrary morality: therefore to them moralizing is nothing but an intolerable platitudinizing. The morality of the grown-up is also very largely a settled morality, either purely conventional and of no ethical significance, like the rule of the road or the rule that when you ask for a yard of ribbon the shopkeeper shall give you thirty-six inches and not interpret the word yard as he pleases, or else too obvious in its ethics to leave any room for discussion: for instance, that if the boots keeps you waiting too long for your shaving water you must not plunge your razor into his throat in your irritation, no matter how great an effort of self-control your forbearance may cost you.

Now when a play is only a story of how a villain tries to separate an honest young pair of betrothed lovers; to gain the hand of the woman by calumny; and to ruin the man by forgery, murder, false witness, and other commonplaces of the Newgate Calendar, the introduction of a discussion would clearly be ridiculous. There is nothing for sane people to discuss; and any attempt to Chadbandize on the wickedness of such crimes is at once resented as, in Milton's phrase, "moral babble."

But this sort of drama is soon exhausted by people who go often to the theatre. In twenty visits one can see every possible change rung on all the available plots and incidents out of which plays of this kind can be manufactured. The illusion of reality is soon lost: in fact it may be doubted whether any adult ever entertains it: it is only to very young children that the fairy queen is anything but an actress. But at the age when we cease to mistake the figures on the stage for *dramatis personae*, and know that they are actors and actresses, the charm of the performer begins to assert itself; and the child who would have been cruelly hurt by being told that the Fairy Queen was only Miss Smith dressed up to look like one, becomes the man who goes to the theatre expressly to see Miss Smith, and is fascinated by her skill or beauty to the point of delighting in plays which would be unendurable to him without her. Thus we get plays "written round" popular performers, and popular performers who give value to otherwise useless plays by investing them with their own attractiveness. But all these enterprises are, commercially speaking, desperately precarious. To begin with, the supply of performers whose attraction is so far independent of the play that their inclusion in the cast sometimes makes the difference between success and failure is too small to enable all our theatres, or even many of them, to depend on their actors rather than on their plays. And to finish with, no actor can make bricks entirely without straw. From Grimaldi to Sothern, Jefferson, and Henry Irving (not to mention living actors) we have had players succeeding once in a lifetime in grafting on to a play which would have perished without them some figure imagined wholly by themselves; but none of them has been able to repeat the feat, nor to save many of the plays in which he has appeared from failure. In the long run nothing can retain the interest of the playgoer after the theatre has lost its illusion for his childhood, and its glamor for his adolescence, but a constant supply of interesting plays; and this is specially true in London, where the expense and trouble of theatregoing have been raised to a point at which it is surprising that sensible people of middle age go to the theatre at all. As a matter of fact, they mostly stay at home.

Now an interesting play cannot in the nature of things mean anything but a play in which problems of conduct and character of personal importance to the audience are raised and suggestively discussed. People have a thrifty sense of taking away something from such plays: they not only have had something for their money, but they retain that something as a permanent possession. Consequently none of the commonplaces of the box office hold good of such plays. In vain does the experienced acting manager declare that people want to be amused and not preached at in the theatre; that they will not stand long speeches; that a play must not contain more than 18,000 words; that it must not begin before nine nor last beyond eleven; that there must be no politics and no religion in it; that breach of these golden rules will drive people to the variety theatres; that there must be a woman of bad character, played by a very attractive actress, in the piece; and so on and so forth. All these counsels are valid for plays in which there is nothing to discuss. They may be disregarded by the playwright who is a moralist and a debater as well as a dramatist. From him, within the inevitable limits set by the clock and by the physical endurance of the human frame, people will stand anything as soon as they are matured enough and cultivated enough to be susceptible to the appeal of his particular form of art. The difficulty at present is that mature and cultivated people do not go to the theatre, just as they do not read penny novelets; and when an attempt is made to cater for them they do not respond to it in time, partly because they have not the habit of playgoing, and partly because it takes too long for them to find out that the new theatre is not like all the other theatres. But when they do at last find their way there, the attraction is not the firing of blank cartridges at one another by actors, nor the pretence of falling down dead that ends the stage combat, nor the simulation of erotic thrills by a pair of stage lovers, nor any of the other tomfooleries called action, but the exhibition and discussion of the character and conduct of stage figures who are made to appear real by the art of the playwright and the performers.

This, then, is the extension of the old dramatic form effected by Ibsen. Up to a certain point in the last act, A Doll's House is a play that might be turned into a very ordinary French drama by the excision of a few lines, and the substitution of a sentimental happy ending for the famous last scene: indeed the very first thing the theatrical wiseacres did with it was to effect exactly this transformation, with the result that the play thus pithed had no success and attracted no notice worth mentioning. But at just that point in the last act, the heroine very unexpectedly (by the wiseacres) stops her emotional acting and says: "We must sit down and discuss all this that has been happening between us." And it was by this new technical feature: this addition of a new movement, as musicians would say, to the dramatic form, that A Doll's House conquered Europe and founded a new school of dramatic art.

Since that time the discussion has expanded far beyond the limits of the last ten minutes of an otherwise "well made" play. The disadvantage of putting the discussion at the end was not only that it came when the audience was fatigued, but that it was necessary to see the play over again, so as to follow the earlier acts in the light of the final discussion, before it became fully intelligible. The practical utility of this book is due to the fact that unless the spectator at an Ibsen play has read the pages referring to it beforehand, it is hardly possible for him to get its bearings at a first hearing if he approaches it, as most spectators still do, with conventional idealist prepossessions. Accordingly, we now have plays, including some of my own, which begin with discussion and end with action, and others in which the discussion interpenetrates the action from beginning to end. When Ibsen invaded England discussion had vanished from the stage; and women could not write plays. Within twenty years women were writing better plays than men; and these plays were passionate arguments from beginning to end. The action of such plays consists of a case to be argued. If the case is uninteresting or stale or badly conducted or obviously trumped up, the play is a bad one. If it is important and novel and convincing, or at least disturbing, the play is a good one. But anyhow the play in which there is no argument and no case no longer counts as serious drama. It may still please the child in us as Punch and Judy does; but nobody nowadays pretends to regard the well made play as anything more than a commercial product which is not in question when modern schools of serious drama are under discussion. Indeed within ten years of the production of A Doll's House in London, audiences had become so derisive of the more obvious and hackneyed features of the methods of Sardou that it became dangerous to resort to them; and playwrights who persisted in "constructing" plays in the old French manner lost ground not for lack of ideas, but because their technique was unbearably out of fashion.

In the new plays, the drama arises through a conflict of unsettled ideals rather than through vulgar attachments, rapacities, generosities, resentments, ambitions, misunderstandings, oddities and so forth as to which no moral question is raised. The conflict is not between clear right and wrong: the villain is as conscientious as the hero, if not more so: in fact, the question which makes the play interesting (when it *is* interesting) is which is the villain and which the hero. Or, to put it another way, there are no villains and no heroes. This strikes the critics mainly as a departure from dramatic art; but it is really the inevitable return to nature which ends all the merely technical fashions. Now the natural is mainly the everyday; and its climaxes must be, if not everyday, at least everylife, if they are to have any importance for the spectator. Crimes, fights, big legacies, fires, shipwrecks, battles, and thunderbolts are mistakes in a play, even when they can be effectively simulated. No doubt they may acquire dramatic interest by putting a character through the test of an emergency; but the test is likely to be too obviously theatrical, because, as the playwright cannot in the nature of things have much experience of such catastrophes, he is forced to substitute a set of conventions or conjectures for the feelings they really produce.

. . . .

The drama was born of old from the union of two desires: the desire to have a dance and the desire to hear a story. The dance became a rant: the story became a situation. When Ibsen began to make plays, the art of the dramatist had shrunk into the art of contriving a situation. And it was held that the stranger the situation, the better the play. Ibsen saw that, on the contrary, the more familiar the situation, the more interesting the play. Shakespear had put ourselves on the stage but not our situations. Our uncles seldom murder our fathers, and cannot legally marry our mothers; we do not meet witches; our kings are not as a rule stabbed and succeeded by their stabbers; and when we raise money by bills we do not promise to pay pounds of our flesh. Ibsen supplies the want left by Shakespear. He gives us not only ourselves, but ourselves in our own situations. The things that happen to his stage figures are things that happen to us. One consequence is that his plays are much more important to us than Shakespear's. Another is that they are capable both of hurting us cruelly and of filling us with excited hopes of escape from idealistic tyrannies, and with visions of intenser life in the future.

Changes in technique follow inevitably from these changes in the subject matter of the play. When a dramatic poet can give you hopes and visions, such old maxims as that stage-craft is the art of preparation become boyish, and may be left to those unfortunate playwrights who, being unable to make anything really interesting happen on the stage, have to acquire the art of continually persuading the audience that it is going to happen presently. When he can stab people to the heart by shewing them the meanness or cruelty of something they did yesterday and intend to do tomorrow, all the old tricks to catch and hold their attention become the silliest of superfluities. The play called The Murder of Gonzago, which Hamlet makes the players act before his uncle, is artlessly constructed; but it produces a greater effect on Claudius than the Œdipus of Sophocles, because it is about himself. The writer who practises the art of Ibsen therefore discards all the old tricks of preparation, catastrophe, *dénouement,* and so forth without thinking about it, just as a modern rifleman never dreams of providing himself with powder horns, percussion caps, and wads: indeed he does not know the use of them. Ibsen substituted a terrible art of sharpshooting at the audience, trapping them, fencing with them, aiming always at the sorest spot in their consciences. Never mislead an audience, was an old rule. But the new school will trick the spectator into forming a meanly false judgment, and then convict him of it in the next act, often to his grievous mortification. When you despise something you ought to take off your hat to, or admire and imitate something you ought to loathe, you cannot resist the dramatist who knows how to touch these morbid spots in you and make you see that they are morbid. The dramatist knows that as long as he is teaching and saving his audience, he is as sure of their strained attention as a dentist is, or the Angel of the Annunciation. And though he may use all the magic of art to make you forget the pain he causes you or to enhance the joy of the hope and courage he awakens, he is never occupied in the old work of manufacturing interest and expectation with materials that have neither novelty, significance, nor relevance to the experience or prospects of the spectators.

Hence a cry has arisen that the post-Ibsen play is not a play, and that its technique, not being the technique described by Aristotle, is not a technique at all. I will not enlarge on this: the fun poked at my friend Mr A. B. Walkley in the prologue of Fanny's First Play need not be repeated here. But I may remind him that the new technique is new only on the modern stage. It has been used by preachers and orators ever since speech was invented. It is the technique of playing upon the human conscience; and it has been practised by the playwright whenever the playwright has been capable of it. Rhetoric, irony, argument, paradox, epigram, parable, the rearrangement of haphazard facts into orderly and intelligent situations: these are both the oldest and the newest arts of the drama; and your plot construction and art of preparation are only the tricks of theatrical talent and the shifts of moral sterility, not the weapons of dramatic genius. In the theatre of Ibsen we are not flattered spectators killing an idle hour with an ingenious and amusing entertainment: we are "guilty creatures sitting at a play"; and the technique of pastime is no more applicable than at a murder trial.

The technical novelties of the Ibsen and post-Ibsen plays are, then: first, the introduction of the discussion and its development until it so overspreads and interpenetrates the action that it finally assimilates it, making play and discussion practically identical; and, second, as a consequence of making the spectators themselves the persons of the drama, and the incidents of their own lives its incidents, the disuse of the old stage tricks by which audiences had to be induced to take an interest in unreal people and improbable circumstances, and the substitution of a forensic technique of recrimination, disillusion, and penetration through ideals to the truth, with a free use of all the rhetorical and lyrical arts of the orator, the preacher, the pleader, and the rhapsodist.